SECRETS I WON'T TAKE WITH ME

JEWS AND JUDAISM: HISTORY AND CULTURE

SERIES EDITORS

Mark K. Bauman
Adam D. Mendelsohn

FOUNDING EDITOR

Leon J. Weinberger

ADVISORY BOARD

Tobias Brinkmann
David Feldman
Kirsten Fermaglich
Jeffrey S. Gurock
Nahum Karlinsky
Richard Menkis
Riv-Ellen Prell
Mark A. Raider
Raanan Rein
Jonathan Schorsch
Stephen J. Whitfield
Marcin Wodzinski

SECRETS I WON'T TAKE WITH ME

HOME, WAR, AND THE STRUGGLE FOR PEACE IN ISRAEL

YOSSI BEILIN

THE UNIVERSITY OF ALABAMA PRESS
Tuscaloosa

The University of Alabama Press
Tuscaloosa, Alabama 35487-0380
uapress.ua.edu

Copyright © 2025 by the University of Alabama Press
All rights reserved.

Inquiries about reproducing material from this work should
be addressed to the University of Alabama Press.

Typeface: Plantin MT Pro

Cover image: Map of Armistice Lines, 1949, adapted from the Atlas of
the Jewish-Arab Conflict by Shaul Arieli, used by permission
Cover design: Sandy Turner Jr.

Cataloging-in-Publication data is available from the Library of Congress.
ISBN: 978-0-8173-2230-4 (cloth)
ISBN: 978-0-8173-6202-7 (paper)
E-ISBN: 978-0-8173-9554-4

For Daniela, my beloved

Contents

Preface ix
1. Angry at Herzl 1
2. "I Just Don't Want Him to Grow Up to Be a Show-Off" 9
3. "Father, I'm Not Going with You!" 15
4. Love Doesn't Diminish When You Divide It 24
5. Cupping Glasses for the Living 30
6. Playing a Silent Cardboard Piano 37
7. The Little Star from Lodz 46
8. I'm Sure You Already Know—There's Going to Be a War 55
9. Like a Cup of Coffee with King David 62
10. A Child of the Establishment 71
11. Just Don't Get Involved in Politics 76
12. It's Not the Time to Hesitate 85
13. All-Out War 91
14. A New Political Forum—Mashov 97
15. Suddenly in the Holy of Holies 105
16. Do You Know Where Shimon Is? 111
17. The Brief Golden Age of Peace 123
18. Schlemiels and Schlimazels 128
19. "It's Unthinkable That a Lowly Bureaucrat Is Shaping Israel's Policies" 135
20. The Sextet vs. the Old Guard 145
21. A Meeting at a Monastery 168

22. The Dismantlers, Inc.	175
23. When Avrasha Returned Home	183
24. The "Secret" Sextet in Cairo	188
25. Oslo at Tandoori	194
26. Better If Arafat Is Here, and Not in Tunisia	200
27. "What If We Propose a Permanent Accord Straightaway?"	209
28. An Engagement, Not a Marriage	218
29. A Tête-à-Tête with Arafat	223
30. Erekat's Astonishing Request	230
31. Don't Leave Us with Half a Party!	234
32. Opening the Locked Door in the Palace	240
33. Yossi, We Have a Trump Card Here!	246
34. Turn on the TV, Rabin's Been Shot!	255
35. No Positions, Only Principles	267
36. How Do We Get Out of Lebanon?	275
37. Hoo Ha—Look Who's Coming	281
38. Pursuing Justice	286
39. The Horses Have Already Left the Stables	293
40. Like a Fellini Film at Taba	306
41. There's Someone to Talk with	313
42. Two Farewells	319
Afterword	323
Acknowledgments	327
Index	329

Photographs follow page 151.

Preface

AN AUTOBIOGRAPHY IS NOT AN OBJECTIVE LIFE STORY, SO I DEBATED for a long time whether to write one. I also recognize that those who try to distance themselves a bit, to admit failures and mistakes, can never distance themselves enough. Each person sees things from their unique perspective. Broadminded people also understand that there are countless other perspectives, and, in principle, they accept the fact that those other perspectives might be more correct. But the ability to see things from another person's perspective is truly uncommon, and I don't think I was blessed with this ability. Thus, I resolved to refrain from writing my life story.

However, after reading the account of my life in the praiseworthy book by the historian Avi Shilon (*The Decline of the Left Wing in Israel: Yossi Beilin and the Politics of the Peace Process*), I realized that my perspective can only be described by me. Perhaps I'm right and maybe I'm wrong, but the story—part of which is the story of many of my contemporaries and some of which is unique—also deserves to be told first-hand.

I apologize to the readers of this book that I changed my mind about not writing. As compensation, I decided not to burden them with footnotes. I tried hard to validate my memories with recorded facts but cannot claim that no mistake has slipped into my recollections.

The book ends with the Geneva Initiative and several related events that occurred immediately afterwards. If I write a sequel, it will discuss my four years as chairman of Meretz and my peace activity in recent years, primarily my efforts to promote the idea of a Palestinian-Israeli confederation as a means of implementing the two-state solution. It will also describe the important project of saving Jewish cemeteries in Eastern Europe, an initiative my partner Daniela and I support via the Beilink consulting firm we established, and my work as chairman of Hillel Israel, the Israeli branch of the global Jewish student organization.

This is the place to thank the wonderful people I have met during my lifetime, in Israel and throughout the world. The list is too long to list everyone who was crucial in enabling me to promote the matters I deemed important. The successes were shared. The failures I take upon myself—and I say this not as lip service, but from a profound sense of responsibility.

Still, I owe a special note of appreciation to the book's editor, Amichai Shalev, because the book would never have been published in its current format without him. The English version could not have been published without the help of my friend Brian Lurie, and without the faithful translation of another friend of mine—Ira Moskowitz.

✳✳✳

The organizing principle of my life is my Jewish identity. I didn't choose it, but it is the lens through which I see the world. I know—it's emotional, tribal and perhaps even too narrow. I'm sometimes annoyed by the fact that it's important for me to know whether someone who strikes me as being Jewish is indeed a Jew, or by the fact that I'm thrilled to discover the Jewish roots of someone I never imagined was Jewish. (One such surprise is described in the book.) The Jewish people is my extended family. I don't think it was chosen by anyone, and I'm unwilling to take any metaphysical authority upon myself. God for me is the moral sensibility that distinguishes human beings from other animals. It is my conscience, and a source of awe and fear.

I'm familiar with the Jewish sources over the generations and they continue to touch a deep chord in me, even if they also include a considerable amount of nonsense. When I'm visiting some far-flung place and hear someone say the *Shma Yisrael* declaration of faith, I immediately feel tears on my cheeks, just like when I hear Israel's national anthem, *HaTikva*, in an unexpected place.

I was shaped by the landscape of my homeland. But for me, Israel is first and foremost the most effective instrument for the continued existence of the Jewish people. I would like very much to see my extended family, the Jewish people, congregate in the Jewish state. It is difficult to believe that this will happen, but the fact that we are approaching a situation in which the majority of world Jewry lives in Israel makes me very happy.

Israel, in my eyes, is the state of the Jewish people and of all its citizens. If there is no Jewish majority, it will no longer be my state. And that majority will not be ensured by pushing the others away, but rather by establishing a border between us and our Palestinian neighbors and ensuring their independence, liberty, and sovereignty. Our self-determination must not come at the expense of another people.

I fear that our supposed patriots—those who wrap themselves in the flag, are enraged that an Arab Supreme Court justice refrains from singing *HaTikva* and enact the superfluous "Israel as the Nation-State of the Jewish People" law—are leading us to a dangerous place, where we'll be a Jewish minority ruling over a non-Jewish majority. I'm also convinced that it is possible to avoid this via a peace accord with the Palestinians, preferable under the umbrella of the Holy Land Confederation (a confederation of two states, west of the Jordan River, in an area sacred to people of various religions.) The confederation could facilitate everyday life in the Holy Land, enable joint planning and action to address environmental challenges, make more effective use of resources, offer an easier solution for Jewish settlements that remain under Palestinian sovereignty, and establish responsibility for defending the confederation partners from common enemies.

It is hard to accept that we are still captive to decisions that may have been right for their time, but today cause severe and unnecessary harm in our lives. One example is the famous "Status Quo Letter" that David Ben-Gurion, then serving as chairman of the Jewish Agency's Executive Committee, sent to the ultra-Orthodox Agudat Yisrael organization in 1947. (The letter presented the Jewish Agency's position on issues of religion and state in the emerging state, and was aimed at convincing Agudat Yisrael to testify favorably before the UN Special Committee on Palestine.)

I'm concerned by the fact that the Orthodox establishment is the sole arbiter of "who is a Jew" and that marital status in Israel is entirely governed by religious law. I believe that Israel, as a state, should recognize the self-definition of anyone who declares that he or she is a Jew (subject to review if suspected of deceit), and to recognize civil marriages or, at least, "matrimonial partnerships." At the same time, I'm concerned about the failure to build bridges between secular and ultra-Orthodox Jews in Israel.

✳✳✳

The coronavirus crisis exposed the ultra-Orthodox community's detachment from the Israeli mainstream. It is an important, rapidly growing group that does not entirely identify with the Israeli success story and distrusts the secular establishment. The non-enlistment of the ultra-Orthodox to the Israel Defense Forces (IDF) is no longer an esoteric problem, but I think it could be resolved by establishing an equal policy for men and women in the Defense Service Law, allowing draft exemptions to those who demonstrate that due to reasons of conscience or family-religious lifestyle they cannot perform defense service. This would be a universal decision that would also enable the induction of Arab Israelis to the IDF or their exemption on grounds of religion or conscience.

I want to live in a state in which there is complete civic equality, where the only distinction between Jews and non-Jews is in the Law of Return. Without the Law of Return, in my opinion, a "Jewish and democratic" state becomes a meaningless phrase. I think that liberals who share my unequivocal belief in the equal value of all persons, can still justify this lone exception to civic equality.

I consider myself a social-liberal who wholeheartedly believes that human rights must not be trampled by collective rights, and who is convinced that there is no replacement for the free market, but that it is imperative to address its flaws, which create wide social disparities and terrible injustices.

I want to live in a state that is part of the world, a state that understands the huge advantage in cultivating ties with other states. I want to live in a world where there is an international organization that only includes democratic states as members—alongside the UN, where membership is not tied to the nature of the member state's regime.

I want to believe that I have helped to advance the objectives I believe in and that I can continue to contribute, even when operating outside the corridors of government power. In any case, no one departs the world having achieved even half of his or her desires, and there will always be someone else to carry the torch.

SECRETS I WON'T TAKE WITH ME

1

Angry at Herzl

My story starts at 24 Kalischer Street in Tel Aviv, in the home that my grandfather Yosef Bregman had purchased. Actually, the story begins much earlier, when he was called Yossel Hosid as the grandson of two rabbinical sages—the Karlin-Stolin Rebbe on his mother's side and the Chernobyl Rebbe on his father's side.

Grandfather Yosef was born in Pinsk, White Russia (today Belarus). At age sixteen, he joined the Hovevei Zion movement and, together with a few friends, formed the Bnei Zion Zionist Society. This was even before the First Zionist Congress (1897). He later joined the Zionist Federation and was a great admirer of Theodor Herzl. But at the Sixth Zionist Congress (1903), when Herzl presented his famous Uganda proposal, my grandfather was devastated. "Traitor!" he shouted at Herzl, shocking many of the delegates; he now became a sworn enemy of the "King of the Jews."

He was a member of Chaim Weizmann's Democratic Faction (an opposition group of young intellectuals that operated within the Zionist Federation during the years 1901–1904) and was close to Menachem Ussishkin in the latter's struggle against Herzl. In parallel to his work as a banker in Pinsk, my grandfather would travel to Jewish towns in the area and try to convince his listeners that Zionism could only be fulfilled in the Land of Israel.

In the five Zionist congresses he attended as a delegate, my grandfather worked at Weizmann's side and devoted a great deal of his time to organizing the Zionist movement in Eastern Europe. Much of this activity was illegal, and he was arrested in 1906 for participating in a clandestine Zionist conference in Vilna, Lithuania.

My grandfather was short, stocky, and bald, and walked with a cane. He had a weak heart, a short fuse and was not inclined to compromise. In his voluminous correspondence with Ussishkin, I found scathing references to Herzl and it was hard to believe that my grandfather had written such things. He could not understand how a Jew could be non-Zionist, and how a Zionist could be willing to settle in any place other than the Land of Israel.

Haya Weizmann-Lichtenstein, the sister of Chaim Weizmann and my grandfather's partner in Zionist activity in Pinsk, wrote in her book *To the Coveted Border* that he was like a volcano in his youth. "At age sixteen, he gave his heart and soul to the Zionist idea. Nothing was difficult for him. The leaders of the Zionist movement sent this devoted and quick-witted young man wherever the organization needed his work, and he waged battle against the opponents of Zionism with fiery rhetoric that exuded confidence and deep conviction. He was among the preachers of Zionist work in the Jewish Diaspora, of cultural activity in all segments [of Jewish society], and of practical work in the Land of Israel."

It is important to note that my grandfather had no formal education. He was the epitome of an autodidact; he devoured entire books in many fields, particular in the fields of economics and banking. He was a believer in cooperative banking and was appointed to manage a savings and loan bank in Pinsk in 1907.

In 1904, he was one of three young Zionist Congress delegates dispatched by Ussishkin to inform Herzl that they would work to depose him if he did not renounce the Uganda idea at the Seventh Zionist Congress. The fact that neither side persuaded the other became irrelevant: Herzl died soon afterward, and the Congress was postponed until 1905.

At age twenty-six, my grandfather married Rivka Shapira. Their son Baruch arrived a year later, in 1907, and their daughter Zehava, my mother, was born in 1910. At home, unlike most of their contemporaries, they read and wrote in Hebrew. As a devout Zionist, my grandfather was eager to move to the Land of Israel with his family. But the movement wanted him to stay and establish a Zionist bank in Yekaterinoslav, Ukraine, and he reluctantly agreed. (In the meantime, Yekaterinoslav was renamed Dnepropetrovsk in the wake of the Bolshevik Revolution and the ascendency of the "Reds"—the Bolsheviks and their supporters, over the "Whites"—the federation of their opponents.)

And so, the family spent a number of years moving from place to place against the backdrop of civil war, until the long-awaited approval to emigrate to Palestine came in 1923. They arrived at the port of Jaffa on the *Campidoglio* on April 26, 1923, and my grandfather very quickly found work at a bakery, lugging sacks of flour. His employers soon realized that he could be more useful as a bookkeeper. The family rented a modest apartment on Bezalel Street (later renamed Tchernichovsky Street) in Tel Aviv. He later took a job at the Mashbir retail organization of the cooperative movement and then returned to banking in 1928 as the manager of the Savings and Loan Bank in Tel Aviv, where he worked for the rest of his life. One of the employees at the bank was the mother of Yitzhak Rabin, Rosa Cohen ("Red Rosa"); my grandfather used to say that she was destined for greatness.

Along with his banking endeavors, he continued his Zionist activity. He played a key role at the Jewish National Fund, was a board member of the Geula land redemption company, a founder of the HaMifade HaEzrahi fund for small businesses, and more. Ideologically, he was situated between Mapai and the General Zionists. He was a strong believer in consumer cooperatives and published thin booklets, with illustrations and black covers, on the importance of credit cooperatives (a form of organization based on sharing the means of production and leveraging the members' collective purchasing power, while maintaining equality among the members).

My grandfather's Zionism was uncompromising. In his view, the world was black and white: Zionists and their supporters versus the opponents of Zionism and the anti-Semites. He loved the Jewish tradition and the melodies from his parent's home but recoiled from religious ritual as if from fire.

My mother Zehava venerated her father and seemed fearful of him even years after his death. The letters they exchanged when my grandfather traveled to Jerusalem or visited other places offer a glimpse at their relationship. For example, she informed him in one letter that she had received her matriculation certificate and wished to continue her studies at Hebrew University:

> My dear father! Perhaps you hoped to hear something different from me. You would have liked to hear that I wish to study agriculture, join a *kvutzah*, a *moshav*, and work the land. I realize that our young people must return to working the soil, to be farmers. . . . But each person has their own special inclinations. I have no penchant for agriculture. I am prepared to work for the homeland, for the benefit of my people and land, but in a different way.

Anyone who didn't know my grandfather might assume that he was swayed by her earnest request. But he responded as follows:

> Have you forgotten that I have always sacrificed my own personal interests, and those of my wife and son and daughter, when I found that the interest of building the land—or more precisely, Zionism—demanded that of me?

But my mother did not relent. Two years later, when he was on another trip to Jerusalem, she wrote:

> I awoke this morning with the burdensome question that has remained unresolved since the day I graduated from high school. My father! Do I need to repeat the things that you're already aware of and that weigh so heavily upon my heart? In any case, I'll reiterate that the second year of my idleness is starting today, and that if I don't continue my studies this year, it's clear that my life will pass without ever continuing my studies. You'd like me to work in some office in Tel Aviv? That is not desirable to me for various reasons: First of all, you know that I'm sick and tired of Tel Aviv, and I'm suffocating in it; second, and more important, is that I'll become the type of person I detest most—a limited person, who has nothing to occupy herself with besides her job and a stroll in the early evening!

My mother wrote unequivocally that she aspired to greater things and even asked her father to help her find work in Jerusalem: "In about another month and a half, classes start at the university. I pray that my studies will also begin then," she concluded.

In the end, my grandfather gave in. A month later, my mother packed her things, moved to Jerusalem, and enrolled in Middle East and Arabic Studies.

✳✳✳

In 1935, Grandfather Yosef acquired the home at 24 Kalischer Street, adjacent to the Carmel open market. A taxi came every morning to drive him to the bank on Herzl Street, at the corner of Yehuda Halevi Street. There was an electric refrigerator in the house, and even a private telephone. It was one of the few such telephones in Tel Aviv; the phone number was 3894. A year after moving into 24 Kalischer Street, Zehava married Zvi Beilin and my grandfather invited them to stay in the house. The temporary arrangement became permanent. In August 1937, a baby boy—my brother Yinon—was born to Zehava and Zvi. The blond, green-eyed child was the favorite of Grandfather Yosef. Unfortunately, however, they didn't have much time to enjoy each other's company. On May 14, 1946, my grandfather went to the bank in the morning. At 3:00 p.m., the taxi brought him home. He didn't feel well, went to rest, and died from a heart attack. He was only sixty-six years old.

A large crowd gathered for his funeral. Among those present were Mayor Israel Rokach, the leaders of the Histadrut labor federation, the chief rabbis, the head of the Jewish National Fund, bank managers and all of Tel Aviv's "who's who." After his burial in the cemetery on Trumpeldor Street, the family remained alone, feeling shocked and orphaned. His study, which was referred to as the "Cabinet," was left untouched—not a single book was moved, not a single picture was replaced. Even his cane remained in its place. For my mother, he was the most important and closest person in the world. She was completely shattered.

A while after his death, my Aunt Riva came to live with us. She was Grandmother Rivka's cousin. During the day, she worked at the Shalva convalescent home on Yavne Street. At home, she would usually walk on her tiptoes, as if afraid that her mere presence would disturb us.

Two years later, when I came into the world, my family was still deep in bereavement, so it was no surprise that the name chosen for me was Yosef. My grandfather's presence was still palpable in every corner of the home. Only the Haganah's weapons cache, tucked into one of the walls, vanished as if it had never existed. When I was old enough to ask about my grandfather, I was told he had traveled to America, and that sounded perfectly logical to me. I remember dreaming about meeting him at the port in Haifa; in those dreams, he would greet me with a big hug and ask about my activities in kindergarten. When I was a bit older, they decided to inform me that he had actually died and would never return. I immediately burst into tears, heartbroken.

✳✳✳

I remember every detail about the house, though the house seems to grow bigger as the memories become more distant. My first memory of the house is from when I was two and a half: I wanted to get to the place where Grandmother Rivka was sitting and had to walk through a long, dark corridor to get there. Even though I was already a big boy, I asked my mother to accompany me. She said that I was already big enough to walk through the hallway on my own, and instead of accompanying me she started to sing—in a loud voice and terribly off tune—"David, King of Israel, alive and existing." And that helped.

In reality, it was a one-story home with five rooms and had cupboards stretching up to the ceiling. The house was situated on a lot of about 3,500 square feet, but for me it was an entire world. The front gate was low and had no lock. Anyone who wanted to could enter the yard, and a multitude of dogs and cats were keen to explore the possibilities the site offered.

I remember the milkman entering through the yard every morning, and the laundry room and the storeroom for the wood used to heat bathwater on Fridays. The house was brimming with Zionism and full of incomprehensible books on finance, an encyclopedia in German (*Meyers Lexikon*) with wonderful pictures that could keep me busy for hours (including transparent pages between the pictures), a huge collection of books in Russian and literature translated into Hebrew (Stiebel Publishing), not to mention volumes of the *HaTekufa* newspaper, *HaShiloah* literary journal and the *Davar for Children* weekly. Yinon would bind all of the issues of *Davar for Children* at the end of each year and I continued this strange practice, without knowing when we might need to use them later in life.

I remember that the toilet was separate from the bathroom, and that there was a metal chain connected to the toilet tank mounted above; to flush, you used the chain to pull a wooden handle. The bathroom contained a bathtub and water tank. You had to open a compartment at the base of the tank, fill it with wood from the wood storeroom, douse the wood with kerosene, light a match, toss it between the pieces of wood and then quickly shut the door to the opening so that the flames wouldn't jump out. In less than an hour, the water was very hot, and it was enough for several showers, one after another. The showers were primarily on Friday afternoons and prior to other festive occasions. During the summer, we could shower in cold water.

We bought the firewood from a peddler who rode on a three-wheeled bicycle; bags of wood were attached to his bike with iron wire. He would peddle his wares by singing "wood for the bath, don't forget." One time, when a regular customer stopped buying wood from him, he stood outside the customer's house and shouted at the top of his lungs, "Have you stopped bathing?" It turned out that the customer had switched to a gas-powered water heating system.

The four doors to our home were ceremoniously bolted every evening: the front door, the door to Grandmother Rivka's entrance, the door to the kitchen and the door to the porch attached to the "Cabinet." There were four hooks installed in the wall, two above and two below, and an iron bar was placed on each of the two pairs of hooks.

In those days, a laundry woman worked for us. Her name was Shoshana, and I liked her very much. She was always in a wonderful mood, and I remember that sometimes, at bedtime, my grandmother would tell me stories about Shoshana, about her family and about the animals she raised in her yard. I believed every word she said as I drifted off to sleep. The real story was different: She was married at a young age to an old man she never loved, and they had one child who died when he was just a young boy. She lived alone for many years in a tiny room in the Neve Tzedek neighborhood. When Shoshana fell ill, I went with my grandmother to visit her. I saw her bed, her meager cupboard, and the bathroom in the courtyard. From that day, it was no longer possible to lull me to sleep with stories about our laundry woman. I suggested to my grandmother that Shoshana come to live with us. I don't know if she gave any serious consideration to my proposal. Even if she did, Shoshana died a week after our visit.

I remember that my room was connected to a hallway that my family used as a shelter during World War II. My grandmother's dining room was to the right of my room and had photographs of Herzl and Weizmann at various ages, and of Max Nordau, a drawing of Maimonides and a picture of Rabbi Yavetz, who had a strange and frightening glare. There was a large cabinet made by the famous carpenter (and future mayor of Ramat Gan) Krinitzi that displayed all sorts of clay dishes and Hanukah menorahs behind its glass doors. The pendulum clock above it always needed to be adjusted. My father would do this; he would skillfully open the glass cover above the hands of the clock, insert the key in the right spot and wind the spring with a serious look on his face, like a professional clockmaker. Between my grandmother's dining room and ours, there was a folding partition that was only opened after she passed away.

My family cooked food on Primus stoves and wicks. It was a period of austerity. We lived on ration coupons and my parents would never consider for even a moment violating the austerity laws and purchasing products on the black market. The minister of rationing and supply, Dr. Dov Yosef, was the most oft-mentioned figure on the radio. According to family legend, my mother fed me porridge one day and started to tell me a story to occupy me during the feeding. "There once was a man," she began, and I promptly completed her sentence, "And his name was Dov Yosef."

We lived on makeshift products. I was so convinced that eggplant salad was chopped liver that the first time I tasted real chopped liver I felt that it was missing the taste of eggplant. Like many others, I was certain that filet was the name of a fish, though it was actually cod fish. It was the only fish I knew besides the live carp that arrived before the High Holidays and went straight into the bathtub. Soon afterwards, its life would come to an end—I never watched that part; it would then be stuffed and topped with slices of cooked carrots.

We never ate at a restaurant in Tel Aviv because "only people who have no home eat in restaurants," and we had a home, thank God. My family only drank wine after reciting the *kiddush* blessing on Sabbaths and holidays. Sugar had a place of honor in nearly every dish: rice with sugar and cinnamon, noodles with sugar and cinnamon, and even cauliflower with sugar. My grandmother also used a lot of garlic, because "garlic is healthy."

Until the age of fifteen, I had never tasted steak, avocado, cherries, and other items that have long been staples of Israeli cuisine. They didn't grow these food products locally, didn't bother to import them or they were simply too expensive. But I never felt that I was deprived, and I was reminded that "there are hungry people in India who would be happy to eat what you left on your plate."

Since I was born straight into the home on Kalischer Street, I never asked myself or anyone else who owned the house. For me, it was "our" house, belonging to everyone who lived in it. It was only when the house was put up for sale that I discovered it was owned by Grandmother Rivka. After she died, my mother wanted to sell the home as quickly as possible in order to avoid any potential inheritance disputes among the family's third generation. My parents lacked the means to buy their own home, so they were living in the home of my mother's parents. In my eyes, nothing could be more natural.

The house was sold when I was in ninth grade, and the proceeds allowed us to purchase a modest apartment in the Hod workers housing project on Frug Street. But I was never able to develop any sentiment toward the new apartment.

2

"I Just Don't Want Him to Grow Up to Be a Show-Off"

My mother Zehava was born in Pinsk in 1910. As mentioned, her parents spoke only Hebrew to her, but her first—and last—language was actually Russian. Near the end of her life, when her faculties were dimming, she suddenly returned to speaking fluent Russian. All in all, prior to the outbreak of civil war she had a comfortable life. At age thirteen, she emigrated to the Land of Israel with her parents and her brother Baruch.

My mother was able to enroll in the Neve Tzedek primary school for girls because she spoke Hebrew fluently and could read and write. She had no difficulties adjusting and immediately made friends, though most of them were two years younger due to the years of schooling she had missed during the Russian civil war. She impressed her teachers with her writing abilities, but her arithmetic skills were less impressive. Upon completing primary school, she was accepted to continue her studies at the Herzliya Hebrew Gymnasium, where she also excelled in Hebrew, literature, history, and Bible, while struggling with chemistry, math and physics. She loved the high school and venerated the teachers, including Haim Bograshov, Baruch Ben-Yehuda, and Ben-Zion Mosensohn. She had a romantic spirit, especially in those years, though this doesn't necessarily mean that she had romantic partners. In any case, if she had such partners, she never told me about them.

Her most vivid memory from that time, which she loved to recount, was about a trip to Petra. The students in her grade (the high school's eighteenth graduating class), traveled to Transjordan for two weeks. It was a real growing-up experience for the teenagers, and when they saw the structures carved into the reddish rock, they rubbed their eyes in amazement. It was my mother's first trip since arriving in the country and her last trip for many years, until she traveled as a very elderly woman to

France for a Bible conference. Every time she told us about Petra, it seemed like a far-off place that we'd probably never have an opportunity to visit. (When I did indeed make it to Petra, I could not send regards to her from that magical place—she had died a year earlier.) Her tales of Petra came against the backdrop of the futile attempts of bold hikers to reach the red rock and Arik Lavie's ballad *The Red Rock*, which played quite often on the radio in those days.

As an undergraduate in Middle East and Arabic Studies at Hebrew University (after finally receiving her father's approval, as described earlier), she didn't feel well one day and hailed a local coachman, got into his horse-drawn vehicle, and asked him in literary Arabic, as her strength was waning, to take her to the emergency room. It turned out that he didn't understand a word she said, but eventually got her to the hospital. The incident apparently changed something in her, reinforcing ideas she had already begun to form. She realized that her Arabic studies were largely useless. She had embarked on her studies with the desire to understand the language of local Arabs, but when she desperately needed to use this language, she couldn't even ask the coachman to save her life. Therefore, just before completing her undergraduate studies, she left the university and returned to Tel Aviv.

My mother worked for a while at the *Davar* newspaper as a reporter's assistant on Middle Eastern affairs and slowly shifted her focus to Bible studies. She read voraciously on this topic and became an expert; she was later among the founders of the Israel Society for Biblical Research, along with people like professors Haim Gvaryahu, Yehuda Elitzur, Yosef Braslevi, and Nechama Leibowitz. She edited books, published articles, and was one of the Bible commentators on Israel Radio (in a five-minute segment aired daily before the 7:00 p.m. news). In addition to a regular Bible study group she led at home, she frequently lectured on the Bible at labor councils, WIZO branches, and in municipal frameworks.

The annual conferences of the Israel Society for Biblical Research were very important events in her professional life. My mother also participated in Prime Minister David Ben-Gurion's Bible study group. Ben-Gurion initiated the study group in 1958, when the Bible was at the peak of its popularity in Israel; the Bible Contest was held for the first time that year and the winner, Amos Hakham, became a celebrity in Israel. The prime minister's group met twice a month on Saturday nights. After the "old man" resigned, President Zalman Shazar became the leader of the study group and my mother continued to participate in it.

My mother often relied on archeological findings in her lectures but was strongly opposed to the school of "biblical criticism" that challenged the authenticity of the Bible's redaction and allowed itself to suggest far-reaching interpretations on various questions. I loved her lectures and went to hear some of them, especially those held on Saturdays at Beit Tavori in Tel Aviv. I was proud of how she was able to captivate her audience and how she shared her impressions of the biblical text with them. I always preferred to sit in one of the back rows and didn't applaud at the end. I thought that as her child, it wasn't befitting or consequential for me to clap.

In any case, as a child I found it very difficult to reconcile her devotion to Hebrew, the Bible and Judaism with her explicit secularity. She wasn't a strident secularist. On the contrary, she kept kosher ("so that a rabbi could eat in our home") and looked approvingly on the fact that I went with my father to the synagogue on special Sabbaths (for example, to bless the new month), on holidays or when famous cantors came to the Great Synagogue. But she herself did not attend synagogue or engage in religious ritual. As in other fields of life, she followed in her father's footsteps in this area.

Her love of the country was not expressed in hiking with a backpack and a walking stick, but mainly in her refusal to tolerate any criticism of the state. Anything connected with Israel was the best and most correct thing, always. Thus, in our home, she filled the role of spokesperson for the IDF and for the Israeli government. When exchanging presents (always books) with my father, they would write to each other "3 years since our redemption" or "4 years since our redemption," marking the time since the War of Independence instead of citing the current date. In my mother's eyes, those who emigrated from Israel ("yordim") were despicable, almost as abhorrent as card games.

My mother was a loyal reader of the *Davar* daily. Her father had been one of the newspaper's first subscribers when it was established in 1925, and she continued the tradition. She had no doubts about the veracity of what the newspaper published. Other newspapers never entered our home.

Though she was very loyal to the establishment, she was not involved in any party-related activity. Her only "political" involvement came in the framework of the Israel Society for Biblical Research, where things could get quite stormy. There was infighting between the active Tel Aviv branch and the Jerusalem branch; people were insulted that their article was not included in a book published in the memory of a deceased scholar, or in honor of the eightieth birthday of another scholar. My mother saw herself responsible for mediating between rival factions and conciliating them.

✱✱✱

I clearly remember the day I graduated from kindergarten. I came home full of excitement and handed over my report card. My mother began reading it and her face turned gloomy. I was sure they had discovered a major flaw in me. I asked her to read it to me. She didn't want to. She said there was no need. I asked her if I was entitled to move up to first grade and she said yes. I calmed down a bit and waited for my father to arrive.

When he came home from work that evening, I asked him to read me the report card. He didn't understand why my mother had refrained from doing so and he read it aloud with great pleasure, clearly enunciating each word. "The child Beilin Yosef is promoted to first grade in accordance with his age and development. He was in the kindergarten under my direction during the year 5714 [1953–1954]. Comments: Intelligent. Excellent learner. Takes initiative in games, especially in building. A dominant type who knows his worth. Gathers most of the children around him and successfully commands them. Excellent rhythm and expression. Talks a lot and his language is very good. Very lively in conversations. Very knowledgeable."

I asked my father whether the report card was okay, and he said yes. I asked why Mother had refused to read it to me, and he didn't know. My mother entered, saw what was happening and told my father that he had made a mistake, that the report was intended for parents and not for the child. She added that she was very concerned, especially by the words "knows his worth." When my father wrinkled his forehead, she explained: "I just don't want him to grow up to be a show-off." Then she told me that I'm a regular and good child, and that I shouldn't let all sorts of ideas get into my head.

On the spot, I promised her that I would never become conceited—as if someone can promise such a thing.

But one time she caught me red-handed. There was a girl on our street, a year older than me, who was a bit mentally impaired. The neighbors' children and I used to laugh at her. One summer day, in the afternoon, she was leaning against the wall of the house across from us and we gathered around her and asked her all sorts of questions that we knew she'd be unable to answer. When she tried to answer, we laughed at her in the way that children sometimes laugh at someone who is weaker. My mother saw what was happening and immediately called me home for a rare scolding. It was unnecessary to explain to me that I had behaved badly. I knew that very well and asked her to forgive me.

But my mother insisted on explaining to me that the girl might be able to help me during difficult moments, and that I shouldn't make fun of anyone—not only because it was really unbefitting for a boy like me, but also because Aesop's fable about the lion and the mouse was relevant to this case: "One day," she said, "you'll be hurrying to school and will forget the notebook with your homework. I know that it would be like the end of the world for you. Imagine that I notice that you forgot the notebook but couldn't bring it to school because I had promised to meet someone. Imagine that I see that girl in the street and ask her to do me a favor and bring the notebook to you, and that she agrees. She'll make you a happy person, in a single moment, when she arrives at school with your notebook. How could you allow yourself to make fun of someone who might come to your assistance?"

It was a very embarrassing moment. Mother's example didn't sound particularly realistic to me, but somehow it was seared into my memory forever. So, when there were moments in my life when I started to pat myself on my shoulder, I would always remember that girl, who never got a chance to bring me the homework I had forgotten. Usually, when I came home with a high grade on an exam, Mother would ask what grade so and so received. And if it was a higher grade, she would praise him effusively. That annoyed me. "Why don't you ask me what grade I received?" She would say that she already knew.

So, on the one hand, she identified with every achievement of mine at school, with the articles I wrote for teen newspapers and with my achievements in chess. On the other hand, she feared that those achievements would change me. I had to assure her each time that I clearly understood that if I let myself get dizzy with success, it would lead to my downfall; and that it's impossible to always succeed and that there are others who excel in areas in which I know nothing; and that those who don't excel in anything can still contribute greatly to society, perhaps more than me.

All in all, my mother invested most of her time in me and Yinon. She marveled at us, imparted a lot of knowledge, documented our activities in writing from the moment we were born, and identified with everything we were experiencing at school and outside of school. She was very active on the parents' committee at school and through that activity was more informed about our school experiences than most of the other parents.

From the time I was five years old, she would record my thoughts in her notebook. I would tell her imaginary stories and dictate poems to her, and she encouraged me to continue. Later on, I would show her all of the products of my graphomania and would receive her uncritical support, even when I didn't deserve it. My mother had a talent for writing that did not turn her into an author or poetess, but she loved to write and compose rhymes, especially for family events.

✳✳✳

During my first year in the army, I remember worrying that my mother might take it hard when I informed her that I had to remain with my battalion and wouldn't be joining the family for the Passover seder. But when I told her, she responded with a sentence that I'll never forget: "I'm so proud that when we all sit at the seder table, you'll be guarding our border!" I almost felt insulted by how easily she accepted my absence.

When I introduced her to my future wife, Helena, my mother told me that Helena was very nice, but that it was too bad she wasn't Sephardi. She was convinced that her sons should personally contribute to the "integration of the exiles."

In 1994, when I accompanied her to her final resting place, I said at the gravesite that I wish to applaud her now, to make up for all those times during her life when I was embarrassed to do so.

3

"Father, I'm Not Going with You!"

My father Zvi, like my mother, was born in 1910. He was in the Haganah pre-state defense force and used to say that his years in that underground organization were the most important of his life. He also joined the Jewish Supernumerary Police Force that operated during the British Mandate to protect Jewish communities from attacks by Arab gangs. This gave him the opportunity to train and use weapons that served the Jewish underground. He was fit and strong, and never fell ill. He prepared himself for retirement, but unfortunately never reached retirement age.

At the beginning of World War I, his mother took him to Russia, and they returned to his father in Warsaw at the end of the war. He learned to speak Hebrew fluently at a Tarbut school, so had no difficulties adjusting after arriving with his parents in Palestine in 1926. He enrolled at the Geulah High School of Commerce and graduated two years later. My father really wanted to join a kibbutz, but he was an only child and his father was struggling to make a living. Consequently, he did not join a kibbutz or study at a university. Instead, he started working at Chile Saltpetre, a British company that sold chemicals used for fertilizer. He was even sent by the company to train at the head office in Cairo. Thus, from a young age, he helped support his parents—with his salary of eight pounds a month! A few years later, he was hired by the General Mortgage Bank (later renamed Leumi Mortgage Bank) to work in the bank's Insurance Department and eventually became the manager of the department. He worked there for forty years. During most of those years, he also held a second job as a bookkeeper for the Journalists' Association, which was then located on Rothschild Boulevard in Tel Aviv.

My father also had a talent for writing, but he wasn't a real journalist, except for a few articles he wrote for Mapai's newspaper *HaDor*. Perhaps that's why he wanted so much for me to become an important journalist. In any case, he was the coeditor of two Bank Leumi newspapers and didn't hesitate to apply some nepotism to publish my first poems and stories. Every article of mine in the school newspaper made him happy. He taught me to professionally proofread and, after the Beit Sokolov Journalists' House was built in 1957, he often took me to the "Newspaper of the Journalists"—an event held every Friday night, in which journalists shared their experiences.

At Beit Sokolov, I heard an elderly Ouri Kessary tell about his meeting with Alfred Dreyfus many years earlier. Another journalist who had visited Jordan with a foreign passport, spoke about the condition of the Western Wall. Beit Sokolov was where I listened to Daniel Barenboim for the first time. Then a seventeen-year-old, he came with his mother and played the piano.

✱✱✱

I remember walking with my father one Saturday along the seashore, past the shooting clubs and toward the Opera House, the site where the Knesset had initially convened before relocating to Jerusalem. Suddenly, we heard loud voices and saw a crowd gathering on the sidewalk across the street. I quickened my step to get away from the commotion, but my father grabbed my hand and wanted to cross the street and join the crowd. "If you're not curious, you won't be a journalist!" he explained.

I said in response that I'm very curious about some things, but not about "some quarrel on the beach." He was not ready to accept my argument.

We often took long walks on Saturdays. With canteens and brimmed hats, my father and I set out on hikes to places connected to the War of Independence. He drew my attention to the marks left by enemy bullets on Herzl Street and elsewhere and showed me Jaffa and the places where Arabs used to fire toward Kalischer Street. Sometimes we would walk as far as the Mikve Yisrael school or continue northward to the great expanse on the other side of the Yarkon River. During those walks, my father would tell me about events from his days in the Haganah, about his childhood in Warsaw, and how he played soccer as a child with a ball of rags. He also told me that when he didn't do well on a test at the Tarbut school, he would tell his parents that "all of the children failed the test." His father always understood the hint.

My father knew Hebrew, Arabic, Polish, Russian, English, French, German and even Latin. In fact, he was the king of trivia. He taught himself from *Reader's Digest* and from pocket-sized paperbacks published by Penguin. Politically, he was not right-wing, but he was much further to the right than my mother. For example, he was very angry that the left had accused the Revisionists of murdering Haim Arlozoroff in 1933 and was sure that the culprits were Arabs. My mother, on the other hand, believed that right-wing incitement had led someone on the right to commit the murder. Arlozoroff's assassination severely divided the Yishuv [the pre-state Jewish community], and my parents agreed not to talk about it. I always had the feeling that this unspoken topic was the elephant in the room.

My father was also opposed to marking May 1 as a national holiday. He harbored unpleasant memories of that day from Poland and, though he was loyal member of the Histadrut labor federation, he insisted on reporting to work on the first of May every year. Sometimes he was the only employee in the bank.

He told me several times, half laughingly, that he was grateful to me for being born on June 12, during the first ceasefire in the War of Independence, because he was able to receive a furlough and didn't have to participate in sinking the Irgun's *Altalena* munitions ship.

During election campaigns, my father would take me to hear Ben-Gurion and Moshe Sharett, Menachem Begin and Moshe Sneh. And, of course, we went to hear Moshe Dayan at the Carmel Market. My father felt it was important to expose me to a range of perspectives. He once told me that Sneh, the communist leader, could have been an outstanding prime minister had he not turned leftward, and he viewed Begin as a dangerous populist. My father never agreed to disclose which party he voted for. When he was on his deathbed and I told him that I had officially joined the Labor Party, he got very angry and felt that he had failed in properly educating me.

He wanted me to be an eminent journalist, erudite, with a deep national perspective, traditional, a man of culture, sociable, someone who keeps a distance from politics and can make essential repairs around the house.

My poor father tried to teach me how to repair folding window blinds, in case one of the slats fell out of place. This involved an entire procedure of dismantling the piece of metal connecting the parts of the wooden blinds and inserting it correctly, and then screwing the screws in place. He explained that I couldn't get married and have a home without knowing how to repair window blinds. So, I was already resigned to the fact that I would never have a home. There was also the task of repairing the electric fuses that burned out and replacing the electric wire in the clay fuse, not to mention fixing leaky faucets by replacing the rubber washers. In short, there was a series of essential repairs that we would usually tackle on Friday afternoons—that is, he would do the repairs and explain, and I would pretend to catch on.

Sometimes, we devoted Fridays to our stamp collection. We would moisten the overseas stamps to peel them off the envelopes, dry them, and then insert them carefully into albums. I saw this as endless, Sisyphean work that would do us no good. My father insisted that it would teach me about many countries. I told him once that Yitzhak Levanon's *Countries of the World*, which I had read twice, and Moshe Medzini's radio program on the United Nations provided me with information that was much more serious than inserting the picture of Queen Elizabeth II a thousand times in an album. But Father did not give up easily.

On Saturday mornings, we sometimes went to see a new exhibit at the Tel Aviv Museum at Beit Dizengoff. I mainly enjoyed the paintings of Marc Chagall; the temporary exhibits didn't always appeal to me. For example, I was fascinated by the exhibit of kinetic art by Yaacov Agam but found his work to be too technical. My father explained to me about different streams in art, and if I passed a painting or sculpture too quickly, he would notice and suggest that I go back and take a closer look. It was impossible to elude him.

He also loved music very much, especially Hebrew songs. When they played the poignant song *Kalaniyot* on the radio, sung by Shoshana Damari, he would melt on the spot. He was also fond of cantorial and classical music. It was important to him that I know the difference between a concerto, even a double concerto, and a symphony, what an oratorio is, and what *a cappella* means.

When they inaugurated the Heichal HaTarbut concert hall in Tel Aviv in October 1957, he got two tickets and divided them between the four of us: He and Yinon heard the first half of the concert, and my mother and I took their seats after the intermission. Isaac Stern and Arthur Rubinstein performed, and Leonard Bernstein was the conductor, his majestic mane of hair swaying from side to side with the music.

Nonetheless, there was also friction between the two of us. He thought I read too many books and didn't play enough soccer. Though he was proud of my grades at school, he was concerned that he was raising a "nerd" even before they coined that term. He sometimes shouted. On rare occasions, he also raised his hand against me—and that hurt. Mother would usually come to my rescue.

Some of our joint outings were not enjoyable for me—for example, going to the amusement park in Jaffa. I didn't understand what was so great about the Ferris wheel or the roller coaster, which frightened me, or the cotton candy that stuck to my face. And when I hit a target and won a teddy bear, I had no use for it. I also didn't like Jabaliyah (Givat Aliyah) Beach (which was so successful until they built a refugee camp by that name in Gaza). Fortunately, the Gordon pool opened in 1956, with its intoxicating fragrance of chlorine, new easy chairs, and a cafeteria—and no tar. Father agreed to split the summer between the pool and the beach—in part because he still preferred his "sleep of the just" on the sand, and in part because the Gordon pool charged an admission fee and money didn't grow on trees.

✻✻✻

I don't know when he decided to stop wearing a kippah. I never saw pictures of him wearing one, but I know that he grew up in a very religious home that was strictly observant. I don't know how his parents reacted to the tradition that he had fashioned for himself.

At home, we kept kosher according to the practice of German Jews: two hours between meat and milk, and half an hour between milk and meat. To eat non-kosher food was unthinkable. There was a complete separation of meat and milk, and the rules of Passover were strictly observed, including the immersion of dishes and tableware in boiling water, the search for *chametz*, and the purchase of new kitchenware. To please my father, Mother lit candles on Friday nights and on the eve of Jewish festivals. Father also refrained from writing on the Sabbath, explaining that writing was his work.

He did not put on tefillin or pray every morning, but, as mentioned, he would attend synagogue on special Sabbaths and on holidays, when great operatic cantors like Jan Peerce and Richard Tucker would sometimes appear. He would occasionally take me to Hasidic synagogues in Tel Aviv, in part to show me a *tische* and how the rebbe's followers ate leftovers from his dish.

I remember one time losing hold of my father's hand in the Tel Aviv Great Synagogue. I found myself lost in a forest of legs and prayer shawls. I couldn't see a thing and panicked, not knowing how I'd ever find my father. After a quick and rational assessment, I reached the conclusion that I would apparently remain alone in the Great Synagogue forever—a conclusion that held force for only a few moments, until my father found me.

And there was the matter of soccer. Father was not a fan of any particular team, but simply loved the game. Occasionally, on Saturday afternoon, he would take me to Basa Stadium (the site of Bloomfield today), where I saw for the first time all of the names that the legendary broadcaster Nehemia Ben-Avraham mentioned on the radio, such as Ya'akov Hodorov, Nahum Stelmach, and Shiye Glazer. It was a bit difficult standing for two hours, especially during the boring parts of the game, but my father enjoyed every moment, and it was certainly more comfortable for him to come with his son than to stand there alone.

This continued until one fateful Saturday. It was one of the special Sabbaths and we went to the Great Synagogue. I was then a few months past my eighth birthday. When the prayers were over, we went out to Allenby Street to wait for a shared taxi to take us to Basa. And then, while we were waiting, I told him, "Father, I'm not going with you. I'm not going to travel on the Sabbath anymore."

This decision had been in the making since my eighth birthday. It was hard for me to understand my father's middle-way approach to tradition. I thought that the most important thing was to preserve the Jewish people after the Holocaust and that the way to do that was to observe the religious commandments, and if so, then we must do this uncompromisingly. In some ways, I could better appreciate my mother's completely secular approach.

My father could not believe this was happening to him. He was furious but couldn't yell at me in the middle of the street. He still hoped to persuade me to get into the taxi that stopped for us. That didn't happen. The driver asked him to hurry up and my father got in alone. I walked home and recounted the episode to my mother.

"You'll get over it," she said.

"Mom, it's not a headache!" I replied, and I grew increasingly fearful that my father would give me an earful when he came home. But that didn't happen. He arrived and calmly asked me to explain what was going on with me. I explained, and he responded by saying that children see everything in black and white, and that as we grow older it becomes clear that the world is more complex. He said that religious tradition is indeed important, but it doesn't mean that things don't change. He added that he greatly appreciates my concern for the future of the Jewish people, but that I won't contribute to its continuity by refusing to travel with him to Basa on Saturdays.

"In biblical times, there were no taxis or elevators, and it's really not work, so people who aren't extremists can allow themselves to carry out the commandments they consider most important," he explained. And if he were a construction worker, he added, he would write on the Sabbath. But since he writes all week, writing is work for him, so he doesn't engage in writing on the Sabbath.

He also thought that I'd get over it. He was right, but I only got over it seventeen years later, during the Yom Kippur War, when he was no longer alive.

✳✳✳

Though my father was completely fluent in German, he never used it and never bought any products made in Germany, except for one time when he decided to surprise my mother with a new mixer and brought it home on Friday afternoon. When he took a closer look at the product, he discovered that it was made in Germany. As if detecting pork on his plate, he immediately packed up the mixer and hurried back to Allenby Street to switch it for another one before the store closed for the Sabbath. He returned home an hour later with a mixer made by Moulinex, a French company.

My father never visited Germany and wanted no connection to Germans. On the issue of reparation payments, he sided completely with Ben-Gurion. He used to say that he couldn't understand why Begin was so intent on allowing Jews' money to remain in the hands of the Germans, and why the survivors and their state should not receive monetary compensation. He was less enthusiastic about Israel establishing diplomatic relations with Germany.

My father was entirely committed and engaged. In the 1950s, for example, he volunteered to teach Hebrew in the transit camps for new immigrants as part of a national campaign to wipe out illiteracy. I don't know how he found time between his numerous jobs, but I remember him returning home several times a week, sometimes completely drenched from the rain, after taking multiple buses to reach a transit camp with a Hebrew book in hand. Private vehicles were only for the wealthy. Father never even learned to drive. He traveled in buses and in shared taxis. Private taxis were for sick people, just as restaurants were for those who have no home. When Mother took me to a movie at the new luxurious "Tel Aviv" cinema (with Technicolor, Hebrew subtitles, and air conditioning), and father discovered that the ticket price was 250 prutot [¼ of an Israeli pound]—he almost fainted on the spot.

My childhood was during a period of austerity, and everything was done sparingly. For example, we wore shoes whose tips had been cut to accommodate our growing feet. My father would cut the tips with a razor. I don't remember conversations at home about the economic situation, but he was always worried that more difficult days may lie ahead and that we needed to prepare for them. As mentioned, it was only later that I realized that my parents did not own their own home.

I remember that as the economic situation began to improve in the early 1960s, my father went on a one-month tour of classical Europe, and we followed the long journey of our personal Marco Polo via the postcards he sent from every port. We missed him terribly. My mother and I went to the port in Haifa to welcome him back. When he disembarked, I noticed that his hair had suddenly turned white! I calmed down a bit only after we got home and I saw the presents he brought—a white wool sweater, white chocolate, and cherries—which until then had only existed in the movies.

✳✳✳

My parents met in 1933 at a party in Tel Aviv. Someone at the party asked, "Why isn't everyone dancing?" The answer was that there was no phonograph or records. Zvi said that his friend had a portable phonograph and volunteered to go bring it. He asked Zehava, whom he had met a few minutes earlier, if she would accompany him—and she agreed. That was the beginning. Their paths later separated, but Tel Aviv was small, and they met again in 1936 and married. Yinon was born a year later.

They were very different from one another. Father wanted to take in the whole world and was never satisfied. Mother loved being at home and was an optimistic person. Yet, they undoubtedly had beautiful moments together. She would call him "Zeb" and he would call her "Zehavti" [my Zehava]. They had a diverse group of friends. Sometimes they went out in the evenings and sometimes they hosted their friends at our home.

Independence Day was the most sacred holiday for both of them. After a festive dinner, they would go out for a rare visit to a café on Dizengoff Street. The IDF Parade on Independence Day was an event we never missed. We would stand on Allenby Street for long hours, waiting on the sidewalk in a crowd of people, or we would wait on the balcony of a relative, the dentist Dr. Mina Meyrovna-Friedman.

In addition, there were family vacations outside of Tel Aviv. Several summers, we traveled to the Beit Hakerem neighborhood in Jerusalem, where my father rented a room for a few days. We'd sightsee and visit relatives, including professor Michael Ish-Shalom, a leading expert on the history of the Crusades in the Holy Land; he also coordinated the preparation for awarding the Israel Prize on Independence Day and directed the event. We would also go to see churches and monasteries, and once even visited the Knesset at the Froumine House during its summer recess, and the university at Terra Santa, before it moved to its new home on Givat Ram. And there was always a visit to the Strauss House, the new headquarters of the Histadrut in Jerusalem. I remember going up to the roof and looking toward the Old City. It was impossible to see the Western Wall, but sometimes we saw Jordanian Legionnaires, as well as quite a few laundry items on clotheslines. But my father's real vacation was on the kibbutz. He had a lot of friends on various kibbutzim, and he would make a round of visits, working a full day each time in the orchards or cowshed.

I certainly remember that my parents often argued. Sometimes the arguments ended in reconciliation; other times, they stopped speaking to each other. On a number of occasions I found myself delivering messages between them, and I hated every moment of that. They certainly were not happy, but they apparently convinced themselves that there were other couples who were far more miserable than them. In retrospect, I think that both of them deserved more suitable partners, but there was no real option for that at the time. People didn't divorce unless their marriage became unbearable.

In any case, after a long battle with cancer, my father passed away twenty-two years before my mother died. During all those years, we thought she never would consider finding a new partner. We were wrong. After her death, we found among her papers copies of letters to a man she met in her Bible-related activities. The letters suggest that there was indeed love between them, though not entirely symmetrical.

4

Love Doesn't Diminish When You Divide It

YINON WANTED A LITTLE BROTHER. HE HAD TO WAIT QUITE A FEW years, until he was eleven years old, before his wish came true. We lived together in the same home for only seven years; he remembers all of them and I only recall four—or maybe four and a half. To a large extent, my brother Yinon, the blond youth with green eyes, took responsibility for me, without even being asked.

Kalischer Street, at least its western part, was within gunfire range of the Hassan Bek Mosque in Jaffa. Therefore, 24 Kalischer became the neighborhood Haganah headquarters and, after the state was established, an IDF command center. At first, the family still lived in part of the house. However, my father was mobilized for military duty and my mother, who was pregnant with me, began roaming to other places of residence with Yinon in tow. They stayed for several weeks in my paternal grandparents' home in Tel Aviv's Kiryat Meir neighborhood. But it was a two-room apartment and one of them was rented out. Living there was not easy. They moved from there to Petah Tikva, to the home of my Uncle Baruch, who managed Bank Leumi in the moshava and was married to Levana. They lived in a spacious apartment in a handsome building, on the town's main street, next to the monument for Baron Rothschild. A fruit-bearing citrus tree grew in the yard. Yinon was enrolled in the local school, and when my mother went into labor on Shavuot eve, she was taken to Beilinson Hospital. The delivery was difficult and protracted.

My father received a furlough from the army and came with Yinon to the hospital the next day. The corridors of the hospital were full of wounded soldiers, groaning in pain, and that image remained implanted in Yinon's mind for many years. Nonetheless, the first lull in fighting had begun and some initial optimism could be felt at the hospital.

My mother was still very weak when she was released from the hospital, and since my father returned to the army, Yinon became my main caregiver. Diapers, laundry, and all the rest. But mother didn't want to abuse the hospitality of her sister-in-law, and after several months accepted an invitation from another relative, Beno Eisenstadt, who lived on Mapu Street in Tel Aviv.

The Eisenstadt family took on a central role in our lives. The mother Zippora (whom we called Tante Zippa) was my grandfather Yosef's cousin. Most of her children lived in Israel, and each had a different last name: Victor lived with his family in Haifa and Hebraized Eisenstadt to Eshet. He succeeded Abba Hushi as secretary of the Haifa workers' council and served in that position for many years. Baruch was a kibbutznik and teacher and lived in Givat Haim Ichud. He Hebraized his name without coordinating it with his brother and called himself Azania. Baruch served in the Knesset for many years, representing Mapai (and its later incarnations), including a stint as chairman of the House Committee. Beno kept the original family name.

In any case, we returned home only several months later, in late 1948, as the war wound down and the military command center in our apartment was evacuated; my father was also released from the army at that time.

✳✳✳

Perhaps because of those six months of itinerancy, or by natural inclination, Yinon continued to be my third parent, and this seemed perfectly normal to me. For example, I remember him using a sterilized needle to remove splinters from my fingers that I got while playing with blocks of wood. He would professionally fold and soften the rough toilet paper before I needed to use it. We would play together with the lead soldiers passed down to us from our only cousin, Oded, and I would drive Yinon crazy.

Yinon would do his homework in Grandfather's "Cabinet," sitting on the black-leathered, square-shaped chair, while I would find a place for myself to stand on the narrow strip of wood at the base of the backrest. I pretended I was a garbage collector standing on the step at the rear of the truck, and shouted, "Garbage truck! Garbage truck!"

Yinon was my role model. I would tag along after him, and even went with him to his friends and to rehearsals for a graduation party where he played in an "orchestra" with a comb and paper napkin. At home, I devoted quite a lot of time to producing classical music from a thin-toothed comb, with only partial success.

We only fought one time, when a lead soldier slipped from my hand and broke. Yinon was furious because he saw Oded's toys as a sort of heirloom, and he slapped my hand. I remember that the slap didn't really hurt, but I felt insulted. He later apologized, and I apologized too. And still, even six decades later, I haven't forgotten that incident.

On Saturday mornings, I would creep into his bed to listen to his favorite radio program with him: *On the Opera Stage*. That was the beginning of my musical education. Often, we would also listen together to *Stages and Screens*, the weekly program about plays and movies.

He loved French chansons, and I loved French chansons. He loved the *Les Compagnons de la chanson* vocal group and I didn't miss any of their performances in Israel. I loved the relatives he loved, the food he preferred and, following in his footsteps, I went to the Dugmai kindergarten on HaShachar Street and the Ahad Ha'am School for Boys (which kept its name even after becoming coed.)

My first year in elementary school was Yinon's last year in high school and it was a magical year. He would often walk me to school on his way to high school, and I felt real pride arriving at the school gate in the morning with such a big brother. Our regular game was to hold hands and create an air pocket by pressing our palms together—and then release them quickly to make quite a loud "pop" sound. Every day, I looked forward to the next morning when he would take me to school again. Some of my teachers had also taught Yinon when he was in elementary school, and it felt special to be his brother.

✳✳✳

Yinon's high school graduation party was exciting; there was an "orchestra" of pots and pans and cups and spoons instead of regular musical instruments, and there was also a skit. I've forgotten so many plays I've seen over the years, but the skit performed at the graduation celebration is etched into my memory. It was about a mute woman and her loving husband. The husband makes extraordinary efforts to enable his wife to speak and finally finds a doctor who cures her muteness (with the use of a hose!). But then, without any warning, the wife starts talking—and never shuts up. She talks on and on, until her husband can no longer bear it. In the final scene, we see him returning to the doctor to check whether it's possible to restore his wife's muteness.

At home, we celebrated Yinon's graduation with a festive lunch. Professor Shmuel Noah Eisenstadt ("Mulik") came especially from Jerusalem for the event. My mother prepared her delicacies, headlined by *gibrotene katshke*—which originally called for roasted goose and was converted to turkey stuffed with prunes. The chubby professor relished it in particular.

Next came Yinon's enlistment in the Nahal Brigade. During his last year of high school, he had joined his classmates in a pre-enlistment group (*garin*) affiliated with the Scouts movement, though he was not in the Scouts. After a long period of basic training as a combat soldier in Pardes Hanna and further training in Ashdot Yaakov Ichud, he served near Eilat in Ein Radian, which later became Kibbutz Yotvata.

We had no telephone at home after my grandfather died, and our only connection with Yinon was through infrequent letters. It was hard for me to adjust to his absence. I dreamed that I was in class and he came to the door and asked the teacher's permission to take me out. I remember that Yinon's unit had to be in Haifa for a particular activity during his basic training, and we rode in Uncle Baruch's car behind the truck transporting the soldiers all the way from Pardes Hanna to Haifa, just to get a glimpse of Yinon from afar. I noticed that he was very thin. He had the letter *tet* on his beret, indicating that he was in basic training [*tironute*], and his rifle was slung over his shoulder. He smiled sort of bashfully when he saw his family tailing him.

Yinon was released on furlough only once every three months—for four days each time, and sometimes five with Saturday. When he came home, it was hard for me to contain my excitement. I sat with him and listened to his stories—about his work in agriculture (part of his Nahal service), his friends, and the heat. He loved Ein Radian, but I loathed the place that stole my brother from me. During his home leave, Yinon would take me to movies. He would leave early in the morning to return to the army, and always left chocolate bars from the army canteen (a *Mikupelet* and a *Noga*) under my pillow.

✳✳✳

Immediately after completing his army service, Yinon moved to Jerusalem to begin undergraduate studies in sociology and literature at Hebrew University in Givat Ram. He later earned a master's degree too. At the same time, he began working in the civil service, first at the Ministry of Transportation (Administration Division), then at the Civil Service Commission and finally at the Ministry of Postal Services, where he directed the Philatelic Service for many years. Yinon served under communication ministers of all political stripes and was a consummate civil servant.

He rented a room in the home of Abba Uri, a teacher. I only visited him there once, but Yinon would sometimes come home to Tel Aviv for the weekend. One weekend, when I was ten years old, he told me that he was going to marry Aliza.

Aliza was the neighbor across the street. When they were together in kindergarten, Yinon and Aliza decided to get married when they grew up, and now they were going to fulfill that promise. Aliza was part of the landscape of my life for as long as I could remember. I loved her dearly, but I couldn't hold back the tears—the army, Jerusalem and now the wedding—all took Yinon away from me.

He was surprised by my reaction, hugged me, and explained that if you spread your love to more people, it doesn't mean that each person gets a smaller share of love. He promised that he would always love me as he had throughout the years, and the fact that he loved Aliza and was marrying her didn't take anything away from our relationship.

It was hard for me to accept his words, but it was Yinon, and he had never lied to me. Then, in December 1958, my grandmother Rivka died suddenly from a heart attack. The wedding was scheduled to take place less than a week later at Beit Shaltiel, a center for immigrants from Greece. (Aliza's father had emigrated from Salonika in his youth.) After checking with experts in Jewish law, it was decided not to postpone the wedding, even if it fell during the seven-day period of mourning. But there would be no orchestra.

My grandmother was active until the end of her life, and I didn't know how my life would look without her. I also didn't know how my life would look after Yinon's wedding. I told myself that it was a test, and that made it easier for me to face it.

The young couple purchased a modest apartment on Shimoni Street, in the Rassco neighborhood in Jerusalem. Aliza worked at Bank Leumi and Yinon continued his studies and his government work. When their daughter Talia was born, I felt a special responsibility and visited them often.

Those were Israel's most secure years, and I didn't have to call home to report that I had arrived safely in Jerusalem—besides the fact that we still didn't have a phone at home, nor did Yinon and Aliza. If I had sent a postcard, I would have arrived home before it.

Jerusalem was an enchanting and different place—with churches, monasteries, priests, and monks. I never missed a chance to visit the Knesset, where I could see Ben-Gurion, Begin, and others whose names I would hear on the radio program "This Week at the Knesset" every Thursday evening. I knew their faces from the pictures of Knesset members that my father would place in a special folder after each new Knesset was sworn in. When I was alone and wanted to get into the visitors' gallery, I turned to one of the two MKs I knew: Esther Raziel-Naor from the Herut party, who had been my mother's classmate, or Baruch Azania.

I also loved to roam through the Mea She'arim neighborhood and see the people walking in black coats in the middle of the summer. My father explained to me once that it was important to observe them because that was exactly how his grandparents had looked. He believed that such customs would soon die out.

5

Cupping Glasses for the Living

My grandmother Rivka lived for Grandfather Yosef. The dozen years that she outlived him were the least important years of her life. While my father was busy working, my mother had her nose in her books, Yinon studied and Aunt Riva worked at the convalescent home, Grandmother served as my mother's deputy in running the home and taking care of me. She was my regular babysitter because she never left the house. She read a lot and did some cooking occasionally.

We spent many hours together poring over entries she showed me in the German encyclopedia. I wanted her to tell me about Pinsk and about her hard years of wandering from place to place in Russia, but she always preferred to translate encyclopedia entries and book excerpts for me. I don't know why. Perhaps she didn't think the time had come to tell me, because people always think that a more appropriate opportunity will arise in the future. Those opportunities, however, almost never arise.

I remember her with three pieces of equipment: 1) an orange rubber bag that we'd fill with ice from the ice closet and plug with a large plug; then she'd place the ice bag on her head; 2) a hot water bottle, also made of rubber and orange-colored; she'd fill it with hot water from the samovar and then place it on her stomach; 3) and cupping glasses.

If my grandmother didn't feel well (she suffered from high blood pressure), my mother would call a private nurse. When she arrived with her box of glasses, the house would turn silent. The nurse would light a fire in Grandmother's room, make sure there was a vacuum in the glasses and press them to my grandmother's back. The suction that pulled the skin and tissues beneath it were supposed to improve blood circulation. At the time, people placed so much faith in cupping glasses that "cupping glasses for the dead" was considered the most fitting and colorful metaphor for futility; they didn't know that cupping glasses for the living are similarly futile.

Sometimes Grandmother would take the square kitchen stool, whose white paint had peeled off long ago, place it next to the gate and sit down and watch what was happening on the street. She did this mainly during the afternoon hours, and then would come back inside at sunset. I didn't understand why she did this. One time, I summoned up the courage and asked her why she wasted her time sitting on the stool outside. She wasn't embarrassed and responded, "One needs to be with people. You all are with people here and there, and I need to go out to the street to be with people."

But the truth is that she had quite a few visitors, especially women of her age. One of them was Hayuta Bussel from Degania Alef, whose husband Yosef drowned in the Sea of Galilee in 1919. She worked as a kindergarten teacher, was the secretary of the kibbutz, a delegate to Zionist Congresses and active in the Histadrut labor federation and Mapai party. Like my grandparents, she was born in White Russia, but left many years before them. My grandmother told me that she was the smartest woman she knew.

Every Saturday night, my father's parents would come to visit, and sometimes did *havdala* [the ceremony marking the end of the Sabbath] with us. We would drink tea and I would explain what I had learned that week. I don't remember if Grandmother Rivka participated in those somewhat contrived get-togethers, and I don't know how she truly felt about her in-laws. The secular world of Grandmother Rivka, with her love for Russian literature, was somewhat foreign to the religious world of Grandmother Rachel (who spoke mainly Yiddish) and Grandfather Ze'ev.

✳✳✳

Grandfather Ze'ev and Grandmother Rachel lived in the Kiryat Meir neighborhood, which was then on the outskirts of Tel Aviv. Father's family arrived in 1926 with an immigration "certificate" that was awarded to people of means and those with professional skills in high demand. My grandfather worked in his father's business, trading in leather and linen. But this was definitely not a profession in high demand, so he presented himself as a carpenter and even arrived in Mandatory Palestine with carpentry tools as proof.

He started out doing manual labor, such as road paving and construction, and though he was already forty years old, he didn't complain. When my father started working after graduating from high school, he helped his parents pay the rent. Later, my grandfather received a job at the Jewish Agency's Bank Idud, where he worked until retirement. He didn't hold a senior position, but his job provided a livelihood and enabled him to purchase a two-room apartment in Kiryat Meir. At one point, he rented out one of the rooms to Misha Kolodny, one of Grandfather Yosef's relatives from Pinsk, who was later elected to the Knesset as a member of the Progressive Party and served as Minister of Tourism bearing a Hebraized name: Moshe Kol.

When I was born, my paternal grandparents already had the two-room apartment, a hen that regularly provided eggs, and a large balcony covered with a green awning where they liked to spend their free time. There were beautiful gardens between the buildings in the neighborhood, the work of landscape architect Yehiel Segal, the first garden planner in Tel Aviv. The first IDF induction center was later built to the east of the neighborhood, and once I even watched from the balcony as Chief of Staff Yigael Yadin arrived in a jeep to visit the new inductees. There was a large open expanse to the south, where the largest bonfires were lit on Lag B'Omer, with the participation of Israel's chief rabbis.

The local synagogue, Ohel Meir, like the neighborhood itself, was named after Meir Dizengoff, the first mayor of Tel Aviv. Chaim Levanon, the current mayor and a resident of the neighborhood, was one of the synagogue's congregants. It was a large wooden shed and Grandfather Ze'ev's life mission was to build a stone synagogue in its place. The synagogue was the center of his life. He wore a large, black, boat-shaped kippah on his head and served as a *gabbai* [sexton] there for decades.

On Saturdays and holidays, he would stand on the *bimah* and use a paperclip to record the sums donated for the honor of reciting the blessings for the Torah readings. I marveled at that technology: There was a box with a card for every congregant, with squares indicating different sums. Grandfather would use a paper clip to mark the square corresponding to the honoree's contribution.

In the end, Grandfather succeeded in completing his mission: A new and beautiful synagogue was built to replace the old shed, and its name was changed from Ohel Meir [the Tent of Meir] to Heichal Meir [the Palace of Meir].

My grandfather Ze'ev had wonderful penmanship and he attributed great importance to calligraphy. From the moment I was officially allowed to learn reading and writing, which only happened in first grade, he prepared notebooks for me to fill with the letters of the alphabet. He would write letters on one line and leave two lines open for me to copy the letters. Then he would fill in another row and I had to copy it on two lines again. I didn't hate this assignment, but I didn't enjoy it either. In any case, I did not achieve brilliant success in penmanship, to put it mildly.

I learned many religious practices from Grandfather Ze'ev, and the most important of them was the search for unleavened bread on the day before the Passover *seder*: preparing the bits of bread, distributing them in four or five places in the home and using a long wooden spoon to collect the morsels of bread we had hidden from ourselves. Then we'd place them on the spoon, wrap and tie it, and then burn the bread the next morning.

There were lots of other chores before Passover, such as koshering the silverware (which we did in the laundry room) and preparing the *charoset* and the special chair for my grandfather, cushioned with a pillow. And of course, there was the *seder* itself. The family on my father's side was very small: Grandfather Ze'ev, Grandmother Rachel and the four of us—six people in all. My father was an only child; I learned only years later that he had a brother who apparently died in infancy. We didn't know anything about the families of my paternal grandparents. Much later, we learned that most of their family perished in the Holocaust. But my grandfather had a sister in the Soviet Union, and they corresponded immediately after the end of World War II.

Grandfather Ze'ev devoted a lot of time to God, to performing the religious commandments, to prayers and to building the synagogue. My father would tell me that Grandmother Rachel was even more religious. When I came to spend the Sabbath with them, I'd sleep between them in their large bed and go with them to the synagogue. There were wide vistas and fields that didn't exist elsewhere in Tel Aviv, which was gray and prematurely worn down.

✱✱✱

Sometimes we know little about the people closest to us, perhaps because when we meet strangers we ask them basic questions about where they live, their background family and education—simply to get to know them. But the people around us—siblings and parents and grandparents—are the landscape we take for granted. It would be strange to ask them where they went to high school and what their grades were. We live alongside them, know some things that they toss out here and there (in the case of my grandparents, some tidbits about their life in the Diaspora and their parents), and then they quickly vanish from our lives. And then we can't forgive ourselves for not having asked them a few simple questions.

I knew that my grandparents had an arranged marriage. Rachel was introduced to several potential grooms one day. My grandfather was the second. She actually liked the first one, but he was missing a button on his shirt. She said to herself that if a man came to such an important meeting without a button, he was not the one she wanted to spend her life with.

They both came from families that were considered middle class, and they lived in Jewish townships that were not far from each other in White Russia: Druya and Dzisna. Soon after their marriage, they moved to Warsaw. When World War I began, my grandmother took her only child and traveled to Russia. What did they do in Russia? What was their livelihood? Where did they live? When did they return to Warsaw? I didn't know to ask such questions and they didn't bother to tell me. Later, they made it to the Land of Israel.

In 1954, Grandmother Rachel became ill with cancer and passed away a year later. A few days before she died, my father asked me to go into the bedroom and say goodbye to her. She was no longer herself, and the way she looked that last time is seared into my memory. I was angry at my father for pushing me to see her. I don't remember whether she said anything to me, or just looked at me. And I don't think I said anything to her more intelligent than "Shalom Grandmother."

During the years we lived together in this world, I hungrily lapped up everything that was going on, so I remember quite a few of her sayings. Most of all, I remember her saying "hopefully next year" [*halevai iber a yor*] every time we met on annual events such as holidays and birthdays. There were also a lot of important guidelines, such as not eating horseradish on Rosh Hashanah, so that the year wouldn't have a bitter taste. In the blessing after meals, she would always be particularly moved by the words "young lions suffer want and hunger" and sometimes even shed a tear. To this day, I don't know why.

***

A few years after she died, Grandfather Ze'ev agreed to move in with us on Kalischer Street. It was hard for him to say goodbye to Heichal Meir, but he soon felt at home at the Jerusalem Synagogue on nearby Gruzenberg Street. I remember accompanying him there, mainly on Friday nights and Saturdays, when only the "first room" was in use, and on holidays when there was also a prayer service in the closed porch, which was referred to as the "second room." When "auctions" were held for the *haftarah*—for example, the great annual auction for *Maftir Yonah* on Yom Kippur—the prices were lower in the "second room."

Tensions ran high during those Yom Kippur auctions. Even though the *Book of Jonah* was read at a difficult hour, in mid-afternoon on a day of fasting, no one was absent from the synagogue—as if it were the *Yizkor* memorial service. Reb Noah, the head *gabbai*, would announce a sum of several shillings (the contributions for Torah honors were given in shillings, with one shilling equal to one-twentieth of an Israeli lira). It was usually a rigged game, and everyone knew that a particular worshipper would ultimately receive the prize. We all looked down at him because he was one of those congregants who only showed up on the High Holidays, or when there was a bar mitzvah or wedding in the family.

But one Yom Kippur, a tough competitor emerged and upped the ante by one shilling every time the usual winner made a bid. When the new rival bid a whole shilling, the usual winner gave up, angrily accepting defeat. It was only then that the great importance of the "second room" become evident.

Reb Noah did not want to anger anyone, especially wealthy donors, so he suggested to the angry man that he compete for *Maftir Yonah* in the closed porch, where the public auction would begin immediately after concluding the auction for the main prayer hall. The man followed Reb Noah's suggestion and easily outbid a few regular congregants of lesser means. Thus, he was able to continue his tradition of buying the honor every Yom Kippur.

Reb Noah, who had immigrated from America, ran the synagogue and was also the chazzan and Torah reader, and would also blow the shofar on occasion. It was a real Fawlty Towers.... Though he had no family, he was cheerful and loved to make others happy. On Simchat Torah, for example, he would help us, the children, tie the men's prayer shawls together by their tassels. And when the men stood up, they discovered that they were attached to each other. They would always get annoyed by this prank, and we would burst into laughter, together with Reb Noah, who became the target of their ire.

When I was a bit older, I sometimes served as the tenth man in the *minyan* [prayer quorum] when needed and was called to roll up and dress the Torah scroll, with the clear knowledge of the enormous responsibility—and reward—that came with this honor. On Simchat Torah, I was frustrated that I had to gather under Reb Noah's large *tallit* with the other children, and I longed for the moment when I could be called to the Torah on my own.

At age thirteen, of course, the moment arrived, and I was well-prepared to read the Torah portion that week, Naso. It was important to my father to organize a bar mitzvah celebration worthy of the occasion. He received a discount from his second workplace, Beit Sokolov, and the event was held in the courtyard there, with many guests in attendance.

The person who helped me prepare for the Torah reading promised to also write a sermon for me that would relate to the weekly portion, as is customary. I told him that I had no intention of reading a sermon that someone else wrote. In retrospect, it was my first political speech. I spoke about the Eichmann trial and its impact on me, and I praised the judicial system and the achievements of the thirteen-year-old state. But then I added:

> Not everything has come to fruition. Our precious Jerusalem is not yet completely in our hands. Many of our brethren remain in the Diaspora, in false abundance. Many want to come, but the exit gates are locked and an iron curtain surrounds them. But problems are not solved in a day. I hope that my generation, which witnessed the birth of the state, will contribute to a solution and that I will be among those who do their part in this.

I used a reference to the weekly portion to deliver a topical message:

> In the portion, we learned about building the tabernacle and heard the wonderful priestly blessing, whose main theme is peace. In the *haftarah*, we read about the birth of our hero Samson. This combination reflects the life of our people in its land: With one hand, it builds its economic and spiritual future, and seeks a life of peace and tranquility. And with the other hand, it guards the state's security and borders.

After my bar mitzvah, I played a much more serious role in the synagogue as a Torah reader, opening the ark, closing the ark, and so on. I put on *tefillin* every day and sometimes participated in lessons conducted between the afternoon and evening prayers. I didn't want to make a display of my religious observance, and since I didn't wear a kippah outside of the synagogue, I wasn't "suspected" of being religious, heaven forbid. The marks of the *tefillin* straps on my left arm usually were gone by the time I got to school.

I felt that I was doing the right thing and that I was more complete than the people in my immediate surroundings. My religious expertise—knowing where to stand during prayers, exactly what to do and when—gave me a special sense of advantage over those less knowledgeable. To a great extent, it was a "secret" that was pleasant for me to keep, and I assumed that I would continue to keep it for the rest of my life.

6

Playing a Silent Cardboard Piano

IN THE FEW SQUARE KILOMETERS IN WHICH I LIVED, THE HOLOCAUST continued to fill a central role, in constant "competition" with the battle for independence. Memorial Day for Israel's Fallen Soldiers and Holocaust Remembrance Day were the most important days in every home. Many of us were born with a historical burden on our shoulders. During my childhood, schools were not yet prepared to teach us about those events. We learned about them in the street, from the radio and newspapers, and realized that we weren't living in normal times. As a child, I particularly remember the burning of Hitler's effigy in Lag B'Omer bonfires, and that I was afraid of Holocaust survivors and uncomfortable in their presence.

On Montefiore Street, for example, there was a quiet man who was always sewing something. His shoes were made of cloth. I don't remember him speaking or panhandling. I don't know what he lived on and, of course, I don't know his story. But to play it safe, I preferred to move to the other side of the street when I saw him. There was also "Madame Ketsalle," a short and wrinkled woman who wore a colorful kerchief on her head and walked with a stick. It wasn't a walking stick, but a stick for flogging. She would run after us, the children, and strike the back of anyone who didn't manage to elude her. My mother explained to me that she came from "there" and that we needed to treat those who came from "there" with great understanding. I accepted her guidance without demanding details about "there."

My father's tailors lived in the Little Tel Aviv area, not far from our home. They were twin brothers who shared a small room that was divided into two areas: One half of the room was devoted to their tailoring work and had a large sewing machine. The other half, separated by a giant khaki blanket, was their living quarters. My father would bring me to them mainly to alter Yinon's old clothes to fit my changing dimensions.

For quite a few years, they rarely bought me any new clothes. There was an unpleasant smell in the tailors' shop. The two brothers spoke little and smiled all the time—the type of fixed smile you see on people who feel embarrassed. I knew that they also came from "there" and I pitied them. But I was angry at myself because I was unable to translate this compassion into affection.

At home, I would listen every afternoon to the "Search Bureau for Missing Relatives" program on the radio, in which people tried to find information on relatives who had disappeared in the Holocaust. The monotonous voice of the announcer who read the names of the lost people was threatening, but I couldn't bring myself to turn off the radio before the program was over.

✳✳✳

Kalischer Street started in the west, went up from HaCarmel Street, crossed HaTavor Street and Mohilever Street, continued toward Gruzenberg Street, where the Jerusalem Synagogue had a place of honor, and then turned toward Nahalat Binyamin. Near the magnificent fashion shop OBG, there was a staircase to the Beit HaShoeva Alley that led to Allenby Street. That was my route to school—I would continue on Allenby and pass the largest department store I knew, Eckmann. Every time I passed the store, there was a sign "This Week in White."

At 81 Allenby Street, I was sometimes joined by one of the trio who lived around the inner courtyard: Baruch, Amikam, and Hannah. All three lived in modest apartments adjacent to their parents' stores. Baruch's parents sold down-filled quilts. Amikam's father sold baby strollers; his family also rented out a room to Ami Assaf, a member of Moshav Kfar Yehoshua who served as a Mapai MK and was later appointed deputy minister of education and culture. Hannah's father was a jeweler. The three of them were my classmates and good friends, and the inner courtyard was big enough for soccer games or for playing hide-and-go-seek. It was one of my favorite places at the time. Across the street lived the Yizraeli family, who converted one of the rooms of their apartment into a dental clinic.

The Moshav Zkanim ["Elders' Place"] Synagogue was the next landmark. When I turned from there to Montefiore Street, I would come to a store that sold orthopedic shoes. In its display window, you could see every day, and even on Saturdays, a mannequin sitting and incessantly moving its head from side to side due to the pain in his feet. From there, I continued on to Bezalel Yaffe Street. Occasionally, I took a different route and passed a book store that also functioned as a library. I was allowed to borrow only one book per day, despite my efforts to persuade the librarian to allow me two books.

On that route, I could also check whether there were pictures from the new plays at the Cameri Theater in Nachmani Hall, and sometimes also by the Ophir Cinema. The disadvantage of this route was the frightening funeral home on Mazeh Street, at the back exit from Hadassah Hospital. I would sometimes sprint past it.

Every morning on the way to school I would feel nervous and nauseous, as if I hadn't done my homework or wasn't prepared for something. My teacher in first grade, Rivka Greenberg, taught us the secret of the squill plant that heralds the fall season, the white wagtail birds with black bibs and the gray wagtails that winter in Israel, as well as the wonder of the different seeds planted in a row in the farm corner, which magically turned into vegetables.

She would visit a different home every weekend to get to know the environment from which each pupil came, and she would bring her son Uri with her. I remember that if she was coming on Saturday, my mother would already start preparing for the visit on Sunday. My teacher and her son would join us for a meal (usually eggplant-based during the austerity period), with quivering red jelly for dessert. In those meetings at our home, Rivka spoke mostly about my good behavior, though I expected her to emphasize my academic achievements.

✳✳✳

As a child, I taught myself not to display emotion. I didn't like it when others felt a need to exhibit their emotions, and I even felt uncomfortable when that happened. People close to me often asked whether I was happy about something, and I usually replied in the affirmative. But I didn't jump for joy—I only rejoiced in my heart. I don't know if I acted this way in imitation of Uncle Baruch or whether I was following my own genuine instincts, but I thought it was more dignified not to display my emotions and that it demonstrated self-control. This exaggerated self-restraint became a part of me. I saw it as a compliment that those around me concluded that people had to know me well in order to discern whether I was joking or serious. In retrospect, I believe it wasn't a compliment.

In any case, I think my real breakthrough occurred in third grade. The new teacher was Galila Selman, a friendly, joyful, and knowledgeable teacher. Her husband was a quizmaster, and we would receive one of his books as a gift on our birthday. I soon became her favorite pupil and, at her request, took first and second graders under my wing and tutored them. She was unwilling to suffice with the regular grades for my report card and created new grades, such as "outstanding" in various subjects, and "exemplary" in conduct. I had an agreement with her that I wouldn't raise my hand in any class, about any subject, and she would call on me only when no other pupil knew the answer.

That's why I decided to always prepare myself for the lesson after the next one, and I continued that practice throughout my school years. The system was simple: First, I'd read the material for the next two lessons. Then, when all of my classmates prepared for the upcoming lesson, I would already read the material for the lesson after it. I'd often use this "extraordinary" knowledge in class, perhaps leading my surprised teachers to think that I knew a lot more than I actually did.

There were also disadvantages to being the teacher's pet pupil. Every Friday, the duties for the following week were assigned: someone to erase the board, someone to flip the chairs onto the table and someone to empty the garbage can. Every Friday, Galila would ask for volunteers. When no one volunteered for the thankless job of emptying the trash, her eyes would gaze at me. I finally told her at one point that I would volunteer to perform that duty for the rest of the school year.

***

I was a real bookworm. I read the Hebrew-language books at home in the order of their arrangement on the endless bookshelves. I received no guidance from my parents—perhaps because they trusted my judgment, or because they never imagined I'd be reading D. H. Lawrence's *Lady Chatterley's Lover* in fourth grade or Lea Goldberg's translation of Tolstoy's *War and Peace*. I also read books from the library on Mazeh Street, where I had to settle for less audacious selections such as *Heart* by Edmondo De Amicis, *Sans Famille* by Hector Malo, *With Fire and Sword* by Sienkiewicz, and all of the *Hasamba* books by Yigal Mossinson. I helped Bina, the school librarian, two afternoons a week. In return, I could take out twice as many books as the other pupils were entitled to receive. I used the rest of my spare time to write—stories, poems, and quizzes.

My mother didn't scold me for my constant reading, but she often warned me that I'd ruin my eyesight. With my father, it was a different story. It's not that he wanted me to be an ignoramus, but he was very worried that I'd become a misanthrope. It made him angry that I didn't play enough with friends. Each time, I'd try to explain to him that I'd never become a misanthrope because I loved people more than anything else, and that I combine my reading and writing and studies with games. I played quite a lot of soccer and a lot of chess. I also started a singing duo with my friend Asher Hollander, drawing inspiration from the *Batzal HaYarok* entertainment troupe. We would go from classroom to classroom, mainly on Fridays, and sing to please the crowd. Nonetheless, my father seemed to remain unconvinced.

✳✳✳

The Sinai Campaign was launched in October 1956. I had just started third grade at the time. My father went with the bank's staff to build fortifications and was called up for reserve duty on the eve of the war. Yinon was also in the army. We did drills in the classroom in the event of bombings, ducking quickly under the desks that were supposed to protect us.

The fedayoun (terrorist gangs operated by Arab countries, including Egypt) threatened us, and we had to launch a war of defense. The only question was when, and the "when" was announced by Ram Evron, the radio broadcaster who described the advance of IDF forces as I joyfully cheered in the background.

This was not the War of Independence, but we surprised the enemy. Instead of targeting Jordan, as everyone expected, we attacked Egypt. We captured the Sinai Peninsula in five minutes, were at Saint Catherine's Monastery, controlled the entire Gaza Strip, reached the Suez Canal and Sharm el-Sheikh was in our hands. Ben-Gurion wrote a letter to the solders of the ninth Brigade, and IDF Chief of Staff Moshe Dayan read it to the soldiers at a victory formation at Sharm el-Sheikh. Ben-Gurion, who served as both prime minister and defense minister, promised the soldiers that "Yotvat, which is called Tiran, will again be part of the third kingdom of Israel," no less. The euphoria was so great it drowned out the news of a plane crash in which Maj. Gen. Asaf Simhoni was killed. I wrote an article for the school newspaper strongly denouncing the two superpowers who dared to threaten us and demand our withdrawal from the Sinai. An article with my father's byline appeared in the newsletter of Bank Leumi employees in which he sadly bid farewell to Gaza.

The following ten years were the quietest in Israel's history. Perhaps as part of the national effort to distance me a bit from my reading, my mother signed me up for piano lessons at a teacher's home in Tel Aviv. I didn't refuse to play the piano, but we didn't have one at home and my parents never imagined taking on such an expense. So, I had a foldable "silent piano" of cardboard that I would use to practice for my lessons. When I "played" on my cardboard, I felt a deep connection with Beethoven, who also couldn't hear what he was playing. But for some reason, I felt I was a bit less talented in comparison to him.

I sometimes played at the home of Mrs. Zeidman, who—like all of the adults on Kalischer Street—had no first name. She lived at number 22, right next to us, and she had a piano. My mother told her that I had started to play the piano. Mrs. Zeidman was very pleased and suggested that I come and practice at her house when Mr. Zeidman wasn't home (because he couldn't tolerate the sound of children practicing the piano). Our generous neighbor occasionally engaged in philosophical discussions with me and during one of them tossed a bombshell: Children love their parents because they provide them with food! That sounded horrible to me, and I immediately rejected the possibility. When I returned home, I asked my mother whether it could possibly be true. She confirmed that our neighbor's assertion was utter nonsense.

All in all, I studied the piano for two years, preparing for my lessons with a silent piano and sometimes at Mrs. Zeidman's home too. When I was nine, there was a recital and I played a popular piece from Bach without mistakes. After that, I felt it was the right time to retire. Convinced that my powers of persuasion were greater in writing than in speech, I wrote my mother a long page. I remember one quite foolish sentence from that letter, but it apparently did the trick: "In the morning, I feel like a king, and in the afternoon, I feel like a slave." It was clear to me that my glory would not come from playing music. And I knew what I wanted: to act in the theater.

Brimming with excitement, I would go to the plays of Tilon, Menachem Golan's popular theater for children and teenagers, and at one point I enrolled in his modest theater school on Shalom Aleichem Street in Tel Aviv. I completed my theater studies after one year, with a certificate signed by Golan himself. Among the plays I saw at his theater were *Lassie Come Home, In Search of the Castaways, David and Goliath, Eight Trailing One* and *Topelle*.

❋❋❋

I also loved the game of chess. My father taught me to play and stopped playing with me when he started to lose. There were also a few children at school who were chess enthusiasts and we organized tournaments. I remember one summer vacation when Yoav and I finished with a record of 400 to 300 in my favor.

Sometimes I visited the Lasker Club on HaYarkon Street and played against adults. We played speed (blitz) chess, tapping the clock after each move. The first thing I'd look for in the weekend edition of *Davar* was the chess column. I'd arrange the pieces on the board and play each move as described in the newspaper. Books such as *Chess Openings* were almost always my request after finding the *afikoman* at the Passover *seder*.

In sixth grade, I decided to participate in the school championship.

The process was quite long, involving dozens of matches, and the entire school felt a sense of suspense, including those who were not crazy about the game. During the final days of the competition, I couldn't fall asleep at night. In the end, I found myself competing against an eighth grader who was an excellent chess player. Everyone expected him to win. I clearly remember that match, even if I can't replay the moves in my mind. The main thing is that I remember winning the match and everyone applauding enthusiastically. I was happy and eagerly awaited the prize: a match against the school principal, Menachem Alon. I really looked forward to that great honor, but for some reason the invitation never came.

It was only two years later, when he awarded me first prize for "outstanding work in the chronicles of Israel"—a prize established in memory of his only son, Shimon, who fell in the War of Independence—that I dared, in great trepidation, to remind the principal that he had yet to play chess with me. The serious and somber man, who was called an "owl" behind his back, looked at me gloomily, and instead of promising to right the injustice, said: "Yosef, I've apparently lost too many battles in my life."

✳︎✳︎✳︎

In fifth grade, a new teacher took over our class. Yosef Vinokur was about fifty years older than us and looked ill-tempered. I was afraid that I wouldn't be able to forge a connection with him like the one I had with Galila. Vinokur arrived in the country in 1907 as a lone teenager to study at the Hebrew Gymnasium (later known as the Herzliya Hebrew Gymnasium) and was in its first graduating class of twenty-two pupils, who included Moshe Sharett and Dov Hoz. He pursued higher education and became a chemical engineer. Somehow, the vicissitudes of life had brought him to teach at my school.

He was no longer a healthy man and had suffered several cerebral hemorrhages. His face was wrinkled, there was always a tear in one of his eyes, and he spoke his own brand of Hebrew. When someone used an incorrect word, he would say that he didn't understand because the pupil was speaking "the language of Ashdod" (meaning: the language of the ancient Philistines). When he reprimanded someone for not behaving well or not listening, he would say, "Are you [too] sick to hear?" And when someone asked him a question that seemed foolish, instead of responding to the question he would say, "I'll inform you by telephone." Notification by telephone was considered something very dramatic, of course, especially when only a few of the pupils had such a device at home.

He was a very educated man, but not much of an educator. The weaker pupils really suffered in his class. He would make fun of them and even hit unruly pupils with a ruler. But those who knew how to draw knowledge from him—benefited. In addition to the exact sciences, he taught us, from first-hand knowledge, the history of the Yishuv, and the history of Tel Aviv, and told us about the history of Zionism and the Hebrew literature and journalism of the ninteenth century, from *HaTzefira* to *HaMelitz*, *HaZman* and many others. He regaled us with the story of Tel Aviv's early days and shared with us his impressions from meeting the people who had all become street names; they had come to meet the first graduating class of the Hebrew Gymnasium, whose members were slated to fill the ranks of the future leadership, as indeed transpired.

Of all my teachers, he ultimately had the greatest impact on me. I found myself unconsciously imitating him, though also arguing with him from time to time.

Vinokur organized many "public tribunals." I almost always defended Ben-Gurion's stance, as a faithful child of the establishment. I remember a fierce debate in which I had to defend the silly proposition that Israel must prevent the import of televisions. I argued that children would stop doing their homework and would become addicted to the device, as was happening in a declining America. I was convinced that Ben-Gurion was justifiably concerned about television corrupting Israel's youth and eroding our cultural level. I also defended the prime minister's stance regarding the Irgun's *Altalena* munitions ship and explained that it would have been disastrous if our young sovereign state had more than one army. This subject stirred a heated debate in the classroom, and Vinokur did not take a stance.

Within a few months, we became friends. He even showed me where he hid his cigarettes from his wife, who forbade him to smoke. Vinokur invited me to his home on Mane Street and gave me private lessons on Jewish religious writings. He was devoutly secular yet bursting with Judaism. And he realized that other children would not have patience for some of things he wanted to share with me.

The most amazing gesture he did for me was in eighth grade, the last year for both of us at school, when it came time for the terrifying *seker* exam—a national standardized assessment that included an essay component graded by the teacher. I didn't expect the essay to pose an especially difficult challenge for me. I chose to write about King David, and I innocently thought that my composition was good. A day or two later, before he returned the essays, he called me to his desk at the end of the day and asked that I come to his home at 4:00 p.m. I arrived early and waited outside before knocking at the door at exactly four o'clock.

Vinokur opened the door for me, led me to the living room and asked what I thought about my essay. I had no particular opinion and asked him if something was wrong with it. He said it wasn't up to my level and that if he had to give me a grade, I'd probably receive an 8—and he didn't want me to leave with that grade after four years as his pupil. On the spot, he handed me official sheets of paper for writing another essay and gave me an hour and a half, the same amount of time allowed in the classroom, to write an essay on one of the other subjects the Ministry of Education suggested. I thanked him very much but asked whether we weren't deceiving the Ministry of Education by doing this. "If I gave you an 8, that would be deceiving the system," he said and walked out of the room.

I finished writing in less than an hour. The next day, he returned the essays to the pupils, and I received a ten. I never told this story to anyone. That grouchy and frustrated man—who fumed at young kids who didn't do their homework, scorned them ("you'll be a wagon driver!" he sneered at one of the children, unaware that there would be no wagons in the streets when we grew up) and struck them with his ruler—did this extraordinary gesture for me.

Some years later, I delivered a eulogy at his funeral. I mentioned many praiseworthy things about him, but I didn't have the courage to tell this story.

7

The Little Star from Lodz

When I was in fifth grade, the Greenbaum family from Lodz, Poland moved into 22 Kalischer Street, next door to us, on the same floor as the Zeidman family with the piano. The father opened a fabric store on Nahalat Binyamin Street. The mother was gorgeous, and all of the neighbors said she was a non-Jew. They had twin boys and an older daughter, Rina, a beautiful girl with a long black braid. She was eleven and a half years old and was accepted into seventh grade at the Ahad Ha'am School. I didn't know what her family had experienced during the Holocaust, and she didn't volunteer any information. She only told me that her father was fifteen years older than her mother. But I knew that Rina had acted in several films as a child in Poland, and I saw this myself, to my great delight, when one of the films, *King Matt the First*, was screened in Israel. My mother viewed my special connection with Rina as my contribution to absorbing Jewish immigrants and was happy about it.

Rina fit in well at school. She was much more open than I was and made new girlfriends. But she assured me that I was her best friend, and even shared secrets with me that only the girls in her class knew. One of them was the name they invented to refer to menstruation: "green fabrics." Rina was smart and funny—and so very pretty. I was able to help her fill gaps in knowledge in such fields as Hebrew literature, Bible, Jewish history, and grammar. We spoke a lot about world events as I stroked her braid. We had a lot in common, but we primarily shared our love for the theater. In a world without telephones, we would call each other with a special whistle—the "Toreador Song" from Bizet's *Carmen*. I don't remember going to her home, but she visited our house almost every day. She was very diligent and a quick learner. I was happy to know that she needed my help.

I knew that she was unattainable, that the wide age difference would prevent us from becoming a couple. But as long as the connection continued, I was thrilled by every moment and feared the day when reality would separate us. I often wondered how Rina viewed our relationship. I assumed that she saw me as a small and positive child, a boy she could rely on and from whom she could learn, without any romantic musings. For me, however, it was clearly the first real infatuation in my life. I knew that because I had read quite a bit about the torment of love, and I indeed was pained by the disparity between our close relationship and the clear knowledge that a real lover would soon appear on the scene, someone her age or perhaps even older, just as her father was older than her mother. I never spilled my heart to her. We continued with our tight and functional relationship until a knight on a white horse indeed arrived.

After we left the house on Kalischer Street, Rina and I didn't keep in contact. She changed her name to Ganor, became a highly sought-after actress, married "Poli" from the *HaGashash HaHiver* troupe and later moved to England. We never met again.

✶✶✶

An amazing innovation entered our school when I was in fifth grade: A loudspeaker was installed in each classroom and an internal communication system was set up in a room next to the principal's office. The principal used it to convey important messages, but also allowed the upper classes to prepare audio skits, broadcast funny things, and use the groundbreaking technology for entertainment purposes.

So, along with the rest of my activities, I was also in charge of my class's broadcasts on the school's internal radio network. This responsibility required me to write feuilletons, update the pupils in the school about new discoveries in science, sum up the political news of the week and decide what each pupil would read (and which pupil would be insulted by not receiving anything to read).

In April 1961, when I was already in seventh grade, the communications network began broadcasting parts of the Eichmann trial. By that point I had already read quite a few books on the Holocaust, but we still hadn't learned about it in an organized way. The trial illustrated things that we couldn't have imagined, and we simply sat in the classroom and wept. It was painful to hear descriptions like that of Ka-Tsetnik (the writer Yehiel De-Nur), who fainted on the witness stand. But we didn't want to stop listening to the court hearings, as the trial was foremost in the minds of many of us.

About two years earlier, I noticed an advertisement in the *Davar for Children* weekly for young reporters to work at Israel Radio for Youth. I sent a few of the columns I had written for the school newspaper and then traveled to Jerusalem, to 3 Helene HaMalka Street, to meet with the legendary radio personality Leah Porat. A few days later, I received a letter from Israel Radio that included a young reporter's ID card signed by Hanoch Givton, who had just been appointed director-general of the Israel Broadcasting Service.

The Broadcasting Service placed a twenty-four-year-old student named Yossi Godard in charge of our group of young reporters, which included about a dozen boys and girls from various places in Israel. He taught us the ins and outs of radio, including how to conduct interviews and edit, and how to find immediate solutions for various glitches. He also revealed some secrets. For example, we learned that Israel Radio had a special collection of records ready to be played immediately upon the announcement of the death of important figures such as the president, prime minister or Knesset speaker. Thus, when the time came, there would be no need to go searching for somber music in the giant piles of records.

We usually met in Jerusalem, sometimes to participate in a fascinating course led by Leah Porat. Other meetings were held in Tel Aviv at Israel Radio's studios in the Kirya, where we saw people whose voices were so familiar to us: Moshe Hovav and his sister Reuma Eldar, Rivka Michaeli and Yitzhak Shimoni, Esther Sofer and Haim Yavin.

Each week, we had to respond to questions on various topics, from the question of ballroom dancing versus youth movements, to the question of whether to demand capital punishment for Eichmann. Godard came up with special tasks for us, such as writing a suspense story, with each of us composing a few lines. He even took us all to a restaurant once. For me, it was a special occasion because we never ate in restaurants in Tel Aviv—after all, "only people who have no home eat in restaurants."

Since I had to travel alone to Jerusalem, I would sleep at Yinon and Aliza's home in the Rassco neighborhood. I felt a sort of independence when I visited the Knesset. There were days when I sat for many hours in the visitors' gallery, watching Ben-Gurion and Begin, Moshe Dayan and Abba Eban, soaking up every word.

I also loved the procedural aspect: the speaker, who dared to interrupt important people in the middle of their speeches because their allotted time was up; the way MKs accepted their punishment and left the hall after being called to order a third time; and the heckling. While I sat watching, I amused myself with the thought that perhaps someday I would also take part in the parliamentary debate at Froumine House [the seat of the Knesset from 1950–1966].

But my precocious sense of maturity was apparently subjective. For many months, I would go to the back entrance of the Habima Theater on

Saturday afternoons and participate in a theater club. The first hour was devoted to "etudes" (imaginary situations that we had to act out). During the second hour, an actor or director came and told us their story. Our group was invited to the dress rehearsals held on Fridays at the theater before the premieres.

I was enchanted by the world of theater, just as I was enchanted by the world of journalism. But a decision was made to limit the theater group to high school students, and I was only twelve, so I had to leave the group. I remember writing a long letter of protest to Shlomo Bertonov (son of the legendary actor Yehoshua Bertonov and an actor in his own right, as well as a gifted narrator). The letter began:

> I have been interested in the art of theater for a long time and I am always looking for a pathway toward it. Not to perform, but to learn and know about it. And then, perhaps I'll continue in it. . . . This entire letter of mine would not have been written if the auditorium was full and you had to reduce the number of participants in Habima's class for youth . . . in that situation, you would set an age restriction. But in this case, the decision really surprises me. Perhaps you would be kind enough to tell me why you cannot allow me to come to your class.

Bertonov responded in a long letter explaining the reasons for setting the age limit. The main reason was that some of those who had appeared before us said they would not come again "because they saw children in the audience." He noted that he personally disagreed with the decision to prevent children from participating, and he suggested that I come to the theater's library, which was under his supervision, any day between noon and 1:00 p.m. and read books about theater. He concluded his letter with a quote from the world of theater: "In one play, the characters discuss the appointment of a certain person to an important position. One of the characters says, 'That person's disadvantage is that he's too young.' Another character responds, 'Never mind. That disadvantage diminishes from day to day.'" I didn't take him up on his invitation to come to the library.

In any event, I was re-accepted into the class a few months later. I don't remember how that happened, but I remained a faithful participant through the end of high school.

In those years, I went to almost every play at Habima, the Cameri, and other theaters. I collected the theater reviews in a thick folder. Backstage was our second home, and we got to know the icons of the theater—Yehoshua Bertonov, Aharon Meskin, Hanna Rovina and Chanale Hendler, Shimon Finkel and Shmuel Rodensky, and others. My thirst for theater was insatiable. I participated in a class that analyzed plays, and sometimes I panned a play, but that didn't dampen my love for theater. On the other hand, as in the case of the piano, I felt that my talent was insufficient. I realized that if I wanted to remain in the world of theater, I would need to work on the sidelines—writing reviews, analyses, and so on. That was interesting, even fascinating, but not enough. I wanted to be an actor. And when I reached the conclusion that I would never become a great actor, I decided that I would no longer make any attempt to act.

But that's not how I felt about journalism. On the contrary. At the end of eighth grade, I was also accepted for a position at *Maariv for Youth* and was assigned many tasks: Together with other young reporters, I interviewed important people, learned about new subjects and had to meet tight deadlines. I now had a significant platform for publishing short stories and poems. Here too I met other teenagers, some older than me and some my age, whose main pastime was writing. Years later, they assumed important roles in the media and beyond. With my press credentials from *Maariv for Youth*, I could enter museums free of charge, even without committing to write something about them! My father, who had spent his entire life on the margins of journalism, believed that I was fulfilling his dream.

✳✳✳

Though I didn't live nearby, I received a scholarship to attend the Herzliya Hebrew Gymnasium. It wasn't considered the city's best high school at that time, but it retained an aura of history and I was thrilled to encounter such iconic figures as Dr. Haim Bograshov, who was the president of the Gymnasium and had taught at the school when my mother studied there. He was so important that he had a street named for him while he was still alive. The fact that he was accorded this honor during his lifetime did not prevent him from changing his family name to Boger. He also served in the second Knesset on behalf of the General Zionists. Another icon was Dr. Baruch Ben-Yehuda, who was the first director-general of the Education Ministry and continued to serve as the school's principal long after reaching retirement age.

Ninth grade was very challenging for me in almost every subject, especially in the beginning. In tenth grade, my grades rose again to where they had been in primary school. I did a lot of writing for the high school newspaper, *Hadim* [Echoes], and edited the newspaper as an upperclassman.

The Talmud teacher, Yitzhak Einhorn, who was called "Shmelke" for some reason and instilled fear in the pupils, found a kindred soul in me. From the moment he entered the classroom, all of the pupils jotted down every word he uttered, and he noticed that I didn't take any notes. When he asked why, I said that it was easier for me to remember when I wasn't writing. I realized that he would try to skewer me the next time. And sure enough, as expected, he didn't let up on me. He asked questions designed to trip me up, and the classroom tensely watched the duel the teacher waged with me. In the end, he admitted defeat.

I loved studying Talmud and understood its Aramaic language. Shmelke was always serious and seldom smiled, even outside of the classroom, but after I won his trust—the sky was the limit. We all studied for the first test, and there was much fear and trepidation. After we received our grades, he festively announced that I was exempt from all future tests and that I would receive a grade of "Excellent" for as long as he continued to be my teacher. He asked if I'd be willing to help prepare the class for future tests, and I answered affirmatively, of course. So, before each test, any classmates who wanted this help would come to my home. During the tests, I would go to the library and Hadassah, the eternal librarian, would tell me about the new books that had arrived.

During my last two years of high school, Dr. Asher Weizer, the Bible teacher, was our homeroom teacher. He was "old school" and invented his own scale of grades (acceptable, almost acceptable). He wore a kippah and loved my penchant for the Bible and Talmud. At one point, he suggested that I transfer to a yeshiva. Though I was still religiously observant (including *tefillin* every morning), it never occurred to me to abandon the secular world.

Besides my curricular activities, I continued to edit *Hadim* and worked at Israel Radio, was very active in the Habima youth program and wrote nearly every week for *Maariv for Youth*. During the summer vacation before my senior year, I wrote my first and last novel. It was several hundred pages long and told the surprising story of an affair between a teenage boy and his teacher, an adult woman. The pages remained in the drawer.

On the eve of Rosh Hashanah, in September 1965, I was invited to participate in an Israel Radio program to recap the year in literature and art. The author Yehoshua Kenaz, whose best-seller *After the Holidays* was published a year earlier, moderated the hour-long discussion. The panel included several well-known literary critics; I represented, as usual, the "young generation." When Kenaz asked each of us to choose the book of the year, I responded, without hesitation: *Where the Jackals Howl*. It was the first work published by an unknown twenty-five-year-old author named Amos Oz. The book was a collection of stories from kibbutz life, with poignant expressions of pain and disquiet. In my opinion, Oz's maiden publication offered very rare insights about the human race, in general. As we were leaving the studio, one of the panelists told me that he really hoped I had cited Oz's book only to surprise, and that I should clearly understand that it was not worthy to be selected book of the year.

Two months later, I received a letter in a double envelope from Israel Radio containing a letter from Amos Oz. I understood that the envelope with his letter had made the rounds of Israel Radio's departments until someone took the initiative to find my address. Oz wrote:

> Shalom Yossi Beilin,
>
> I just listened to the literature and art broadcast, including your remarks. I was moved by what you said about the sorrow you felt while reading. Indeed, you read my words in the same way I wrote them. However, I take issue with the ranking you assigned to my book: I believe there are better ones in this year's crop of prose (and I'm objective—after all, I myself am the object) . . . In any case, I wish to thank you. Could you find a little time to "pop over" to Hulda for a face-to-face discussion? Let me know and I'll be waiting for you. And if my suspicions are correct and you also engage in literary writing, bring something with you. I'm curious to read something of yours. Have I falsely suspected you?
>
> With gratitude, Amos Oz, Kvuzat Hulda, Mobile Post—Nahal Ayalon.

Of course, I found "a little time." I sent my response (and did not save a copy) and received a postcard in reply, in which the young author explained that there was a direct bus to Hulda at 2:30 p.m., leaving from HaGdud HaIvri Street at the Central Bus Station. And indeed, I met him and his young wife Nili on the proposed date. We talked for several hours until a bus came and took me back to the Central Bus Stations, this time making stops along the way.

Our relationship continued until his death in 2018. I was always wary of burdening him too much my affairs, robbing him of precious time that he could have devoted to his writing. He asked to see the novel I had written several months earlier, but I never showed it to him. I sent him my short stories from high school and from the period of my army service, and he took the trouble to comment; he offered compliments and was brutally critical. His most important warning was not to write "Agnon-like." He explained, for example:

> Agnon is a mighty and domineering sheriff for beginning storytellers. For most of them, their real literary existence begins with a "declaration of independence"—in short, with their liberation from the jaws of Agnonism. There is no question about Agnon's greatness. He has no equal. And here's the thing—there's no place for an Agnon and a half, and certainly no place for an Agnon and another few tenths.

Amos was also my confidant during the two years (1993–1995) of secret negotiations I conducted with Mahmoud Abbas (Abu Mazen) to draft a permanent accord. When I led the Geneva Initiative, Amos agreed to join the Israeli negotiating team; and when I chaired the Meretz party, he was ready to lend a hand whenever I needed him. I cannot stop grieving his death and cannot put the accusations leveled against him by his daughter Galia Oz out of my mind.

✼✼✼

Helena Einhorn was in my class during all four years of high school. We were good friends and even visited in each other's homes. Both of us were considered outstanding students, and we had a lot in common, including a love for the Bible. We would go every Saturday morning to hear our teacher, Weizer, lecture on the weekly Torah portion at the Ohel Shem hall on Balfour Street in Tel Aviv. We laughed each time he said something like "Rashi [a medieval sage] had difficulty"—as if talking about something that occurred yesterday.

Helena sometimes came with me to hear my mother's lectures. We traveled together during Passover week in 1965 to the national conference of the Israel Society for Biblical Research. We arrived in Jerusalem and met my mother at the Eden Hotel, where she was staying. (It was the very same hotel where Grandfather Yosef had stayed and written his letters to her.) On the way back to Tel Aviv, Helena and I spoke, half-jokingly, about which teachers would attend our wedding if we married one day. When we got to my home, it still wasn't very late. My father was at Beit Sokolov, and my mother had remained in Jerusalem, and we moved our relationship to a higher level.

She was my first and only girlfriend, and we remained a couple for thirty-six years. I disclosed to her that I didn't travel on the Sabbath and that I kept kosher. She was surprised but accepted it. After completing my military service, an army rabbi married us.

✳✳✳

A few weeks before the end of twelfth grade, Weizer, our homeroom teacher, entered the classroom, radiant with joy. I had never seen him look so happy. "I have a surprise for you," he said. "The outstanding pupil in this graduating class is a pupil in our class!"

I remember that for some reason I didn't think that he was referring to me. Perhaps I thought that if it were me, he would have informed me personally before announcing it to the entire class. And then he called my name.

I felt goose bumps running up and down my body, but, as usual, I wore an expression that did not betray my emotions. He also mentioned that the prize included tuition for the first year of university. It was an extraordinary feeling, like winning a competition in which I hadn't participated. I spoke on behalf of the students at the graduation ceremony, in front of my father and mother, who were unable to hold back their tears. I couldn't have wished for a more exciting final chord before embarking on the next stage two months later: basic training.

8

I'm Sure You Already Know—There's Going to Be a War

I HAD NO IDEA WHAT AWAITED ME IN THE ARMY. AT THAT TIME, THEY didn't present options to future recruits. I wasn't gung-ho—and the Hebrew slang to describe such military intoxication ("mooral") wasn't even part of the vernacular yet.

Still, I was an excited and very proud soldier. I viewed military service as a national obligation and considered draft evasion as akin to treason. However, I had no plans to pursue a military career and hoped that my period of service would go by quickly.

At the time, it wasn't customary or permitted for families to accompany their children to the induction center or recruitment bureau. I went to the recruitment bureau in Jaffa and from there was transported, along with other new recruits, to the Tel HaShomer base, where we received the famous kitbags, mess kits, and long woolen coats. Surplus British or American gear, familiar to us from WWII movies, were waiting for us there in all their glory.

Initially, we were assigned chores on the base and ardently painted the tree trunks. We would assemble every day in the afternoon, and the all-knowing master sergeant would call out names and order the soldiers whose names were called to climb aboard the truck to the basic training camp.

After a few days passed, I began worrying that they had forgotten me. But then I was called to board the vehicle heading into the unknown. When we arrived at the training base, it turned out that we had disembarked from the vehicle too slowly. The corporal who received us ordered us back onto the truck so that we could get off again and reach the square within twenty seconds. After we succeeded in doing so, only after five failed attempts, I realized that we were lazy weaklings and that this was what basic training would be like. Then they assigned us to large tents, twenty soldiers in each tent, with one lantern per tent for us to use. A very strict inspection was held every morning in which we had to show our beds, shaving gear, mess kits, and so on. I presented both of my mess kits—one for meat and the other for dairy.

It was the late summer and early fall of 1966. The security situation was good. There were no threats from the air and no danger of infiltrators or terrorism. In conversations among the soldiers, we spoke half-seriously and half-jokingly about the fact that our parents or older brothers had had the good fortune of fighting in both the War of Independence and the Sinai Campaign, while we would have no such opportunity.

The training was not easy. There was "water discipline" (limiting our water consumption, which was later recognized as a mistake), sudden wakeups and formations, and nights when we slept in our boots so that we'd be able to make it to the formation area within thirty seconds of wakeup. Some guys were assigned the punishment of wearing their helmets all day because they didn't finish lunch in time. There were a lot of collective punishments, and there was a great fear of falling asleep while on guard duty at the end of a crazy day. If someone dropped his rifle during formation, or sand was detected in his rifle barrel, the weekend furlough would be canceled for all of us.

There was also kitchen duty, which consisted primarily of scrubbing gigantic pots. The sergeant in charge of the kitchen was brutal, and there were threats of having to repeat basic training if we didn't pass muster (though we knew of no soldier who was forced to do basic training twice). There were also long runs, with a steel helmet and Czech rifle or Uzi, in full battle gear, with a full water canteen. And some *gazlan* ("robber") would show up in the middle of nowhere, precisely at the point where the run ended, to sell us refreshments at exorbitant prices. Sweating, exhausted, and breathing heavily, we were ready to pay any sum for a warm bottle of Tempo, a popular soft drink at the time.

The radio operator's course that began immediately after basic training was a sort of vacation. I quickly learned all about HF and VHF devices, speech devices, simple encryptions, and primarily a new language—Morse code. We had a civilian teacher, a nice man who was proud of his Iraqi heritage, and we learned with him to work at a speed of eighteen words per minute—and were tested on this at the end of the course. We were the last cohort of soldiers to have a six-digit army ID number, and our course was one of the last to learn Morse code.

During our compulsory service, the length of conscription was extended twice. When we were inducted, the mandate was to serve for two years and two months. A few months later, four additional months were tacked on to the period of compulsory service. In the wake of the Six-Day War, it was extended for another six months, and we received a monthly payment of one hundred lira during those six months of additional service. The "temporary" extension continued through the next generation of IDF soldiers.

All in all, the physical effort during my first months in the army was not easy. I was not terribly excited by the radio operator's course. I also wasn't interested in going to officers' course and serving another year in the standing army, as I was asked to do at the end of my additional six months of service. However, I didn't appreciate at first how much the army had contributed to shaping my behavior and even my way of thinking. It enabled me to recognize my limitations and to predict what I could do and what I couldn't. It taught me to decide quickly and to act quickly. It introduced me to young people I would never have gotten to know so well in any other circumstances. And it exposed me to phenomena I was unaware of, or at least whose scope I was unaware of, such as the phenomenon of drug use.

After the course, I was placed in one of the most highly sought-after units. My unit provided communication services to the chief of staff and senior members of the IDF General Staff, and also specialized in facilitating communication between ground forces and aircraft, managed the army's large wireless networks, allocated frequencies for networks and temporarily assigned Communications Corps personnel to various units for operational purposes. I was amazed by what I saw at my assigned post. It was so different from anything I had seen in the army, including both basic training and the radio operator's course. It was no longer a collection of surplus equipment from the British or American army. It was "America" itself: state-of-the-art equipment, modern and user-friendly buildings, and almost no saluting while serving with senior commanders whose faces I had previously encountered only in the newspapers.

On November 13, 1966, a few days after being posted there, a few communications vehicles set out from my unit to participate in the attack on the village of Samu, the IDF's largest operation since the Sinai Campaign. I asked to join one of the unit's vehicles. "We don't take rookies," they politely explained to me. I was insulted, but of course I accepted the decision. I made a promise to myself that I would quickly learn everything I needed to know, so that I wouldn't be passed over the next time.

The next significant operation occurred about six months later. In early May 1967, my direct commander summoned me and told me to report the next morning with the communications vehicle at 5:15. I didn't understand where to report, and he repeated, "at 5:15." I still didn't understand. He explained that he was referring to the secret 515 unit (later renamed 848 and, after the Yom Kippur War—8200), which had been assigned a secret mission in the Negev. He noted that the duration of the mission was unknown and instructed me not to ask questions during the mission and to forget I was there after its conclusion.

I finally felt that I was about to do something significant. I told my parents that I was being attached to one of the units for an exercise, something I had already done in previous months. And at the appointed hour, a team of three radio operators reported to the captain who was commanding the mission.

We rode in a convoy of military vans. The path to the summit of Mount Sagi was not designed to accommodate such vehicles, but we somehow reached the top and started to set up. I remember the happy moment of making initial contact with the command group; you aim the antenna in the right direction, move to the current frequency (which changes day and night) and start to broadcast, without being sure you'll receive a response. And then, when you hear the familiar sound and you can even guess who's on the other side by his special way of broadcasting—you feel like a movie character who's trying to hang onto a helicopter and suddenly a strong arm reaches out from the door and pulls him inside.

The members of the unit were particularly nice. No differences in rank could be discerned between the officers and soldiers on the hilltop, and for the first time in my army service I found myself doing guard duty with a captain. We received the daily supplies, together with the daily newspapers, from a Piper plane that tossed us this intellectual and material sustenance. We had two roles: to transmit encrypted telegrams to the command center and to take turns guarding the facility we had set up. During the rest of the time, we could read, play chess, and engage in philosophical conversations with our mysterious comrades from 515.

After a week on the plateau summit, we were instructed to pack up immediately. No one asked questions. We proceeded slowly down the path to the foot of the hill until we reached the paved road. We traveled this time via Beersheba and stopped for a break in the courtyard of the Southern Command in Beersheba's Old City. An officer approached us and asked where we were coming from. We didn't say a word. "So, I'm sure you already know—there's going to be a war!" he said. We didn't take his words seriously.

Immediately upon returning to my base, I was sent to one of my unit's branches. I was there for a number of days until they called from headquarters and told me to quickly report and join an air support squad that was slated to be attached to the eighth Brigade. There were four of us in the vehicle: Alon Levine, who was already a corporal and commanded the squad; Arie Dichtwald, a religious soldier; Toledano ("Tole"), the driver; and me. Tole was instructed to proceed to the brigade's headquarters. On the way, we had to pass through Sde Teman, north of Beersheba. Sde Teman was built by the British to counter a possible eastward thrust by the Nazi army, and huge hangars remained at the site.

The road to Sde Teman was incredible: a chaotic mix of countless military and civilian vehicles, with military policemen helplessly trying to direct the traffic, while almost everyone ignored their efforts. It took us about five hours to get there. From Sde Teman, we were sent in the direction of the brigade's headquarters in the Paran desert. We arrived late in the evening, in the middle of nowhere. Somebody knew we were coming. We filled in forms in order to be officially attached to the brigade, set up two pup tents on the sand and fell asleep.

We had learned the story of the eighth Brigade, which was born two weeks before me, as part of the history of the War of Independence. It was the IDF's first armored brigade and was dubbed "The Old Man's Brigade," in reference to Yitzhak Sadeh, who was already fifty-eight when he took command of it. It was disbanded a year later and then reestablished, this time as a reserve infantry brigade. Three years prior to the Six-Day War, it returned to its original mission as an armored brigade, with one tank battalion and two armored infantry battalions. Its commander was Col. Albert Mandler, who led "Samson's Foxes" in the War of Independence and was killed in the Yom Kippur War. By 1973, he had reached the rank of major general and commanded the Sinai Division. For me, joining the brigade was sort of a continuation of my history studies, as if I were personally living the sequel to the War of Independence that I had read about.

Parked next to us was a communications vehicle that had also been mobilized for the brigade from another communications unit and was manned by four reservists. A mustached sergeant arrived and gave us instructions. He was our contact person with brigade headquarters and explained what was expected of us. We understood that there would be no fresh food, only battle rations. The water would be given to us sparingly, so to save water we would forgo bathing and shaving. We would also have to bury the toilet paper we used so that it wouldn't fly all over the brigade. "The desert is one big bathroom for you," the sergeant said. He explained that we needed to maintain radio silence and refrain from any wireless communication. That would change only if we received the code word. We could only call home in exceptional cases via the carrier wave device. The preferred mode of communication was to write letters, but we must not write anything that could disclose our place of deployment or write any other foolish things because each letter would be examined by a military censor.

In retrospect, the weeks of waiting weren't so long, but we had no idea when the period of waiting would end. We latched onto every bit of information, to no avail. The smug Gamal Abdel Nasser met with his officers and boasted about the certain destruction of Israel. He could no longer wait for the "meeting" with Rabin. In Tel Aviv, they turned Gan Meir into a possible cemetery. Talk of another Holocaust also reached the Paran desert. Pessimism reigned in the reservists' communications vehicle. H. M. was a twenty-six-year-old lawyer who took Nasser in complete seriousness and was convinced that Israel was not prepared for a confrontation. There were arguments between the two vehicles that escalated into shouting.

I was one of the only ones there with a small transistor radio, and I was able to tune into Israel Radio. Prime Minister Levi Eshkol, in his "stammering" speech, managed to also make us, the younger ones, pessimistic for a moment. But then Chaim Herzog entered the arena as the national voice of calm and that quickly improved our mood.

An opportunity arose for one of us to go home one weekend. Of course, I was longing to go home, like all of the others, but the moment the sergeant asked us to choose the lucky one to receive the weekend furlough, we all shouted out the name of the demoralized H. M., that twenty-six-year-old lawyer who would go on to become one of the leading spokespersons for the political right—self-assured, eloquent, and more patriotic than anyone else. I never disclosed to him why he was unanimously chosen to go on home leave.

We received a directive to remove the camouflage netting from the communications vehicle three times, and twice we were told to put it back on. The others in my squad, like me, hoped each time that it would be the last time and that we'd finally head off to war. We were angry about the government's hesitance. Meanwhile, beards sprouted on our unshaven faces and we didn't change clothes. The "aunties" from the Committee for the Soldier visited us a couple of times and we drank lots of Tempo for free and ate wafers. On one of those occasions, we had the chance to taste Coca-Cola for the first time. Alon, the commander of our squad, managed to open the bottle cap with his teeth. The women from the Committee for the Soldier also brought a film, and hundreds of soldiers crowded near the sheet on which it was screened, with a translation on the side.

One time, IDF Chief of Staff Yitzhak Rabin arrived in a helicopter. We observed him from afar, from the small hill of sand on which we were encamped. I remember his visor cap and his upright gait. He didn't convene the soldiers or deliver a speech, but his visit still had a calming influence on me. I understood that the most important person in the army knew we were there, dispersed in the Paran desert, eager to defeat the enemy and ready for his order.

A few days later, Moshe Dayan's appointment as defense minister added a refreshing dose of reassurance. No one around was so revered, and the fact that he took this position upon himself suggested that he knew something about Israel's chances of winning, and about whether a war would really erupt soon and when.

Years later, when there was discussion about the IDF's attempts to avoid calling up reservists for duty in the security zone in Lebanon, I recalled our lack of fear on the eve of the Six-Day War. In retrospect, I think that it can mainly be attributed to our youth, rather than to our great heroism.

9

Like a Cup of Coffee with King David

ON JUNE 4, IN THE AFTERNOON, THE MUSTACHED SERGEANT CAME TO our two communications vehicles to inform us that the war would start the next morning. He added that radio silence was still in effect and that we should keep the camouflage netting on but start to dig foxholes. The sergeant also brought scallions with him, and each of us received our first fresh vegetable in many days. We devoured it immediately, as if it were an ice cream cone.

While still munching on the scallion, it hit me: It was no longer a history lesson, no longer Haim Gouri's poem "Here Lie our Bodies," which I would read at the annual Memorial Day ceremony. It was now the real thing, which could turn my life into a short episode.

The fear was replaced by adrenaline and the determination to prove to myself that I could also meet this ultimate challenge. Still, I was very worried about Yinon; he was a reservist in an armored brigade, and I had no idea where he was deployed. Writing, as always, was my refuge. I took a notebook with red margins from my kitbag and wrote a few pages, as a sort of intellectual last will and testament. (After the war, I considered it a bit too "literary," and the fact that I wasn't wounded made it superfluous.) Then I dug a deep foxhole for myself and bedded down in it but wasn't able to fall asleep.

At 6:00 a.m., we all stood in the foxholes, and the sergeant came to check that they were deep enough. I prepared myself for staying four or five years in my foxhole, but after less than three hours, the sergeant informed us that it was over.

What exactly was over? How was it that the radio now announced that the IDF had acted in response to belligerent activity by the Egyptian army, while they already had told us about the war the previous afternoon? And what would happen now? Could we return to brigade headquarters? Shorten our length of service? But you didn't ask questions in the army, and if you did ask—you paid a price.

A few hours later, it became clear that we were back to the waiting mode. The Israel Air Force (IAF) had done the main work, but we had to advance into Egyptian territory and establish Israel's control there. When would we start advancing? "We'll receive an order." Should we take off the camouflage netting? "Not yet." Now a new fear arose: The IDF would conquer the entire Sinai and would forget us in the Paran desert.

Since our code word had already been broadcast, we contacted headquarters and managed to send encrypted telegrams. We kept our ears close to the transistor radio that broadcast what the IDF Spokesman's Office had approved. We also listened to the Voice of Thunder, a Cairo-based radio station that broadcast propaganda in Hebrew, and wondered when they would stop fabricating stories about Egyptian victories and the downing of Israeli planes.

We were still on the Israeli side of the Green Line on June 7 when we received news of the IDF's capture of the Old City in Jerusalem. I never believed such a thing would happen in my lifetime. We thwarted Nasser's threat—and we captured the Western Wall! I was happy, but still knew nothing about Yinon's situation. I wrote to my parents, sharing my feelings about the capture of the Old City. And though I didn't want to add to their worries, I asked if they had heard anything from Yinon.

In the evening, we received an order to remove the camouflage netting and head out. The hardest thing in such moments for an ordinary soldier is the lack of information. No one considers it necessary to waste time updating the troops. The only thing we were told was to get into the vehicles and join the endless convoy. We were warned about Egyptian soldiers we'd encounter en route. Some of them were hungry or frightened, we were told, and they might shoot one of us if we got out of the vehicle to relieve ourselves. The rumor was that we were heading toward the town of Nakhl, in central Sinai, which had already been significantly "softened" by the IAF.

It was the slowest trip in my life; it lasted about ten hours, maybe more, nonstop, bumper to bumper. There was no need for a map or directions. It was enough that we felt contact with the back end of the vehicle in front of us to know that we were heading in the right direction. When someone needed to relieve himself, another soldier would go out with him, armed with a Czech rifle. Afterwards, they could easily catch up with our slow-moving vehicle, without even having to walk quickly. We slept most of the time. The vehicle's headlights were off, but there was no need to see where we were going. We couldn't ask Tole to drive the whole time, so each of us took his place for a while. No one asked whether we had a driver's license, and rightly so—it wasn't really driving, but rather a dialogue of bumpers.

At the entrance to the dusty town, situated in the heart of the Sinai Peninsula, we were greeted by a pile of charred corpses of Egyptian soldiers. All of their clothing was completely burned, except for their steel helmets. For some reason, their penises were erect and that made us laugh. All of them had been killed by bombs the IAF had dropped from low altitudes. Despite the laughter, I felt horrified, and I assume the others felt likewise. I don't remember if I asked myself whether the bombing was really essential, considering the fact that Egypt had already been defeated in the first hour of the war. I don't think I did.

We were directed to a site where we assumed we'd be deployed for the following weeks. An army canteen (Shekem) van parked near us. A line stretched toward the window of the vehicle, and we had to climb three metal stairs to reach the window. When the happy moment arrived, I ordered a *Mikupelet* chocolate bar. Suddenly, under the top stair, I noticed the bullet-ridden body of an Egyptian soldier. I didn't give up my place in line or forego the *Mikupelet*. I paid and made way for the next soldier in line. Though I ate the chocolate bar with great appetite, the images of that bullet-ridden soldier and the charred remains of the other soldiers I had seen earlier remain with me till today.

In the town itself, we saw no Egyptian civilians or soldiers. Some of our guys removed armchairs and couches from the homes and rested or slept on them. I preferred to sleep on the sand. I was already bearded and filthy, and I had become accustomed to it. We still had no idea what we were supposed to do there or how long we would remain at the site. But a day later, the next order arrived: We're going to the Golan Heights.

✷✷✷

We set out on Friday in a long convoy; I couldn't see where it ended. Our objective was to reach Syria and join the brigade's forces that were already deployed there. Signs of the Egyptian army's hasty retreat were visible on the roads in the Sinai, reminding me of photographs from the Sinai Campaign.

One image is etched in my memory: a large truck lying on its side in the middle of the road. It was carrying cans of beans for the Egyptian troops and never reached its destination. The convoy's slow pace allowed our soldiers to hop off the vehicles, grab cans of beans and return—without delaying the convoy. When I told one of the soldiers I knew, that I thought it was unethical to take these Egyptian supplies, he said I was being sanctimonious. The cans of beans were just sitting in the scorching sun and would never reach their intended destination, so it wasn't a case of looting. Maybe he was right.

We passed Egyptian soldiers who had been gunned down along the way—lying in the spot where they died. Like statues. Like part of the landscape. Neither threatening nor threatened. On the other hand, I had no idea how many of our soldiers had been killed or wounded. The radio made no mention of that.

As night fell, we arrived at the Hadera Junction. There was a long stand of sweets and drinks arranged by the "aunties" from the Committee for the Soldier. I got out of the vehicle, approached one of the women and asked whether the number of Israeli casualties was known. She said no numbers had been announced, but the rumor was that we had lost about four hundred soldiers.

I was shocked. I had assumed that such a swift and easy victory would not involve such heavy losses. But it turned out that even when it seems relatively easy, many young people pay with their lives. The mood in our communications vehicle changed immediately; the euphoria we had felt in the initial days faded as we sadly realized that every victory comes at a cost.

As we neared the Golan Heights, a message was passed from vehicle to vehicle that any Syrian soldiers we see on the sides of the road should be taken prisoner. We headed up to Quneitra and were surprised by the number of corpses covered with a blanket—IDF casualties waiting to be collected and taken on their final journey.

Just before our arrival in Quneitra, I suddenly noticed three Syrian soldiers walking toward us. They looked old and exhausted. We immediately jumped out and aimed our fearsome Czech rifles at them. It was three against three. They were exhausted, and we were after a sleepless night; it was really not a scene from a Western. They put up no resistance when we took them prisoner. We found rope to tie their hands and had them sit at the side of the road until the Military Police arrived. It was an unexpected opportunity to use my high school Arabic and bring pride to Mr. Haddad, my immortal teacher.

The POWs were not surprised. They told me they had nothing against Jews and said a few things about the battle fought a few hours earlier. Meanwhile, a few of our soldiers gathered around them, and one of them tried to snatch a wristwatch from one of the prisoners. I immediately barked at him, freezing him in his tracks. I told him that we hadn't come to the Golan Heights to plunder and that it was not a Jewish thing to do. I was happy that other soldiers spoke up in support of my stance. The would-be looter desisted, mumbling something about "bleeding hearts" and standard wartime practice.

✳︎✳︎✳︎

Quneitra was a ghost town. We found ourselves in an orderly and handsome neighborhood, apparently reserved for the families of officers. The door to one of the houses was wide open. Our squad entered out of curiosity. It seemed like the war had passed over the home. But when we entered the bedroom, we found the corpse of an officer lying on the bedspread of the double bed, which was neatly made. The other dead men I witnessed had been killed in the midst of doing something, without having resigned themselves to a life cut short. This dead officer seemed to have calmly come to terms with his own demise, and it seemed that we accepted his death in the same way.

On Saturday evening, June 10, the war came to an end. Now, after seizing the Golan Heights, we were redeployed again. Instead of returning to our home unit, we continued with part of the brigade to a Jordanian army base near Jerusalem. The convoy was much smaller this time, and we advanced relatively quickly. We passed through Ramallah and were surprised to see the beautiful homes and well-arranged streets. There were white flags in some windows, but no one was in the streets. A strange idyll.

When we arrived at the base, it was completely abandoned. It was clear that the Jordanian soldiers had been ordered to evacuate it without warning and immediately left behind their belongings and breakfast plates. Photographs of King Hussein were strewn on floors. Some of us stepped on the photographs as if to nail down our victory.

I took advantage of the wireless device and asked headquarters to call my parents and let them know that all was well with me and to inquire about Yinon. The response came quickly, and I let out a sigh of relief: Yinon was fine. I learned only later that he had fought in the battles for Gaza, which were not so easy.

We quickly settled into the rooms of the abandoned Jordanian base and prepared for a period of service as a garrison force. No one at headquarters seemed to know how long this period would last. We were still plastered with the accumulated filth of the recent weeks and all wanted just one thing: to shower. A day or two after we settled in, we were told that we'd be taken by bus to the Schneller base in Jerusalem to shower. But in the same breath, they informed us that there was no hot water there. Indeed, that's how it was: a wonderful cold shower and clean clothes. Real luxuries.

The driver wanted to take us back immediately after we showered and changed. But I mustered the courage to ask that we stop first at the Western Wall. He explained that this detour was not included in the order he had received. But after other soldiers supported my idea, he felt obliged to comply.

As soon as we got off the bus, I saw the familiar stones—it was like meeting King David for a cup of coffee. And I wasn't the only one with tears in my eyes. We walked back and forth along the exposed wall, and I couldn't help remembering an evening at Beit Sokolov with my father when a journalist with a foreign passport spoke about his recent trip to Jordan, describing the broken tombstones on the Mount of Olives and the forlornness of the Western Wall. Hearing about a place that was so close, yet so far, had convinced me that I would never see it with my own eyes. And suddenly it was happening. Suddenly it was in our hands, after battles that were so swift, though exacting a steep price. It was still hard to take this all in.

On June 16, our communications vehicle returned to headquarters, and our attachment to the brigade ended. We turned in our gear and were released for a weekend furlough. A birthday present from my parents was waiting for me on the desk in my room: *Beit Hanivharim* (later published in English as *The Knesset: The Parliament of Israel*) by Asher Zion, the Knesset secretary. The inscription was in my father's handwriting: "To our dear Yossi, on your nineteenth birthday and your first furlough upon the conclusion of the Six-Day War and the redemption of the Land. With love, Mother and Father. 8 Sivan 5727, June 16, 1967."

✸✸✸

Soon afterwards, I was sent to an advanced communications course, and I felt like someone returning to his old home. We learned about additional communication devices and developed faster Morse speed. After completing the course, I was sent to Qantara, situated along the northern part of the Suez Canal.

The communications vehicle was already there, operated by another soldier from the unit, whom I was sent to replace. My job was to contact headquarters every day at a certain hour and be available to the field unit for air support missions. I was told right away that I'd be added to the rotation for guard duty at the entrance to the army post.

Three months after the war, in September 1967, the Palestinians were still reeling in panic, while we were still basking in a state of euphoria. The Egyptians—after Nasser retracted his resignation due to popular demand—started to bombard the eastern side of the canal. It was quite surprising to discover they were still around, feisty, and impudent.

On the way to Qantara, I stopped in Gaza City and walked down the main street with a backpack and a Czech rifle, on my own, as if it were

Allenby Street. I even went into a toy store and bought something for Yinon's daughters. I could pay with Israeli currency, and the price they requested was ridiculously low. Only afterwards, I was alarmed by the thought that perhaps they had given me a special discount because my rifle had intimidated them. Did they see me as a ruthless soldier? While these thoughts ran through my head, a boy, about ten years old, suddenly approached me and asked in Arabic-accented Hebrew, "Shoeshine?"

My military shoes were indeed dusty, but I couldn't imagine having someone shine them for me. On the other hand, perhaps his mother was ill and had sent him out to make some money, I thought. In the end, I offered him a lira, but he refused to take it because I had rejected his pleas to shine my shoes. I still can see the boy's face in my memory.

I told myself at the time that perhaps that short encounter summed up the entire story. I saw myself as someone who was defending his country against an arrogant Egyptian leader's threats of destruction. A ten-year-old boy saw me as a conqueror who was not even willing to let him shine my shoes and thought I could buy him off with money. He either hated me already, or he'd hate me later.

※※※

I didn't know anybody in the unit deployed in Qantara. I reported to the communications vehicle and replaced the soldier there. I was told that the Egyptian bombardments usually came in the mornings. No one had been killed yet, but there was no reason to be the first one. When the bombardment starts, I should run to the place where I'm supposed to sleep every night: a sort of dugout next to a guava tree (whose fragrance is not to everyone's liking). Most of the guys were nice, except for the master sergeant, who was a real jerk. The cook, a reservist, invested his skills in providing us meals, but we had only battle rations for breakfast.

I brought a good number of books with me from home, so there was no chance of getting bored in that distant and dull place. I soon developed a routine: After reading the daily papers, which arrived two or three days after the rest of the world saw them, my day was divided between reading books; doing guard duty at the gate; writing letters to my parents, girlfriend, and Yinon; lunch together with my fellow soldiers, and then writing down some of my thoughts—for my own eyes only.

One morning, while I was still eating my battle ration, a bombardment suddenly began. I immediately left everything and ran to the dugout, which offered protection that was largely psychological. It was an especially heavy barrage. When they told us we could come out, I returned to my usual place by the communications vehicle. When I arrived, I saw that a shell had hit my ration, slicing it right down the middle; in fact, I could have eaten the half that remained. Of course, I chose not to do that and tossed what remained in the trash. Somehow, being in such strange proximity to the angel of death did not instill fear in me or leave a particularly profound impression.

I never missed the appointed hour for contacting my home unit. Even when there were bombardments, I'd make contact and report on the situation. But if the bombardments were during other hours, I'd make sure to run to the dugout. After all, it had already proven itself.

We called the central part of the encampment "the courtyard of the national institutions." The commander's office, dining hall, bathrooms, and showers were there. (They were built of asbestos, long before the world discovered that the material was toxic.) There were only two female soldiers in our encampment; they served in the commander's office. About two weeks after my arrival in Qantara, I was in that "courtyard" and saw them—with wet hair, wrapped in large towels and wearing sandals—hurrying from the showers to their tent, where they'd get back into their regular field uniforms. Everyone in the courtyard had their eyes glued to them, while the master sergeant, a Holocaust survivor from Poland, shouted: "Why don't they give? Why don't they understand that we've been here for weeks upon weeks? It wouldn't be like that in any other army!"

For a few seconds, I stood frozen in place. I couldn't believe that a soldier with ranks would say such a thing. But then I felt I couldn't remain silent like the others and responded to him: "Then we're very fortunate not to be like any other army!"

"Boy, go back to your Gymnasium," he replied, as if he actually knew that I came from there. This time I didn't answer him.

After a little over a month, I received notice from the unit's headquarters that I would be replaced on a particular day, and that a vehicle would come to take me north. And when "Cushi" emerged from the vehicle, I jumped for joy. Sergeant Major Nissim ("Cushi") Lavi was my direct commander, a veteran wireless operator, who had come to the Communications Corps from the navy; his Morse speed was very high. He had an impressive and even tough presence, but in reality, he was far from it; he knew how to be both a commander and a friend. Cushi said that he felt duty-bound to personally pick me up at Qantara because of my daily broadcasts to the unit. He explained that they knew very well when our site was under bombardment and clearly saw that the shelling did not prevent me from broadcasting on time.

I told him that I was very happy that he came, but the justification he gave was incorrect. "I'm just a 'square' who follows orders," I explained. Somehow, my response reached the soldiers in the unit. So, when I was appointed to a command position, I was dubbed "Commander Square."

Cushi remained my friend. He later went off to officers' course and reached the rank of lieutenant colonel in the Communications Corps. And when I ran for chairman of the Labor Party, thirty years after serving together, he volunteered to help my campaign.

✳✳✳

During my last year of compulsory service, I commanded more than sixty soldiers and played a prominent role at the headquarters unit. On my last Independence Day eve in the army, I was selected as the unit's outstanding soldier, out of hundreds of guys, and I felt I was mature enough to dive into civilian life.

For me, the Six-Day War was a direct continuation of the milieu in which I lived, another link in the chain. In my eyes, the names carved into the marble slabs were proof that my generation was also ready to do its part. As I hung up my army uniform and prepared to step out into the world, it seemed to me that I was now facing the real moment of truth.

10

A Child of the Establishment

INTENTIONALLY OR NOT, I FOLLOWED IN YINON'S FOOTSTEPS BY marrying at age twenty-one and combining work and academic studies. In those days, no one imagined post-army treks in India or South America, and tours of classical Europe were only for the wealthy. And even if all those options were open to me, I probably would not have opted to travel.

Living together with your girlfriend before marriage was also not an accepted practice then, and Helena and I really had no need to get to know each other better—we had been together for three and a half years. She had already completed her first year of law studies at Tel Aviv University, and I was accepted to study Hebrew literature and political science there. So, it was only natural for us to get married at the Students' Club on campus. The two sets of parents bought a two-room apartment for us on the fourth floor of Arba Aratsot Street and visiting us was a challenge for elderly guests since there was no elevator.

Two weeks after the wedding, I started working as a reporter for the *Davar* daily. I had responded to an advertisement in the newspaper for an economics reporter. It was a bit nervy of me to apply because I didn't know much about economics. But I figured that the knowledge I did possess, along with my writing ability, would compensate for my lack of professional knowhow. I sent copies of articles I had written and met several times with the head of the editorial staff, Chaim Isaak, and with others. I was still in the final days of my army service when I received the happy news that they had decided to hire me. This saved me from the need to work in student jobs until finding permanent employment.

Davar was a fascinating school. I was assigned to cover the Histadrut labor federation, and I became thoroughly familiar with its merits and its ailments, which prepared me for proposing reforms in the 1980s. In addition, I wrote feature articles for the *Davar HaShavua* weekend magazine. I interviewed just about everyone I wanted to, wrote about almost everything I wanted to, and worked night editing shifts to supplement my modest salary. My economic knowledge was indeed inadequate, so I occasionally consulted with my father during the initial years.

The editor of *Davar* in those years was Dr. Yehuda Gotthelf. He was a friendly man, gray-haired and highly esteemed, and a veterinarian by training. He shifted for many years between Mapam and Mapai, and supported Pinhas Lavon in the latter's conflict with Ben-Gurion. The conflict centered on the "Unfortunate Affair"—a false flag operation in Egypt in which Israeli agents planted bombs at various American and British civilian sites. The idea was to make it look like the Egyptians were responsible for the bombings, and thus drive a wedge between Egypt and the US and convince the British to keep their troops deployed at the Suez Canal. The operation failed and thirteen members of the Israeli terror cell were arrested. The newspaper was torn asunder by the affair but showed openness and gave a platform to both Lavon's supporters and Ben-Gurion's supporters.

In any case, my first assignment from Gotthelf was to write a feature article on the old central bus station in Tel Aviv, before its demolition. I did indeed write the article, but another forty years passed before the station was actually demolished.

Despite the newspaper's political affiliation, no one asked me about my political views or which party I vote for. At *Davar HaShavua*, which was edited by Ohad Zmora, there was a young and liberal atmosphere compared to the newspaper itself, which was a bit more conservative.

I remember once preparing a long article on one of the automobile companies, based on information I had received on what was going on there. The article never saw the light of day. Hanna Zemer, who had meanwhile replaced Gotthelf as editor-in-chief, explained to me that the same automobile company was running a daily front-page ad, and that sometimes the newspaper had to make compromises in order to pay the journalists' wages. Another time, she asked me to write a "promotional" article for a special supplement celebrating the Solel Boneh conglomerate. After she rejected my request to decline this assignment, I asked if she would agree to publish it under a pseudonym. She promised to give me an answer within a day. And indeed, she informed me the next day that she would reluctantly honor my request. My article appeared under the byline Yosef Kashash—and only I knew that 'Kashash' was an acronym in Hebrew for "done under duress."

During that period, such talented reporters as Eli Mohar, Doron Rosenblum, Ehud Ya'ari, Nahum Barnea, and Danny Rubinstein roamed the corridors of *Davar*. There were also journalists from the older generation, including Yehoshua Meshulah, who proposed that every Jew in the world buy an Israeli product daily for one dollar, and then the Israeli economy would prosper, and thrive.

Zemer was a great editor, and I learned the profession from her, even though I thought I already knew everything. Every change she made in the newspaper was received with angry criticism by the shrinking readership. When she added two red stripes under the name *Davar*, people remarked sneeringly that it was her lipstick. And when she decided to remove the vowels (*nikud*) from the newspaper's name, they ridiculed her by starting to call it "Dever" (Hebrew for "pestilence").

For several years, I had a regular column that I called "The 5th Floor and the Other Floors." It described what was happening inside the Histadrut. I spared no criticism of the illustrious organization, which did not know how to adapt itself to the changing reality, and I became the scourge of the Histadrut leadership. "Why don't you like me?" Yeruham Meshel, then secretary-general of the organization, once asked me. "I'm also from Pinsk," he added in desperation, half-jokingly and half in earnest.

During my last years at the newspaper, I was also the TV and radio critic, and that was one of my favorite jobs ever. My articles engendered some rancor (or appreciation) among the subjects of the reviews, and some of those I critiqued have never forgotten what I wrote, even fifty years later. Meanwhile, I continued to write short stories and published most of them in the *At* monthly magazine for women. The editor, Tommy Lapid, asked for more than I could write. When he stepped down in 1974, I suddenly realized that in a sense I had finished that role and stopped writing prose.

✳✳✳

Helena was doing secretarial work in the morning hours and studying law in the evenings. I had more control over my schedule, and I raced back and forth on buses between *Davar*'s offices and my classes at the university. The literature classes were pure pleasure, with teachers such as Dan Meron, Uzi Shavit, and Lily Rattok. The political science department was completely different. Two years after the war, there was a salient presence of young lecturers from the United States, who immigrated to Israel after completing their studies and, in some cases, after having already begun to teach at American universities. Some taught in English or rudimentary Hebrew; only a few were fluent Hebrew speakers. Most of them favored the behavioristic approach (which focuses on analyzing behavior rather than its motives) and introduced new American ideas, which mainly involved extensive reliance on in-depth surveys—much to the consternation of the political science teachers at the Hebrew University of Jerusalem, some of whom came to teach us in Tel Aviv.

Life was very intensive. In retrospect, those were beautiful years—two students who had no time to participate in extracurricular student life for even a moment. We were building our nest, working for a living, meeting on the fourth floor only late in the evening and on weekends, doing some of our schoolwork on the buses and the rest in the evening, at home. We crammed for tests, waited anxiously for the results, walked to visit our parents on the weekends and had almost no time to go out and meet with friends. We had no TV in our apartment, and we'd watch the "Hedva and Shlomik" TV series on Friday evenings at the home of Helena's parents.

Politics had yet to enter our lives. Those were the years of blindness between the Six-Day War and the Yom Kippur War. To a large extent, I continued to be a child of the establishment: I preferred Golda Meir to Ben-Gurion, and I didn't like the Rafi party that "the old man" headed. I wasn't involved in student politics either and didn't even vote in the elections for the Students' Association. I was glad the Alignment (*HaMaarach*) was formed in January 1969, and I was pleased that for the first (and last) time in history the ruling faction comprised a majority of Knesset members (63 of 120). I was also happy when Begin and his colleagues left the national unity government in August 1970 in protest over UN Security Council Resolution 242. In those days, I simply placed my faith in the state's leaders. Even the Alignment's crazy campaign advertisement in 1973 failed to shake this trust: "Quiet prevails on the banks of the Suez. Also in the Sinai desert, in the Gaza Strip, in the West Bank, in Judea and Samaria, and in the Golan. The borders are secure, the bridges are open, Jerusalem is united, Jewish settlements are being built, and our diplomatic standing is strong. This is a result of sound, bold, and far-sighted policy. This is proof of the nearsightedness of Gahal's leaders. We've achieved this with your help. And with you—we'll continue."

***

Sadly, bereavement touched our family in May 1970. Yossi Bregman, the oldest son of Oded, my only cousin, was killed by a shell near the canal. Yossi and I were named for the same man—my grandfather and his great-grandfather. He was three years younger than me, which made me "big Yossi." In those years, Oded's family (he, his wife Shula, and their four children) and Oded's parents, Baruch and Levana, lived as neighbors on HaMa'alot Street in Ra'anana. Baruch was a senior manager at Bank Leumi, and Oded also worked for the bank. Baruch was a reserved person, cynical and wise. Oded was convivial and loved music; he played the accordion and had a mustache like those of the Palmach fighters.

We visited them often, and we loved them dearly. I felt a sort of shared fate with Yossi because of our identical name; and since I was three years ahead of him at school and in the army, I served as a source of information for him on almost everything that awaited him in his near future. He had asthma but tried not to make a big deal about it and enlisted as a combat soldier.

On that terrible morning, my sister-in-law Aliza called to tell me that Yossi had been killed at the canal. The news struck me like a bolt of lightning. I rushed to Oded's home in Ra'anana. He was walking from wall to wall in the kitchen. Shula wept, and the three younger siblings were in shock, but Oded asked that I go check on his father. He was very concerned about Baruch's weak heart and didn't know whether his father could bear this awful news.

I was afraid to meet Baruch and had no words of wisdom to offer him. Levana sat by the table and cried. Baruch sat in his armchair and wept bitterly. I had never seen him cry and didn't think he was capable of such weeping. I didn't say a word to them. I kissed Levana, and sat in silence next to Baruch. I realized then that you can only console strangers. Later, when I had to speak to bereaved families on Memorial Day for Israel's Fallen Soldiers, I never chose the military cemetery in Ra'anana.

11

Just Don't Get Involved in Politics

IN SEPTEMBER 1971, MY FATHER WAS DIAGNOSED WITH CANCER, which had apparently gone undetected for several years and was the cause of the severe pain he suffered. The doctors operated on him but gave up the attempt to remove the growth. Father quickly recovered from the operation and was led to believe that everything would be fine if he strictly maintained the right diet. It wasn't customary then to reveal the stark truth to patients, and he was supposed to understand the situation himself. He lived for another year and two months in pain, shriveling physically while trying desperately to live a regular life. One day, about two weeks before his death, he sat in his office at the bank, and a woman walked in and asked what happened to Mr. Beilin who used to sit in that office. When he said that he was Mr. Beilin, she thought he was joking around with her, and she left the room. That incident broke his heart.

Gil, our first-born, arrived three months before my father's death at age sixty-two. From Gil's very first day, he was strikingly beautiful. I was then twenty-four years old and already a father. And three months later, I was fatherless.

I remember being at his bedside that morning at Ichilov Hospital, helping him eat. That afternoon, my mother telephoned to say it was over. I returned to the hospital just to see him one last time. I was glad he had lived long enough to see Gil and to hold him in his arms. I was also able to inform him that the university had offered me a position as a teaching assistant in political science. He was much less pleased when I told him I had joined the Labor Party. "Just don't get involved in politics," he warned.

The crazy pace of life didn't allow me a sufficient chance to grieve for my father, though I did make sure to recite the mourner's prayer in a *minyan* (quorum of ten). He wasn't perfect, and I didn't like his stormy temperament, the punishments he meted out to "educate" me, and his silly grudges with my mother. But I loved him and knew that he always was and always will be my personal minister of defense. When he was approaching home, and I heard the telltale sound he made when clearing his throat, I felt reassured that everything was all right. And I felt the same way when I woke at night and heard him snoring in the next room. Just knowing that he was always there had a calming effect.

His death tore down a wall between me and death. I felt that now I myself was exposed to the end, without any means of defense. Looking back, I recognize that I inherited from him the sense of living in a young state—that we must forgive it for the mistakes it makes and shed a tear when hearing *HaTikva* (the national anthem); that Independence Day is the most important holiday, when we recite the *Hatzi Hallel* psalms; and that the blessing Rabbi Isaac Halevi Herzog added to the prayer book for the nascent State of Israel (and its ministers and advisors) is no less sacred than the *Vayehi Binso'a Ha'aron* prayer chanted at the beginning of the Torah service.

✱✱✱

After I completed my bachelor's degree with honors in both departments, I decided to pursue a master's degree in political science and to bid farewell to the literature department. An MA in literature seemed like a sort of luxury to me. Then the head of the political science department, professor Asher Arian, called and invited me to join a new track that bypassed the master's degree and proceeded directly to a doctorate. I immediately accepted his offer. It turned out to be a mistake that prolonged my period of studies instead of shortening it.

We were three students in the track, and the department invested great effort in teaching us. Important professors visiting from abroad were asked to come and lecture to the three of us. Though the track was prestigious and groundbreaking, it went on for too long. I asked to take the tests for the master's degree along the way, and finally completed my PhD dissertation and all of the difficult exams for the doctorate only in 1980.

My dissertation was entitled "Inter-generational Friction in Three Political Parties in Israel," and my main conclusion was that there is no political (or other) significance in the generational changing of the guard in politics—unless generational units are created that formulate their own worldviews and challenge the conventions of the older groups.

Meanwhile, Helena also completed her studies and started an internship at the Central District Court. In light of our many commitments, I found myself dividing my life between *Davar* and the campus (where I split my time between my work as a teaching assistant to professor Aharon Klieman and my doctoral studies). Gil's main caregiver was Helena's mother, Irena. Thus, our lives took on an established routine, and we felt a considerable sense of self-fulfillment.

As a reporter for *Davar*, I was asked to interview Yitzhak Rabin in mid-1973. He had just completed his term as ambassador in Washington and had joined the Labor Party; word had it that he would receive the twentieth slot on the party's list for the upcoming Knesset elections. I arrived at his home in Zahala carrying a page with a long series of questions. Since I covered the Histadrut beat, I naturally asked him questions concerning social welfare policy, workers' rights, and social disparities. I saw signs of dissatisfaction in his face, and a few minutes later he told me that the questions "aren't good." He wasn't the first interviewee who was unhappy with my questions, but none of the others had expressed their opinion so bluntly.

He asked me for the list of questions. I hesitated. It was an unprecedented request, but it was Rabin, and I remembered him with his visor cap visiting the eighth Brigade in the Paran desert. I handed him the page. He read my handwritten questions intently, returned the questions to me as if he had expected something else, and that's when he said, "The questions aren't good." Nonetheless, he answered all of them. They were the responses of a typical American right-winger. The questions disappointed him. His responses disappointed me, but I published all of them without comment.

In the end, he indeed entered the Knesset in the twentieth slot on Labor's slate of candidates. And, of course, I could never have guessed how our paths would cross in the future.

✳✳✳

And then Yom Kippur came and everything changed. I was praying at the nearby synagogue on Yehoshua Bin Nun Street and returned home during the short afternoon break. The sirens went off at 2:00 p.m. At first, I thought it must be a technical fault in the warning system. After all, in the quiet tranquility of Yom Kippur afternoon, no one could possibly think of waging war.

It soon became clear that the fault wasn't in the warning system. Israel Radio, which goes off the air on Yom Kippur, began broadcasting. The neighbors hurried down the staircase, even though no bomb shelter awaited them below, only a small entryway. The memory etched in my mind is of Gil, who was still learning to speak, pointing at the baby shoe that fell from his foot on our way down the four flights of stairs. We held up the convoy of neighbors for a moment to retrieve it.

The IDF call-up squad worked quickly, and I received an emergency mobilization order (*Tzav 8*) and hurried to the "Pit"—the command center in Tel Aviv. The atmosphere was one of uncertainty, shock, and frantic activity of people hurrying to no place. Communication networks were opened with the mobilizing units, and I was in charge of a shift, responsible for ensuring a reliable connection between headquarters and the field units, and for submitting the handwritten radio logs recorded by the wireless operators.

In the two wars I experienced during my period of compulsory IDF service (the Six-Day War and the War of Attrition), I operated in a narrow world, without seeing the context in which my unit operated. This time, the full picture was spread out before me: the maps, the arrows drawn on their plastic sheeting and, in particular, the true data from the field in real time.

Suddenly, it seemed that the entire order had collapsed; for me, as a veteran radio operator, any violation of communication procedure was blasphemy. The soldiers spoke on the wireless network without codes, without any caution, as if they were speaking on the telephone. Cries of desperation from the military posts, the terrible arguments between the most senior commanders (generals Gorodish-Gonen and Sharon, for example), the derogatory names, disputes over tactics, and especially the terrifying helplessness that could be heard as the Syrian army rapidly advanced toward Kibbutz Gadot, and as the Egyptian army, undeterred by the famous Bar-Lev line, quickly moved eastward.

Retired generals, dressed in uniform, arrived at the Pit to ask if they could help in some way, and no one knew what to tell them—at least not at the beginning of the war. The omnipotent defense minister, Moshe Dayan, in his khaki clothes, hurried to the war room, ashen-faced. Dado (David Elazar), the IDF chief of staff, was frighteningly serious. During the following days, there was only one voice on the network that sounded like someone who knew what he was doing. It was Haim Bar-Lev, who illegally moved from his position as minister of commerce and industry to the role of commander of the southern front. (To avoid firing the recently appointed GOC Southern Command, Gorodish-Gonen, in the midst of war, he was allowed to retain his position but was subordinated to Bar-Lev.) On the network, Bar-Lev received the number 1,000 and radiated a sense of calm. Still, the situation continued to seethe.

In retrospect, my life can be divided between everything that occurred up to October 1973 and everything that has happened since. The terrible ease of sliding from the euphoria of victory to the despair of defeat shaped my political worldview. The awful number of casualties; the awful number of POWs and their ranks; the awful number of MIAs and their families' efforts to discover what happened to their loved ones; the photographs of Israeli soldiers displayed at Beit Sokolov in Tel Aviv so that their families could identify them; the good people, some of whom I interviewed, who walked around like shadows of themselves while awaiting word of their missing sons—all this together gave me a sense of the mortality of the gods.

The Yom Kippur War, experienced from the vantage point of IDF headquarters, also put an end to my religious observance. For the first time in my life, I wrote on the Sabbath, and I never returned to the synagogue except when representing Israel overseas or for family celebrations. I stopped keeping kosher. From Helena's perspective, this made life much easier. From my perspective, it was an upheaval.

Politically, from someone who had supported a territorial compromise on all fronts but was waiting, together with Dayan, for a "phone call from Hussein," I became someone who no longer viewed the territories we captured in the Six-Day War as bargaining chips, but rather as a terrible burden that had led to war. The speed with which the Syrian army had attacked the Golan Heights; the danger posed to the children's homes on kibbutzim; the impotence of the Bar-Lev line in the Sinai—all made it crystal clear to me that the territories I had helped to conquer were not a security belt, and that it was imperative for Israel to reach agreements with Egypt and Jordan, and to end the occupation.

I was furious at Golda Meir, the kindly and smiling grandmother figure, who had forbidden Nahum Goldmann, the president of the World Jewish Congress, from meeting with Nasser in 1970 and then later rejected the proposal of Gunnar Jarring, the UN secretary-general's emissary, to try to work out an accord with Egypt's new president, Anwar Sadat, in February 1971. Acceptance of the proposal might have spared us the Yom Kippur War. I couldn't forgive Dayan for his smugness (quoting Jeremiah—"Have no fear, my servant Jacob," and declaring, "Better Sharm el-Sheikh without peace than peace without Sharm el-Sheikh"), nor could I forgive Yisrael Galili, the minister of information, for the disastrous advice he offered. I had accepted many of their assessments as established facts, but now I learned that no leadership should be given a blank check.

My desire to enter politics was not born in October 1973, but it certainly grew stronger, along with my views on a range of subjects—from Israel-Diaspora relations and Jewish continuity, to the need for a separation of religion and state. But my primary objective was to promote the chance of reaching peace with our neighbors, based on the realization that avoidance of such accords in order to allow Jewish settlements to remain in the Sinai, Golan, and West Bank—endangered our future.

I was very surprised that the Labor Party's central committee almost unanimously supported Golda Meir as the party's candidate for prime minister in the December 1973 election (originally scheduled for late October but postponed due to the war). On the other hand, I was glad that the protest waged by Motti Ashkenazi and his friends forced her and her close associates to resign a few months after winning the election.

While Pinhas Sapir had proposed Golda's candidacy in 1969 as a way to sidestep the anticipated clash between Moshe Dayan and Yigal Allon, the top ranks of the party were now stepping down, and there were no natural candidates. I met with the justice minister at the time, Haim Zadok, and tried to persuade him to compete for the party's leadership, but he was not interested. I had no clear preference between Rabin and Shimon Peres. My interview with Rabin several months earlier had convinced me that he lacked sufficient experience and a social-democratic worldview. Peres had the image of someone who knew how to get things done; he held hawkish views, had pushed to form the national unity government with Begin and spoke about the enormous importance of science in a way that failed to spark my enthusiasm. In addition, his close relationship with Dayan did not add to his credit in my eyes.

In April 1974, I sat in the Ohel Theater as a journalist covering the central committee meeting that would elect a new Labor Party chairman. The two candidates, in their early fifties, sat in light-blue shirts in the first row, side by side, and they seemed to have an excellent relationship. I learned that the two had just come from a lunch meeting where they had agreed that whoever loses the race for party chief would serve as defense minister, and perhaps that explains their high spirits, even before the results were announced. In the end, the party establishment backed Rabin, giving him the majority with 298 votes, versus 254 for Peres. The younger generation and critics of the establishment preferred Peres and lost.

I hoped that the Alignment would embark on a new path and overcome the mistakes for which the outgoing leadership was responsible. But this didn't happen. The relations between Rabin and Peres quickly deteriorated, turning into a burning hatred that continued through the next two decades and cast its shadow over everything that occurred in the party.

✸✸✸

At the same time, I started to be active in the Labor Party in various capacities. I became active in the party's *Bet* branch on Ben-Yehuda Street, which was previously run by Yossi Sarid. There was a hot water urn, teabags, and cookies, and every few weeks a member of Knesset or government minister would appear, and the elderly party members would ask mundane questions. There were also internal meetings in which we'd discuss the issues of the day, such as how to address inflation; our conclusions were never presented to anyone else in the world.

I also volunteered to recruit members for the party in our area. Thus, for the first time, I got to know the upper floors on Ben-Yehuda Street. I met older people, living a hardscrabble life, with memories and grievances. The membership fee was ten lira, and it was a lot of money for some of them. A few took pity on me and paid under protest. They didn't like Rabin, who had made some controversial statements about Israeli émigrés (*yordim*) and others. They didn't understand why Peres was feuding with him, and they missed Levi Eshkol, the late prime minister. Anyone who dared to say they missed Golda received a long lecture from me. I explained to the potential party member why he was wrong to long for the days of Golda, taking into account the possibility that it might ruin my chances of recruiting him.

Another sphere of my political activity was the Young Guard of the Labor Party. The party's headquarters on 110 HaYarkon Street was teeming with life. After all, the Alignment had 56 Knesset seats. The headquarters included departments for new immigrants, women, Arabs, and municipal issues, as well as divisions responsible for information campaigns, organizations, external relations, and more. The Young Guard was for members from ages 18 to 35. It included various groups, and its leaders historically saw themselves as destined for greatness. When I joined, it was led by Natan Ra'anan, with Haim Ramon as secretary of information, Muli Dor as secretary for organization, and Mario Tuval as the Young Guard's international secretary. Serving alongside Tuval was Daniela Sielski, who was married to Natan Ra'anan at the time and is now my wife.

After joining this impressive group, I was asked to edit the Young Guard's mouthpiece, *Ramzor*. Soon afterwards, I was elected to chair the Young Guard's political policy committee. All of us were more dovish than the central stream of the party and were critical of the Histadrut's conduct. (We demonstrated, for example, against Solel Boneh for building homes in the occupied territories.) The magazine I edited gave very prominent expression to the opposition we mounted.

✱✱✱

In that same year, 1975, I traveled with other Young Guard activists for meetings in Europe. It was my first flight abroad, and I was already twenty-seven. The main destination was Germany, for a joint seminar with Jusos (the youth wing of SPD, the social-democratic party in West Germany).

We landed in the capital of France and walked its length and breadth, with the Paris aficionados among us serving as tour leaders. The next day, we flew to London and met with Prime Minister Harold Wilson. It was the first time I met someone of his rank, and it wasn't as a journalist but as a political activist. Mr. Wilson was impressive and interesting, as expected.

The encounter with our German contemporaries was complex. The young socialists of Jusos criticized us in regard to Israel's treatment of the Palestinians and the Palestinian issue, and it was hard for us to accept such criticism from them. In the following decades, several of them went on to become Bundestag members, government ministers, and even chancellor (Gerhard Schröder). Most of them adopted a more balanced approach over the years, but at the time our positions on ending the occupation and making peace with our neighbors were not enough to satisfy our hosts.

My international activity in the framework of the Young Guard grew more intensive, and I was elected to serve as its international secretary. I was a member of the International Union of Socialist Youth (IUSY) and represented the Young Guard at various conferences; I became familiar with this sort of activity and learned how to draft resolutions. Most importantly, I formed relationships with people whose worldview was close to mine. In retrospect, the network I cultivated in those days was helpful on many issues I addressed in my work in subsequent decades. However, I also learned how difficult such activity is. My friends and I, who were tagged as leftists in the Israeli political system, were often accused in the international arena of being "collaborators" with the "occupation regime."

In 1976, at the IUSY's annual congress, our delegation decided to walk out of the session after the approval of a German-sponsored resolution opposing the two-state solution and calling for the establishment of a single democratic, secular state. Before leaving the hall, we delivered several speeches about the real meaning of Zionism. Daniela contacted the office of Willy Brandt, the former chancellor, and he invited her to meet with him in Bonn. She traveled to Bonn from Stuttgart to complain about the conduct of the SPD's youth wing. He asked her to see a copy of the resolution and then tore it into pieces.

Daniela was born in Buenos Aires to a family that had immigrated to Argentina from Germany. She studied at a Hebrew school her parents had helped to found, spoke Spanish, German, English, Hebrew, and Portuguese, was a passionate Zionist and came on her own to settle in Israel immediately after high school. Her familiarity with international issues and fluency in multiple languages enabled her to forge relationships and stay in contact with important figures hosted by the Labor Party.

The Yom Kippur War, the global energy crisis that followed, the UN General Assembly's "Zionism is Racism" resolution, the anti-Israel terrorist activity in Europe—all made our activity very challenging. We were warned not to wear or carry things that identified us as Israelis and not to speak Hebrew in public when we were abroad. I was even given special training in using a pistol and served as a security person on some of the Young Guard's overseas trips.

ALONG THE ROADSIDE

I met Shimon Peres for the first time in 1963, when he was deputy defense minister. Several young reporters for "Maariv for Youth" were selected by the editor to interview him, and I was one of them. With great awe and reverence, we walked through the gates of the Kirya in Tel Aviv and entered the old building of the Defense Ministry. He greeted us with a politician's smile and devoted an hour to us.

The second meeting took place in 1975, when I interviewed him for "Ramzor." We spoke about the various issues of the day, including the interim agreements with Egypt and Syria. When I was teenager, Peres was a star of the Geva and Carmel newsreels that were screened at movie theaters before the main attraction. He lacked Moshe Dayan's charisma and Abba Eban's eloquence, but he was active-effective and always at Ben-Gurion's side. Peres was the symbol of the technocratic generation that would replace the idealistic pioneers of the Second and Third Aliyah (waves of immigration) who spoke Hebrew with a heavy Russian accent. He also was very familiar with the corridors of government. Many saw him as "Mr. Security," a centrist in his social views, an opponent of territorial compromise and a great believer in a diplomatic arrangement with Jordan that would allow the Palestinians a type of self-government. Though he lost to Rabin in the competition for the party's leadership, he was still perceived as the more likeable of the two.

In any event, when I broached the subject of Jewish settlements in the territories during that interview for "Ramzor," I was astonished when Peres declared, "The settlements in Judea and Samaria are the roots and eyes of the State of Israel." While I knew that he didn't oppose the settlements, I never expected him to make this sort of statement, which in some sense continues to echo in my mind to this very day. Until then, I had thought that even though the settlers claimed Peres as their champion, he was not a whole-hearted supporter. I was wrong.

12

It's Not the Time to Hesitate

DESPITE THE ENTEBBE OPERATION IN 1976, THE RABIN GOVERNment lost the public's appreciation and trust. In December of that year, Rabin disbanded his government in the wake of a conflict with the religious parties, thus triggering early elections. Peres demanded that the Labor Party conduct a vote to choose its candidate for prime minister, and the party's 3,000-member convention met in February 1977 to decide the race between Rabin and Peres. The tension was enormous in the run-up to the vote. Most of the Young Guard's activists supported Peres—not because of his worldview, but because they believed that only he, a popular defense minister who was perceived as a centrist, had a chance of leading the Labor Party to victory in the Knesset elections.

At that time, I was very far from belonging to the "Peres camp." I regarded him as a sort of right-winger on issues of war and peace, though I didn't view Rabin as a leader in that sphere either. Rabin, in my eyes, held right-wing views on social and economic issues, and some of his caustic remarks didn't sit well with me either. I preferred not to affiliate with either camp, but I soon realized that it would be very difficult to sit on the fence as an activist in the party. And though I didn't identify with either of the candidates to lead the Labor Party, I never considered joining a small and antiestablishment left-wing party—not because I looked down on such parties, but because I never saw myself as someone who could belong to them. I wanted to change things from inside.

I wrestled with the question and finally decided to support Peres, mainly because of the circle in which I found myself in the party. Most of my new friends in Labor supported him and saw Rabin's term as prime minister as a colossal failure. A number of Labor MKs such as Uzi Baram, Micha Harish, and Yossi Sarid also supported Peres, and I decided to join them. Of course, I didn't know to what extent that almost coincidental decision would identify me as a Peres loyalist in the following decades, even when our opinions sometimes sharply diverged.

Peres lost by only forty-one votes, but he assumed the mantle of party leader after Rabin decided to withdraw his candidacy when it was revealed that his wife had maintained a US bank account (in violation of Israel's foreign currency law at the time).

✳✳✳

As the 1977 elections drew near, *Davar* prepared to cover the rival parties. Since the veteran and esteemed journalist Teddy Preuss chose to interview the presumptive winner, Peres, I was assigned to interview the perennial loser, Menachem Begin. But on the evening of May 17, Haim Yavin declared on Israel TV that the election results marked a political "upheaval."

Despite the exit polls showing a tight race, I found it hard to believe that this threatening man—the one who had goaded his followers to throw rocks at the Knesset during the historic decision on reparation payments from Germany, who had opposed the UN partition, and whose organization was responsible for the massacre at Deir Yassin and the bombing of the King David Hotel—was going to be the prime minister of Israel. The thought that I'd be one of the first journalists to interview him after his victory made me shudder.

I arrived at 1 Rosenbaum Street early in the morning and proceeded to Begin's apartment, which was famous for being extremely modest. Eliyahu Ben-Elissar, the Likud's spokesperson, whom I knew from covering events related to his party, gave me a warm welcome. Begin was even more effusive in welcoming me. I understood from him that he read *Davar* every morning and always read what I wrote. He didn't agree with everything but could definitely accept much of it. He smiled a lot, answered my questions in detail and said that he was sure the interview would appear the next day true to its source. And indeed it did.

A month later, Peres invited me to his office at the Labor Party's headquarters. The building that had teemed with life was now quiet and half-empty. Peres sat in the large conference room. As I arrived, he was signing a check. When I sat down, he showed me the amount and smiled wistfully: It was a check for one hundred lira. The everyday management of the party had fallen on him because there was no secretary-general, until Haim Bar-Lev agreed to assume the position. Peres told me he had been forced to fire long-serving and good employees; that was never easy, he added. After an obligatory conversation about the Begin government and its intentions, he asked me if I'd agree to serve as his advisor and as the party's spokesperson.

I was shocked. It was almost the last thing I wanted. Though I had a full schedule—*Davar*, the university, and the Young Guard—I could control my time to a large extent and was engaged in things I liked to do. As a journalist, I was courted by spokespersons and knew that the communiqués they sent me were usually only half true, at best. Several ministers had asked me to serve as the spokesperson for their ministry, and I had rejected their offers without a moment's hesitation. And in regard to serving as an advisor—the ideological gap between Peres and me was so wide, I didn't think it would be possible to fill such a personal role.

I thanked him for his expression of confidence in me but explained that it would mean leaving my work at the newspaper and probably also require me to stop teaching at the university. It would also hurt my chances of completing my doctorate in three years. He said that on the personal matters, "we'll work things out," and that he'd be amenable to any request concerning my academic work. I didn't want to leave the subject open with a "let me sleep on it" response, so I told him my answer was no. Peres didn't accept my decision and immediately tried a more political argument. The party was in its deepest crisis ever, he asserted. Everyone must overcome personal and other impediments to lend a hand and save what the Labor Party represents.

In order to conclude the stressful meeting, I suggested that if he didn't find another candidate to take on the job within the next few weeks, he could call me again, and I'd consider it. He agreed. I wanted to believe that this agreement would put the matter to rest, but I was invited to another meeting a few weeks later. Peres said that he hadn't found anyone else he deemed appropriate and proposed that I take the job for one year only. I could continue to lecture at the university during that year, he reassured me.

At this stage, I raised the subject of my family. I said that I understood I'd need to accompany him on his travels and be away from home. He confirmed that this would indeed be the case. Afterwards, he invited Helena for a meeting and mainly presented a case for party patriotism. "It's not a time for hesitation," he argued, and said he needed someone like me. Peres appealed to Helena to convince me to accept his offer. He also reiterated that it would only be for a limited period and wouldn't disrupt my academic career.

In light of the situation, I spoke with Hanna Zemer about taking an unpaid leave of absence for one year. There were a number of precedents at *Davar* of journalists who left to become the Labor Party's spokesperson and later returned to write for the newspaper.

Thus, I started my job at the party on October 4, 1977. I never returned to *Davar*. I never would have guessed that I was embarking on the longest chapter in my life, spanning thirty-one years.

✳✳✳

Year after year, it was the same ritual: I asked to resign, Peres requested that I stay on for just one more year, and I agreed. In the end, I held these two posts—advisor to Peres and party spokesperson—for seven full years. They were years of hope for the party's rapid rehabilitation and a return to power; years of frustration and renewed hope; years of internal conflicts that threatened to split the party.

A few weeks after starting my new role, the Egyptian president, Anwar Sadat, made his historic visit to Israel. I was happy. Among the Labor Party's leaders, the happiness was also mixed with some bewilderment over why Sadat had not come sooner. A complex discussion was conducted in the party, and there was considerable tension in the meetings of its political policy committee, which was made up of former ministers and other senior figures.

Suddenly, I realized that until now I had been a journalist who was fed leaks, while now I was the one worried about tendentious leaks and the one who issued and explained the press releases. Most importantly, I suddenly was sitting in the room with icons like Rabin, Abba Eban, Haim Bar-Lev, Yisrael Galili, Golda Meir, and others, and I heard them speak with each other in a way that was so different from the way they spoke in the media. It was a very sharp transition. Only the transition from the role of spokesperson to the role of cabinet secretary, seven years later, was sharper yet.

The process the Labor Party underwent in 1978, which ultimately gave Begin the majority he needed to win Knesset approval for the Camp David Accords, drew me closer ideologically to Peres. Despite opposition from Labor Party hawks, Peres made extraordinary efforts to ensure that the party would help his inveterate rival make peace. And I did everything I could vis-à-vis the media to assist in these efforts.

I also traveled overseas with Peres several times that year. The most significant trip was in July 1978, and the primary objective was a meeting with the president of Egypt at a stage when it seemed that the talks between Israel and Egypt had failed. The meeting took place in Vienna under the auspices of the Socialist International. Peres—who ten years earlier, when Labor united with Rafi, had objected to any mention of "social democracy" in the merger documents—now served as vice chairman of the Socialist International and quite enjoyed the formal and informal political frameworks the organization provided him. He was invited to a meeting whose participants included Sadat (as leader of Egypt's National Democratic Party, a member of the Socialist International), Austrian Chancellor Bruno Kreisky, and Willy Brandt, the former chancellor of West Germany who was then serving as the president of the Socialist International. The event included a press conference with all of the participants, a separate meeting between Peres and Sadat, and lunch at the famous Hotel Sacher.

Sadat told us that the main issue of dispute between him and Begin was the Israeli prime minister's refusal to accept that UN Resolution 242 also applied to the West Bank, which meant that its occupation would end when the parties reached an agreement. He revealed that he had offered in exchange to lease the city of Yamit to Israel until 2001 but Begin remained steadfast in his refusal.

The truth is that this was and has remained the real dispute between the left and the right in Israel: the willingness of the left to divide the western Land of Israel in order to ensure a Jewish majority in the Israeli democracy, versus the enlightened right's opposition to dividing the land. Begin, who expressed this right-wing position to a large extent, was willing to grant Israeli citizenship to Palestinians. His hope was that masses of Jewish immigrants to Israel would maintain the demographic balance in favor of the Jewish side.

Sadat acted like an old friend and was quick to laugh. He spoke with optimism and self-confidence, but without arrogance. He was confident that the Egyptian people supported him and that the Arab world would also follow his lead if he signed a peace treaty with us. I asked him which Arab state he thought would be the second to sign an agreement with Israel, and he responded, without hesitation or doubt: "Saudi Arabia."

The participants in the Vienna meetings also discussed the situation in Iran, expressing concerns that the shah might be deposed and uncertainty over who might replace him. Nonetheless, everyone supported his continued reign and were convinced that he would overcome the uprising against him. My impression was that the shah had lost public support and would be overthrown, but after hearing the earnest opinions of these experienced and wise elders, I realized I was wrong.

We heard a similar assessment in London. We met there with the prime minister, James Callaghan, and with his young foreign minister, David Owen. They both were worried about the events in Iran, but said that the shah's military might, especially his air force, would prevent the overthrow of his regime.

The last stop on that trip was Rabat, the capital of Morocco, for a meeting with King Hassan II. We flew there from the airport in Le Bourget in the king's plane, which had been dispatched to France especially for us. It was the first time I flew under a false identity. I was very surprised to see a group of Israelis greet us as we alighted from the plane. For some reason, Peres was sure that I was aware of the fact that the Mossad had a considerable presence in Morocco. At the nocturnal meeting with the king, the possibility of an Israeli-Egyptian peace accord was discussed, of course, but another subject received no less attention—the situation in Iran. Hassan II also expressed confidence in the shah's resilience.

When Ruhollah Khomeini seized power seven months later, I noted to myself that the fact that intelligent people in key positions are convinced that something will happen does not mean that they are necessarily right. It was one of the important lessons I learned in international relations.

A few days after returning from this diplomatic tour, our son Ori was born. His big brother Gil took him under his wing and helped to take care of the beautiful blond infant, who was smart and playful. I felt guilty about not devoting as much time with Ori as I had with Gil during his early years. Between the endless work at the party, my studies at the university and teaching duties there, I was less and less at home. I consoled myself with the quality hours that we did spend together, but that didn't do much to assuage my guilt feelings.

13

All-Out War

THE DAYS LEADING UP TO THE KNESSET VOTE ON THE CAMP DAVID Accords were tense and difficult. It wasn't a given that the Alignment would support the agreement Begin presented. Yisrael Galili was opposed to evacuating the kibbutzim in the Sinai. Representatives of the kibbutz movement descended upon the party's headquarters, demanding that the Labor Party's leadership join the right-wing opposition to the agreement. Yigal Allon also said he couldn't agree to the proposed evacuation. He suggested conducting two votes: one on the agreement and one on the evacuation of the Sinai settlements. In the Labor faction's meeting prior to the decisive debate in the Knesset, it was still unclear which view would prevail. In the end, with sighs of relief by many on both sides of the political divide, a large majority coalesced in support of the accords.

In the Knesset vote, the Alignment gave Begin the majority he needed to implement the framework agreement. Allon abstained. Shlomo Hillel, Yehezkel Zakai, Amos Hadar, and Shoshana Arbeli-Almozlino voted with the extreme right against the agreement. For Peres, it was an ideological and personal achievement, and I was happy to have been involved in the effort to persuade the wavering MKs.

Begin won a place in history through the peace treaty with Egypt and had to compromise many of his principles in doing so. Still, he was a pathetic leader in many respects, captive to his own slogans, outdated in his manners and in his sarcastic speeches. He focused on building Jewish settlements in the territories, did not understand much about economics, spouted hollow and populist slogans, and allowed his finance minister, Simha Erlich, to lead the Israeli economy into spiraling inflation.

Thus, the government provided plenty of reasons to criticize it, despite the peace agreement. The new and promising party, the Democratic Movement for Change (Dash), led by Yigael Yadin, which was the great hope of the 1977 elections, winning fifteen seats (nearly all at the expense of the Alignment)—also very quickly turned out to be a disappointment. As its weaknesses were exposed, it lost support in the polls. In this context, it seemed that the opposition could sail back into power. However, the ongoing conflict between Rabin and Peres weighed heavily upon this chance and, against my best interests, I found myself on the front lines of this conflict. I served as the spokesperson for the entire Labor Party, but in this war of Gog and Magog between the two camps, it was impossible to remain neutral.

The party's elected chairman was under fierce attack by Rabin, who on the one hand had supported Peres's selection as party chief, while on the other hand used his memoirs (*The Rabin Memoirs*) to lambaste him. The book was also exploited by right-wingers to cast doubt on Peres's trustworthiness. Even before the book was published, there were rumors that Rabin intended to badmouth Peres. But when the book was published, it was a major political bombshell. The book itself was interesting and important, especially its description of operations such as Operation Danny—the conquest of Ramla and Lod and the expulsion of their Palestinian residents in the War of Independence. But his references to Peres stemmed from the enormous anger Rabin harbored from the three years in which he served as prime minister and Peres as defense minister. In particular, Rabin's description of Peres as an "indefatigable schemer" is etched in the public memory.

Rabin acted like someone who had withdrawn from public life and had no interest in conforming to what was "politically correct." I found myself in television studios denouncing his remarks, as did many former ministers, some of whom were considered to be his supporters.

Soon afterwards, Peres convened the Labor Party bureau, which voted by a large majority to censure Rabin. It was my job to brief the press on this meeting and its decisions. As the spokesperson of the party that had officially denounced Rabin's harsh critique of Peres, I was perceived as a spokesperson for the "Peres camp" versus the "Rabin camp." Again, this was hardly in my best interests. The worst episode in this conflict, from my personal perspective, was when Rabin ridiculously accused me of fabricating and disseminating a statement about him from Moshe Sharett's diary. The notion that it was possible to forge a quote from a diary that had already been published and could be found in every public library, could only have been concocted in those days of all-out warfare. Rabin's complaint was ultimately arbitrated by the party's venerable oversight institution and was rejected. However, the tension between us remained unabated in the following years.

Rabin almost never visited the party's headquarters at 110 HaYarkon Street and didn't exchange a word with Peres. At one point, it appeared that Labor's leadership would be contested between Peres and Allon, Rabin's former commander who had served as a minister in his government. But after Allon's sudden death on February 29, 1980, Rabin returned to lead the rival camp and unsuccessfully competed against Peres for the party's leadership.

The self-definition of party activists, starting in 1974 and continuing through the next twenty-one years, was first and foremost a question of their affiliation with one of the two camps, even if they preferred to see themselves as party patriots before anything else.

✳✳✳

In parallel with my political activity, I had already collected the materials and interviews for my PhD dissertation. But I needed several months without interruption to write the dissertation, as well as to prepare for an exam on 120 books. Peres told me he'd approve an unpaid leave of absence but asked that I recruit someone as a temporary replacement.

I had gotten to know Gideon Levy in the political science department, where he stood out as a brilliant young man. He was working as a journalist for Army Radio. I asked him if he'd agree to replace me, and he answered in the affirmative. In order to keep abreast of party affairs, I still came to headquarters on Thursdays, the busiest political day, to attend meetings. But most days I sat at home with a pile of material and occasionally pounded away on the Hermes Baby typewriter my father bought me for my seventeenth birthday. My two thesis advisors, professors Asher Arian and Mike Aronoff, invested considerable efforts in discussing and commenting on my work until the final product emerged.

I suppose that if I had done a doctorate in the life sciences, my worldview would have remained completely separate from the subject of my research. This is not the case in the social sciences. The materials I read influenced me greatly, at least in two areas: the importance of working as part of a group and a timely retirement from politics. It's not that lone wolves have failed to reach positions of influence. Moshe Dayan was a lone wolf, for example. However, working in a group framework whose common denominator is both generational and ideological can offer a greater and more lasting influence—provided that there is no constant competition for the group's leadership.

The second lesson—a timely retirement—derived from my understanding that insistence on remaining in the political arena, and thus delaying the entry of a younger generation, almost inevitably, like a law of nature, leads political systems to degenerate. Old age distances people from the evolving reality, making them—despite their best intentions—unable to truly represent their constituents' problems and preferences. Elder statesmen often genuinely feel that they cannot abandon the arena because they must continue doing the things that led to success in the past, or because there is no one capable of replacing them. Most of them feel that they have devoted their lives to the common good and that their absence is likely to harm the state. They find it hard to understand why young people are in such a hurry to push them out instead of appreciating what they have done for the nation.

The activity in the Young Guard convinced me of the merits of working in a group, and I resolved that if I pursued a political career, I would retire at age sixty, on my own accord.

Years after submitting my dissertation, I had a heart-to-heart conversation with Peres in which he uttered the immortal words: "I would happily end my political career if I saw someone who could replace me. . . ."

***

In January 1981, Begin called for early elections, moving them up to June 30, over the tangential issue of teachers' wages. The government's popularity had plummeted, and the surveys predicted a decisive victory for the Alignment, led by Peres. Perhaps that is why, along with the right's fear that its victory in 1977 was a fleeting episode, the 1981 elections became the most violent in Israel's history. I resumed my full-time work at the party and split the heavy workload with Gideon, including traveling around with Peres. Each campaign outing with him was like going into battle.

The election campaign turned into a sort of ethnic battle. Peres symbolized affluent Ashkenazi Jews, though a rumor circulated about him having an "Arab mother." The absorption of immigrants from Arab lands in the state's early years was portrayed in the 1981 election campaign as ugly and discriminatory exploitation by Mapai, the precursor of Labor. Among many Israelis, feelings of deprivation and discrimination were expressed through fierce hatred of the state's founders and their successors. It was very difficult to counter this wave with learned explanations that would refute the accusations. There were serious disruptions at every election rally, nearly drowning out Peres. The police had difficulty keeping order.

I remember a huge gathering in Petah Tikva where the crowd responded mainly by pelting the stage with tomatoes and eggs. In Kiryat Shmona, it was much worse. After a tough confrontation with the crowd, we were escorted to our car by a security officer and were able to get in and sit down. But a mob surrounded the car, started rocking it, and didn't allow us to move. The security officer wanted to fire a shot into the air, but Peres didn't allow it. The police were summoned to help and managed to free us from the mob after a long quarter of an hour. It was impossible to stop this craziness. A decision by Peres not to appear in a particular place would be seen as surrender but continuing this nightmarish campaign tour did not offer great advantages either.

✶✶✶

In any case, the optimistic polls still showed the Alignment ahead, though its lead was starting to shrink. The bombing of the Osirak nuclear reactor in Iraq on June 7, 1981 (whether essential or not), along with Begin's speech in response to Dudu Topaz's remarks about the Likud's *chachchahim* (a derogatory reference to Jews of North African descent), were apparently the deciding factors in that wild election campaign. The Likud won forty-eight Knesset seats, while the Alignment garnered forty-seven, receiving ten thousand fewer votes. Thus, the Israeli voting map coalesced into a state of ongoing parity between the center-right and the center-left.

Begin very quickly formed a government after the elections, building a coalition with the Tehiya party, the ultra-Orthodox parties, and the national-religious parties. There were emissaries who urged Peres to bring the Alignment into a national unity government with the Likud, just as he had pressed Eshkol to invite Begin to join the Labor-led government on the eve of the Six-Day War. The hawks in the party supported this idea. I was among the resolute opponents. In the end, Peres decided not to join Begin's coalition and did not even raise the question for discussion in the party's central committee.

The results were disappointing, of course, but the Labor Party managed to turn Dash into a short-lived episode and win back the voters it had lost in 1977. It was clear that the Labor Party was the only alternative to continued rule by the Likud, and that we had to put our frustration aside, examine our mistakes and reorganize for the next elections.

ALONG THE ROADSIDE

As Peres himself admitted, he loved to participate in family celebrations as part of election campaigning. The photographers would swoop in on him, and the family members would gather around him to receive kisses. When the youngsters came up to him, he'd always check their biceps and say he foresees great success for them in sports.

At this stage, I would already find my way back to the car to do some work by the light of the back seat. I swore to myself that if I ever embarked on an independent political career, I'd refrain from visiting wedding and bar mitzvah celebrations. (I indeed kept this oath, with a few exceptions.)

In the car, when he wasn't napping, we'd sometimes engage in long conversations. I recall, for example, a complaint he often voiced regarding the import of mineral water from distant lands. It was absurd, he insisted, and must be stopped. Though his audiences accepted his assertion without argument, I told him that the bottled water was imported under economic agreements with the exporting countries and that it wasn't right to attribute the blame to Begin's policies. He remained unconvinced.

Later, soon after becoming prime minister, Peres invited Mordechai Barkat, the customs director, to his new official residence. He asked Barkat to bring a list of the main import items, and they sat all night going over the list. Peres arrived at the office the next day with heavy eyelids. I asked him what happened at night, and he told me, somewhat sheepishly, that he had made a fool of himself. He now realized that mineral water and other imports were included in Israel's trade agreements, which we had no interest in harming.

Before his appearances, I always prepared a few points—lessons from previous events, his mistakes, or an attempt to prevent future mistakes. For example, when he spoke about the township of Yeruham in the Negev, he would call it "Kfar Yeruham"—an earlier name from when it was still only a village ("kfar"). I warned him not to insult the local residents by repeating this mistake. He promised to heed my warning. But, of course, he began his speech there the next time by saying how happy he was to be in Kfar Yeruham. I clearly remember the silence that settled over the crowd.

14

A New Political Forum—Mashov

IN THE SUMMER OF 1981, I TOOK UP A FASCINATING OFFER FROM THE American Embassy in Tel Aviv and embarked on a one-month tour of the United States, which included several meetings in Washington. The embassy designed this program for Israelis it identified as future leaders. It wasn't a political-diplomatic visit of the type I had become familiar with since becoming Peres's advisor in 1977, nor was it a tourist excursion. Instead, it was an opportunity to get to know other sides of America, especially the Midwest, to meet people who thought and spoke differently than those I had met in Washington, New York, Los Angeles, and San Francisco. Years later, when Donald Trump was elected president, I recalled the Americans I had met in the Midwest, most of whom viewed the world in black and white. They were prominent among Trump's supporters.

After consulting with a few people who had participated in this program, I prepared a detailed plan for the month-long journey. It was particularly important to me to visit parts of America I hadn't seen, especially the Midwest and the West Coast. It was indeed an extraordinary experience, and Helena—who was already a senior criminal prosecutor for the Central District of the State Attorney's Office—joined me.

Soon after returning to Israel, I founded the Mashov group. My friend Yisrael Peleg, the spokesperson for Labor's Knesset faction, suggested the name. *Mashov* means "feedback" in Hebrew, but the word was also used here as an acronym for "the Guard and its alumni." My intention was to form a circle of people in their thirties who would discuss the central issues on the public agenda: the doctors' strike that was underway at the time, the unrecognized Bedouin communities in the Negev, the Israeli-Palestinian conflict and everyday life in the territories, and the ownership of companies by the government and by the Histadrut.

It wasn't easy to form a new group in the party. Most of the old-timers didn't understand what purpose it could serve. After all, there was a party, its institutions, its branches, and the groups that already existed. In addition, according to the party's bylaws, the party bureau had to approve any new group; so I appeared before the bureau and explained my intentions. In the end, a narrow majority of members supported my request, and the forum was launched.

Mashov was very different from other groups that discussed current affairs. It was an ongoing seminar that set out to analyze certain phenomena and propose practical solutions and recommendations, which would then be presented to the party's convention, where policy decisions were made. Young people with expertise in various fields gravitated toward Mashov. Most of them were experienced enough to be angry about the status quo and sought to propose alternatives. Many viewed us as a group of spoilsports who failed to understand that everything was actually fine. For example, they would always tell us that people from around the world were coming to see how the Histadrut had succeeded in combining a "workers' society" with a trade union, and that we were the only ones refusing to join the chorus of admirers.

On a personal level, I found myself in amusing situations: On the one hand, I was the party's spokesperson; on the other hand, I was leading a band of rebels. I remember a particularly embarrassing moment, about two years after forming Mashov. I was in Peres's office in Tel Aviv when he turned on the radio to hear the news. The lead story reported that the Mashov group in the Labor Party had denounced the US invasion of Grenada (in the wake of a military coup that toppled the prime minister, Maurice Bishop). Peres heard the report and slammed his fist on the desk. "Who is this Mashov anyway?" he thundered. A moment later he remembered: "Oh, it's you!" And he burst out laughing.

✳✳✳

In any case, unlike some of the other Labor Party groups that included both doves and hawks, Mashov was a defined ideological circle. For example, it supported the Yariv-Shem Tov formula that defined three conditions for Israel's recognition of the Palestinian Liberation Organization: The PLO would have to recognize Israel, accept UN Security Resolution 242 and be willing to make peace with Israel. Many of us taught at universities; others were familiar with the inner workings of the political system based on personal experience. Some of the members of our circle were adept at writing succinct position papers and often presented them to the media (which angered the party's old guard, which demanded that any such paper be brought before the party's institutions before finding its way to the media). Mashov also did not hesitate to criticize the party for opposing a no-confidence motion when the government launched the Lebanon War in 1982. The truth is that until the war broke out, the party's leaders were united in opposing a war in Lebanon.

At the meetings of the party's political policy committee during the first half of 1982, the prospect of war was a central topic of discussion because some of the participants were familiar with "Little Pines" and "Big Pines" (two contingency plans for an IDF incursion into Lebanon), and feared that the new defense minister, Arik Sharon, wanted to reshape the Middle East and was eager to find an excuse to justify a war in Lebanon. Everyone tried to guess what that excuse might be, and the sense was that despite the cautious nature of the former ruling party, this time Labor would not try to be part of the consensus and would warn against the war before it started. The former IDF chiefs of staff—Rabin, Bar-Lev, and Motta Gur—were convinced that Begin would fall into "Arik's net."

When members of Abu Nidal's organization severely wounded our ambassador in London, Shlomo Argov, it provided a sufficient excuse to go to war after an 11-month ceasefire negotiated by the American mediator Philip Habib. Begin promised that Operation Peace for Galilee would last no more than forty-eight hours and would not extend beyond forty kilometers from Israel's northern border—and the Labor Party voted against a motion of no-confidence. Yossi Sarid was the only one who abstained, and he was fiercely criticized for that.

I had already been called up for reserve military service, which lasted for several months. Still, I managed to publish an op-ed in the *Haaretz* daily on June 16, 1982, calling for an immediate withdrawal from Lebanon. I wrote:

> Again they'll say—it can't be that our sons have fallen in vain and that we withdraw from Lebanon without achieving our objectives. Again, we'll wait for a telephone call, or for an independent Lebanon, and again we'll remain "for now" in territory that isn't ours . . . . Naomi Shemer will write a new anthem about the Beaufort operation, Gush Emunim will build a settlement in Tyre and Rabbi Kahane's men will barricade themselves in Damour to prevent a withdrawal.

✷✷✷

After completing my reserve duty, the Mashov forum became much more active on the Palestinian issue. We met with a number of Palestinian leaders from East Jerusalem, from the West Bank, and from the Gaza Strip.

This activity was coordinated by Dr. Yair Hirschfeld, who had developed good personal connections with Faisal Husseini, Hanan Ashrawi, Ibrahim Haddad, Raymonda Tawil, and other key figures. We learned from them about everyday Palestinian life, about their complex attitudes toward Israel, about specific problems that weren't too difficult to resolve vis-à-vis the Civil Administration, and about their views regarding the PLO. Without these meetings, the Oslo process would have never come about. They outlined for us the range of views held by the Palestinian leadership at the time. One of the people they mentioned was Issam Sartawi, who started his political path as fanatically anti-Israeli but eventually became an advocate of peace with Israel, emphasizing the advantages in neighborly relations with it. I never imaged that soon our paths would cross.

It happened on April 9, 1983. Peres and I were on a train from Lisbon to Albufeira ("Balfouria," according to Peres) in southern Portugal to attend a conference of the Socialist International. The journalist Tamar Golan was traveling with us to cover the event and noticed Sartawi in the same car of the train. She immediately asked if we'd agree to exchange a few words with him. Though the law prohibiting Israelis from meeting with PLO members had yet to be enacted, Peres opted not to speak with Sartawi. His somewhat strange response was: "What would happen if I meet him today and tomorrow there's, heaven forbid, a Palestinian terror attack against Israelis?"

I tried to persuade him to speak with the Palestinian man who was risking his life to promote dialogue with Israelis. Peres knew exactly who Sartawi was, but still stubbornly refused to talk to him.

Sartawi comported himself like someone who did not wish to impose himself on us, and since he realized that Peres was not interested in striking up a conversation with him, he continued to read a book.

The next morning, after already settling in, a discussion began on the proposed appointment of Walid Jumblatt—head of the Progressive Socialist Party in Lebanon and its top Druze leader—as vice president of the Socialist International. After his appointment was approved without opposition, a general discussion on the matters of the day began. Then suddenly gunfire was heard.

At first, the participants thought the noise might be something else, but they very quickly realized that their ears had not betrayed them.

I hurried out of the hall toward the hotel lobby and was the first to do so. Sartawi lay on the floor in a pool of blood. His eyeglasses had flown far from his body. It later turned out that Abu Nidal's organization was responsible for the murder.

The local security personnel feared that we'd be next in line for assassination, though we were apparently not targeted by the organization. The Socialist International conference came to an abrupt end. The assembled leaders returned to their countries, and I assume they all noted to themselves that those who speak or act courageously in politics may end up paying with their lives. The fact that only hours earlier we had sat in the same train car, and he had wanted to talk with us—and we had refused—weighed on me.

In any case, we were quickly shuttled back to Lisbon. On the way, I said to Peres that when he had spoken about an act of terror the previous day, he certainly did not have this in mind. Peres was still reeling from the murder of Sartawi but made it clear to me that if I was asking him whether he regretted not speaking with Sartawi, his answer was no.

✽✽✽

Begin resigned on August 28, 1983, following months in which he really hadn't functioned as prime minister and his associates had covered for him. The soaring inflation and the sense that the Lebanon War was a great failure (culminating in the Sabra and Shatila massacre), along with the uncertainty about how it would end, made it impossible for the new prime minister, Yitzhak Shamir, to keep the coalition intact. He was compelled to call for early elections, moving them up from November 1985 to July 1984. Efforts to form a national unity government under his leadership and thus avoid early elections were unsuccessful.

In a conversation with professor Arian in early 1984, he encouraged me to take on a tenured position at the university but noted that it would require me to do a post-doctorate overseas. Consequently, I applied to the Kennedy School at Harvard and told myself that I would go and study there if accepted. Nonetheless, the upcoming election was also a factor when weighing my options.

It was the last time that a selection committee determined the Labor Party's list of candidates for the Knesset. I tried to get onto the list. Peres chaired the committee, which apportioned the slots on the list according to a complicated formula of Peres-Rabin, Rafi, and Ahdut Ha'avoda, as well as other calculations typical of selection committees. In the end, I found myself in the fifty-fourth spot on the list. Only a few very optimistic polls predicted that we'd win fifty-four seats, so my chances of entering the Knesset were slim to none.

At party headquarters, I was responsible for polling and also took on the task of managing Peres's 100-days team. The concept was apparently conceived by John F. Kennedy's staff on the eve of the 1960 presidential elections. The idea was to prepare the first months of Kennedy's term, hour by hour, based on the assessment that whatever he failed to accomplish during his initial months in office would be very difficult to do in subsequent months. I read about the 100-days team formed in Portugal, and I proposed to Peres that we put together a similar team to prepare a detailed plan for his first hundred days as prime minister. The plan would include saving the economy, exiting from Lebanon, enacting essential legislation, making symbolic gestures toward Israel's Arab citizens and other sectors in Israeli society, and more.

He said he would give the idea some thought. Soon afterwards, he gave me the green light to proceed: I would present him with a list of proposed members of the 100-days team for his approval; the team would prepare a first draft and sit with him to understand what was acceptable to him, what he wanted to expand, and what he preferred to delete. He promised to be patient and to listen the team's appeals regarding ideas he chose to reject. The team included people I had met at the university and in the framework of Labor Party activity—Dr. Nimrod Novik, Dr. Ehud Kofman, and Amnon Neubach.

In the heat of the election campaign, the first hundred days seemed far-off in the future. Nonetheless, the 100-days forum met with Peres many times and formulated, under his guidance, a document that outlined activity for every single day. The document was kept under wraps until Peres was sworn in as prime minister because we didn't want to be criticized for being overconfident and "counting our chickens before they hatched."

Most of the members of the team, along with Uri Savir, who became Peres's spokesperson, and Avrum Burg, whom I recruited to serve as his advisor on Diaspora affairs, were appointed as official advisors after Peres became prime minister. The media dubbed us "Beilin's blazers" because most of us always dressed in a blazer and a tie.

Election Day arrived, and the Alignment won forty-four seats and the Likud only forty-one. However, the map of blocs in the Knesset left no alternative but to form a national unity government with a rotation of prime ministers: The Labor Party returned to power after seven very long years, but Peres would have to step down as prime minister after two years and hand over the reins of government to Shamir.

In the midst of the negotiations between the parties, a letter arrived from Harvard: I received a post-graduate fellowship at the Kennedy School. Thrilled, I informed Peres that I planned to start my studies at the beginning of the spring semester and return a year later.

Peres asked me to stay on and work closely with him as director-general of the Prime Minister's Office or as cabinet secretary, whichever I preferred. He argued that I'd be making a mistake if after seven years of "wandering in the desert," I gave up the experience of serving in a senior role in the Prime Minister's Office. I told him that if I turned down the fellowship from Harvard, it would almost certainly mean giving up on an academic career forever. His response was that I was still young enough to keep my options open.

After struggling with my dilemma for several days, I informed Peres that I wanted to serve as cabinet secretary. I didn't regret my decision, but sometimes, in particularly trying moments, I thought of the road not taken.

ALONG THE ROADSIDE

In principle, Peres did not like to criticize me in person. Perhaps it was because in each of the seven years of opposition he asked me to stay on for just one more year and didn't want to risk receiving a negative response. Perhaps it was his nature. When he was displeased by something I said, by an article I wrote or an interview with me, I would always hear about it from his secretaries. "You know that Shimon didn't like what you said on the radio yesterday?" they would inform me, as if sharing a secret. I don't know if they were indeed leaking secret information or whether he was using them as a conduit to convey his response.

But it didn't always work this way. Years later, when I was already his deputy at the Foreign Ministry, I was interviewed on Israel Radio's morning news program while traveling to Jerusalem. When I arrived at the office, I went to see him to discuss a certain issue that we had left unresolved the previous day. I saw immediately that something was troubling him and asked him what happened.

"I heard you on the radio," he said.

"And?" I asked.

"You said something and emphasized that it was the view of the Rabin government."

"And?" I asked again.

"It's the government of Israel!" he replied in anger.

Nothing could infuriate him more. . . .

The media always played an important role in Peres's conduct. False information about him made him especially angry, but it was also difficult for him to accept criticism that wasn't tainted by distortions. One day, he handed me an article from one of the newspapers. The article mentioned that when he was angry at people, he often referred to them as "farts."

"How could they write such lies?" he asked. "I sometimes get angry at people, but calling them 'farts'? I never use that stupid word!"

"Except for ten times a day," I replied.

He looked at me in deep disappointment.

Nonetheless, I believed that part of my job was to make unflattering comments about his appearances in the media or in public. After each appearance, he would ask me, "So, how was I?" And almost always, I'd note some mistakes, some unsuccessful statements, or unintended insults. He really needed to hear positive feedback and took criticism to heart. More than once, he repeated the same mistake, even after ostensibly internalizing the lesson. "Yes, I know," he would admit. "It slipped out from me again."

15

Suddenly in the Holy of Holies

THE TRANSITION FROM POLITICAL THEORY TO PRACTICE WAS VERY rapid. After a long security background check, I found myself in a place where I had never been: in the holy of holies of state secrets and top-secret discussions.

I was not there as a "fly on the wall"—I was often asked to take part in the discussions, though I used this privilege sparingly. Every day, the journalist in me found headlines that would never see the light of day. Every day, the researcher in me found subjects for professional articles. I was exposed to people I had never known and frameworks I never knew existed. Initially, at least, I felt considerable pride in those who maintain the systems of government.

In later years, I filled roles that were more senior than cabinet secretary, but my twenty-five months in that position were unique—and not only because it was the first chamber I entered in the complex structure called the government. After seven years of reacting to government actions and conversing with journalists about the Labor Party's internal processes, I had the sense that now we were dealing with the real things.

One of the first issues we faced was the exit from Lebanon. It was one of the key election promises of the Alignment, and of the 100-days team. Peres was also keen to quickly clear this issue from the agenda. Personally, I believed that it would be best to leave Lebanon in the framework of a peace accord between Israel, Syria, and Lebanon. Since there was no chance of reaching such an accord in a rotation government with the Likud, it was best to get out of Lebanon as quickly as possible and stop bleeding there for no reason.

But it wasn't so simple. The Likud opposed a unilateral pull-out from Lebanon because it would raise the question of why Israel had waited so long to make this move. In addition, most of the Likud ministers warned that Israel's Galilee communities would be exposed to endless barrages of Katyusha rockets if the IDF retreated from Lebanon. Several Labor ministers and I divided the work of persuading the undecided ministers.

The cabinet meeting on January 14, 1985, was fascinating. Rabin, as defense minister, outlined four options for the future of southern Lebanon. Each option was presented by a different IDF general, and the IDF chief of staff, Moshe Levy ("Moshe and a half," because of his height) discussed the option that was ultimately selected: demarcating a strip of a few kilometers in which the SLA (the South Lebanon Army, under the command of General Antoine Lahad) would operate with Israel's financial backing and with assistance from about 100 Israeli "mentors." The idea was for the latter—IDF officers and soldiers—to train and advise SLA personnel, but not get involved in battle. In the end, the IDF greatly increased the number of its troops in the security strip (especially after Moshe Arens took over as defense minister in 1990).

The fact that the IDF presented different options to the decision makers and did not suffice with the option preferred by the chief of staff and defense minister was both impressive and rare. The discussion was also serious, and culminated in the approval of the preferred option, with sixteen ministers voting in favor (all of the Labor ministers and two Likud ministers—David Levy and Gideon Patt). Shamir criticized the withdrawal plan as irresponsible, warning that it would set the Galilee aflame. I was pleased that the government, after just a few months, had succeeded in accomplishing one of the central objectives that justified its existence.

I remember walking down the stairs with Rabin to the lobby where the media was waiting. I read out the detailed cabinet decision with considerable excitement, and the defense minister explained why it was the best option and responded to questions. I didn't know then that the one hundred mentors would drag the IDF back into Lebanon, that the SLA would be unable to bear the burden of securing the buffer zone, and that we would need to endure another sixteen superfluous and bloody years before making a complete withdrawal from Lebanon.

✳✳✳

The staff at the cabinet secretariat was unique; nearly everyone continued working there until they reached retirement age. The fourteen members of the staff included the deputy cabinet secretary, assistants, secretaries, and typists. Aryeh Zohar, one of the senior members of the staff, provided a glimpse into the work of this group in his book *In the End, the Protocol Remains*. He typified the special and noncompetitive human makeup of this group of people—their professional integrity, their complete discretion, their wonderful ability to fill in for each other when necessary, and the fact that they didn't use the cabinet secretariat as a springboard toward a more senior government post.

Indeed, the staff was uncommonly dedicated, knowledgeable, and ready to help. I felt that everyone was there to help me in managing the largest government in Israel's history (as of then) with twenty-five ministers. The job required me to work with Likud ministers I had often criticized during the previous seven years. I had never met some of them. The need to listen to them, hear their comments and questions, and respond to their requests was no small challenge.

I soon realized that one of my most important roles was to formulate the government's decisions. After each cabinet meeting, the secretary sits with his notes, and sometimes with the full minutes of the meeting, and drafts a government decision that specifies the date a particular initiative will begin, the ministries that will be involved in its implementation, and the minister responsible for the project's execution. The cabinet secretary also draws out details from the discussion and the prime minister's summary. However, before the decision is released, a sort of negotiation is conducted with the pertinent ministers. Sometimes each minister understands the agreed-upon course of action in a slightly different way.

I would sometimes ask the relevant ministers to meet after the cabinet meeting in order to agree on the final wording of a decision, and I'd have to facilitate compromises between them. Most of the issues were administrative rather than political. Sometimes I had to settle disputes between two Labor ministers, and sometimes between two Likud ministers.

Two months after the government was formed, I asked my friend professor Yehezkel Dror to prepare recommendations for improving the efficiency of the cabinet secretariat. He proposed sixteen efficiency measures, some of which I implemented. The most important idea was to create a joint forum of all directors-general of government ministries, under the chairmanship of the cabinet secretary. I learned that these directors-general did not regularly meet and some of them did not even know each other. I thought that if we could shift some of the administrative conflict resolution from the ministers to their directors-general, it would greatly enhance the government's efficiency.

Every Wednesday, the ministers received the agenda for the cabinet meeting scheduled for the following Sunday. A line was drawn on the agenda to separate the topics slated for discussion at the meeting from topics that probably would not be discussed. The rule was that the prime minister was not obligated to place a subject on the agenda just because a minister so requested, even if that minister had already told the media that he demanded discussion of a particular matter at the next cabinet meeting. Therefore, I thought that the forum of ministry directors-general could address some of the issues that appeared "under the line" on the agenda and recommend decisions that would not require discussion by the cabinet, only a vote.

When I spoke to Peres about this, he agreed to discuss it with a few ministers and get back to me. Finance Minister Yitzhak Moda'i strongly opposed the creation of the forum, fearing that a "government of directors-general" would present the cabinet with faits accomplis. Other ministers were not enthusiastic but didn't reject the idea. I didn't give up. I spoke with Moda'i and convinced him that there was no danger of creating a regime led by directors-general, and he withdrew his opposition.

Since the directors-general of government ministries were among the busiest people around, I invited them to only two meetings a month, at an hour when it was difficult for them to cite previous commitments as an excuse for not attending: 7:30 a.m. Gradually, the forum gave the directors-general an opportunity to address bilateral issues on the sidelines of our meetings, simply because they were meeting face to face. We resolved quite a few problems together; we refrained from addressing issues of a political or ideological nature, and we found solutions for many interministerial questions without involving foreign interests. In time, ministers themselves would suggest that a particular matter that arose in the cabinet meeting be referred to the forum of directors-general for preliminary discussion.

For several years, the forum remained informal and operated behind the scenes. Later, it expanded to include the civil service commissioner, the director of the courts, and two top Finance Ministry officials: the head of the Budgets Division and the accountant general. In 1987, the government—then led by Shamir—approved the following decision: "The forum of directors-general of government ministries, which operates under the cabinet secretary, will provide consultation and staff work for preparing recommendations for the government on topics requested by the prime minister, the government, a ministerial committee or ministers. This does not prevent the forum from addressing, if requested by forum members and without infringing upon the authorities of the ministries, subjects of inter-ministerial coordination in order to improve the government's activity." The forum continued to operate until the time of Ehud Olmert's government in 2006.

***

The role of the cabinet secretary is defined in Basic Law: The Government. Like many positions, it can be narrow and bureaucratic, but it can also be very influential. For example, it isn't written anywhere that a cabinet minister who previously served as the Labor Party's spokesperson should mediate between the hawks in the Likud.

In March 1986, a meeting of the Likud's central committee burst into chaos. A Likud activist, Gaston Malka, crashed the stage and raised a chair against MK Roni Milo, while Malka's cohorts cut off the microphone of the elderly MK Yohanan Bader. Shamir decided to go home, and David Magen stood and sang *HaTikva* in an attempt to put an end to the farce. The tension between the David Levy/Arik Sharon camp and Shamir's camp was so great that Levy asked if I, as someone who was not suspected of being a Likud member, could step into the fray. So I found myself shuttling between him and Moshe Katzav, exchanging lists of Likud activists for the party's various institutions, until I realized that the challenge was too much for me.

The cabinet secretary is sometimes called upon to interpret the intentions of ministers. A minister who has to leave a meeting can leave a note with the cabinet secretary to indicate how he wishes to vote on a particular matter, and the note is counted when the votes are tallied. On April 30, 1985, in one of the most tense meetings on the economic plan that saved Israel from astronomical inflation, a meeting that lasted for a full day, Minister Yitzhak Peretz from Shas wrote me a note saying that he planned to go out to pray, and that if there was a vote, I should add his name to the proposal that doesn't hurt the poor. . . .

ALONG THE ROADSIDE

My first argument with Peres occurred a little over a month after I started working at party headquarters. The argument arose in the context of Sadat's historic visit to Jerusalem. Peres drafted a speech for the Knesset plenum, where he was scheduled to speak after Begin. I went to Peres's home on Saturday morning and saw a pile of drafts on his desk. He showed me the latest version of his speech and asked for my opinion. I read his words, which were beautiful and gracious. But in his great excitement, he wrote that he would be honored to serve as Israel's first ambassador to Egypt after the signing of a peace treaty.

I asked him to delete that sentence, arguing that someone who aims to be prime minister cannot offer to serve in a diplomatic post. Moreover, this sentence could become the main headline from his speech. He insisted on keeping the sentence, saying that the media always expected some meaningful statement beyond the usual words of praise, and that this statement could stir interest.

I agreed with him in principle and told him that there were a number of points in his draft that merited headlines. But there really might be peace with Egypt soon, and the entire media would ask him whether he still wanted to be the ambassador. What would he say then? That he had just wanted a headline and didn't really mean it?

Peres was not ready to give up. Sonia, who sat in her corner in the living room, supported my opinion. That didn't help. I asked him if he would be willing to give me the names of two people who were close to him and whose judgment he trusted, so that I could consult with them. He immediately gave me the names: the editor of *Davar*, Hanna Zemer, and the author S. Yizhar.

Yizhar received me at his home in Rehovot, read the draft closely and told me unequivocally that Shimon must not volunteer to serve as ambassador to Egypt. Hanna, who had still been my boss two months earlier, was more scathing: "Tell Shimon that this is utter nonsense." Armed with these two opinions, I returned to Tagore Street in Ramat Aviv. He reluctantly surrendered.

Two days later, the historic event took place at the Knesset. I listened intently to Peres's speech, fearing that he might decide at the last moment to rely on his inner voice. To my great relief, he didn't. He also never mentioned this matter again, even when the peace accords were signed.

Though we spent countless hours together, we almost never spoke about personal matters. I remember only one time—when he complained to me about his financial burden, which included supporting his father. All those years, we kept a sort of distance between us, and I suppose I was the one who was primarily responsible for that. I always thought twice before phoning him, and don't remember ever calling him "SHIMon" (instead of the more formal pronunciation with the accent on the second syllable—"ShimON"). However, especially during overseas trips, we'd often share lists of books we had read. He liked to suggest reading lists and would later ask my opinion about books he had recommended. So, I had little choice but to read many of the books he recommended, even if I wasn't thrilled about all of them.

16

Do You Know Where Shimon Is?

IN 1985, AFTER A HIATUS OF OVER TEN YEARS, CONTACTS BETWEEN Israel and Jordan were resumed at the highest echelon. Lord Victor Mishcon, a well-known Jewish-British lawyer, offered Peres the use of his country house for a meeting with King Hussein, and Peres gave his consent. Mishcon and Hussein had known each other for years, since the time the king's sister and Mishcon's daughter were classmates in England. When Mishcon suggested to Hussein the possibility of meeting with Peres, the king immediately agreed.

Mishcon was a prominent figure in the British Labour Party and had earlier served as vice president of the Board of Deputies of British Jews. His father had immigrated to Britain from Russia and was a rabbi in south London. Lord Mishcon himself was completely secular, with lots of *Yiddishkeit* ("Jewishness). He was a great supporter of Israel, though often harshly critical of Begin's policies.

Peres told me that the meeting with Hussein would be on a Saturday, and since it was conditional upon complete secrecy, he decided not to tell anyone about it—except for the relevant Mossad and Shin Bet officials. He would be incommunicado for most of the weekend, so he asked me to cover for him. I prayed for a quiet weekend and that nobody would need to urgently contact Peres. And I was very curious to hear from him after the meeting.

Everything went smoothly until Saturday morning, when the phone rang. "Yossi, do you know where Shimon is?" Rabin asked in his deep voice.

The last thing I needed was to get into trouble with Rabin. I took a deep breath and told him that Peres was tending to a personal matter and wasn't available, but that I could try to get a message through to him. He asked that I try to get hold of him. "There's a problem with a suspicious ship approaching our territorial waters," he said, adding that he wanted to receive approval in principle to fire at the ship in order to keep it from drawing closer, and was taking into account the potential for escalation.

I promised to get back to him as soon as possible but had no way of reaching Peres and had no one to consult with. I clearly remembered the *USS Liberty* incident of June 8, 1967, when the Israeli Air Force sunk an American spy ship, killing its thirty-four crew members, after mistakenly identifying it as a hostile vessel. The IDF chief of staff at the time was Rabin.

I phoned Rabin and informed him that Peres wanted to refrain from opening fire at this stage and to receive updates on the ship's route. To my surprise, this did not anger Rabin, and he didn't insist on speaking directly with Peres. A few hours later, he called back to inform me that the ship had changed course and was no longer approaching our waters. After hanging up the phone, I let out one of the biggest sighs of relief in my life.

When I met Peres prior to the weekly cabinet meeting on Sunday, I updated him on the instruction he had ostensibly relayed to Rabin so that he could ask him for more details on the suspicious ship. Peres took this in stride and filled me in on his meeting with the king. He said that Hussein was very relaxed and updated him on his efforts to form a Jordanian-Palestinian confederation with Arafat, despite the strong animosity between them. The king also raised several semi-technical issues that required cooperation between Jordan and Israel. A minute before the cabinet meeting began, Peres asked me if I'd be willing to take upon myself "the Jordanian portfolio" and to accompany him on subsequent meetings with Hussein (who had come to the meeting with the minister of his royal court). Needless to say, it was a rhetorical question.

The Jordanian portfolio was fascinating and undefined, and I devoted a considerable amount of time to it during the following two years, culminating in the London Agreement, concluded just before Passover on April 11, 1987.

I was not the only one focusing on Jordan, of course. The Mossad was the most significant organization in this regard, and its representative traveled with us to all of the meetings with the king. The IDF's intelligence branch also kept close tabs on Jordan. Amos Gilad, then a young and promising lieutenant colonel, joined the small team that knew about the Peres-Hussein conversations. Gilad gave us detailed accounts of the situation in Jordan and the talks between Hussein and the PLO; he also helped us to prepare documents for the upcoming meetings and to address issues that arose during the conversations. For each meeting, we flew on Friday afternoon or early Saturday morning and returned on Saturday night in an Arava plane, traveling under assumed names. Despite the scant chance of someone recognizing me, I still was subjected to a makeover (mainly around my eyes and hair) until I could barely recognize myself in the mirror. Still, my heart skipped a beat or two from fear of being identified when we landed in England.

The second meeting with the king was held a few weeks after the first tête-à-tête, again at Mishcon's country estate. The old home was situated in the heart of endless lawns. Mishcon reminded me of the actor Ray Milland, who played the gruff father of the hero in the film *Love Story*. "Jolly good" was his response to many questions. At that time, he also served as Princess Diana's lawyer (before the royal couple had their falling-out).

Hussein arrived after a kingly tardiness of twenty minutes. The "weanling" as Golda and Dayan disparagingly referred to him, was no longer a child. I immediately recalled the pictures of him in uniform strewn on the floor at the Jordanian base near Jerusalem in 1967. Most of those pictures were torn under our soldiers' boots. The king was a convivial man who smiled politely under his moustache—with no crown, keffiyeh or even a military beret. I looked for some royal mannerisms in his dress and finally found one: A crown was etched in his belt buckle.

The five of us sat down: the king, his cousin and royal court minister Zayed bin Shaker, Peres, Mishcon, and me. (One of the tasks of the king's minister was to bring a cigarette from Hussein's jacket from time to time, despite the latter's promise to Queen Nur that he had quit smoking.) We immediately began the first part of the meeting: a tour d'horizon. King Hussein and Prime Minister Peres analyzed the situation in the Middle East and did not spare any leader from criticism. I enjoyed the analyses, but already knew they should be taken with a grain of salt. Peres was particularly interested in the conversations between the king and Arafat, and it seemed that the option of a joint political framework encompassing Jordan, the West Bank, and the Gaza Strip was still feasible.

Hussein said that he'd very much like to start peace talks with Israel but would not make a separate peace like Sadat had done. In order to begin peace talks, he would need international and pan-Arab backing—that is, an international conference that would launch bilateral dialogue and would not impose anything on the sides. The king already knew that Peres was prepared to face the risks involved in such an initiative. However, Shamir was firmly opposed because he feared that an international conference, even if not designed to do so, would ultimately impose an undesirable solution on Israel.

At a certain stage, Lady Mishcon—who was younger than her husband, tall and elegant—heated up a lunch for us, and we were invited to dine on salmon with a special British flavor. I took advantage of the lunch break to ask the king a few questions about his view of the Allon Plan and his meeting with Yigal Allon and Abba Eban in London in early 1968. The Allon Plan—presented to the Israeli government in 1967, but never approved—proposed that the territories captured in the Six-Day War be divided between Israel and an autonomous entity controlled by the Palestinian residents of the territories, independently or in a confederation with Jordan. The king confirmed what Abba Eban had told me: When Allon presented the plan to the king, Hussein replied that it was unthinkable for Jordan to accept only 70 percent of the territory captured during the war, when Israel was offering Egypt and Syria 100 percent.

During our conversations in the next two years, the king made quite a few references to historical events, but when I once tried to understand from him how Golda had responded to his warning of imminent war on the eve of Yom Kippur in 1973, I sensed that he didn't feel comfortable talking about his ostensible betrayal of the collective Arab trust. I never brought this subject up with him again.

We spent several hours in the afternoon discussing current issues. The king complained about the spotlight installed on the air control tower at the Eilat airport: The light was blinding pilots—including him—when landing at the Aqaba airport, he said. Another issue Hussein raised was the amount of money permitted to carry across the Allenby Bridge; he asked to raise the permitted amount to five thousand dinars. The king also proposed a collaborative effort to combat a plague of flies in the southern region of the long border between Jordan and Israel.

We raised the possibility of reopening Jordanian banks in East Jerusalem; the banks had not operated since the war in 1967. The king suggested re-establishing the branch of the Cairo Amman Bank and sending the bank's CEO to meet with me. And indeed, we arranged for the banker to come for meetings in my Jerusalem office. I asked Peres's economics advisor, Amnon Neubach, and the Bank of Israel's supervisor of banks, Galia Maor, to join the meetings. After several months of intensive negotiations, the branch was re-established and became the harbinger of the return of Jordanian banks to East Jerusalem.

On the flight back after the second Peres-Hussein meeting, I wrote a summary of our discussions at Mishcon's country home and took upon myself the duty of reporting to Shamir. The next morning, before the weekly cabinet meeting, I went to his office at the Foreign Ministry and presented my summary. He read intently and handed the paper back to me without comment.

But I insisted on asking for his opinion.

"Peace won't emerge from this," he said, "but talking is better than waging war."

★★★

The meetings with the king were held about once every two months. I coordinated the implementation of agreements we reached and prepared the responses and topics for discussion prior to each meeting. To address some of the issues, I worked with Jordan's foreign minister, Taher al-Masri, and prime minister, Zayed a-Rifa'i. I would meet with them in Europe in preparation for the meetings with the king.

In Israel, I worked with the head of the Mossad, Nahum Admoni, and with Efraim Halevy, a future Mossad director who then headed its Tevel division. Several people at the cabinet secretariat were aware of the secret meetings and helped me manage the project, which soon took on the proportions of a mini government ministry and demanded a considerable share of my time. Dealing with flies and spotlights and helping to re-establish a bank were certainly not part of my formal job description, just as it had not included mediating between rival Likud leaders.

I remember a particularly poignant meeting with the king one Friday evening in Israel, held near the Williams House, between Eilat and Taba. Hussein was slated to arrive in his yacht from Aqaba. On the Israeli side, we were Rabin, Peres, and me. The helicopter that took me there had earlier transported an IDF team that was responsible for setting up a large tent, an air conditioning system, and a kitchen. The Israeli Navy was ordered to turn off its radar for a few hours to avoid a catastrophe, without explaining the reason why.

Peres and Rabin arrived in a helicopter, and I was asked to go to the port so that the king would see a familiar face upon arrival. A few minutes after I reached the dock, the yacht appeared, the king at the helm, and laid anchor. Since the dock was much higher than water level, the king had to climb a considerable number of rungs on a ladder to get onto the dock. A group of security men were waiting to ensure the king's safe reception. Hussein took off his orange life jacket as soon as his feet touched the ground and looked around. Of course, he didn't recognize anyone until his glance fell upon me. The calm that swept over him at that moment was palpable. He smiled broadly and embraced me as if he were meeting his long-lost brother. A moment later, we were already in the stately car waiting to bring us to the tent in the desert.

On the way, Hussein complained about a persistent pain in his ear. He told me that he had undergone various treatments, which had only provided partial relief. I couldn't help thinking the whole time about the discarded pictures of him at the military base after his defeat in 1967. I informed the king that Rabin and Peres had already arrived and were waiting for him. He smiled and asked whether they remember the harm they caused him in 1974. He was convinced that if an interim accord had been reached between Israel and Jordan, the Arab League would not have dared to recognize the PLO as the exclusive representative of the Palestinians. The king noted that he had never raised this criticism with Peres, and of course, he didn't mention it that evening either.

The dinner was unlike any other official military meal I had seen. It was the only meeting in which Rabin also participated and the only time the king arrived alone. The atmosphere was wonderful. Rabin emphasized security concerns, while Peres focused on the possibility of a "noncoercive" international conference.

It was the last meeting with Hussein before the rotation with Shamir. By the time the next meeting was held, Peres had already left the Prime Minister's Office and was serving as foreign minister. Our intensive effort to reach an accord with Jordan while Peres was still prime minister was unsuccessful. On the other hand, we managed to resolve issues that made life easier for both sides—for example, the flies. . . .

✷✷✷

Several days before Passover, on April 10, 1987, I flew with Peres to Heathrow Airport in London. It was the only time we met with Hussein at Mishcon's London home and not at his country house. Again, we traveled in disguise, under assumed names. I was then serving as Peres's number two at the Foreign Ministry with the title of "director-general for political affairs," while continuing to hold the "Hussein portfolio."

En route, Peres suggested that we prepare a paper—one that both Hussein and Shamir could accept—calling for an international conference whose sole purpose would be to launch negotiations. I pulled out a pad of paper, jotted down some ideas Peres raised, added some points on the structure of the conference and on the inclusion of Palestinians (in the spirit of the Yariv-Shem Tov formula). By the time we landed in London, a draft was ready.

The meeting this time was held with the knowledge of Margaret Thatcher, the British prime minister at the time, who had an excellent relationship with Peres. Nonetheless, we went through passport control under assumed identities, and all the way to the hotel I focused on my new name so that I'd pronounce it effortlessly during check-in at the hotel.

One vehicle that awaited us at the airport was for Peres, and it took him to Lord Mishcon's home. Efraim Halevy waited for me in another vehicle and drove me to a hotel in London where we would both be staying. He did not observe the speed limit; perhaps he felt he could permit himself to speed since he was born and raised in Britain. But then a police car ordered us to pull over.

I felt the world collapsing on me. Here we were in the capital of a friendly state (at least since the end of the British Mandate), and we had no logical explanation for speeding. I was plastered with makeup and could barely remember my new name, and there was no reason preventing them from detaining us, which meant we would miss the meeting with the king. I could already envision the interrogation room and hear the probing questions that I was not at liberty to answer.

But Efraim, as usual, remained cool-headed and acted as if he were meeting an old friend. I can't remember even a single word of what he said to the policeman, but the speeding incident ended with just an oral warning.

We drove to Mishcon's home the next morning. The king and his prime minister, Rifa'i, arrived soon afterwards. After catching up on the events that had occurred since our last meeting, we proceeded to discuss current topics. We engaged in a long discussion this time on Jordan's severe water shortage and how Israel could help.

Then we came to the main issue: a proposal for an international conference that could facilitate a resolution of the conflict. At Peres's request, I presented the basic idea: a formula that would be presented to the Reagan administration as a secret and informal agreement between Jordan and Israel. If the administration agreed, it would propose the conference as an American initiative. According to the proposal, the secretary-general of the UN would then send invitations to an international conference to the five permanent members of the Security Council and the parties involved in the Arab-Israeli conflict. The ultimate goals were to reach a comprehensive peace accord based on Security Council resolutions 242 and 338, bolster security in the region and enable the Palestinian people to exercise their legitimate rights. The plan was to establish bilateral committees in the wake of the conference, and the committees would then directly engage in peace negotiations.

The third part of the proposed agreement was intended to remain confidential. It included a number of mutual understandings between Israel and Jordan: The international conference would not impose an agreement; the negotiations would be direct; the Palestinian issue would be discussed in meetings of the Jordanian, Palestinian, and Israeli delegations; and participation in the conference would be limited to parties that accepted resolutions 242 and 338 and renounced terrorism and violence.

I had no idea how Hussein and Rifa'i would respond, but when I finished presenting the document, I saw that the king was excited. He said that it was an excellent idea and might turn out to be a historic move. The king told us that he would like to stay and go over every line in the document in order to reach agreement on everything but had a prior lunch commitment. Therefore, he would leave us under Lord Mishcon's auspices, and he suggested that his prime minister and I work out the details of the document. He would then return in the afternoon and the four of us could finalize the document.

However, it turned out that his two bodyguards were not waiting for him in the next room and, of course, he couldn't leave the premises without them. In jest, I offered the king my good services. I told him that with four war decorations, he could definitely rely on me to protect him from anyone who dared to attack him in London. He, uncharacteristically, burst out laughing.

After lunch, I discussed every word in the paper with Rifa'i. Peres and Mishcon entered the room from time to time. Halevy sat in another room. We didn't have serious arguments, but there were certain points that were important for him to emphasize and didn't require much of a compromise from me. Most importantly, we were able to reach a joint memorandum of understanding.

Peres read the document and had no objections. When the king returned, he met privately with Rifa'i for some minutes and then joined us to go over the document together. An hour later, after making very minor last-minute revisions, we had the draft of a complete agreement; the last section stated that the understandings were subject to approval by the governments of Israel and Jordan.

Still, we all felt that something was missing—but we couldn't put our finger on it. A toast? Speeches? Embraces? On the one hand, the paper could change the Middle East. On the other hand, it wasn't even signed. And then the king found a partial alternative; he asked me to write at the bottom of the document: April 11, 1987, London. In this way, the draft seemed a bit more significant than a collection of sentences that were not attributed to anyone and which no one had signed. We parted in high spirits.

On the return flight to Israel, Peres and I were unable to fall asleep. I wrote up a summary of the day's meeting. Shimon read a newspaper that

Lord Mishcon had given him. Afterwards, before landing, Peres told me that this time he should be the one to brief Shamir on what happened in London and asked me to update Rabin. Both of us were overly optimistic about the prospect of winning support for this initiative from Likud ministers. Ostensibly, the third part of the document outlined exactly what they had aspired to achieve: a conference that would not be empowered to impose anything on the sides, to be followed by direct negotiations, with conditions that would effectively preclude the PLO's participation or compel it to radically change its stripes.

Prior to the cabinet meeting, which convened on Sunday as usual at 9 AM, I sat with Rabin, gave him a detailed account of the meeting in London and showed him the document. He studied it and said, "If this is all true, it's simply phenomenal." Rabin was seldom so effusive. His reaction made me even more optimistic that the political right in Israel would also find it difficult to reject this sort of surprise.

Immediately afterwards, I had a moment to exchange impressions with Peres. He said that he showed the paper to Shamir and thought it went okay. I told him about Rabin's rare enthusiasm, which made Peres very happy. He asked me to inform the American ambassador, Thomas Pickering, whose previous assignment was ambassador to Jordan.

I spoke with Tom and asked if he could come to Jerusalem, even though Sunday wasn't a regular work day for him. He laughed and said that his only condition was that I have good news to share. The ambassador soon arrived, and after I filled him in about the joint document, he emphasized that we must not miss this opportunity. He suggested that I fly immediately to Helsinki and update the secretary of state, George Shultz, before his meeting in Moscow with the Soviet president, Mikhail Gorbachev.

The upcoming meeting in Moscow was expected to be particularly important. Shultz had set up a small team in Finland to prepare for his discussions with Gorbachev on various issues related to the waning Cold War. A possible resolution of the long conflict in the Middle East could make an important contribution in further reducing friction between the superpowers. Shultz was planning to stay in Finland for another twenty-four hours before heading to Moscow.

Meanwhile, the weekly cabinet meeting in Jerusalem had already begun. I asked Peres to step out for a moment, and I told him about the American ambassador's reaction and suggestion. Peres, without thinking twice, asked me to fly to Helsinki.

When I left Tel Aviv for work that morning, I had no idea I'd be flying a few hours later. I didn't have my passport with me, not to speak of any basic items for a short overseas stay. I asked my mother-in-law to grab my passport and pack a few things for me, and to take a taxi to the airport, while I made my way there from Jerusalem. It was the only time I've flown without a plane ticket.

It wasn't a direct flight. At the stopover, Foreign Ministry personnel were waiting to escort me to my connecting flight to Helsinki, where the embassy took me under its wing. I set off for Shultz's temporary headquarters, stopping at a hotel on the way to drop off my small travel bag. Charles Hill, Shultz's close advisor, greeted me and said that Shultz was already "bursting" with material, but was very curious to learn about our meeting with Hussein the previous day. Shultz had asked Hill to meet with me and then present him with a written summary. I immediately updated Shultz's advisor. He was pleasantly surprised, jotted down some notes and promised to deliver them to Shultz in full and contact me the next morning.

I received a phone call from my office the next morning informing me that my visit in Helsinki was the main headline in *Haaretz*. That was the last thing I wanted. It could have led to the premature exposure of the initiative at a time when secrecy was so crucial, particularly for the king. Charlie phoned me later that morning. He said that Shultz considered our agreement with the king a breakthrough and important background for his talks with Gorbachev.

When I returned to Israel and reported to Peres on the American response, I saw that he was worried. His conversation with Shamir did not go well, particularly because of the way it ended: The prime minister asked to see the document, and Peres told him he couldn't share it with him because he had promised Hussein to keep it secret. I told Peres that he should have given Shamir the document, and that he too would have gotten angry if Shamir had withheld a document like this from him.

In the end, the political right in Israel based its rejection of the London Agreement mainly on the fact that Shamir didn't receive it from Peres, though that was not the real reason.

ALONG THE ROADSIDE

I remember that in January 1981, during our second secret trip to Morocco, we stayed at the king's palace in Marrakesh. After a day of sightseeing, Peres wanted, as usual, to attend some sort of cultural event. The Moroccan security personnel looked at him in astonishment and explained that it was impossible due to security concerns.

He didn't argue, and we thought that the matter was closed. But about two hours later, we were informed that a dance troupe had come to perform for us. They ushered us into one of the halls in the palace. There were only two chairs. The dancers were already waiting there and started their performance as soon as we sat down. They danced for over an hour and a half for the audience of two; we applauded after every number, hoping that it was indeed the end of the number.

Peres loved life, enjoyed a good meal and fine wine, loved theater and music and literature. He didn't take vacations and was very glad that I never took time off either. He occasionally scolded me for what he called my "asceticism" and never gave up trying to mold me into someone else, perhaps more similar to him.

Paris was his beloved city outside of Israel. He loved its urban landscape, its restaurants, and its nightclubs. He would often stand and look up at the balconies. "There's a balcony on every floor," he would explain, "and there's always one that is different from the others!"

I remember one evening, after a long and exhausting day of meetings, we were heading to our respective hotel rooms when he asked if I'd like to go with him to the Chez Rachelle nightclub. I had never heard of that place and had no interest in any nightclub. I told Peres that I was planning to prepare for the meetings scheduled for the next day and then go to sleep. He found my reply totally unacceptable and demanded that I join him.

I failed to understand (and, in fact, still don't understand) what attracts people to those nightclubs. The music is deafening; bored people sit around small tables with little plates of olives and nuts; old men dance with younger blondes who are not their daughters.

Since we didn't dance, we remained sitting at the table. Peres ordered a whiskey and I ordered an orange juice. "You don't want milk?" he asked mockingly.

I tried to talk with him about the meetings planned for the next day, but the loud music prevented us from hearing one another. I knew that he was determined to "educate" me, but I didn't believe he was really serious about it. It turned out I was wrong.

The next day—after the flight to Morocco was delayed, requiring us to spend another night in France—he asked me, in a mischievous tone he rarely used, "Have you ever been to Nice?" I replied in the negative. He suggested that we take a trip there and promised to use the day to teach me how to drink. I told him that I planned to learn many things in life, but drinking was not one of them. He didn't give up, of course. We were like two kids skipping school, and soon we found ourselves on a plane from Paris to Nice.

There was something melancholy about the French Riviera in January. We stayed in an old building—a castle renovated and converted into a hotel—and we walked along the boardwalk, almost devoid of tourists. At our meals, he ordered a double helping of rolls and butter, and taught me to spread the butter on a roll, take a sip of wine, and then another bite of the roll. Actually, it was okay. That is, the roll was tasty, the butter was excellent, and the wine was sandwiched between them so that it was almost palatable.

He would later proudly look back on that day in Nice as his great triumph as a wine steward and educator. But I have to say that this claim was quite an exaggeration.

17

The Brief Golden Age of Peace

ON MAY 1, SHULTZ DECIDED TO VISIT ISRAEL IN ORDER TO CLARIFY with Shamir and Peres the role they wished the US to play in the context of the understandings reached between Hussein and Peres. Shamir recruited Moshe Arens to persuade Shultz not to engage in the matter, on the pretext that it involved an internal Israeli political dispute. This indeed deterred Shultz, and he canceled the planned visit.

Meanwhile, I conducted conversations with Likud ministers who were members of the inner cabinet. The most surprising talk was with Moshe Nissim, who was then the finance minister. When I sought to present what I considered the great benefits of the understandings with Hussein, I saw that Nissim was not ready to listen. Until then, I had regarded him as one of the most rational and serious Likud ministers. He looked me straight in the eye and said-asked: "Yossi, do you really expect the Likud to go to elections next year on Peres's peace plan?" (Nissim later denied that he ever said that.)

Only then did I realize there was no point in continuing my efforts to persuade. The opportunity to pursue peace fell victim to the political rivalry between the two large blocs. If the Hussein-Peres agreement were put to a vote in the inner cabinet (composed of five ministers from each side), the result would be a tie: five in favor and five opposed, effectively rejecting the agreement.

When it became clear that there was no chance of approval, I asked Peres not to bring the matter to a vote so that it would not be recorded in the annals of Israel that the government rejected this document. Peres was furious at Shamir and wanted to do the opposite: to submit it to a vote that would end in a tie and thereby officially cast the blame on Shamir for undermining the London Agreement. Ultimately, Peres was convinced to refrain from doing this, and the agreement was never discussed by the cabinet plenum or inner cabinet.

In retrospect, perhaps he was right and I was wrong. In any case, it was one of the bitterest disappointments in my public life. The plan was not contrary to the Likud's platform; we had ostensibly found a formula that both the Likud and the Hashemite kingdom could live with. The document contained no reference to partitioning the land, and it made no mention of the PLO. The fact that none of the Likud ministers suggested giving serious consideration to the document, (unlike their conduct in the lead-up to the dramatic votes on the security buffer in Lebanon and on the economic recovery program), convinced me that it was impossible to remain in a joint government with the Likud.

✻✻✻

The Labor Party ministers gathered for weekly meetings at Peres's Foreign Ministry office during that period. I handed Peres a letter of resignation prior to one of those meetings. (As a civil servant, I didn't participate in that Labor Party forum—just as I refrained from participating in the meetings of Labor's Knesset faction or other party meetings.) I told Peres that I would not be true to myself if I continued serving in my role as cabinet secretary after the government had stymied such an initiative. I couldn't treat it as just another topic when it was in fact the most important issue and the one that justified our unnatural partnership with the Likud. I told him that I was certain that he too could not explain to himself how he could possibly remain in the government. But if he wasn't going to quit, I would quit myself.

Peres asked me to wait before taking any action. First, he wanted to gauge the mood of "our ministers" and their readiness to quit the government. In particular, he wanted to see where Rabin stood on this question. Secondly, he wanted to check whether he still had the support of the majority of ministers—if not, he wouldn't make it to the end of the term in any case. Thirdly, he argued that if I resigned, the media would have a heyday with this and portray him as a politician who was clinging to his seat. They would compare him to his director-general, who was faithful to his ideological principles, and "you certainly don't want that," he said. My resignation was shelved for the time being.

At the meeting of "our ministers," Rabin presented a firm position against breaking up the unity government. His main justification for staying in the government was to block dangerous decisions by the right if it indeed managed to form an alternative government of a uniform ideological bent. Most of the ministers supported Rabin's approach.

Our meetings with King Hussein were not resumed. Shamir did meet with him and even reported that the meeting was "good." However, the

London Agreement was dead. Hussein later said that Peres disappointed him, because he had promised to resign if the government rejected the agreement. I wasn't there when Peres made this promise to the king, if indeed he made this promise, but Hussein's disappointment was understandable. Resigning and going to elections with the London Agreement would have been the right course to take, both in terms of our commitment to Hussein and from a political perspective.

✳✳✳

On December 9, 1987, the first intifada began in Gaza and then spread to the West Bank. On July 31, 1988, the king announced that he was severing Jordan from the West Bank and revoking the citizenship of its Jordanian residents, in violation of international law, in an effort to help establish a Palestinian state.

Benjamin Netanyahu and I appeared on the evening news program, *Mabat*, on Channel One, which was then the only TV channel. Bibi, who had just returned to Israel after resigning his post as UN ambassador, welcomed the king's decision, saying that it created a vacuum that would enable Israel to exercise its historical right to the Greater Land of Israel west of the Jordan River. I, who was then serving as the Foreign Ministry's director-general for political affairs, said the king's move was liable to be very detrimental because Israel would not remain a Jewish and democratic state if it annexed the West Bank. "Israel needs a border, and on its eastern side, Jordan would be better than any other alternative," I argued.

Three years later, in late October 1991, the Madrid Conference was convened. Ironically, Shamir came to the conference as the head of a narrow right-wing government. The Palestinian side agreed to be part of a joint delegation led by Jordan. After each round of talks, the Palestinians, with Shamir's acquiescence, traveled to Tunisia to receive instructions directly from Arafat before resuming negotiations.

However, the talks ran aground due to disputes over issues that were completely marginal—perhaps because of Shamir, who later admitted that he had no interest in making progress in the negotiations, and perhaps because of Arafat, who wanted to prove that no progress could be made without the PLO's direct participation.

The negotiations also remained deadlocked during the early period of Rabin's government, which took over the reins of power in 1992. Shamir's cabinet secretary, Eli Rubinstein, continued to head the Israeli delegation under Rabin. This stalemate prompted me to embark on the Oslo process. The Jordanians were angry that the Palestinians had established a channel with Israel without updating them. In fact, the Palestinians officially remained part of the joint delegation with Jordan until the signing of the Declaration of Principles (Oslo I) between Israel and the PLO.

Against the backdrop of the Jordanians' anger over the fact that the Palestinians had bypassed them, the Israel-Jordan Common Agenda was signed on September 14, 1993, a day after the festive signing of the Oslo I Accord at the White House. Fourteen months later, on October 26, 1994, Israel and Jordan signed a peace treaty. The signing ceremony in the Arava Valley was very moving. I came as deputy foreign minister with Rabin, and again met the king in a large tent for the dignitaries in attendance. Hussein seemed relaxed and proud of his achievement.

Our next meeting occurred less than a year later. To celebrate Lord Mishcon's eightieth birthday, the king hosted him and his wife, and Peres and me, at his palace in Aqaba. Hussein again used his skills as a skipper and sailed his yacht from Aqaba to the coast of Eilat. This time, there was no need to shut down the radar. . . .

The atmosphere at the meeting was reminiscent of a "graduation" party. The king spoke about Mishcon's important role in renewing the contacts between Israel and Jordan, and he criticized other leaders in the Arab world, as usual. We also discussed the preparations for the upcoming regional economic conference in Amman in November 1995.

By the time the conference was held, I was no longer deputy foreign minister: I had been appointed minister of economics and planning. In this capacity, I coordinated the preparations for the conference on the Israeli side, including joint ventures planned with the Palestinians and the Jordanians. We didn't know then that the economic conference in Amman would be the concluding ceremony of the brief golden era of peace. It seemed in those days that we were writing a new chapter in the history of the Middle East, and it felt like only the sky was the limit for cooperative endeavors. On the Saturday after the conference was adjourned, Rabin was assassinated.

✳✳✳

Three years later, in August 1998, I met with government leaders in Washington together with three other former contenders for the leadership of the Labor Party—Ehud Barak, Shlomo Ben-Ami, and Ephraim Sneh. King Hussein was hospitalized at the time at the Mayo Clinic in Minnesota, and we asked to meet with him, though we realized he was very ill and that a visit was unlikely. However, we received permission to visit, cancelled what was planned for that day and flew immediately to Minnesota.

I had pictured the Mayo Clinic as a futuristic place for millionaires, but from the inside it looked like a regular hospital—that is, except for the king's floor, where a large home carpet was spread and the dominant aroma was of re-boiled Turkish coffee.

They ushered us into the guest room, and the king soon joined us. Instead of a patient's hospital gown, he was dressed in a suit befitting a leader. He was very happy to see all of us and made an effort to appear that he was on the mend, even though he looked emaciated and his face was gaunt. He told us that he was about to start the last round of chemotherapy and would return to Amman within two months at full strength. We wanted to believe him.

There was talk at the time of convening a summit meeting of Clinton, Netanyahu, and Arafat to discuss the continued implementation of the interim agreement of 1995 (Oslo II). Hussein asked how serious Bibi was. Each of us gave his answer, and if there was a bottom line, it could be described as cautious optimism. After about a half an hour of talking about the contemporary situation in the Middle East, Hussein asked if it was possible to return to November 3. It took us a moment to understand the question. He was asking whether it was possible to return to the era prior to Rabin's assassination. We looked at each other and answered with a hesitant "yes," without offering any basis for this response.

It was the last time I met King Hussein, who passed away six months later.

18

Schlemiels and Schlimazels

TWO AFFAIRS WEIGHED HEAVILY UPON PERES'S SECOND YEAR AS prime minister. The first was the Bus 300 Affair. On April 12, 1984, during Shamir's term as prime minister, four Palestinians, about eighteen years old, seized control of a bus heading from Tel Aviv to Ashkelon and forced the driver to head toward the Egyptian border. They threatened to blow up the bus with its forty passengers if Israel didn't agree to release five hundred terrorists. The IDF's Sayeret Matkal commando unit stormed the bus, killing two of the hijackers. The two others were captured and taken to an isolated location where they were murdered by Shin Bet agents, who were acting upon a directive they had received from the director of the Shin Bet, Avraham ("Avrum") Shalom. The photographer Alex Levac caught the two Palestinians on film after their capture, alive and uninjured, and the photo was published in the *Hadashot* newspaper. It was therefore clear that they had not been killed during the IDF's assault on the bus and the successful rescue operation.

An internal review committee was formed by Defense Minister Moshe Arens to determine who was to blame for killing the terrorists after they were apprehended. Shin Bet agents, again following Shalom's instructions, lied in their testimony to the committee, obstructed the investigation and pinned the blame on Brig. Gen. Yitzhak Mordechai, who commanded the rescue operation. The Shin Bet men emerged from the affair with impunity at this stage.

Three senior Shin Bet officers who learned the truth about the affair and believed that such flagrant lying was unacceptable, met with Shalom and demanded that he resign or openly acknowledge that he had ordered the murder of the captured hijackers and the false testimony. Shalom refused and fired the three from the Shin Bet, claiming that they had mounted a rebellion. The three met with the attorney general, Yitzhak Zamir, who then met with the forum of prime ministers (Peres, Shamir, and Rabin) and demanded Shalom's dismissal. The prime ministerial trio rejected Zamir's demand, preferring to accept Shalom's claim that the three Shin Bet officers were plotting a mutiny.

At this stage, Zamir asked to meet with me, in my role as cabinet secretary, and told me what he knew. There were two options, according to the attorney general: Shalom's immediate resignation or the launching of a police investigation. I was shocked by the story. From the beginning of my term as cabinet secretary, I had developed a close friendship with Zamir, and I was certain that he was presenting the true picture. He also told me that he had decided to postpone his announced resignation in order to bring the affair to a close, one way or another. I encouraged him not to resign.

I recalled that Friday in mid-September when Peres sat in the prime minister's chair for the first time and Shamir came to brief him for the handover of power. I was sure that it would be a long meeting, but it lasted exactly twenty minutes. I mentioned to Peres that when positions are handed over at much lower echelons, the briefings can stretch over several days. I asked Peres what Shamir had managed to say in their short meeting. Peres replied that Shamir's main message was "take care of Avrum!"

When I heard that the first time, I laughed. After the conversation with Zamir, it no longer sounded funny at all.

In any case, Zamir asked me to meet with the deputy state attorney, Dorit Beinisch, and with senior attorneys Yehudit Tzur and Yehudit Karp. Beinisch laid out the story for me in full detail, and then I met with the three dismissed Shin Bet men, who impressed me very much. Next, I met with Peres. I told him that he could not allow himself to be part of such a terrible cover-up, and that the three men who were fired had justice on their side.

Peres told me that he hadn't said anything to me about the affair, even though it had been on his mind a lot in recent days, because he knew that I wouldn't support him on this matter. During this conversation, he was "Mr. Security": He expressed complete confidence in the Shin Bet director and was convinced that the three were acting out of line. According to Peres, anyone interested in ensuring that this sensitive system operates properly cannot lend a hand to this sort of revolt. For the first and last time in our relationship, he wasn't even willing to listen to my counterarguments.

For several weeks, there were Friday afternoon meetings at the Prime Minister's Residence with Shalom, attorney Ram Caspi, and a few others. Peres asked me to participate in all of those meetings, which were long and very gloomy. Shalom strongly resisted the suggestion that he resign (ostensibly for reasons unrelated to the Bus 300 affair), claiming that it would be a terrible blow to the Shin Bet. I remember the amiable man sitting on the sofa, weeping bitterly.

Nonetheless, Zamir informed Shalom that if he didn't resign, he would instruct the police to open an investigation against him. And indeed, an investigation was launched. The forum of prime ministers decided that the only remaining option was to quickly find a replacement for Zamir. However, as noted, Zamir had retracted his resignation. In the end, the justice minister, Yitzhak Moda'i, proposed appointing Judge Yosef Harish as Zamir's replacement, and the cabinet approved the proposal. Everyone understood that the appointment was aimed at enabling Israel's president to pardon Shalom and those who organized the false testimonies.

The cabinet meeting on this matter began at 10:00 p.m.and continued until dawn. Caspi presented the case for granting a pardon before a trial, rather than after it. Though such action would be very unconventional, it would be legal, he argued. The new attorney general expressed his support and noted that a pardon entails an admission of guilt. For that reason, some of the Shin Bet personnel who were slated to receive a pardon did not hurry to request one, and only did so at a later stage.

Since the cabinet secretary is also the liaison between the government and the president, I was responsible for presenting the cabinet's decision to President Chaim Herzog. The official meeting was scheduled for late in the morning. I asked to meet with him privately two hours earlier. When I arrived, he asked why I had requested two meetings with him. I explained that the second meeting would be between the president and the cabinet secretary, while the first meeting was between Vivian (his nickname) and Yossi. I acknowledged that I was doing something highly unconventional but was imploring him not to accept the official request I'd be presenting him two hours later. I saw that this made him uncomfortable, and I shared with him everything I knew about the affair. I told him that the decision to grant a pre-trial pardon of those who had ordered and executed the killing of bound prisoners would leave a black stain on his presidency and would make a mockery of what is called, justly or not, the "purity of arms."

However, I saw right away that I had no chance of persuading him. Herzog was part of the same group as Peres, Shamir, and Rabin, men who had stood by the cradle of the State of Israel at its birth, and whose patriotism was expressed, in part, by defending Israel's security personnel at any price, even when they violate the norms of proper conduct.

And indeed, Herzog pardoned Shalom. The High Court of Justice gave its stamp of approval (with a dissenting opinion by Aharon Barak) and Shalom resigned. (Years later, he joined me in the Geneva Initiative.) Those who received a pardon became ineligible for government jobs. The three senior officials who exposed the true story remained outside the Shin Bet. Anyone directly or indirectly connected to the Bus 300 Affair couldn't escape its shadow and perhaps also couldn't help feeling that other affairs, undetected by the media, continued to occur.

***

In November 1985, the Pollard Affair descended upon us. Peres summoned me and briefly explained that it involved a young Jewish-American who worked as an intelligence analyst for the US Navy. The man, Jonathan Pollard, had approached an Israeli officer at the end of a lecture in the US with an offer to pass on information to Israel in exchange for payment. The officer, Col. Aviem Sella (who happened to be the son-in-law of Haim Zadok, the justice minister in Rabin's first government), referred Pollard to Israel's LAKAM (a Hebrew acronym for Science Liaison Bureau) organization, which became his espionage operator. When the Americans discovered what Pollard was doing, he tried to flee to the Israeli Embassy in Washington. However, the embassy refused to open its gates for Pollard, and the FBI arrested him.

Peres was furious about the employment of Pollard and ranted about the "schlemiels and schlimazels" responsible for this affair. He said he had no idea that Israel had engaged the services of this strange spy. If he had known, he would never have approved such an arrangement, but the prime minister is not involved in recruiting and running operatives.

The mood was somber in a meeting Peres convened with Rabin, Shamir, and Rafi ("Smelly") Eitan, who ran LAKAM. It was clear that Israel was facing an unprecedented crisis with the United State and that the most important task was to clarify that while Pollard had indeed delivered classified information to Israel, it was done without the approval of Israel's top echelon.

At the Sunday cabinet meeting, Peres described the affair to the ministers, and it was agreed that a government statement, in Hebrew and in English, would emphasize that it was a "rogue operation." After the meeting, attorneys and security officials came to my office, and we composed the statements. The media was already waiting impatiently downstairs in the lobby.

The news about an American who was caught spying for Israel made headlines in many newspapers around the world, and the world was waiting in suspense for Israel's explanation. I walked down the stairs like someone who'd been caught with bloodstains on his hands to read a clever and evasive statement, like a parrot, after announcing in advance that I would not field any questions. A news photographer snapped a picture of me reading the statement, and the picture was published in the world press. The caption claimed that the person reading the statement was apparently the head of the Shin Bet. In those days, the names and pictures of the heads of the Shin Bet and Mossad were not allowed to be published, and the newspapers assumed that Israel had changed its secrecy policy in the wake of the Pollard Affair. The fact that I was mistakenly identified as the Shin Bet director created considerable difficulty for me in later years.

In some circles, Pollard came to be seen as a sort of "prisoner of Zion," despite the information that later surfaced about him: that he apparently offered his good services to China and Pakistan before turning to Israel; that the CIA rejected his application for employment, that his security clearance was temporarily canceled, and more. Senior Israeli politicians made pilgrimages to the American prison where he was incarcerated, and he was awarded Israeli citizenship during his imprisonment. Pollard was released under parole restrictions in 2015. Those restrictions were lifted in 2020, which allowed him to leave the US and settle in Israel.

Pollard did not save the State of Israel, and it was a reckless decision to engage his services. The effort to portray him as a sort of "Eli Cohen" [the Israeli spy who developed close ties with Syria's leadership in the 1960s, was caught and hung] was foolish and adversely affected Israel's relations with the US and American Jews, who were again accused of dual loyalty.

***

In the fall of 1986, Peres prepared to transfer the premiership to Shamir as stipulated in the rotation agreement. Some party members urged him not to honor the agreement and to call for early elections in light of the strong public support he had won and the wide acclaim for this statesmanship. The Labor Party convention met to discuss this question, and Peres persuaded the members not to adopt a decision that violated the coalition agreement. Indeed, it had never occurred to Peres to renege on the agreement.

Peres told me that he wanted to suggest my name to Shamir as a candidate for ambassador in Washington. I thanked him, but said I wasn't interested in serving as a diplomat and that I was planning to compete for a seat in the next Knesset. I added that in the meantime I was considering a position at the Technion's Neaman Institute, which had offered me a professorship. He asked me not to make any commitment.

Meanwhile, the media reported that Peres had decided to appoint me ambassador to the US and that Shamir was opposed, and that this dispute was delaying the handover of power from Peres to Shamir. Shamir called me the next morning and asked that I come to meet with him. I told him I had no interest in any diplomatic appointment and that I understood that he wanted the ambassador in Washington to be someone who was ideologically close to him. He said that the media reports were untrue and that he didn't oppose my appointment but knew that Peres was debating between me and Maj. Gen. (Res.) Avrasha Tamir as his appointee for the position of Foreign Ministry director-general. He asked me to accept the appointment and showered me with compliments, saying that despite our different views, he trusted me. If Avrasha is appointed director-general of the Foreign Ministry, Shamir said, he would not allow him to be a member of the "Heads of Delegations Committee" that normally included the Mossad director, the Shin Bet director, the police commissioner, the head of military intelligence, and the director-general of the Foreign Ministry. He also promised that I would continue to participate, as a regular invitee, in all of the cabinet meetings.

I didn't want to be the one delaying the implementation of the rotation, but Ezer Weizman felt superfluous and frustrated as a minister without portfolio, and one of his demands before the rotation was to appoint Tamir, who had entered politics with him, as the Foreign Ministry's director-general. Despite the special connection between Ezer and me, he told Peres that he felt a special obligation toward Avrasha and was unable to compromise on this matter. Ezer felt deprived: He was the one who had given Peres the possibility of the rotation agreement, yet he remained without a ministerial portfolio. Tamir's appointment was a sort of sedative for him.

Meanwhile, the story became a central item in the political news. The Likud leaders scrambled to find creative ways to appoint me, including a legislative amendment that would allow someone who is not a member of Knesset to serve as a deputy minister, or the invention of a new position called "vice minister."

Peres suggested that I accept a position as "director-general for political affairs." However, since the title made it sound like the position would be subordinate to the director-general, Peres would clarify in a letter to Tamir and me that I would be his "number two," while Avrasha would be his "number three" at the Foreign Ministry. The letter would also state that I would be the permanent member of the Heads of Delegations Committee and chair the ministry's appointments committee (for appointing ambassadors and the heads of other delegations).

I preferred this administrative arrangement to a change in legislation on my behalf. It was agreed that in light of my appointment, no deputy minister would be appointed (to avoid padding the bureaucracy) and that my position would be erased at the end of the national unity government's term in November 1988.

To a large extent, it was déjà vu: Just like two years earlier, when I accepted the job as cabinet secretary, I again gave up an opportunity in academia, I was again presented with a request-demand-plea from Peres, and I again had a conversation with Helena, this time by phone, who counseled me to accept the appointment.

When I arrived at the courtyard of the Foreign Ministry's old asbestos compound, I was far from convinced that I had made the right decision. I felt at first like I was swimming toward a particular destination and continually being swept off course by the waves I encountered. That was not my feeling when I left the job two years later.

19

"It's Unthinkable That a Lowly Bureaucrat Is Shaping Israel's Policies"

THE FOREIGN MINISTRY WAS FASCINATING. IN LATER YEARS, VARIous roles were stripped from it. But at the time, its voice was heard in meetings of the cabinet plenum and inner cabinet—even if less powerfully than it would have preferred. I attributed great importance to the ministry's Center for Political Research and spent considerable time meeting with ministry staff members and preparing for meetings of the appointments committee. In addition, I cultivated a wide network of relationships with the heads of foreign ministries in various countries.

However, the most important issue on which I focused and fought was Israel's relations with South Africa. My first encounter with this issue was in early 1963, when I interviewed professor Arthur Goldreich as a reporter for *Maariv for Youth*. The interview was not for publication. He was then thirty-four years old, with sandals and a smile, and his story was mesmerizing. Goldreich was born in South Africa to a proud Jewish family, was active in the Zionist movement there and came to Israel to serve in the IDF during the War of Independence. Two years later, he returned to his studies in South Africa and later completed them in London.

Goldreich told us—the teenage reporters at the secret meeting with him—how he had met Nelson Mandela, then still a law student, and what a strong impression Mandela made on him. He decided to join the struggle of black South Africans—as long as it was non-violent. In 1963, the "Spear of the Nation" underground began to engage in violence, and Mandela became a wanted man. He and his associates were captured, while Goldreich and a few other activists went into hiding and escaped to neighboring countries. Goldreich was tried in absentia and sentenced to death. He came to Israel because his wife was Israeli and because he was already familiar with Israel from his period of military service. He traveled dressed as a monk and thus managed to elude the long arm of the apartheid regime.

Goldreich described to us how racial separation affected the daily lives of South Africans, how they suffered from deprivation, and how they were torn from their neighborhoods and transferred to Bantustans (the unofficial term for the ten "homelands" created by the apartheid regime for the country's black inhabitants). This resettlement plan was enacted in 1959 under Prime Minister Hendrik Verwoerd, an extreme nationalist. It aimed to enable blacks to work in the white cities but then return to their "native reserves," where they could exercise their rights without disturbing the prosperous white minority.

Goldreich also told us about the prohibition on interracial couples, and the segregation on buses and in all public places. We clung to his every word in astonishment. I found it hard to believe that only a few years after the defeat of Nazism, a regime that purported to be Western, and even democratic, dared to concoct such a system, and I was proud that Jews like Goldreich had joined Mandela and his just cause. I later read everything I could find about the events in South Africa and hoped that one day I'd be in a position to help sever the connection between the Jewish state and that racist regime.

In 1976, when Yitzhak Rabin hosted South African Prime Minister John Vorster in Israel, I strongly condemned this. I really couldn't understand how it was possible to host someone who had supported the Nazi movement and had become the most prominent spokesman for racial separation in his country. The conventional explanation was that nearly all of the African states had cut off diplomatic ties with Israel in the wake of the Yom Kippur War, and that Israel was not in a position to renounce its few friends.

South African governments had invited me and my wife for visits when I was working as a journalist, when I served as Labor Party spokesperson, and when I was cabinet secretary. They wanted to show us the "real" South Africa—where the blacks received a superior education in comparison to other African states and where they could ostensibly fulfill their right to self-determination in the Bantustans. My response to all of the invitations was that I wouldn't set foot in their country until they put an end to apartheid.

When I began working at the Foreign Ministry, I told myself that now I had the opportunity to do something beyond my personal boycott. (It occurred to me that my personal boycott of South Africa was not unlike my father's refusal to speak German or buy German products.) I thought that the world's growing awareness of the white minority's repression of the black majority in South Africa, which reached new peaks in the summer of 1986, along with the increasing demands for sanctions, would make it easier for me to lead a change in Israel's policy. Even so, I knew that I'd be accused of political naivety in challenging the knowledge, experience, and pragmatism of the Israeli defense establishment.

The first action I took was a small structural change: I asked that the ministry's desk dealing with South Africa report directly to my office, and I appointed my advisor Alon Liel to head the desk. (Liel would later serve as Israel's ambassador to South Africa and as the director-general of the Economics Ministry and Foreign Ministry.) It was clear to me that Israel's relations with South Africa could not be directly managed from afar. Anyone who seeks to institute change should realize that systems tend to preserve the status quo, and without close personal monitoring, the desired change will be stymied.

When I began to plan the change in policy, I came to the conclusion that we should act on two tracks: to cultivate relations with the black leadership in South Africa and to lobby the Israeli government to support the sanctions imposed in the world at that time, included an end to arms deals. The subject of military collaboration with South Africa was sensitive, of course.

Alon and I conducted meetings, collected material, and prepared to take action. I learned about the important project initiated by my former teacher, professor Shimon Zelniker, which focused on bringing black South African union activists for courses in Israel in the framework of the Histadrut's Afro-Asian Institute, led by Yehuda Paz. The project was kept secret so that the South African government wouldn't cancel it out of fear that the Histadrut was fomenting opposition to the regime.

In this framework, we brought people to Israel who later became part of the South African leadership; they got to know the various sides of Israel and developed friendships with Israelis. The government of South Africa suggested that we host the Zulu leader, Chief Mangosuthu Buthelezi, who represented a much more moderate approach than other black leaders vis-à-vis the apartheid regime. We did indeed invite him, while recognizing exactly who he was—a classic example of a top black leader who was willing to compromise with the policy of apartheid.

At a certain stage, Shlomo Gur, a Foreign Ministry official, was appointed deputy ambassador to South Africa. From my perspective, his principal role was to serve as an ambassador to the leaders of the black majority. I asked him to try to reach the highest level possible in the black leadership, regardless of the regime's assessment of its legitimacy, and to forge connections in anticipation of the morning after apartheid. He reported to me on his activities, performed his role with great wisdom and considerable success. Later, when I served as deputy foreign minister, he was my bureau chief.

I found two camps at the ministry: those who supported the "realistic" approach and believed that I was taking an unreasonable risk in the policy I was leading, and those for whom Israel's policy toward South Africa was a black stain and who welcomed the possibility for change. (The latter group included, among others, the legendary deputy director-general Hanan Bar-On and the deputy director-general for Asia, Africa, and Oceania, Avi Primor.) Without the change that began in American policy toward South Africa, perhaps my efforts would have failed. In any case, the threat expressed in decisions made by the US administration and Congress in 1986 and 1987 certainly helped me in the struggle to change Israeli policy.

The US Congress formed a committee to review the relations of various countries with the apartheid regime. We were shown a draft of the committee's report, which revealed the scope of transactions between South Africa and Israel, and the number and types of weapons they included. The report, which was slated to be published on March 31, 1987, was liable to provide abundant fodder for congressional initiatives to cut aid to Israel. I used the report as my primary weapon in conversations with ministers and heads of the defense establishment. My efforts became public, and most of the media was sympathetic. My demand was for Israel to adopt a series of sanctions against South Africa. In my media appearances, I said that the Jewish state could not allow itself to maintain intimate relations with a state that was carrying the banner of racism.

Of course, there were many who opposed the policy I advocated, and argued that the American administration needed Israel no less than Israel needed America. According to that view, the talk about cutting or cancelling aid was mere nonsense. Rabin was even quoted in the press as saying that "it's unthinkable that Israel's policies are being led by a lowly bureaucrat"—a snide reference to me. Peres called him to task for this in an exchange of notes, and Rabin responded that the quote was inaccurate and that he had merely said that it was unthinkable that a bureaucrat (not a "lowly" one) was shaping government policy.

✱✱✱

By December 1986, Israel remained the only democracy in the world that hadn't joined the boycott of South Africa. Peres wasn't thrilled about my "quixotic battle," as he called it, but he didn't stop me either. As someone who tried to avoid head-on confrontation, he invited me to a three-sided conversation in his office. The third interlocutor was the director of the Mossad, Nahum Admoni. Peres knew that I held Nahum in high regard.

The foreign minister was silent, and the Mossad director spoke. Nahum roundly complimented the moral campaign I was leading, but said it was dangerous and could undermine another moral objective—the security of the State of Israel. Moreover, he contended, the apartheid regime would not fall; the effort I was leading would not make the blacks fall in love with us; and the whites possessed the military means to prevent the black majority from taking over South Africa. "They understand—rightly so, from their perspective—that relinquishing power would mean their collective suicide because the blacks would simply massacre them. So it simply won't happen," he asserted. But what could happen, he added, is that the South African government could decide to terminate its special relations with Israel, and that would result in irreparable harm. It could be inferred from his words that he did not consider a cutoff of American aid to be a realistic possibility, but only saw it as a threat that we could overcome.

I was bold enough to disagree with his analysis and to contend that the apartheid regime would not long endure the burgeoning sanctions and increasingly tight international stranglehold. If Israel, even at a stage when its shameful security relations are exposed, does not join the sanctions, we'll find ourselves treated like a leper state, I argued. The day will come when the black majority rules in South Africa, but we'll become its number one enemy.

Soon afterwards, Ora Namir, who chaired the Knesset's Labor and Welfare Committee, asked for a meeting. She never believed she'd be initiating such a conversation, but life leads people to unexpected places, she explained. After opening with some flattering words about my campaign, she said that terminating Israel's security ties with South Africa could result in the layoff of about five thousand workers, most of them at the Histadrut-owned Koor Metals factory. This also had to be taken into account, she argued.

I told her that a serious effort would be needed to help those workers find alternative employment, but that someone made a terrible mistake in fostering the relations between the two states, and that we now had an opportunity to rectify this mistake. I added that people like her, who believed like me in the inherent equality of all human beings, must not condone the continued intimacy between Israel and the symbol of racism in the world.

But the really difficult conflict was with Mendel Kaplan. Mendel was one of the leaders of South African Jewry, an energetic and fiery millionaire who built steel factories in his country and in Israel, and a philanthropist for Jewish causes. He was later elected chairman of the Jewish Agency's Board of Governors. When he came to Israel on a visit, he burst into my office without warning and started hollering about us making decisions that don't take into consideration Diaspora Jewry and that imposing sanctions on the regime in South Africa would lead to a second Holocaust. On the spot, he demanded that I cancel the meeting of the inner cabinet, which was slated to discuss the sanctions.

I tried, with partial success, to calm him down. I explained to him that an Israeli decision to join the punitive measures against the apartheid regime would be a sort of insurance policy for the Jews of South Africa. In regard to the cabinet session, I reminded him that I wasn't the prime minister or a minister, and that I wasn't empowered to convene or cancel cabinet meetings. He looked at me and said that he had just come from a meeting with Rabin, who had told him, "Speak with Beilin. He's the one who created the whole mess." I thanked him for thinking that I wielded such power but tried to convince him that it was an inflated assessment.

Nonetheless, I was concerned about the conversation he had scheduled with the prime minister, and when I received a call about two hours later from Shamir's office, I was afraid that the battle was lost. I was summoned to meet with Shamir that same afternoon.

To my complete surprise, Shamir informed me that he supported my initiative. He said the sanctions decision was of vital importance and asked that we work in coordination to win the support of the inner cabinet. He believed that his Likud colleagues were "a lost cause," but said he'd speak with Misha Arens and try to persuade him to support the sanctions. In regard to the Labor ministers, Shamir was worried about Weizman's vote and believed that Bar-Lev and Navon "will be okay." And he knew that Rabin was angry about the sanctions, but since the US was very important to him, there was hope that he'd change his mind in order avoid coming across as anti-American. The prime minister asked that we coordinate the work leading up to the cabinet session and that I prepare the proposed resolution.

While still surprised by this development, I spoke with Ezer. He sided with the opponents of the sanctions and also did not believe that the US would punish us. At the end of the conversation, he said that I had not persuaded him, but promised to vote for my proposal because "we're good friends."

There was considerable tension leading up to the cabinet vote on March 18, 1987. Some expected the resolution on the sanctions to fail on a tie vote between the Labor and Likud ministers. The South African media devoted front-page headlines to Israel's deliberations, as did many newspapers in the West. Before the voting began, Shamir informed me that Arens would be "against us." And indeed, Arens was the fiercest opponent of the proposal. Rabin also accepted the view of the Likud ministers, but said that we couldn't afford a rift with America.

In the end, the five Labor ministers voted to approve my proposal, and Shamir joined them, making the vote six to four. It was a surprising outcome and the only one of its kind in all of the years of the national unity government, from 1984 to 1990.

The cabinet resolution included a decision not to sign any new weapons agreement with South Africa, and to establish a committee to recommend a list of sanctions against South Africa. The committee, which I chaired, included the directors-general of the Finance Ministry and Ministry of Industry and Trade, along with senior officials from the Defense Ministry and other ministries. There were fierce disagreements and some shouting too, but we kept on schedule and finished the work within two months.

Shamir did not hurry to bring the full resolution on the sanctions to a vote, and it was placed on the agenda of the inner cabinet only on September 16, shortly before the American decision on punishing foreign aid recipients that refrained from adopting sanctions against South Africa. The proposal included a suspension of Israeli investment in South Africa; a prohibition on granting Israeli government loans to South Africa; a prohibition on importing bars of gold from South Africa; a prohibition on travel by Israeli civil servants to South Africa; a termination of science agreements between the two countries; a call to refrain from cultural and athletic ties; and the creation of an Israeli fund for training blacks and "colored" South Africans in Israel. The result of the vote was again six to four: Five Labor ministers supported the sanctions, and Shamir joined them, while the four ministers from his party voted against the proposal.

I had to be at a meeting in Europe that afternoon, and when my meeting ended in the late evening, the telephone rang in my hotel room. It was from the Prime Minister's Bureau with a call from Shamir. He informed me that the resolution was well-received in the international community; the US was appreciative and South Africa would not sever relations with Israel. He did mention, however, a tough phone conversation with the president of South Africa, Pieter Willem Botha, who was particularly enraged about the funding of training for non-whites in Israel. Botha angrily claimed that Israel was the real racist state, because it was discriminating between whites and blacks in its training program. I replied to Shamir that it would be no problem to extend the funding to whites too.

In one way or another, the issue remained on the agenda. Several prominent figures decided to challenge the sanctions resolution, visited South Africa, and claimed that the resolution was only designed to placate the Americans and would not be implemented. The Israeli tennis player Amos Mansdorf, for example, decided to travel to South Africa for a tournament where he would be the top player since all of the players from the West were boycotting the event. I invited him to my home on Saturday, and Alon and I tried to persuade him not to go. He explained his reasons for wanting to participate in the tournament, and we failed to change his mind.

Nonetheless, the overall picture changed dramatically. In practice, Israel indeed cut its ties with South Africa, and seven years later the unbelievable occurred: Nelson Mandela became the president of South Africa. In 1992, Alon was named Israel's ambassador to South Africa, and this was a closing of the circle from our perspective. There was no longer the need to appoint a special diplomat to focus, in secret or openly, on cultivating relations with the black majority.

Among the heads of state participating in Mandela's inauguration in Pretoria in May 1994 was President Ezer Weizman. Five years later, Mandela visited Israel. We met for a long conversation at the President's Residence. During this conversation, Mandela said to Weizman, pointing to me, "If it wasn't for this guy, I wouldn't have come here." Ezer undoubtedly recalled the gesture of friendship he had made for me by casting a decisive vote in the cabinet meeting on the sanctions resolution.

✳✳✳

The ominous forebodings about the fate of South African Jewry did not materialize, of course, and the blacks did not massacre the whites after ascending to power. Diplomatic relations with South Africa were maintained under the Mandela government, even though these relations had no military component. In later years, I met Mandela twice, both times in South Africa. In 2001, I met for a long talk with his successor, Thabo Mbeki, and Mandela joined us. Mbeki asked how South Africa could help promote peace in the Middle East. I suggested that he invite a group of Palestinians, a group of Israelis, and a group of South African leaders, black and white, to discuss several questions: Do the conflicting narratives allow room for reconciliation? What concessions are necessary to achieve reconciliation? And what is the role of symbols and gestures in this process? I didn't think he would take up my suggestion.

I heard nothing more from Mbeki for several weeks, and then he surprised me with an offer to host a three-way seminar, as I had proposed, at the famous Spier wine farm near Cape Town. The plan went forward, with ten participants on each side. Saeb Erekat led the Palestinian group, I led the Israeli group and Mbeki headed the South African group, which comprised ten current or former ministers, five blacks and five whites. The Israeli delegation also included senior political figures—former ministers and members of Knesset.

Those were magical days. Tough questions were asked, issues were raised that had never been addressed, and we worked hard to address them. Of particular interest was Pik Botha, who had served as his country's foreign minister during the apartheid period and also under Mandela's presidency. In my eyes, he was the most prominent defender of apartheid, and his arrival at this special confab took me by surprise. It was fascinating to hear his analysis of how people like him failed to understand what the last white president of South Africa, Frederik Willem de Klerk, had understood, and how they continued to believe that their country was entitled to maintain the apartheid regime it had concocted, and that it was possible to do so.

Botha described cabinet meetings that were interrupted by reports of violence, including the murder of innocent whites by blacks and massive rioting. The violent clashes were not initiated by the regime, but by its opponents. The conference room of the South African government was where the most important decisions were made. Those decisions were made exclusively by white people who couldn't understand how the world failed to see the "reality" in which educated people, some of them liberals, who did not want to resort to violence, were simply compelled to defend themselves.

Only after the picture changed and he found himself in a joint government of blacks and whites, Botha understood that the big mistake of those in the all-white conference room was the fact that they were stuck in a mindset that left no room for another view of the reality. The world was then divided between terrorists-communists and peaceful citizens who only wanted to protect their families. The intelligence information wasn't wrong and wasn't intentionally misleading, but it saw the reality from a very narrow perspective, and the decision makers felt that they had to make decisions based on the undisputed information and to defend their citizens.

The meetings went on for several days and enabled each side to make comparisons and draw conclusions about acknowledging the other's narrative. It also gave each side an opportunity to describe its hardships and fears, and the way it viewed the contemporary and historical reality, without this hampering our ability to work together. We also learned the need to preserve, remember, and cite the past in a nonprovocative way.

It is important to understand that what later transpired in South Africa, particularly in the years after Mbeki's presidency, was very problematic—in terms of economics, relations between blacks and whites, and the relationship with Israel. The period was characterized by considerable corruption, yet the bottom line is that the prophets of doom were wrong. South Africa is still contending with difficult challenges today, with partial success, and it's hard to believe that until fairly recently a dark and brutal regime ruled that land.

20

The Sextet vs. the Old Guard

IN 1988, I VISITED SWEDEN AND MET WITH TOP OFFICIALS AT THE Swedish Foreign Ministry. The Israeli ambassador, Moshe Arel, invited me to his home for dinner and asked me to suggest people to invite. I suggested Gunnar Jarring, a linguistics professor and diplomat whose career included serving as his country's representative at the UN and its ambassador in Washington. In 1967, while serving as Sweden's ambassador in Moscow, Jarring was surprised by a request from the UN security-general to act as the UN's special envoy to the Middle East, as stipulated in Security Council Resolution 242. The resolution, which became a cornerstone of agreements signed between Israel and its neighbors (as well as unsigned understandings), states that the Security Council "requests the secretary-general to designate a special representative to proceed to the Middle East to establish and maintain contacts with the states concerned, in order to promote agreement and assist efforts to achieve a peaceful and accepted settlement in accordance with the provisions and principles in this resolution . . . [and] to report to the Security Council on the progress of the efforts of the special representative as soon as possible." Jarring agreed to take on this assignment, but Golda's intransigence made his mission synonymous with a Sisyphean effort.

After dinner, we met in a smaller forum, and I asked Jarring to share with us his impressions from his talks with the parties to the conflict. The 81-year-old said with a smile that he was still the secretary-general's special representative to the Middle East, perhaps because they had forgotten to terminate his appointment. Jarring spoke mainly of the principles for peace between Israel and Egypt, which he had presented to the two sides in February 1971. Sadly, they were very similar to the terms of the Egypt-Israel peace treaty signed eight years later, after the superfluous bloodshed of the Yom Kippur War.

Jarring said that he was very impressed by Sadat, who was ready to accept his proposal, and was surprised by Golda's rejection of it. He concluded that Meir was unable to see the difference between Nasser and Sadat, was unwilling to believe in the genuineness of Sadat's intentions, and failed to understand that the Egyptian president was obliged to condition his acceptance of the Jarring initiative by stating that a comprehensive peace would require Israel's withdrawal from all of the territories it had captured. Instead of jumping for joy that Sadat, unlike his predecessor, was ready for peace with Israel, she latched onto that conditional proviso, which everyone knew was mere lip service for the Arab world. Jarring was one of the heroes of my book *The Price of Unity* (1985), which focused on Israel's years of blindness, from 1967 to 1973. The conversation with him in 1988 reinforced my assessment that Golda had not understood, or had not wished to understand, the significance of Egypt's acceptance of his proposal. Her decision to reject Sadat's readiness for a diplomatic accord with Israel in exchange for a withdrawal from the Sinai was the direct precipitant of the Yom Kippur War. That failure to understand, in my eyes, made her the worst prime minister in Israel's history.

✱✱✱

In 1988, before the elections for the twelveth Knesset, I resigned from my position at the Foreign Ministry in order to compete for a seat in the Knesset as a representative of the Labor Party. For the first time, the party's slate was selected in a democratic process, in a vote conducted among the hundreds of members of its central committee. Each candidate had to announce in advance which slot of ten candidates he or she wished to compete in (1–10, 11–20, 21–30, etc.), and the central committee members had to vote separately, time after time, for each group of ten. When the results for one group of ten were announced, unsuccessful candidates had to choose whether they wished to compete for the next group or drop out of the race. Abba Eban, for example, was not elected to the first group of ten and quit without competing in the next group, and that was quite stunning.

Members of the two ideological groups in the party (Kfar HaYarok, led by Haim Ramon and Nissim Zvili, and Mashov, which I led) competed for places on Labor's Knesset list. I tried to apply the conclusions of my dissertation and made an effort to prevent a situation in which each of us waged all-out war against his friends.

We shared common objectives: to demarcate a border between Israel and the Palestinians, end the occupation and secure Israel as a Jewish and democratic state, and to institute changes in the Histadrut and in the relations between the labor federation and the party. We believed it was untenable for the Histadrut to continue to represent both the workers and the employers in the large enterprises it owned (due to the blatantly clear and inherent conflict of interests between workers and employers). We also didn't believe that someone who wanted to join an HMO other than the Histadrut's Clalit HMO should be disqualified from membership in the Labor Party. (At the time, membership in the Histadrut was a requirement for membership in the Labor Party. And anyone who left the Histadrut's HMO had to leave the Histadrut, which meant leaving the Labor Party.) These issues placed us at loggerheads with the party's old guard, especially with the generation born in the 1920s and early 1930s. In the end, we were all elected to the Knesset: Haim Ramon, who had already entered the Knesset in 1983, Amir Peretz, Avrum Burg, Nawaf Massalha, Hagai Merom, and me.

Some party officials spoke disparagingly of the "theories of the ivory tower," claiming that the true university is "the university of life." Nonetheless, those theories worked this time. On that election eve, I suggested that the six of us, together with Nissim Zvili (who did not compete in those elections), meet regularly to plan our work in the Knesset and in the party. Thus, the "Sextet" was born, which became the "Octet" in the 13th Knesset with the addition of Zvili and Yael Dayan.

However, the Labor Party did not fare so well in the elections. It received 39 seats (without Mapam, which left the Alignment when the national unity government was established in 1984), while the Likud garnered forty seats. The members of the Sextet opposed the formation of another national unity government led by Shamir, who did not have to agree to a rotation agreement with the Labor Party this time: The rightist-religious bloc he led constituted a majority without us. Shamir had limited affection for the ultra-Orthodox and religious parties, and he preferred a broad government that wouldn't be dependent upon them. After it already appeared that he would form a narrow government, he turned his back on them, and approached Rabin (not Peres, the chairman of the Labor Party) with an offer to create a national unity government. Rabin was in favor. Perhaps he also preferred serving as defense minister in a Shamir government to serving in that role in a rotation government. Peres was offered the Finance Ministry. The kibbutz movement, which was very strong in the party, lobbied for accepting this distribution of ministerial portfolios, hoping that Peres could help economically distressed kibbutzim as finance minister. Most of the veteran party members also supported joining the Shamir government.

We prepared for the decisive meeting of the Labor Party bureau (an executive committee, much smaller than the party's central committee).

We worked together with Uzi Baram, the party's secretary-general, and other members opposed to resuming the unnatural partnership with the Likud—and now from a position of inferiority. Rabin and Peres explained that the continued partnership was essential for preventing escalation vis-à-vis the Palestinians, who had launched the first intifada a year earlier. We argued, in response, that we were turning ourselves into a sort of fifth wheel, without any real power, solely to receive ministerial roles for the benefit of the sectors closest to us.

Surprisingly, we won. The bureau voted to reject the proposal of Peres and Rabin and not to join the Shamir government. The media sang our praises, noting that despite our lack of experience in the Knesset, we were not rookies in public life. It was our first joint political victory, and we patted ourselves on the back—both because of the power we had demonstrated and because of the essence: The Labor Party had rejected Shamir's invitation.

But the story didn't end there. The two leaders, despite the constant tension between them, joined forces to appeal the bureau's decision before the party's central committee. The show was repeated, this time open to the media, which didn't miss a single nuance. The Sextet failed as the party establishment mustered a majority to support its leaders. The Labor Party was now ready to enter a Shamir-led unity government for the next four years, with Rabin as defense minister and Peres as finance minister.

It was a bitter disappointment. However, when it appeared that the die had been cast, MK Shmuel Halpert from the ultra-Orthodox Agudat Yisrael party contacted me and said that he and his colleagues were furious at Shamir, mainly because Shamir had suggested they could "put in a frame" the coalition document formulated between the Likud and the ultra-Orthodox after the Labor Party expressed readiness to join his government. The ultra-Orthodox felt they had been used and discarded. Thus, they were ready to negotiate a coalition agreement with the Labor Party and form a government led by Peres, without Shamir. Halpert proposed that we jointly draft an outline that would serve as the basis for negotiations between the ultra-Orthodox and Labor.

From my perspective, this made all the difference in the world: a government for the full term, with Peres as prime minister and Rabin as defense minister, which would promote an international conference to launch negotiations with all of Israel's neighbors, versus a Shamir government that would stubbornly refuse to accept a conference even if it promised in advance not to impose any solution on the sides. I updated Peres on Halpert's initiative. He was not enthusiastic but did not oppose the idea. I met with Halpert, and we drafted the principles for negotiations; we planned to continue our talks the following Sunday.

After telling Peres about the draft document, I felt that we had—for the first time since 1977—a real chance of forming a Labor-led government that would launch a serious diplomatic process. I flew to Paris to deliver a lecture, feeling very optimistic. But this optimism was premature. After a few hours in the City of Lights, Peres telephoned and said that Rabin had gotten wind of my meeting with Halpert and had lambasted "the efforts of Peres's poodle" to form a narrow government. Peres asked me to return to Israel as soon as possible.

Rabin's reaction was typical; he had a habit of coining pejorative phrases that quickly made headlines (reproaching Israeli emigrants as "weaklings," describing Peres as an "indefatigable schemer" and referring to me as a "lowly bureaucrat" and "poodle"). On the coalition issue, there was really no cause for him to fume: After all, the Knesset election was a virtual tie; we had yet to sign any agreement with the Likud, and there was a real possibility of forming a government under our leadership.

Ostensibly, Rabin should have become the target of criticism for preferring a Shamir-led government and for portraying the effort to form a Labor-led government as illegitimate. But unfortunately, Peres did not put up a fight, and Rabin ultimately had the upper hand. He maneuvered Peres into accepting the finance portfolio, though Peres had no interest in it. (I was appointed deputy finance minister.) In the end, a short-lived government was formed that rejected any progress toward a diplomatic accord with the Palestinians or with Jordan.

ALONG THE ROADSIDE

Four years earlier, in 1984, Rabin did not plan to challenge Peres for the party's leadership, and the political threat came from an unexpected source: Yitzhak Navon, a close friend of Peres who, like Peres, had been one of Ben-Gurion's young protégés. Navon, who had completed a term as a very popular president in 1983, was considering running against Peres with the aim of serving as prime minister. The polls bode well for him and some prominent figures in the party, including Uzi Baram, encouraged him to throw his hat into the ring.

As tensions rose in the party, Navon and Peres met for lunch at the Shemesh restaurant in Jerusalem. The exact content of their conversation the two men took with them to their graves. But by the time the dessert came around, Peres had convinced Navon that he was better suited for the Foreign Ministry than the Prime Minister's Office.

Chapter 20

The problem was that Peres had already promised the Foreign Ministry to Abba Eban. Peres asked me to go to Herzliya and inform Eban of the change in plans. "He's your friend," he said. "It will be easier for him to accept it if it comes from you."

It was one of the least pleasant missions I had ever been assigned. Aubrey (the name people really used) and his wife Suzy waited for me at the entrance to their home. They realized that I wasn't coming to announce they had won the lottery. Suzy asked if I had come to tell them that Aubrey would not be appointed foreign minister. I nodded. Aubrey was quiet and glum, saying only that he wasn't surprised.

At that moment, I recalled the first time I had seen him, from afar. It was prior to the elections in 1959. My father took me on Saturday to the Eden cinema to hear the young genius, who was serving simultaneously as Israel's ambassador at the UN and in Washington. I had seen his pictures in the Carmel and Geva newsreels and in the Davar newspaper.

The legendary figure now slumped into the chair in his office, and Suzy started to weep. I tried to explain the situation, to say that it was the only way to dissuade Navon, that it hadn't been planned, that nothing deceitful had been done. But nothing helped.

And here, four years later, in 1988, I met again with Abba Eban, now sventy-three, at his home. I was nearing the end of my term as the Foreign Ministry's director-general for political affairs and came to consult with him about a sensitive matter on the agenda. Eban was then serving as chairman of the Knesset Foreign Affairs and Defense Committee. Since every candidate had to choose which group of ten to compete in (and, as noted, those who failed to be elected could continue to compete in the next group of ten), Eban said he would compete for one of the top ten slots. I told him I had decided to compete for a place in the second group of ten.

He seemed embarrassed by the new situation that forced him to woo the members of the party's central committee. On his desk was a list of the names and phone numbers of the hundreds of central committee members, and he called them one after another. "Most of them don't believe it's actually me, and think that it's Tuvia Tzapir," he said, referring to a well-known comedic impressionist. Part of every conversation was devoted to persuading his interlocutor that it was indeed Abba Eban on the line. I suggested that he hire someone to place the call, tell the party member that Abba Eban wished to speak with him or her, and then hand over the phone. He was concerned that it would be perceived as a type of haughtiness. Then I heard him speak with a central committee member who was returning his call.

He arrived with his wife Suzy at the election event. They didn't approach people, but quite a few people went up to them and exchanged pleasantries. The first stage of voting was for the top ten spots on the party's Knesset list. The results were announced about a half hour later—Eban was not elected.

The couple was genuinely astonished. Eban had perhaps reconciled himself to be excluded from the top three in the party, but apparently had not prepared himself for the possibility of being denied one of the top ten slots. I remember the two walking slowly, alone, in silence. I approached them and tried to convince Eban to compete for a seat in the second group of ten. He said that would mean competing against me and that he wouldn't do that.

I told him that if that was the issue, I'd immediately announce that I'd only compete for a spot in the third group of ten. He thanked me and asked me not to do that, saying that even if I did, he would not change his mind. After such a slap in the face from the party members, the situation was clear to him. Suzy was also unwilling to even consider the possibility of Aubrey competing for a lower slot on the Knesset list.

Eban served as deputy prime minister, foreign minister, education minister, and MK, after previously serving as Israel's UN representative and ambassador to the US. Many viewed him as the No. 1 diplomat. All this was still not enough to get him elected.

They got into their car and drove off. Eban never returned to the Labor Party. As I stood and watched the car fade into the distance, I was swept by a wave of sorrow.

1. Prime Minister Menachem Begin (on the left with glasses) and Dr. Eliahu Ben Elisar (in the middle), 1977. Courtesy of the Yad Tabenkin Archive.

2. Egyptian President Anwar Sa'adat and the author, 1979. Courtesy of the Yad Tabenkin Archive.

3. *Left to right*, Yossi Beilin, Ambassador Meir Rosen, Prime Minister Shimon Peres, President George Bush, and Benjamin Netanyahu at the White House, Washington, DC, 1985. Courtesy of the White House.

4. Secretary-General of the United Nations Boutros Boutros-Ghali and the author, 1993. Courtesy of the United Nations.

5. Pope John Paul II and the author, 1993. The Vatican Press Office.

6. Official visit to Oman 1994. Courtesy of the Yad Tabenkin Archive.

7. The author and Yasser Arafat, 1995. Courtesy of the Yad Tabenkin Archive.

8. US Secretary of State Madeleine Albright and the author, 1996. Courtesy of the Yad Tabenkin Archive.

9. Dr. Nabil Shaʻat and the author, 1996. Courtesy of the Yad Tabenkin Archive.

10. Nelson Mandela at President Ezer Weizman's Residence, 1999. Courtesy of the Yad Tabenkin Archive.

11. Secretary-General of the United Nations Kofi Annan and the author, 2000. Courtesy of the Yad Tabenkin Archive.

12. US Attorney General Janet Wood Reno and the author, 2000. Courtesy of the Yad Tabenkin Archive.

13. President Mbeki (in the middle) and Saeb Erekat (on the left with glasses). 2001. Photograph by Daniela Beilin.

14. Richard Gere and the author, 2004. Courtesy of the Yad Tabenkin Archive.

15. President Bill Clinton and the author, 2009. Photograph by Daniela Beilin.

16. Secretary-General of the United Nations António Guterres and the author, 2017. Photograph by Daniela Beilin.

21

A Meeting at a Monastery

NO ONE CAN DENY SHIMON PERES'S DETERMINATION IN CHAMPIONing the economic program that saved Israel's economy in 1985. Nonetheless, he viewed his role as finance minister as a sort of exile or punishment, even if he never said so explicitly. As his deputy at the Finance Ministry, it was important for me to appoint outstanding people to head its various departments. I interviewed people from inside and outside of the ministry and facilitated the appointment of Yoram Gabay as director of state revenues, Moshe Gavish as income tax commissioner, and Eli Yones as accountant general. Peres approved all of the appointments.

During the first weeks at the ministry, I worked late into the evening with top officials from the Capital Markets Division to gain a deeper understanding of the field. I also initiated a forum of senior officials from the ministry and from the Bank of Israel that met weekly to discuss financial topics such interest rates, inflation, the shekel-dollar ratio, government bonds, the possibility of issuing municipal bonds, and more. As expected, serving as deputy finance minister was not my favorite job, but I knew it would allow me a wide range of activity—including work involving political-diplomatic policy, which always remained my keenest interest.

The fact that Peres and I did not see eye to eye on whether to talk with the PLO was already known in political circles. For example, we were both interviewed on the same morning radio program and responded in opposite ways to the decision approved by the Palestinian National Council (PNC), meeting in special session in Algiers in November 1988, to recognize UN Security Council Resolution 242 and declare a Palestinian state. It was the sort of thing that both of us could live with, but not something to be taken for granted.

In the wake of that decision, Faisal Husseini asked Yair Hirschfeld and me to convene a meeting with a number of participants to discuss the possibility of rapprochement between Palestinians and Israelis. The meeting took place on February 15, 1989, at the Notre Dame monastery-hostel in Jerusalem, in an area that had been defined as "no-man's land" between Jordan and Israel before the Six-Day War. Besides Hirschfeld and me, the Israeli participants included part of the team that had worked with Peres since 1984 (Nimrod Novik and Avrum Burg), as well as Ephraim Sneh, a former head of the Civil Administration in the West Bank, Arye Ofri from the Prime Minister's Office, and Boaz Karni, who coordinated the Mashov group. In addition to Husseini, the Palestinian group included Sari Nusseibeh, Hanan Ashrawi, Ziad AbuZayyad, Saman Khouri, and Ghassan Khatib.

The Israeli side hoped that if peace talks were initiated, the Palestinian negotiators would be the group we met with at the monastery. We knew them as high-quality people who were familiar with Israelis, having lived among or alongside them; we believed that the likelihood of reaching a historic resolution was much higher if we negotiated with them rather than with the PLO leadership. The conversation was frank and good, and focused primarily on the question of elections in the West Bank. This question rose to the fore after Shamir proposed that the Palestinians elect a delegation to negotiate with Israel. The Palestinians at the meeting asserted that the PLO would have to be a party in such negotiations, especially in light of the new situation created by the PNC's Algiers decision, and that elections in the West Bank could be held at the end of negotiations but not before them.

However, the Shamir government continued to shun the PLO leadership and insisted that the Palestinians form a delegation exclusively comprised of residents of the occupied territories. Indeed, the formation of a joint Palestinian-Jordanian delegation in the framework of the Madrid Conference in 1981 was in compliance with this Israeli demand. And in 1992, when the Palestinian delegates flew to Tunis after every round of talks with Israel to personally receive instructions from Arafat, Israeli officials were ready to deceive themselves and the public and insist that Israel was not speaking with the PLO.

Some later argued that instead of engaging in the Oslo talks with the PLO, we should have given an opportunity to Palestinians from the territories to reach an agreement with us. Everyone who participated in the conversation at Notre Dame understood that it was not an option. More than once, our Palestinian interlocutors complained about top PLO officials living in swanky hotels and speaking in their name, without really knowing what it meant to live under occupation and what it felt like to wait for hours at a checkpoint. But at the moment of truth, they had to admit that they had no mandate to speak on behalf of the Palestinian people. The PLO held that mandate, whether or not they (or we) were happy about it. Any attempt to circumvent the PLO would be rejected by the Palestinian refugees in the world and by the Arab states, which recognized the PLO in 1974 as the sole representative of the Palestinian people. Husseini and his colleagues told us that they wanted to be part of any Palestinian delegation in the future, but not the delegation itself.

The meeting at Notre Dame drew extensive press coverage, and we came under considerable criticism for having met with PLO-affiliated Palestinians. From our perspective, however, it was one of the most important milestones en route to the Oslo process three years later.

❋❋❋

Jewish immigration (*aliyah*) from the Soviet Union was always a high priority for the governments in which I served. There was a determined core group of Zionists there, many of whom were arrested, tried for the crime of engaging in Zionist activities, and sentenced to long prison terms. The young dissidents became household names in Israel, and the demand to "let my people go" bore their images. The problem was that most of the Soviet Jews (like previous waves of immigrants) were primarily looking to escape their bleak economic condition; they wanted to emigrate to the West, primarily to the US, where they were accorded refugee status, with all the rights that entailed—most importantly, the right to settle in the country. Thus, hundreds of thousands of Jews settled in America. The Israeli leadership, from both the right and left, felt deeply insulted that those Soviet émigrés preferred the US, even when Israel was no longer a poor country and could offer them reasonable conditions.

To bring the émigrés to Israel, two things were needed: direct flights from the Soviet Union to Israel (since most of the émigrés were interested in other destinations and did not continue on to Israel) and termination of the US policy of granting refugee status to Soviet Jews. I had a number of conversations with American leaders in which these points were raised. On one such occasion, I was asked by Assistant Secretary of State Richard Murphy to stay for a private conversation after we concluded an official meeting. He said that he didn't understand why we were making such requests. I explained that it was very difficult for Israel to accept a situation in which the US defines Jews as refugees even though a Jewish state exists as a refuge for them. If the US wanted to open its gates to Jews, that was fine—as long as they weren't classified as refugees. "And in regard to the direct flights, no one will forcibly keep the Soviet emigrants in Israel, but they should be given an opportunity to understand what awaits them there. And if they decide the place doesn't suit them, they can leave, of course," I added.

In preparation for his talks with his Soviet counterparts, the assistant secretary of state asked me to recommend an annual quota of Soviet Jewish emigrants.

I remained silent.

"Twenty thousand?" he asked.

"You won't extract a number from me. No number would be enough for me," I replied.

In October 1989, we learned that dramatic changes would occur within a month. On the one hand, the Soviet Union would allow free emigration for all; on the other hand, the US would limit the number of Jewish immigrants from the Soviet Union to forty-thousand annually and would no longer grant them refugee status.

It was hard to describe my joy. I had already learned to accept that such dreams would never come true in my lifetime. Still, no one knew how the anticipated "opening of the gates" would look in reality. It was impossible to know the real number of Jews in the Soviet Union, how their eligibility for immigration under the Law of Return would be determined, and how many of them would come to Israel.

In any case, I prepared a document on the subject and presented it to the finance minister, Peres. I proposed forming an "absorption cabinet" under his leadership and with the participation of the minister of immigration and absorption, the chair of the Jewish Agency, and other ministers and public figures outside of the government. The plan was for this forum to coordinate the efforts of the Jewish people in Israel and in the Diaspora in preparation for the expected wave of immigrants. Peres agreed that this was the correct course of action, provided that I chair the proposed cabinet in practice—conduct its meetings, facilitate its decision-making, and monitor the implementation of its decisions. I prepared a proposal for him to present to his ministerial colleagues, and he encountered no opposition. A Jewish exodus from the USSR was still viewed as hypothetical, and the proposed absorption cabinet was seen at that stage as just another ministerial committee, one of dozens.

The idea was to estimate the cost of absorbing a large wave of immigration, and we decided to prepare a "realistic" plan for a hundred thousand immigrants, though the number seemed a bit inflated to us. The plan would be used for a fundraising campaign to be conducted in the framework of the United Jewish Appeal (UJA). The various ministries submitted their estimates of the additional resources they would require. The main difficulty was to coordinate between the ministries and to resolve a number of dilemmas: whether to house the new immigrants in absorption centers or directly in rented apartments; whether to provide them an absorption allowance or direct services; whether to disperse the immigrants in Israel according to our preferences, or to accept the fact that they would decide where to live according to their preferences.

The treasury's Budgets Division worked overtime on the "100,000 Plan," while the absorption cabinet had to overcome internal disagreements that sometimes escalated into boycotts and the severance of communication. For example, Simcha Dinitz, the chairman of the Jewish Agency, refused to speak with the immigration and absorption minister, Yitzhak Peretz, and the two institutions were unwilling to cooperate. I've believed for years that the Jewish Agency is an outdated organization that is no longer needed in its current form and should be replaced by another framework representing the Jewish people. On the other hand, it was clear to me that the experience the Jewish Agency had acquired, and the professionalism of its staff made it more efficient than the Ministry of Immigration and Absorption, and that it should play a central role in the absorption effort. In the end, dialogue resumed among all of the entities and the 100,000 Plan was completed and delivered to the UJA, and we conducted grueling discussions on how to absorb the anticipated wave of immigrants.

I was opposed to bringing the new immigrants from the Soviet Union to absorption centers for a period of learning Hebrew. The policy I proposed took into account the fact that the percentage of immigrants with academic degrees was three times higher than the percentage in Israel. Therefore, I contended, we should allow them maximal freedom and trust that they will make every effort to learn Hebrew in order to integrate into the job market. I preferred to provide them with an absorption allowance that they could spend as they choose. I opposed the stance of the immigration and absorption minister, who wanted to disperse the immigrants in rented apartments in the periphery.

I remember some very difficult conversations with mayors. For example, the mayor of Ma'alot, Shlomo Bochbot, insisted that we steer the immigrants to specific locales rather than let them decide on their own. I told him that although I was a fan of the film *Sallah Shabati* (which lampooned Israel's absorption efforts in its early years), I didn't want to recreate the same images of new immigrants dropped off in places where they didn't want to live. My greatest fear was that unsuccessful absorption would convince many potential immigrants to bypass Israel and head to Germany, which was the most available alternative at the time. In the end, the numbers were amazing. In early 1990, about thirty-five thousand immigrants arrived in a single month, about the same number that arrived in all of the Second Aliyah (1904–1914)! It was clear that history was occurring before our eyes, and I asked myself every day how we could minimize our mistakes, knowing that it would be impossible to prevent them completely.

I went everywhere possible. I would sit at night alongside the Interior Ministry's representative at Ben-Gurion Airport and watch the planes land from Russia and the families disembarking. With the assistance of an interpreter, I asked the immigrants where they wanted to go. I quickly realized that their preferences were based on recommendations they had received from immigrants who had arrived in the previous wave, in the early 1970s—whether to join them and whether there were jobs there. For example, when a young man from Moscow was asked where he wanted to bring his family, he replied without hesitation, "Tiberias." I asked him why he preferred Tiberias, and his answer was not surprising: His good friend from his student days had settled there and found work and wrote to him saying that he could also find a job in the city.

I later visited the apartments the immigrants rented. Many of them opted to cram two families, including three generations, into a single apartment in order to save money from the absorption allowance they received. The immigrants told me that it would allow them to spend money on what they really wanted—such as instruction in Russian and Hebrew in private day care facilities. Still, it was hard for me to see new immigrants walking instead of taking a bus so they could save the travel allowance they received. However, when I spoke to them about this, almost all of them said they preferred the freedom to choose how to allocate their allowance rather than being issued a free bus pass.

Since the numbers of immigrants exceeded expectations, we had to double the 100,000 Plan, time after time. But when it came to constructing public housing, I preferred to wait. I asked to check the inventory of vacant apartments in Israel (by examining water bills that showed no water use), assuming that at least some of them could be rented out. We soon learned that there were nearly fifty thousand vacant apartments that could house about two hundred thousand immigrants. I knew that it would not suffice to call upon the owners of those apartments to rent them out, so we decided to dramatically reduce the tax on rental income, with the exception of luxury apartments. Immediately after the Knesset approved this tax cut, thousands of apartments became available for the immigrants.

※※※

The wave of immigration from the Soviet Union was a huge boost for the Zionist dream and a sort of closing of the circle from the mass migration of Russian Jews that began in 1881, in the wake of the murder of Tsar Alexander II; most of the 2.5 million Jewish emigrants in the following decades headed to the United States.

Still, despite everything we did, a small percentage of the immigrants who arrived in the 1990s did not find their place here and eventually resettled in other countries. Even today, many immigrants from the former Soviet Union still carry the scars of migration, in particular those who had to settle for employment that did not utilize their skills and education. Some find it hard to understand why the state doesn't recognize them as Jews, despite their full integration into Israel's Jewish sector. The fact that hundreds of thousands of secular immigrants who see themselves as Jews are not registered as such, and the repeated proposals for making religious conversion fast and efficient, are a sad expression of our weakness.

22

The Dismantlers, Inc.

As deputy finance minister, the issue of customs duties kept me especially busy. I regarded Israel's high customs as one of the main reasons behind the high cost of living, and I knew we could gradually reduce the rates. I realized that exposing Israeli products to competition was like to adversely affect some traditional industries, especially the food industry, but the challenge was to find the right balance point.

In the end, together with the director of state revenues, Yoram Gabay, we prepared the groundwork for an agreement with the European Union on an incremental reduction of customs duties over a period of seven years. The agreement led to lower prices in Israel, and traditional Israeli industries received well-considered and gradual remedies.

In this context, I visited the Ministry of Finance and the Customs Administration in the Netherlands. The visit provided an opportunity for an indirect diplomatic initiative vis-à-vis the PLO, mediated by my friend Max van der Stoel, the former foreign minister. After I explained to him that, unfortunately, Israeli law prohibited contacts with the PLO, he offered to serve as an intermediary and thus eliminate the need for face-to-face meetings. The law did not prohibit this type of process, so I gladly accepted his offer. The formal pretext was Van der Stoel's responsibility for drafting the Dutch Labor Party's platform on the Middle East, in preparation for the party's upcoming convention. I asked Yair Hirschfeld to meet with him first in Paris, and the mediation initiation was scheduled to coincide with my working visit as a guest of my counterpart at the Dutch Ministry of Finance, Henk Koning.

When we arrived at Schiphol Airport in Amsterdam, a military detachment awaited us. It was clear that the Dutch were attributing exaggerated importance to the proximity talks we were slated to conduct. I had yet to inform Peres about the "scheme" behind the innocent meeting on customs issues. I didn't want to implicate him as a partner, and, of course, if he had rejected the initiative, I would not have been able to pursue it.

The meetings at the Dutch Ministry of Finance were interesting and taught me new insights on customs duties, particularly in regard to non-fiscal considerations. However, the more important part was undoubtedly the proximity talks that Van der Stoel orchestrated between two hotels in The Hague. (The Palestinians were staying in a hotel in the city center, and we were in Scheveningen, in the southern part of the city.) Van der Stoel was assisted by Robert Serry, the head of the Middle East Department at the Dutch Ministry of Foreign Affairs. On the Israeli side, it was just Hirschfeld and me. On the Palestinian side, there were three participants: Abdallah Hourani, one of the most senior PLO officials; Afif Safieh, the PLO's representative in Holland; and Hassan Asfour, the Communist Party's man in the PLO. Three years later, Asfour participated in the Oslo talks.

Proximity talks between sides that have never seen each other before are usually very cumbersome. There's something instinctive in wanting to see the other side—their reactions, their conduct, and especially their eyes. We tried to determine whether the Zionist peace camp could find significant common ground with the PLO after its historic decision to adopt Security Council Resolution 242 about six months earlier. The positions the Palestinian group presented were unacceptable to us, but we saw in most of them an opening for understandings based on the readiness of both sides to adopt the two-state solution, while addressing the issues of security, borders, Jerusalem, and the Palestinian refugees.

Our conclusion, and apparently their conclusion too, was that there was something to talk about. I realized that there would eventually be official negotiations between Israel and the PLO, and that Israel would recognize the Palestinian right to self-determination, provided that it would not be at Israel's expense. When I returned to Israel, I updated Peres. He took note of the matter, but it did not seem to make a strong impression on him.

On July 19, Van der Stoel published a document for his party's convention that was based on the proximity talks in The Hague. The document, which did not stir great interest, expressed support for the famous Security Council decisions and the Palestinians' right to self-determination, denounced terrorism and expressed the need for an interim agreement to pave the way toward a permanent solution between the two sides.

However, when news of the proximity talks in The Hague reached Shamir, he quickly dispatched a long letter to Peres, demanding that he fire me. The prime minister explained that the talks, even if they were indirect, violated the prohibition on contacts with the PLO, and that anyone engaging in such contacts was not worthy of serving as a deputy minister. Peres replied in an angry letter that I had not violated the law and that he had no intention of firing me.

There was a momentary frenzy in Israel, with headlines suggesting that the crisis might trigger the government's collapse. Shamir checked whether he himself was authorized to fire me, and soon learned that only a minister was legally empowered to fire his or her deputy. Tzachi Hanegbi, a Likud MK, hurried to fix this "lacuna" by submitting a private member bill that would enable a prime minister to fire deputy ministers. But by the time the legislation was enacted, the Labor Party had already quit the government. The law, incidentally, remains on the books today.

Meanwhile, nothing changed in the diplomatic arena. The Shamir-Rabin axis offered a few proposals concerning municipal elections in the territories, but no one took the proposals very seriously—not in the Arab world and not in the United States. President George H. W. Bush's dynamic secretary of state, James Baker, tried to promote Arab-Israel negotiations and posed a series of questions to Shamir that had been secretly composed by Baker and Foreign Minister Moshe Arens, who had become more pragmatic, as befit his new position. Shamir continued to oppose any notion of an international conference, but it was clear that there would be no talks between Israel and the Palestinians without the umbrella of an international conference.

✳✳✳

At the same time, the Sextet continued to support dismantling the government, regardless of the fact that some of us were serving in it. We spoke a lot in various forums, and Rabin—a master in assigning disparaging nicknames—found a new nickname for Ramon and me—"the Dismantlers, Inc." Peres was not enthusiastic about breaking up the government. (If that happened, Peres would say, we'd have to look for ourselves at the bottom of page 7 in the *Davar* daily.) And it was clear to us that the party establishment would only support this move if it led to the formation of a Labor-led government.

Then Aryeh Deri appeared. He was elected to the Knesset as a Shas representative in 1988 and was appointed minister of interior at the tender age of twenty-nine. He was intelligent, dynamic, determined, confident, and convinced that he was very familiar with the secular world and its interests. His short black beard and the pipe that never left his lips were his trademarks, along with his non-stop uttering of "yes" and "unfortunately."

Less than a year after joining the government, he concluded that it wasn't going anywhere and should be disbanded. Shamir's treatment of the ultra-Orthodox parties during the coalition negotiations may have also been one of the reasons he decided to support a no-confidence vote and the formation of a new government led by Peres.

Deri approached Ramon and me one day and complained that we weren't doing enough to achieve our declared objective of dismantling the unity government. According to Deri, the ultra-Orthodox parties would be willing to help form an alternative government. He urged us not to miss such a historic opportunity, noting that it had already been twelve years since the Labor Party had led the government on its own. We told him he was preaching to the choir and that he needed to speak with the Labor ministers, and primarily Rabin and Peres.

Deri followed our advice and spoke with the Labor ministers. It was a simple calculation: The right-religious bloc included sixty-five MKs, and the center-left bloc had fifty-five MKs; if thirteen ultra-Orthodox MKs moved to the center-left bloc, it would give Peres a stable government of sixty-eight MKs, enabling him to promote a peace process. Deri said that Rabbi Ovadia Yosef, the Shas party's religious authority, supported a peace process and was very angry at Shamir for undermining any chance of progress toward peace. The Labor ministers were persuaded that there was an unprecedented and realistic opportunity here.

In the end, Rabbi Yosef wrote a letter to Shamir in his beautiful and rare handwriting, calling upon the prime minister to pursue every chance of a peace process with the Palestinians, and criticizing Shamir's refusal to respond positively to Baker's proposals. The letter demonstrated that Deri was not only speaking for himself, and the Labor Party decided to back a no-confidence motion.

Shamir, who was closely following the developments, dismissed Peres from his position as finance minister, which led to the resignation of all of the other Labor ministers even before the no-confidence vote. The deputy ministers lost their jobs the moment their respective ministers resigned or were fired.

Though my role at the Finance Ministry was fascinating, especially my work with the absorption cabinet, I felt a genuine sense of relief when the Labor Party decided to leave that faulty government. And I believed we were making history—toppling one government in a no-confidence vote and forming a Labor/ultra-Orthodox government immediately afterwards, a government that would answer Baker's questions affirmatively. However, only the first part transpired.

***

The vote in the Knesset plenum on March 15, 1990, was tension-filled. Until the last moment, many found it hard to believe that a no-confidence vote, which then seemed to be just another meaningless Knesset ritual, would bring down the government. It was a roll-call vote, and all 120 MKs were present in the parliament. Sixty MKs, including all of the center-left-Arab bloc and the ultra-Orthodox MKs from Agudat Yisrael and Degel HaTorah, voted no-confidence in the government, while fifty-five MKs from the right-national religious bloc voted against the motion. The Shas MKs, except for Rabbi Peretz, exited the plenum and didn't vote.

Ostensibly, all we needed for a Knesset majority to approve a new government was for one more MK to join the sixty who had just voted to topple the Shamir government. In practice, this turned out to be much easier said than done. A negotiating team was formed that included Peres and Rabin, Micha Harish (the party's secretary-general at the time), Haim Ramon, me, and other Labor members. I took upon myself the mission of meeting with the ultra-Orthodox religious leadership: the respective rabbinical councils of Shas and of Agudat Yisrael/Degel HaTorah.

The conversations were fascinating, especially with Pinhas Menachem Alter, the son of the Ger Rebbe (who inherited that role several years later), and with the rebbes of the Vizhnitz and Belz Hasidic courts. I also had an interesting meeting with Rabbi Yosef Elyashiv, who reminded me of the story of the Vilna Gaon because of his asceticism, modesty, and short sentences. The strangest meeting was with the aged Rabbi Elazar Menachem Man Schach, in his apartment adjacent to the Ponevezh yeshiva in Bnei Brak. Someone brought me into a large room where he sat with quite a few people. He was drinking leben, part of which trickled into the thicket of his white beard. He wore round reading glasses on his nose, and the words emerged from his mouth slowly and laboriously. He thanked me for being attentive to the ultra-Orthodox in my work at the treasury and compared me to a member of the Polish Sejm (parliament) who was also very helpful to the Jews. I didn't make out the name of the man and wasn't sure it was a compliment.

Rabbi Schach then asked me why people were driving cars on the Sabbath on Nahalat Binyamin Street in Tel Aviv. I tried to understand why he was asking specifically about that street, and I didn't come up with a particularly convincing answer. But then he dozed off. At such moments, you ask yourself whether you should continue talking and pretend you're not aware that your interlocutor is sleeping, or whether you should simply keep silent and wait until someone notices and wakes him. I decided that it would be most respectful to continue speaking, and I said what I had to say. Near the end of the meeting, the rabbi woke up on his own. Someone signaled that my allotted time was up, and I felt the joy a schoolchild experiences when the bell rings at the end of a boring lesson.

I couldn't understand from the meeting whether his small party, comprised of two amiable rabbis (Avraham Ravitz and Moshe Gafni) and inclined toward dovishness (though it was not a salient factor in their political conduct), was with us or against us. On the way out, the rabbi's aide who escorted me said, "It was a very good meeting." I couldn't restrain myself and broke into a broad smile.

"Why are you smiling?" he asked.

I told him that the rabbi was asleep for most of the meeting.

He quickly explained that the rabbi was able to listen attentively to every word while snoozing. I nodded as if persuaded by the profoundness of his response.

In the end, we came to sign a coalition agreement with the Agudat Yisrael MKs, convinced that we had secured a block of sixty MKs. However, one of the Agudat Yisrael MKs (Avraham Verdiger) deceived us, pretending to sign the agreement while not actually signing it. Another Agudat Yisrael MK (Eliezer Mizrahi) did not bother to come to the signing event and did not intend to vote for the Peres government.

Joining ranks with the Labor Party was not a simple matter for the ultra-Orthodox parties. Their voters—according to all of the surveys in the past generation—are the group most hostile to Arabs and to any agreement with them. In addition, a Jewish-democratic state is not a priority for them. Many of them believe that Jews could just as well live in the Land of Israel as a minority, and that the Zionist enterprise violated the "three oaths" the people of Israel swore to God when sent into exile: not to forcibly reclaim the land, not to hasten the time of redemption, and not to rebel against the nations. Democratic principles are not the guiding lights in the education of their youth. They do not see themselves as partners of the center-left, and their dovishness derives from the lack of importance they ascribe to the state and not from a desire to protect its values. The issue of exemption from military service also plays an important role, because the right does not threaten them with changing the status quo, while the center-left demands equality in bearing the military burden.

From the ultra-Orthodox MKs' perspective, playing a key role in transferring power to us would be much more difficult than simply joining a majority that we had already marshaled. Even their loathing of Shamir would not be a sufficient motive. They were under heavy pressure, and they always emphasized to us the pressure of the synagogue; one of the greatest challenges of religious MKs is to constantly face criticism from other worshippers. There was also pressure this time from the Lubavitcher Rebbe, Rabbi Menachem Mendel Schneerson, who instructed the ultra-Orthodox parties not to join a Peres government. Rabbi Schach once remarked, with a sardonic grin, that the religion closest to Judaism is the Chabad-Lubavitch movement. This time, the two ancient rabbis found themselves on the same side.

Chaim Herzog, who as Israel's president at the time was responsible for assigning an MK the task of forming a new government, wrote in his autobiography *Living History* (1996):

> Things got more complicated when, a few hours after my inconclusive meeting with Shas, Chief Rabbi Ovadia Yosef, the Shas mentor, called me and begged me to ignore everything that the Shas delegation had said, imploring me 'in the name of God' to nominate Peres. Late at night, Rabbi Aryeh Deri, the Shas leader and minister of the interior, came and told me that they now favored Shamir. Brushing aside my questions about Rabbi Yosef, he explained that Shas now opted for Shamir. It was difficult to fathom what kind of political negotiations and promises were being brokered behind the scenes. I'm not sure I even *wanted* to fathom them.

Rabbi Schach, who had suddenly recalled the cars traveling on Nahalat Binyamin Street on the Sabbath, decided that he couldn't allow his Degel HaTorah MKs to join us. However, in addition to his small party, he also had "founder's shares" in Shas and steered its course in partnership with Ovadia Yosef. Thus, Deri was torn between his two "giants of the generation." Schach was angry at Deri for promising us to support a Peres-led government without his permission. The young and dynamic man was thrilled when the elderly rabbi offered him a piece of chocolate after he promised not to defy the rabbi's directives. It was hard to contend with such argumentation.

If Peres had decided to submit his proposed government to a vote of confidence on April 12, 1990, and had put Shas to the test, he may have been surprised to see the dominant influence of Ovadia Yosef. However, Peres decided not to take the risk. When he learned that two Agudat Yisrael MKs had fled from the Knesset, and as everyone was waiting in the plenum and in the corridors for him to present his government, he asked the Knesset speaker to postpone the vote. Peres met with President Herzog and received a two-week extension to try to form a government.

Peres always tried to hide his disappointments, and usually failed to do so. This time too. After the meeting with the president, I rode with Peres from Jerusalem to his home in Ramat Aviv, and he invited me up to his apartment. His wife Sonia's face said it all. She seldom accompanied him to official events, but this time had acceded to his request and came to the Knesset—and witnessed his helplessness.

23

When Avrasha Returned Home

ONLY ONE DAY LATER, PERES WAS ALREADY SETTING HIS SIGHTS ON another potential partner for a new government: the Party for the Advancement of the Zionist Idea. I didn't view that Knesset faction as a "natural partner," but we weren't in a position to be choosy. It was founded by former members of the Liberal Party, which had fully merged into the Likud party two years earlier (and some twenty-three years after the Liberal Party formed the Gahal alliance with Begin's right-wing Herut party, providing Gahal a measure of centrist legitimacy). The Party for the Advancement of the Zionist Idea was led by Yitzhak Moda'i and included Avraham Sharir, Pinhas Goldstein, Pesah Grupper, and Yossi Goldberg. The five MKs, feeling powerless and disgruntled in the Likud, submitted a request to form a separate Knesset faction in February 1990, just weeks before the historic no-confidence vote. The Likud did not object to their request, despite its monetary implications, provided that the new faction promised to refrain from voting no-confidence in the tottering Shamir government.

The five MKs promised and kept their promise. But from that moment on, they felt free of any obligation to Shamir. They, like the ultra-Orthodox parties, had plenty of grievances about Shamir's disparaging attitude toward them, and when we put out feelers to them about joining us in forming a government, they didn't reject the idea out of hand. The negotiations with them were not official; they preferred to conduct them in secret. However, we had little success in dodging the media. We arranged to meet at the Dan Hotel, and the cameras were waiting for us at its steps. After a quick consultation, it was decided to move the meeting to my home, and all of the cars headed toward 31 Zeitlin Street, where I was living at the time.

The gathering in my living room included Rabin, Peres, Moda'i, Grupper, and other MKs from both teams. Grupper, the heaviest of the group, landed on the floor when the chair he sat on broke into two pieces.

Orit Shani, who was then my bureau chief, volunteered to help clear the pieces of the broken chair and prepare refreshments. Helena arrived home an hour later and was shocked to find police and security personnel by the entrance; they also rode up the elevator with her as an extra precaution.

The topics we discussed had nothing to do with the government's response to Baker's five questions or anything similar. The allocation of portfolios in the future government was the central issue. It seemed like it would not be difficult to reach agreement.

At this stage, it appeared that we could form a government centered on Labor and other center-left parties, with the ultra-Orthodox parties and the Zionist Idea faction joining us as political "marriages of convenience." The color returned to our faces, but not for long. Moda'i, as usual, was volatile; he changed his opinion several times a day. Clearly, it was not a simple matter for this group to effect a change in power.

Moda'i promised an answer but kept us waiting. Finally, on a bitter Friday morning, while our negotiating team was sitting in his Tel Aviv office, he called to inform us that his answer was "no." Peres took the call in another room, and when he remained there long after the call ended, I went in to check on him. His eyes were red, and he didn't want us to see him like that.

Avraham Sharir, a former minister of justice who had not received a suitable position in the Likud government Shamir formed in 1988 and was thus the most peeved member of the new five-man party, was still interesting in negotiating with us. In the current 60 to 60 stalemate, one vote would be enough to break the tie.

I wasn't involved in the conversations with him, but I was told that he was offered a guaranteed slot on the Labor list for the next Knesset and a ministerial post in the new Peres government and in the government formed after the next Knesset elections, if Labor won. On the other hand, he was under enormous pressure not to join forces with us. This included personal pressure from Shamir, who made an emotional plea—"Avrasha, come home"—in a speech to a Likud forum. That sentence became one of the most familiar political expressions of the decade. And indeed, Avrasha returned home.

After exhausting all options, Peres informed the president that he was unable to form a government. The Likud turned to Labor MK Efraim Gur and offered him a position of deputy minister and membership in the next Knesset. Gur accepted the offer, and Shamir formed a government. In an interview that week with Dan Shilon on Army Radio, Rabin referred to the unsuccessful negotiations as "the stinking maneuver." It was a private settling of accounts with the Labor ministers who had scornfully described his firing of two National Religious Party ministers in the F-15 affair in 1976 as "the brilliant maneuver."

Of course, the moment he chose to use this unparliamentary language, the right-wing camp eagerly pounced on it and turned it into an established fact. The same phenomenon occurred ten years later, when Ehud Barak declared that Israel had no Palestinian partner for peace talks.

The move to topple the national unity government in light of its rejection of Baker's points, and the attempt to form a government with the ultra-Orthodox parties, left the Labor Party outside of the government. The party now prepared for the 1992 Knesset elections, which ultimately crowned Rabin as prime minister. Our group in the Labor Party, the Sextet, was convinced that we would not have returned to power if we had remained in Shamir's government and accepted his policy. The effort in 1990 to form a new government with the ultra-Orthodox parties and the five Zionist Idea MKs was legitimate, and Rabin was part of this effort and, indeed, among its leaders.

✴✴✴

In the end, Shamir formed a coalition that was more right-wing than any previous ruling coalition in Israel. It included professor Yuval Neeman's Tehiya party, Rafael (Raful) Eitan's Tzomet party, and Rehavam Ze'evi's Moledet party. But perhaps precisely because the right held the reins of power on its own, it did two important things: It refrained from retaliating against Iraq in the first Gulf War and agreed to participate in the Madrid Conference.

Two months after the new government was formed, Saddam Hussein invaded Kuwait, contending that he was simply reclaiming part of Iraq's historical territory. Most of the Arab world denounced the Iraqi tyrant. King Hussein, whose caution was his byword, sat on the fence, while Arafat lined up in support of Saddam.

During that period, another meeting of the "Notre Dame group" was supposed to take place. Sari Nusseibeh sat with me at length one morning to jointly draft a summary of understandings, though we realized that the invasion of Kuwait would now overshadow everything else. In our conversation, neither of us tried to defend Arafat's stance. We recognized that there was no point in publishing a joint position paper because the Israeli side would need to denounce the invasion, while the Palestinians could not permit themselves to join in such condemnation, since it would contradict Arafat's position.

At that time, Yossi Sarid published an article critical of the PLO entitled "Don't Look to Me!" and that certainly didn't help our efforts to find a formula for involving the organization in future talks, based on the assessment that it would be impossible to reach an accord without the PLO.

***

As a member of Knesset, along with the demanding parliamentary committee work (Foreign Affairs and Defense Committee; Constitution, Law and Justice Committee; Immigration and Absorption Committee), I devoted my time to organizing a Mashov meeting that would prepare a range of proposals to present at the Labor Party's next convention. The various teams addressed socio-economic questions such as government transfer payments, and political-diplomatic questions such as the conditions for negotiating with the PLO, support for a Palestinian state and revocation of the "Meetings Law" that prohibited contacts with PLO officials. Some party members criticized us for ostensibly creating a "party within a party." But there were also others, including those who held different views from us, who appreciated our systematic approach and our effort to propose solutions and not just complain.

The barrage of Iraqi missiles that fell on Israel certainly did not leave us indifferent. For six weeks, we all went around with gas masks (especially those who remained in the Tel Aviv area), drank a glass of water as advised by IDF Spokesman Nachman Shai and received phone calls from our children in the army who were worried about our situation on the urban warfront. In meetings of the Labor faction, Rabin said that while going down the stairs to the bomb shelter of his home, he reached the conclusion that the public would not easily accept additional wars. He would later cite this realization as one of the reasons for his change of mind about negotiating with the PLO. Some people said that Saddam's attack on Israel demonstrated that missiles were hardly an existential threat to the state. But for quite a few others, the threat of missiles bearing chemical warheads raised the specter of another Holocaust. Some hurried to label Israelis who fled to Eilat "deserters."

Some appreciated the fact that Shamir decided not to strike against the missile batteries in Iraq—because he was wary of jeopardizing the friendship of the US and understood that Israel could cope with the damage caused by the missiles. Others asserted that when a right-wing government lacks the fig leaf of the left, it cannot blame the latter for a policy of restraint and must make cautious decisions on its own. I also thought that the likelihood of retaliation against Saddam would have been higher if we had remained in the government—not because our ministers would have pushed for a response, but because the right would have demanded retaliation and some of our ministers would have joined their call in order to avoid being seen as cowards.

In any case, it was clear that the Arab world viewed Israel as a legitimate target for attack and would continue to do so as long as the conflict with the Palestinians remained unresolved.

24

The "Secret" Sextet in Cairo

THE MASHOV CONVENTION IN MAY 1990 WAS SUMMED UP BY AVRUM Burg in the most succinct way as "the convention of three separations": separation of Israel from the Palestinians, separation of religion from the state, and separation of the Histadrut from the Clalit HMO. The three separations were not of equal importance, but we believed that their implementation could change Israel and save the Labor movement.

After the convention, we went out to the party branches to present our solutions. We received a lot of criticism, as well as considerable support. What was most important to us, however, was the dialogue with the party's activists. We listened to their counterarguments, as well as their complaints about the never-ending feud between Peres and Rabin.

I believed—and stated in the "Peace Process" chapter in the convention platform—that there was a window of opportunity for promoting a diplomatic initiative in the wake of the Gulf War. I proposed recognizing the right of self-determination of the Palestinian people and engaging in talks with any Palestinian entity that recognizes the State of Israel's right to exist, rejects terrorism, and adopts UN Security Council resolutions 242 and 338. I added that in the absence of an agreement, we should consider unilateral steps aimed at a political separation between the two people, preferably starting with a withdrawal from Gaza.

The forty-first president of the United States, George H. W. Bush, did not win a second term, but was one of the best American presidents. He acted correctly in sending the US military into Iraq after Saddam's invasion of Kuwait and acted correctly again by limiting his war objectives. The president won legitimacy from the Arabs and their support for his military campaign. And together with his secretary of state, James Baker, he sought to leverage the victory on the battlefield to facilitate peace between Israel and its neighbors. It seemed like something was about to move.

Egypt also showed interest in helping to broker peace. I traveled to

Cairo for talks with several key figures: the newly appointed foreign minister, Amr Moussa, whom I had met when he was serving as his country's representative at the UN; the minister of state for foreign affairs, professor Boutros Boutros-Ghali; and the president's advisor, my long-time friend Dr. Osama El-Baz. Moussa thought that the new situation after the Gulf War could lead to an international conference, without which there would be no political breakthrough. El-Baz assessed that the extreme weakness of the PLO, the loss of direct monetary support it had previously received from the Gulf states, and the expulsion of Palestinians from Arab states would compel Arafat to accept options that he had rejected in the past—in particular, an interim accord. Boutros-Ghali asked how to best conduct a dialogue with the Israeli peace camp, and I suggested that he invite our group, the Sextet. He had heard about the group and immediately said he would invite us.

A month and a half later, on June 12, 1991, we were received in Cairo as guests of the Egyptian Ministry of Foreign Affairs. As expected, this did not go unnoticed in Israel and raised a stir. The invitation of a specific political group within a party was highly unusual. The accepted practice was to address an invitation to a party, which then decided which party members to send on its behalf. Here, the Egyptians took it upon themselves to decide whom to invite. Dr. Mickey Bar-Zohar was angered by the Egyptian "chutzpah" and sent a complaint to Egypt's ambassador in Israel, Dr. Muhammed Bassiouni.

In any case, the conversations with the Egyptian figures were quite open, especially the long conversation with El-Baz. Those of us who were not accustomed to such conversations were very surprised. I already felt almost like a tour guide in Cairo. But I was still shocked to see the hundreds of thousands of people living in the "City of the Dead"—the huge cemetery where people were born and lived their entire lives until they too were buried there.

Upon our return home, we were not spared criticism. The Likud issued an official statement declaring that our visit was detrimental to the peace process. In addition, we were criticized for appointing ourselves as emissaries to Egypt; our critics emphasized that the government had not sent us and had not asked us to convey messages. In interviews with us, we noted that Israel is a democratic state and that a visit to the only Arab state that has a peace treaty with Israel does not require government approval; the only requirement was an entry visa from the Egyptian Embassy in Israel.

At the same time, the political world was starting to realize that we were a determined group of MKs with clear worldviews, who were not only interested in manning key positions, but also sought to shape the character of the aging party.

Leading up to the party convention, we made efforts to expand the list of our supporters and mobilized Ezer Weizman, Lova Eliav, Uri Gordon (a top Jewish Agency official and a personal friend to most of us), and Uzi Baram, the eternal youngster of the Labor Party. They did not embrace all of Mashov's proposals, and so, for example, we had to delete the term "Palestinian state" from the group's platform. However, the compromises we made to win their support were justified in our view. Our next objective was the party convention.

✳✳✳

The ceremonial opening of the convention, with the red flag alongside the Israeli flag and the singing of *The International*, gave the feeling that we were still somewhere in the 1950s. We demanded that the party put aside the red flag and *The International*—primarily to avoid driving away potential supporters from among the new immigrants from the Soviet Union, who viewed these two symbols as the most blatant expression of the Communist Party, while our party was completely different.

The convention proceeded as usual: the speeches, the self-assurance, the feeling that all we needed to do was to keep doing what we had done so far, and applause at the appropriate moments, when the most simplistic things were said. No innovation, no admission of error. When we left the auditorium and headed to the parking lot, I told Ramon that if the next two days are like the opening session, I don't think I could continue to represent the party in the Knesset. He told me that I had taken the words straight out of his mouth. However, everything changed the following day. Nearly all of our proposals were approved—except for allowing a non-member of the Histadrut to join the Labor Party.

It was a fascinating convention, and the media reported on all of its sessions. The voting was frequent, and the results were close. The sense was that most of the convention delegates were with us. Amir Gilboa described such a feeling in his well-known lyrics: "Suddenly a person gets up in the morning and feels that he's a people."

In regard to the peace process, the convention approved my proposals to delete the disqualification of the PLO as a negotiating partner, to work toward revoking the law preventing all contacts with PLO officials, and to commit a government under our leadership to freeze settlement activity in all of the territories, without distinction between the different regions. Another proposal that was approved was to prevent discrimination against Arab citizens in Israel in awarding child allowances. (This discrimination conditioned the allowances on military service by a family member, and most Arab citizens do not perform military service. At the same time, the great majority of ultra-Orthodox Jews were able to receive allowances without serving in the IDF because they managed to find relatives who had served.)

Avrum Burg delivered a moving speech on the need to separate religion and state. And for the first time in history, this proposal won a majority at the convention. The decision, which would have enabled civil marriages in Israel, made great waves. Both Peres and Rabin were alarmed, fearing that the religious parties would refuse to join a Labor-led coalition in the wake of this groundbreaking decision. They asked us to initiate another discussion of the matter and to present a softer version. In the end, we were sons of the establishment: We ultimately left the decision to Avrum, and he managed to soften it.

Another proposal of ours adopted by the convention was to conduct primaries in the party to elect Labor's Knesset slate and party leader. We believed that this significant democratization would inject new blood into the weary party. In retrospect, the convention definitely marked a fundamental change, and we were recognized there as the most influential political group in the party. By preparing specific material instead of echoing the conventional and hollow slogans, and by operating as a cohesive group, we demonstrated that sometimes a minority can become a majority.

***

Soon afterwards, the Madrid Conference was convened. Its principles were almost a carbon copy of the London Agreement of 1987. The conference was a very dramatic development, and Yitzhak Shamir surprised everyone by agreeing to negotiate in parallel with the Jordanians and Palestinians, the Syrians, and the Lebanese. He later said that he had agreed because he planned to drag out the talks for a decade.

The foreign ministers of the various sides were invited to the conference, but Shamir insisted on personally leading the Israeli delegation, shunting aside his foreign minister, David Levy. Levy was insulted to the depths of his soul and announced that he would not participate in the conference—even though he knew that his deputy, Bibi Netanyahu, whom he despised, would take his place. Ruby Rivlin, who was close to Levy, asked me to try to persuade the foreign minister to travel to Madrid. From my modest place in the opposition, I joined Rivlin and Levy at the Knesset cafeteria, and the three of us sat for a difficult conversation. I told Levy that Shamir would have a podium for proving his extremism and that it was important for Levy's voice to be heard, to express a much more pragmatic Israeli view. Levy spoke bitterly, insisting that it was out of the question for him to participate in the conference in such circumstances, when his honor had been publicly trampled. And indeed, he kept his word and did not travel to Madrid. Netanyahu replaced him and fully exploited the event to build his image as a world leader.

✳✳✳

Rabin challenged Peres for the party's leadership in the wake of the latter's failure to form an alternative government after leading Labor out of the unity government. This time, all members of the party could participate in electing its leader. It was decided that if more than two candidates run, a candidate would need to garner 40 percent of the votes to win. If no candidate reached this threshold, the two leading candidates would face off in a second round of voting.

Besides Rabin and Peres, there were two other candidates competing for the party's leadership: Yisrael Kessar, the secretary-general of the Histadrut, and Ora Namir. Kessar drew most of his support from the Peres camp, while the majority of Namir's voters were affiliated with the Rabin camp. Peres assessed that Rabin would win the first round of voting but fall short of 40 percent and hoped that Kessar's supporters would vote for him in the second round, enabling him to emerge victorious. However, there was no need for a second round: Rabin managed to win slightly more than 40 percent of the votes. Peres was defeated.

I was with Peres when he received the election tally. It was very hard for him to accept. People in the room urged him to telephone Rabin and concede defeat. He waited another long hour before doing so. I feared that it was the end of the Labor Party because in many respects Rabin's positions in the preceding years seemed to closely mirror those of the Likud. His statements during the first intifada, his collaboration with Shamir on plans vis-à-vis the Palestinians that focused solely on the municipal level, and his ongoing opposition to a Palestinian state and to negotiations with the PLO—all led me to fear that even if he became prime minister, he would not agree to take bold steps to promote peace.

The Sextet remained intact during the election campaign for party leader. Each of us helped our preferred candidate, Rabin or Peres, but we didn't quarrel at any stage. At one point, when we learned that Amir Peretz was considering shifting his support from Rabin to Peres, Nissim Zvilil, though he was one of Peres's key advocates, spoke with Peretz in an effort to dissuade him from doing so, arguing that it was in Amir's best political interest to remain in the Rabin camp. Peretz was indeed convinced not to "change horses."

Prior to the primaries for Labor's Knesset candidates, I suggested that we create a new model and run as a group, with each of us speaking on the other's behalf instead of speaking about ourselves. Some of the group agreed, and we ran our campaigns (primarily Ramon, Burg, and me) from a joint headquarters. In the end, we were all elected to realistic slots on the party's list. We were also joined by two more prospective MKs: Nissim Zvili, who was making his first bid for the Knesset, and Yael Dayan, a member of the Mashov group and an icon in her own right. Thus, the Sextet became the Octet, and we reached the peak of our influence. Eli Ben-Menachem and Yona Yahav also joined us.

In the Knesset elections, I was a "foot soldier" of the party's campaign headquarters and traveled almost every evening to a different locale in Israel. In the Jewish sector, I often participated in public debates; and in the Arab sector, I participated in parlor meetings in which I had to explain why the prevailing opinion on the eve of the election—that there was no real difference (*ma feesh farq*) between Labor and Likud—did not reflect the reality. On panels in high schools, where the representatives of the different parties felt like members of a traveling circus, it seemed that Raful's right-wing Tzomet party and Shulamit Aloni's left-wing Meretz party would sweep the elections. In those panels, the two giants at loggerheads—the Likud and Labor—seemed like dinosaurs fighting a hopeless war.

25

Oslo at Tandoori

ON APRIL 29, 1992, IN THE MIDST OF THE ELECTION CAMPAIGN, DOV Randel from the Histadrut labor federation's International Relations Department phoned to inform me that a Norwegian by the name of Terje Rød-Larsen wanted to meet with me. Terje, who headed the Norwegian Confederation of Trade Union's Fafo research institute, invited me to lunch at Tandoori, an Indian restaurant near Dizengoff Square in Tel Aviv. I didn't eat a thing because I can't tolerate spicy food. Instead of eating, I spoke.

In retrospect, it was the start of the Oslo process.

Terje told me that in the past, as a researcher, he had never focused on the Middle East conflict, but had become more knowledgeable in recent years after joining his wife Mona Juul in Cairo, where she worked at the Norwegian Embassy. He had met with various Israel and Palestinian figures and had read a lot of material—including a comprehensive study of health services in Gaza that had pleasantly surprised him. He also told me about his meetings with Faisal Husseini and with the PLO's finance chief, a man named Ahmed Qurei (Abu Ala), who led him to believe that peace with Israel was possible. Larsen proposed that after the elections, assuming that I'd be assigned a role connected to the peace process, I would try to establish an informal channel for meeting with Palestinians in Oslo.

I told him about the conversations and meetings we—Hirschfeld, others, and I—had conducted with Palestinians living in East Jerusalem and the territories, and about proximity talks we held in The Hague. I shared with him my feeling that, unfortunately, we would not be able to reach a peace accord by negotiating only with the residents of the territories, and that I really hoped that my private member bill to lift the ban on meetings with the PLO would be put to a vote again after the elections. Then we could conduct talks with representations of the PLO, following its decision in 1988 to endorse a two-state solution. I told Larsen that the upcoming talks in Washington—with the joint Jordanian-Palestinian delegation led by the hardliner Dr. Haidar Abdel-Shafi, and the Israeli delegation headed by Yitzhak Shamir's faithful cabinet secretary, Eli Rubinstein—would lead nowhere.

I also told him that if we won the elections, we'd be able to identify the real obstacles to reaching agreements with the Palestinians. My assessment was that the PLO would not be satisfied with debriefing Palestinian members of the joint delegation after each session in Washington; Arafat would very likely want to show everyone who's the boss and would not allow his representatives much leeway in Washington.

It is important to note that I had already checked other possibilities for secret talks with the Palestinians (in Britain and in the US), so even if Larsen had not contacted me, I would've pursued a secret channel with them. In any case, I told him that I was thinking about several places where we could conduct discreet conversations. I suggested starting with Husseini, who was a member of the Palestinian team, and then meeting with an official representative of the PLO after amending the Israeli law banning such meetings.

I thanked him for his offer to host talks in Norway, and he noted that the proposal had the blessing of his country's prime minister and foreign minister. I said that I'd want to include my partner on the Palestinian issue, Dr. Yair Hirschfeld, in the talks, and Larsen suggested that the four of us meet during his next visit to Israel: Faisal Husseini, Larsen, Hirschfeld, and me.

I wasn't sure there would be a follow-up to this conversation. But indeed, six weeks later, the four of us met at the American Colony Hotel in Jerusalem. Husseini described the talks in Washington as a dialogue of the deaf and emphasized the need to find a constructive way to bridge the gaps, almost all of which pertained to the authorities of the Palestinian autonomous entity. He liked the idea of conducting a secret channel with us while continuing the official meetings in Washington, but he strongly recommended including PLO officials from Tunisia.

✳✳✳

On June 23, 1992, elections were held in Israel. The Labor Party's victory (forty-four seats in the Knesset) blurred the fact that the right-wing bloc had actually received eleven thousand more votes than the left-wing bloc. It was only thanks to raising the threshold percentage for entering the Knesset that we managed to cobble together a small coalition headed by Yitzhak Rabin. Peres returned to his post as foreign minister, and I resumed my number two role at the ministry—this time in the official capacity of deputy foreign minister, which allowed me to get involved in policymaking. My feeling was that we had received a mandate "by accident"—a fortunate one, from our perspective—and that we must not squander the opportunity to facilitate a historic resolution of the Arab-Israeli conflict. I soon realized, however, that I was again caught in the never-ending Rabin-Peres saga, and that if I acted "by the book," I would be unable to make any progress. For example, when I updated Rabin that I was scheduled to meet with an undersecretary of state in Washington, he instructed me to cancel the meeting, without explaining why. The situation forced me to make some decisions that I hadn't planned when taking on the position.

In the Washington talks, conducted as part of the Madrid process, the situation was gloomy. On Syria, Rabin replaced Yossi Ben-Aharon—the director-general of the Prime Minister's Office under Shamir, who was even more Shamir than Shamir vis-à-vis the Arabs—with professor Itamar Rabinovich, considered Israel's top expert on Syria. Rabinovich was appointed to serve as Israel's ambassador in Washington. In the talks with the joint Jordanian-Palestinian delegation, the prime minister retained the services of Eli Rubinstein, an admirable and fair-minded person with hawkish views. Negotiations with Lebanon, which were conducted by the director-general of the Foreign Ministry at the time, Yossi Hadas, were completely dependent on negotiations with Syria. In practice, there was only movement toward discussions with the Syrians, while the other tracks remained frozen.

The Arab delegations tried to coordinate their moves. Prior to each round of talks in Washington, they met in Damascus under the auspices of Hafez al-Assad, who sought to slow any progress on the Jordanian-Palestinian track. On the other hand, at the end of every session, the Palestinians reported to Arafat in Tunisia, and he too wanted to make sure that progress wasn't too rapid. All of these components combined to ensure that indeed nothing would advance.

Jan Egeland, the deputy of Norwegian Foreign Minister Thorvald Stoltenberg, offered to come to Israel for a working visit, noting that he'd be glad to have a confidential conversation about the Norwegian track Larsen and I had discussed. In September 1992, just a few weeks after starting my new job, Egeland arrived in Israel with Mona Juul (then serving as his bureau chief), her husband Terje Rød-Larsen and several Norwegian Foreign Ministry officials. I hosted a quick meal in his honor at the Dan Hotel in Tel Aviv, where he was staying, and then we went up to his suite to discuss the truly important subject. Hirschfeld and my bureau chief, Shlomo Gur, joined me.

At this stage, the idea was for me to meet with Faisal Husseini with the goal of untangling the knotted situation in which the Washington delegations were mired. None of us knew exactly what we wanted to create, or how to connect any progress made in Oslo with the official delegations in Washington. We only knew that the talks were stuck, and that the experience we had accrued and the connections we had made with the Palestinian leadership in Jerusalem might be beneficial.

Egeland said that the Norwegian channel would indeed be conducted under the auspices of Larsen's Fafo institute, but that the government of Norway would provide the funds, security, and logistics, with Stoltenberg's full backing. So, the only thing missing now was Israel's consent to launch the talks. I promised to promptly raise the matter with Peres, hoping that he'd give the green light or ask Rabin for a green light. I noted that I could not, of course, promise their approval.

It is important to emphasize that nothing thrilling had yet occurred; secret talks are not unprecedented in statecraft. Norway was willing to host such talks, and that was also nothing extraordinary. I was interested in the talks and wanted to present the proposal to my superiors, and there was nothing surprising, out of the ordinary, or exciting about that.

In most of the countless books and articles written about the Oslo process, the story goes like this: Larsen offered Beilin the meeting place; Beilin asked for Peres's approval; Peres asked for Rabin's approval; and thus the channel was launched in which I supposedly led the Israeli delegation.

In reality, it did not happen that way at all.

A few days after Egeland concluded his visit, I grabbed my brown binder labeled in white script "To Discuss with Shimon," and went to Peres's office for our usual brief evening updates. When I entered, I saw that he was not in good spirits and assumed that it again had something to do with Rabin. It soon became clear that my hunch was right. Until that evening, Peres had not told me about their problematic agreement. A few weeks earlier, on the eve of forming the government, it appeared that Rabin preferred a government without Peres. However, his advisors told him that it would lead to an open confrontation and rift in the party, and that it was preferable to keep Peres inside the tent with his wings clipped.

And indeed, his wings were clipped. Rabin told Peres that he'd be appointed foreign minister on the condition that he would not be involved in Israel-US relations or in any of the bilateral negotiations launched at the Madrid Conference. The only peace talks Peres was authorized to manage were the multilateral discussions on refugees, arms control, economic cooperation, water, and the environment. The multilateral track was one of

198 | Chapter 25

the surprising accomplishments of the Madrid Conference. With thirteen Arab states participating—along with the US, Russia, and other countries—these talks led to joint projects (primarily in the field of water desalination) and financial cooperation. But here was the catch: The Arab states had insisted that the talks be held on the subministerial level, so Peres could not take the reins of this project, and I was assigned the role.

So Peres lost out on both ends and remained empty-handed.

Peres clearly did not feel comfortable telling me about his demeaning agreement with Rabin, but apparently felt compelled that evening to tell me about his meeting with Rabin earlier in the day. He had reported to the prime minister, almost incidentally, that he had scheduled a meeting with Faisal Husseini. Rabin demanded that he immediately cancel the meeting, insisting that it violated their agreement. Until that moment, Peres had thought that Rabin did not want him to be involved in formal negotiations but had never imagined that Rabin would also prevent him from meeting with Arab political leaders.

Peres apparently still tried to clarify or apologize to Rabin. He argued that he would not be intervening in the talks between Israel and the Palestinians by meeting with Husseini, an important East Jerusalem leader with whom he converses from time to time, and nothing beyond that. "Rabin turned red and pounded on the table. 'If you meet with him, you'll no longer be foreign minister!'" Peres quoted him. At that moment, I faced the most important question of my public life. If I updated Peres, I would have to drop the idea—and Oslo would never have seen the light of day. Peres would not have even checked with Rabin about the possibility of creating the channel. At that moment, I decided to frame the meeting in Oslo as a sort of seminar, like the occasional conversations between unofficial Israeli figures and Palestinians from the territories; I decided that I myself would not participate in the talks. My intention was to test the effectiveness of the channel and to inform Peres only if and when the two sides were ready to agree on an initial position paper.

But I also realized something else at that moment, something that I only came to fully understand on my way home to Tel Aviv: If I don't travel to Oslo, neither will Husseini. And whoever travels in his place will undoubtedly be a PLO official. So, if we don't amend the law prohibiting meetings with PLO members, we won't be able to take advantage of the Norwegian offer to host the talks.

I immediately updated Hirschfeld about the sharp turn in the plot, leaving out the embarrassing details. I told him that I didn't plan to travel to Oslo and that I was assigning him the job. Now, we only needed to find the right partner. The next day, I informed Larsen that I wouldn't be coming to Oslo for the talks with the Palestinians, and that we'd probably need to find a replacement for Husseini too. I assured him that I'd stand behind Yair and would still be closely involved, even if not personally present. He wasn't pleased.

The next mission was to rapidly repeal the so-called "Meetings Law." The Labor Party ministers were ostensibly committed to this after a resolution to this effect was approved by the party convention in 1991. The lifting of the ban on meeting with PLO members was also stipulated in the coalition agreement between Labor and Meretz. Nonetheless, Rabin was in no hurry to do so. It was clear to me that a political threat would be more effective than any attempt at political persuasion. I spoke with the leaders of Meretz, who served as ministers in Rabin's government, and—without mentioning the Oslo option—prodded them to insist on implementation of this section of the agreement. They were glad to oblige.

Rabin told them that other matters were more urgent. But from their perspective, they argued, it was a commitment they had made to their voters. On December 2, 1992, the Knesset approved a first reading of legislation overturning the prohibition. Rabin emphasized that lifting the ban did not signal Israel's readiness to negotiate with the PLO, but only meant that it was no longer a criminal offense to meet with members of the organization.

And so, a significant first obstacle was cleared from the path, but it was certainly not the last one.

26

Better If Arafat Is Here, and Not in Tunisia

ONE OF THE ISSUES THAT INITIALLY DELAYED ISRAELI-PALESTINIAN dialogue after the formation of the Rabin government was the continued, obsessive debate in Israel over which Palestinians should be allowed at the negotiating table—at both the bilateral and multilateral levels. The Palestinians wanted to include people identified with the PLO in their delegations. We, the Rabin government, behaved as if Shamir were still prime minister, canceling or postponing meetings whenever IDF Military Intelligence informed us that a Palestinian interlocutor was not an innocent professor at a certain British university, but actually a member of an organization that was connected in some way to the PLO. I had a hard time understanding this obduracy yet hoped (and was right) that the moment the Meetings Law was repealed, this foolish practice would cease and such Palestinian interlocuters would be rendered "kosher." We'd then be able to concentrate on the issues in dispute, rather than waste time on pointless matters that lead us nowhere.

Until this happened, some of the PLO-affiliated committee chairs on the Palestinian side did not participate in the meetings that followed the Madrid Conference. Instead, they sent instructions to the members of their delegation from a nearby hotel in the city where the talks were being held. The person in charge of the Palestinian delegation on the steering committee of the multilateral talks (whose official chairman was Faisal Husseini) was Abu Ala.

On December 4, 1992, two days after we managed to amend the Meetings Law in a first reading (by a single vote, 37–36), the steering committee of the multilateral talks met at the famous Guildhall building in London. The meeting with Saudis, Omanis, and Bahrainis, not to mention Egyptians and Jordanians, was special and fascinating.

The American assistant secretary of state, Edward Djerejian, chaired the meeting, together with his deputy, Daniel Kurtzer. (Kurtzer and I were friends since his days at the US Embassy in Israel.) Terje Rød-Larsen was also in London for a meeting of European trade union representatives. Hanan Ashrawi, who had recommended Abu Ala to Hirschfeld as a negotiating partner, informed Terje that Abu Ala would be in London around December 4, and Terje managed to arrange a meeting between Abu Ala and Hirschfeld. And so it happened that most of the key players in the Oslo process, which had begun to take form, found themselves that Friday in London.

When the plenum session of the steering committee was over, Djerejian and Kurtzer accompanied me to my hotel room. They were both hungry and ordered sandwiches. The plan was for us to summarize the morning's discussion and to brainstorm about the best way to proceed. But I steered the discussion in another direction. I told them that, in my opinion, the talks in Washington were leading nowhere, and that I wasn't sure whether the lack of progress with the Palestinians stemmed from Israeli ideological constraints or from the fact that the PLO wasn't interested in seeing the talks succeed. In any case, I continued, if we don't take the bull by the horns and speak with the PLO, there will be no progress. Therefore, I plan to conduct a secret channel with the PLO after we put the Meetings Law behind us, I confided to the two American diplomats. I informed them that there was a Norwegian option, but that I'd prefer to conduct the channel in the US, and that I hadn't yet shared this information with Peres or Rabin "because it was too early." In any case, I asked them to keep this information confidential.

They both nearly jumped from their chairs. They thought it was a good idea, and even an essential one, but told me that the legal situation in the US "lags" behind that of Israel, and that such a move would still be considered illegal there. Nonetheless, they encouraged me to pursue the idea and said they'd be happy to hear if it develops into something.

Later, Hirschfeld phoned and asked to meet with me at the hotel on an important matter. I didn't understand what he was doing in London and how he knew my whereabouts. He got straight to the point and informed me that he had met in the morning with Abu Ala, the PLO's finance chief. Larsen organized the meeting and also participated in it. Yair explained that he didn't want to tell me about it in advance so that I wouldn't make the mistake of officially approving the meeting. Instead, he took the risk upon himself.

Yair said that the conversation was excellent and that Abu Ala had expressed willingness in principle to reach several significant agreements with us, without wasting time on formalities or demands of marginal importance. Yair asked me whether the repeal of the Meetings Law would pass its second and third readings by January 20, when the first meeting in Norway was scheduled. I promised to do my utmost to make this happen and noted that otherwise we'd have to postpone the initial meeting. I thanked Hirschfeld for meeting Abu Ala that morning "behind my back" and told him about my conversation with the American diplomats. Since I knew he was also friends with Kurtzer, I encouraged him to also speak with him on this matter.

It was important for me to ensure that there were officials on the American side who were aware of the initiative, but without requesting an official "green light" from them and without a formal need to update or report. Throughout the year, in meetings in Washington or other places in the world, I updated Kurtzer and Aaron David Miller, who was appointed in 1993 to serve as Deputy Special Middle East Coordinator. I offered these reports when we met in circumstances unrelated to the Oslo process; they did not contact me to request updates.

Meanwhile, we prepared for the second and third readings of the bill to repeal the Meetings Law. However, on December 17, the Rabin government made one of its worst mistakes: Rabin, who was serving as both prime minister and defense minister, ordered the arrest of about twelve hundred Hamas and Islamic Jihad militants, with the intention of expelling several hundred of them to Lebanon. The action was taken in response to the abduction and murder of an Israeli border policeman, Nissim Toledano, several days earlier. Rabin checked the matter with senior Justice Ministry officials, who argued that Israel's High Court of Justice would not condone such expulsion—not necessarily because it violated international law, but rather because Israeli judicial rulings allowed expulsion only in the case of individuals convicted of committing a criminal offense. One way or the other, collective expulsion was impossible.

In a lapse of judgment, the attorney general and justice minister did not render the move illegal, and no effort was made to ensure that Lebanon would agree to take in the expelled militants. On the morning of December 16, the government debated the expulsion. Rabin presented the move as if Israel's security was almost entirely dependent on it, and the ministers found it hard to oppose him. In the end, even the Meretz ministers voted for the expulsion. I was regularly invited to cabinet meetings but didn't participate in meetings of the government plenum. Thus, it was only from the media that I learned about the decision to expel 415 Hamas militants to a barren hill in Lebanon. Peres was out of the country at the time.

The Hamas men were taken in buses to the north, without even being allowed to inform their families about the expulsion. But they did manage to submit a petition to the High Court, whose president, Meir Shamgar, scheduled an urgent hearing for early the next morning, December 17, before a panel of seven justices. The hearing lasted fourteen hours. To the surprise of many, the court ultimately decided to allow the mass expulsion. Aharon Barak (who later succeeded Shamgar as president) admitted in retrospect that his support for the expulsion was one of his mistakes as a Supreme Court justice. Meanwhile, Lebanon absolutely refused to take in the Hamas men, and Israel had to build a camp for them in Marj a-Zuhour—sovereign Lebanese territory that was then part of Israel's security zone.

I refused to appear on CNN and other networks to explain what was impossible to explain. When I saw Dan Meridor the next day at the Knesset, he said to me, "Only the Mapainiks [Mapai was the precursor of the Labor Party] are capable of doing something so convoluted and blatant as this." According to Meridor, IDF Chief of Staff Ehud Barak had proposed this move several times to Shamir, who rejected the idea. Meridor was convinced that Barak had suggested it again to Rabin, who was looking for an unconventional way to respond to the abduction and murder and had adopted this folly.

The world, as expected, seethed over the Israeli response, but not over the acts that had precipitated it. Photos of hundreds of Hamas men freezing on the hill on Christmas Eve reached every TV set. Rabin announced that the expulsion would be for two years only, and then, under American pressure, shortened it to one year. The Hamas militants, meanwhile, turned that year into the most important "boot camp" of their lives.

I spoke with the minister of education and culture, Shulamit Aloni, who admitted to me that she had made a mistake and had thought the number of expellees would be much smaller. She and her Meretz colleagues came under fierce criticism in left-wing circles, and I urged her to take remedial action and demand that Rabin expedite the second and third readings of the Meetings Law repeal. And that's what she did. Rabin, who understood the predicament the Meretz ministers were in after voting for the expulsion, acceded to her request.

The Hamas militants could never have imagined that their expulsion enabled the repeal of the law that would have prevented us from meeting in Oslo at the scheduled date.

✳✳✳

Before the meeting on January 20, Hirschfeld introduced me to Ron Pundak, a former student of his who wrote a PhD dissertation on Jordan.

Hirschfeld wanted Ron to join him at the Oslo meetings (actually, most of the meetings were held in Sarpsborg) and asked for my approval. My conversation with Ron was short. I knew his father well: Nahum Pundak was my colleague as a journalist for the *Davar Hashavua* weekly and divided his time between Tel Aviv and Copenhagen, where he edited the prestigious daily *Politiken*. Ron's brother was killed in the Yom Kippur War, and Ron enlisted soon afterwards, served as an intelligence officer, and later worked for several years in the Prime Minister's Office.

I thought that Ron was an excellent choice, and we drew up the policy guidelines for the impending meeting in Norway. The objective was to identify the gaps between the two sides and check the PLO's flexibility vis-à-vis each of the disagreements in order to later sit together and see whether we could offer proposals to bridge those gaps. Two people at the Foreign Ministry were in the know: my advisor and bureau chief, Shlomo Gur, and my office manager, Orit Shani. The Meetings Law was repealed in second and third readings at almost the last moment from our perspective, and Yair and Ron could now fly to Oslo and become the first Israelis to take advantage of the law's repeal.

It was a tense weekend. We feared that a single problematic statement by Abu Ala might be enough to kill the process before it even got started—for example, if he declared that a peace accord would only be possible if Israel agreed to the full implementation of the right of return for every Palestinian who so desires. Hirschfeld called me several times during the weekend. He reported that there was a friendly atmosphere and that the Palestinians had come with ideas. He also praised the generous hospitality of the Norwegian hosts and noted that they strictly avoided entering the room where the two sides were conducting their conversations. Yair informed me that Abu Ala had brought with him Hassan Asfour, a member of the PLO delegation in the proximity talks in The Hague two and a half years earlier, and Maher al-Kurd, an economist who would later be appointed deputy economics minister in the Palestinian Authority. It was clear from Hirschfeld's updates that the initiative was not a failure and that the talks would continue.

Helena asked me what all my conversations with Yair were about. I couldn't tell her, so I just responded, "He's doing sacred work."

Immediately upon their return from Norway, Ron and Yair came to my office to update me. The great surprise was the proposal that Abu Ala presented, which hadn't been discussed in the Washington talks: Gaza first.

The idea of transferring authorities to the Palestinians in Gaza and later extending autonomy to the West Bank was a central feature in various Israeli proposals over the years. In a television interview in 1991, I proposed recognizing a Palestinian state in Gaza as a first stage in a comprehensive accord between the two peoples. Such proposals were not enthusiastically received by either side. There was opposition in Israel to the very notion of a Palestinian state, even if limited initially to Gaza. On the Palestinian side, there was a fear that "Gaza First" would become "Gaza Last," and that Israel would sacrifice Gaza in order to strengthen its hold on the West Bank.

The fact that the Palestinians themselves brought up the idea demonstrated that they were devoting serious thought to the issues and realized that without softening some of their positions, it would be impossible to reach an agreement. Clearly, the elephant in the room was the question of who stood behind the people in that room. Abu Ala said that a small group of senior PLO leaders, including Arafat, were in on the secret. Yair was much more vague but noted that he was close to me. Later, from reading books written by the participants in the talks, it was clear that once Abu Ala understood that I was involved, he concluded that Peres was also in the picture, and hence Rabin too. He had no way of imagining the real muddle on the Israeli side

※※※

I had originally thought that we'd use the secret channel to resolve the problems hampering the main channel of talks in Washington. However, after the report on the first meeting in Norway, it became clear that the secret channel would focus on reaching agreements on a new model. The model would grant extensive autonomy to the Gaza Strip under an international or other framework, laying the groundwork for transferring powers that would later be exercised in the West Bank too.

I asked Yair and Ron to shift into a new "mode" of work and to prepare a statement of principles addressing both the surprising Palestinian proposal and the prospects for peace, without going into details on solutions for each of the fundamental issues. We had to have the paper ready in time for the second meeting, scheduled for February 11. The preparatory work, primarily by Yair, was completed and approved on the eve of the second meeting.

When the two returned from Norway after the second meeting, they came straight to me with the good news: The Palestinians had agreed to the principles laid out in our paper and the changes they proposed were very minor. We now had a draft of a statement of principles that centered on a proposal to establish a temporary Palestinian entity in Gaza.

Nonetheless, it seemed that the negotiations had finished too quickly. In order to move forward, we needed the approval of the highest echelon, which was still in the dark about the talks in Norway. A third meeting was set for March 21, and I had until then to obtain a green light to continue in this channel and thresh out the details of an accord based on the statement of principles. I thought the best way to raise the topic with Peres would be to hand him the draft and inform him that Yair and Ron had reached agreement with the PLO team, and that with his consent, we'd continue on this path of negotiations with the PLO—this time under his auspices. I presented it as one of the routine topics on our agenda. He took the document and placed it in his briefcase.

Meanwhile, the clock was ticking toward the next meeting. Yair asked if I had spoken with Peres and whether he had read the draft. I suggested that we wait patiently. Two or three days later, I asked Peres whether he had had a chance to read the paper I had given him. He said that he was busy with a lot of other things and promised to read it by the next evening and give me his response. Peres indeed read the document and was generally impressed, though critical of some parts of it. He asked me to summon Yair and Ron and said he would have to present the subject to Rabin after hearing them. I felt relieved that Peres was now in the picture. In the meeting with Yair and Ron, he asked a lot of questions about the nature of the channel and how it was being conducted, expressed criticism about several points and voiced appreciation regarding other points. It was clear that the surprise we had presented, which posed a challenge for Peres vis-à-vis Rabin, did not displease the foreign minister.

※※※

Rabin and Peres met alone for an hour each week to update each other, without recording any notes from the meeting because of Rabin's constant fear of leaks. Their next meeting was scheduled for the following day. Peres told me that he'd present the paper to him and ask for his approval to continue the talks in Norway. But how would he do it? I asked myself. Surely, the moment Peres tells him about this channel, Rabin will call him an "indefatigable schemer" [as he described Peres in his autobiography]— and, ostensibly, this time he'd be quite right. After all, Peres had agreed to serve as a foreign minister with clipped wings. Rabin wouldn't believe for a moment that Peres wasn't the driving force behind the secret channel, conceptualizing it and instructing me to implement it. Therefore, I believed there was no real chance of winning Rabin's approval.

As the two met, I was already coming to terms with the demise of the

Oslo channel. But when I saw Peres's face after the meeting, I immediately realized that he had achieved his objective. There was no need for him to say a word, but he said, "Yitzhak approves." I was curious, but I didn't ask him for an account of exactly what he had told Rabin and what the prime minister had said in response. I assumed that he had taken the same tactic I had applied: keeping a low profile. Something like: "Two of Yossi's academic friends met with a few PLO officials, with Arafat's backing, and there's apparently a chance of advancing the idea of 'Gaza first' with them. What do you think?"

In fact, Rabin read the paper and said there was still a lot of work to do but realized that it was an opportunity. He didn't want to break his main campaign promise: to reach an agreement with the Palestinians within six to nine months. Rabin was facing severe criticism over the sloppy and ill-advised expulsion of the Hamas men, along with the fact that no negotiations were underway with the Palestinians. (The talks in Washington were held through the end of 1992 but came to a halt after the collective expulsion.) This criticism made an impact. Over nine months had passed since becoming prime minister, and he could not point to any progress on the diplomatic front. It's reasonable to assume that Rabin was angry at Peres and didn't believe that I had kept Peres in the dark about the Oslo channel, but the prime minister's pragmatism prevailed.

In a meeting prior to the third round of talks in Norway, Peres suggested that Arafat could come to live in Gaza after the two sides reach an accord. He asked Yair and Ron to raise this option with the Palestinians, and the two were thrilled to receive this bargaining chip. I personally wasn't sure this possibility should be discussed at this stage, but kept my mouth shut at the meeting and expressed my reservations to Peres only after it was adjourned. He explained that he preferred Arafat close at hand rather than in Tunisia, and quoted what President Johnson reputedly said about FBI Director J. Edgar Hoover: "It's probably better to have him inside the tent pissing out, than outside the tent pissing in."

In later April, prior to the fourth round of Oslo talks, Rabin asked us to tell the Palestinians that we would only come to Norway if the official Palestinian delegation returned to the negotiating table in Washington. (As noted, the Palestinians had pulled out of the talks in the wake of the expulsion of Hamas militants to Lebanon.) Rabin was concerned, and rightly so from his perspective, that the Oslo channel had become more important to the PLO than the Washington channel. He wanted to restart the official negotiations, primarily to maintain good relations with the American administration. The suspension of the talks in Washington was a threat from his perspective. In addition, he wanted to test his new partners and use them to sustain the Madrid process.

We conveyed the Israeli demand and proved the importance of our channel: The PLO decided to immediately resume the discussions in Washington, and Rabin realized that the Oslo channel was much more than an interesting academic seminar.

In the following months, we occasionally found ourselves making requests in Oslo and receiving answers in Washington. One of these was Rabin's almost inconceivable request to replace the head of the official Palestinian delegation, Dr. Abdel-Shafi, with Faisal Husseini. (To our surprise, we promptly received an affirmative response.) But the quarrels that continued to characterize the Washington talks were not a feature of the Oslo channel. It's not that we agreed on every issue. On the contrary, there were crises and even exits and tears, but there was ultimately a shared desire to reach solutions.

The Norwegian involvement was upgraded when the defense minister, Johan Holst, moved to the Foreign Ministry to replace Thorvald Stoltenberg, who was assigned by the UN to mediate the crisis in the former Yugoslavia. I already knew Holst from his previous role. His wife Marianne Heiberg was a senior researcher at the Fafo institute and knew the Middle East well. While Stoltenberg went only as far as approving the secret process, Holst made it the main focus of his short term, which ended with his surprising death in January 1994.

Holst was personally involved in the contacts and did not shy away from mediating at a later stage, during the negotiations on mutual recognition between Israel and the PLO. We kept in close contact, and I received an urgent call from him one Friday afternoon as he was about to enter a meeting with the US secretary of state, Warren Christopher. Holst asked me what he could tell him about the Oslo channel. I replied that the best way to convey information to the Americans while also preventing their unnecessary involvement was to use intonation that downplays the importance of the subject. I suggested that he refrain from speaking about the Norwegian backchannel at the beginning of the conversation, unless Christopher raised the subject, and perhaps mention near the end of the meeting that the Israelis and Palestinians were engaged in an informal, seminar-like initiative in Norway.

After the meeting, Holst called and informed me that the mission was accomplished and that Christopher did not ask probing questions.

27

"What If We Propose a Permanent Accord Straightaway?"

Peres really wanted to get involved in the nitty-gritty of negotiations and lead the Israeli delegation vis-à-vis Abu Ala. He felt that his exclusion from the bilateral negotiations was over, and the direct involvement of Holst encouraged him to raise the issue with Rabin. But Rabin still refused to grant Peres this role, perhaps fearing that the latter would "steal the show" from him. In any case, Rabin told Peres that it was important to keep a low profile on this channel. If it became known that Peres himself was involved in Oslo, the Americans and the delegations in Washington would realize that the Israeli government attributed greater importance to the talks with the PLO than to the official negotiations that sprung from the Madrid Conference.

In the end, it was agreed that the new director-general of the Foreign Ministry, Uri Savir, would lead the delegation in Norway. Savir, Peres's confidant, a brilliant man with a rare sense of humor, was an experienced diplomat and committed to peace. Hirschfeld and Pundak were the other members of the delegation. On the one hand, the decision to appoint Savir was a milestone that made the talks official. On the other hand, Israel's top political echelon was still not involved.

I immediately gave Uri a crash course on the Oslo story. He was surprised that this process had been conducted so close to him without his knowledge, and heaped praise on the initiative. He led the delegation to Norway on May 20 and quickly developed a special chemistry with Abu Ala. In the May meetings, Abu Ala raised the Palestinian need to add the Jericho area to the self-governing entity in the Gaza Strip, primarily because of Jericho's proximity to the Allenby Bridge. The Israelis were surprised by the new demand but did not reject it out of hand and promised to look into it.

Uri was very impressed by what he saw in Oslo and shared his sentiments with me upon his return. He suggested adding an Israeli international law expert to the team. I had already spoken with Joel Singer, whom I had met when he led the IDF's International Law Department and was involved in consultations on Taba in 1986. [Taba, in the northern Sinai, was then a bone of contention between Israel and Egypt. It was eventually awarded to Egypt in arbitration.] He was now working at a law firm in Washington. In coordination with Shlomo Gur, I asked Singer to serve as the Foreign Ministry's legal advisor, and he agreed. His addition to the delegation was approved by Rabin and Peres.

There was now a significant number of people who knew about the secret channel We felt that the work was becoming more methodical and that we were nearing the conclusive stage when difficult decisions would be required—on both sides. Rabin convened the "Forum of Four" that included him, Peres, Joel, and me. The forum met once or twice a week, usually at the Ministry of Defense in Tel Aviv, often late in the afternoon on Friday. We also met sometimes at the Prime Minister's Residence at 3 Balfour Street in Jerusalem, at his office in the government complex in Jerusalem or, on Saturdays, at the Dan Accadia Hotel in Herzliya, where Yitzhak and Leah were staying while their home in Ramat Aviv was under renovation. This gave Rabin an opportunity to play tennis.

Rabin did not want to involve anyone who did not have "a need to know." His bureau chief, director-general, and military secretary all apparently knew something was afoot but were excluded from the meetings. When I suggested at one point that he include his military secretary in the forum, he expressed concern about leaks.

At the meetings, Joel would summarize the progress achieved in the latest round of talks in Oslo and present the dilemmas we'd face in the next round. We all contributed comments about the negotiations conducted during the past week and offered guidance for the team's work in the coming week. Rabin would summarize the meetings, and the absence of someone from his bureau was salient. At one meeting, Joel reported that he had received a positive response from Abu Ala on a particular issue that Rabin had raised. Rabin was furious and turned red. He shouted at Joel, insisting that he had never broached that subject with him and that Joel had acted without his authorization in discussing it with the Palestinians. Their positive response placed him in a bind, he raged.

Joel was not intimidated and replied, "Prime minister, I have to tell you that the subject came up in the previous meeting and you asked me to speak with Abu Ala about it. If you hadn't asked me to do so, I wouldn't have spoken with him."

Rabin was further enraged by Joel's "chutzpah." Peres apparently did not recall the discussion about this issue in the previous meeting, and I felt the need to defend Joel. I told Rabin that I clearly remembered the discussion that took place the previous week, and that he had indeed asked Joel to raise the issue with Abu Ala. At this stage, Rabin pulled out a briefcase I had never seen before, angrily opened it, and started rummaging through a pile of papers.

I thought this would only make it harder to get to the truth, but lo and behold, he found what he was looking for, pulled out a piece of paper and read it. Then he laconically said, "Okay, you're right." That was it. Without any apology over his anger or anything else. As if to say, "Joel is a colonel, Yossi a sergeant major and Shimon never served in the army at all, only in the Ministry of Defense. I'm the IDF chief of staff and I have a right to make mistakes. I have no obligation to apologize." At least that's how Joel and I summed up the episode after we left the room.

Nonetheless, these regular meetings created a sort of shared responsibility and a certain level of candor. Often, when Peres and Joel were abroad, the forum was only Rabin and me. In one of these private conversations, I told Rabin that I sensed that the stars were aligning: the Gulf War, which had weakened Arafat, forged an Arab-Western coalition and created an American need to advance the Middle East peace process without entailing tensions with the dissolved Soviet Union; his election victory; and the fact that we finally had a Palestinian partner willing to compromise and accept an interim solution—despite the Palestinians' fears since 1978 that any interim accord would be a trap for them. This alignment of the stars, I added, would not last long, and though it would be preferable to do more preparatory work, we mustn't miss this opportunity. I believed that the framework established in Oslo could allow us to go beyond the Camp David formula of five years of autonomy prior to a permanent accord. I contended that it was in Israel's interest to reach a permanent accord as soon as possible, an accord that would take into account our red lines and those of the Palestinians.

Rabin thought otherwise. His answer had two parts: First, it was important to him to continue along the road paved by the right. In his eyes, the 1978 Camp David Framework for Peace in the Middle East agreement between Begin and Sadat accorded him legitimacy in the face of anticipated right-wing criticism. He also asked us to use the terminology from that agreement ("redeployment" instead of "withdrawal," a "strong local police" on the Palestinian side, etc.); he was convinced that by using the same lexicon we could neutralize the opposition. Second, Rabin argued that if we embarked on permanent status negotiations and reached an impasse, the Palestinians would be unwilling to return to discussions on an interim accord, fearing that the gaps between the two sides were unbridgeable. On the other hand, if the talks on an interim accord failed, it would not preclude returning to negotiations later on.

In parallel to exploring the possibility of leaping with Rabin straight to a permanent accord, I sought to gauge the Palestinians' readiness to pursue this route. I asked Husseini about this when we met in Moscow in May 1993 at a meeting of the steering committee for the multilateral talks. He replied that he didn't think the Palestinian side was ready for that yet. It would be better to establish political institutions first ("like you had before '48") and use them to build a state.

"And what would you do if we proposed foregoing the interim accord and proceeding straight to a permanent accord?" I asked.

"In that case, we couldn't turn you down," he replied.

✷✷✷

When the Oslo process started, Faisal Husseini knew nothing about it. The Palestinian group that conducted the process, under Arafat's guidance, maintained such a high level of secrecy that even Hanan Ashrawi, who had recommended to Yair that he speak with Abu Ala, was also in the dark about the backchannel. Faisal also didn't know that his sudden appointment to head the Palestinian delegation in the Washington talks was Rabin's initiative, conveyed via our conversations in Norway.

During the period of talks in Norway, I met a number of times with Faisal and said nothing about Oslo. When we met in Moscow in May 1993, I asked him what he thought about establishing a Palestinian-Jordanian confederation, despite King Hussein's relinquishment of the West Bank. Faisal looked at me and asked whether I was serious. I was very serious.

"The only confederation the Palestinians need is with Israel," he replied. "The hostility toward Israel among Palestinians does not contradict their admiration for what the Jews have accomplished here. They view Israel as an object of emulation and understand that when peace comes, they'll be able to work with Jews in many fields, including the field of security. A confederation of two impoverished states wouldn't contribute a thing to either of them."

That conversation planted the roots of the Holy Land Confederation idea, which I developed later. I still think a confederation could help solve many difficulties, including the problem of Jewish settlers in the West Bank. A confederation would enable the settlers living east of the future border to remain in their homes as permanent residents of the Palestinian state and as citizens of Israel. An equal number of Palestinians would be allowed to settle in Israel as permanent residents and as citizens of Palestine.

In any case, it wasn't easy to manage the parallel negotiations in Washington and in Oslo. The breaking point occurred in June, when Rabin decided to send a letter from his office to the foreign minister's office, demanding a halt to the Oslo talks because they were allegedly hampering the negotiations in Washington. This demand hit us totally out of the blue, and we feared that the secret process had come to an end, along with all of the progress achieved in it. The letter was sent on the eve of another round of meetings in Oslo and caused great consternation, especially in light of Rabin's blunt wording. Only several days later, when Rabin realized that the Norwegian channel was paradoxically breathing new life into the talks in Washington, he changed course and approved the continuation of the Oslo process.

The fact that such a central and strategic issue was not managed by the cabinet or by an ad hoc forum of ministers, and the fact that Rabin's political power was then much greater than that of Peres, meant that throughout the Oslo process (from the date of revealing it to Peres and Rabin, through the public ceremony on September 13, 1993), it was subject to the fluctuating moods of the prime minister.

✳✳✳

In the summer of 1993, Joel asked Peres and me an innocent question: Who will be responsible for implementation on the Palestinian side? We made peace with Egypt, and it was clear that the Egyptian government was responsible for its implementation. We were trying to reach peace with Syria, with Jordan, and with Lebanon, with the understanding that their governments would be responsible for carrying out their signed commitments. But the Palestinian delegation in Washington, which was a formal part of the joint Palestinian-Jordanian delegation, was neither a government nor an organization.

As we approached the conclusion of the negotiations in Oslo, this question gained practical urgency. I was glad that a "centrist" and responsible person like Joel raised the question rather than me. It was clear that I'd support his proposal of mutual recognition between Israel and the PLO, including a number of conditions the Palestinian organization would have to meet in order to win this recognition.

Peres did not summarily reject the proposal but said that it was still too early and that Rabin wouldn't agree under any circumstances. We didn't plan to raise the subject with the prime minister. In any case, we didn't become a "faction" of three (Peres, Singer, and me) in the Forum of Four, and our preliminary consultations were non-committal. Nonetheless, as we entered Rabin's office, I encouraged Singer to present his proposal.

At a certain point in the conversation with Rabin, which was especially cordial, Joel indeed raised the problem and when the prime minister asked, "So, what do we do?" Joel proposed negotiating with the PLO on mutual recognition. Rabin was not surprised but dictated the framework: Joel would not raise the subject in the conversations between the two delegations but would take Abu Ala aside for an "informal" conversation and ask him about the PLO's readiness to negotiate terms for mutual recognition. If he answered in the affirmative, Israel would insist on keeping the negotiations on mutual recognition separate from the understandings reached in Oslo, which could also be completed without mutual recognition.

Rabin asked Peres for his opinion, and the latter repeated his banal statement that it might be a premature step. Since Peres didn't elaborate or express strong opposition, there was nothing stopping Singer from carrying out Rabin's directive. "I assume that it's superfluous to ask you, Yossi," Rabin said to wrap up the meeting.

A week later, Singer returned with an answer. He reported that Abu Ala was surprised by the question but told him that he believes the PLO's leadership would agree. Abu Ala arrived at the next Oslo round with agreement in principle, and negotiations ensued on the terms for recognition. The main conditions was the old formula of Aharon Yariv and Victor Shem-Tov from July 1974, in the days of Rabin's first government (1974–1977). The two spoke then about amending the PLO's charter, recognizing the sovereign existence of Israel and rejecting terrorism as conditions for negotiations between Israel and the PLO. The first Rabin government, like Golda Meir's government before it, rejected the possibility of mutual recognition. Rabin said at the time that Israel prefers to negotiate with states, and that in the Palestinian context, the address is Jordan.

We now presented the PLO with seven conditions, followed by several weeks of negotiation on nearly every word. As noted, Holst joined the talks at a certain stage, when he realized that once the possibility was raised that the PLO would be responsible for implementing the declaration of principles, it would be almost impossible to separate recognition of the PLO from the Oslo declaration of principles.

※※※

By mid-August, the two sides had come to terms on nearly all of the issues, and it was clear to us that the road was paved for initialing an agreement. With Rabin's approval, Peres traveled to Oslo for a secret meeting to sign the accord with Abu Ala. The Norwegians were pleased by the upgrade of the Israeli delegation.

Negotiations between Peres and Arafat on August 19, which ran late into the night and included intensive mediation by Holst, facilitated a poignant signing ceremony at the official guest house. The table on which the accord was signed was also used by representatives of Norway and Sweden to sign the agreement that separated the two states. Abu Ala, moved to tears, sent me a short message: "This evening I missed the man who got everything started."

We continued to keep the accord secret. We didn't want it to be publicized before the American administration was informed or for the news to appear in the Israeli media before its publication in an official government announcement. Throughout the months of negotiations, there were news items on unofficial contacts with Palestinians in Europe, and when journalists asked me to confirm or deny these reports, I drew from my seven years of experience as a spokesman to prevaricate, without lying. Now, however, it became more difficult to stop the headlines, and we needed to quickly update the US secretary of state.

Members of Christopher's staff later told me that Hafez al-Assad's unenthusiastic response to the "deposit" Rabin had given Christopher (Israel's willingness to withdraw from the Golan Heights if its security demands were met) prompted the secretary of state to ask his staff to "vote" on whether to continue the shuttle diplomacy between the sides or to take a vacation. The minority voted to continue to shuttle between Damascus and Jerusalem, while the majority (some of whom cited family commitments after long months of intensive diplomatic work) voted to take a vacation.

Some members of the American team contend that Rabin's disappointment from Assad's cold response and from what appeared to be an American capitulation, convinced him to decide to sign with the Palestinians. Before returning with the American team to Washington, Christopher asked Rabin in a private conversation how serious the Oslo channel was. Rabin belittled the importance of the process with his dismissive wave of the hand.

Immediately after the secret signing in Oslo, Holst, and Peres asked to meet with the secretary of state during the latter's sacred vacation on the West Coast, and the Norwegian foreign minister's plane took Peres and him to a meeting whose outcome was impossible to guess. But when Christopher heard, in astonishment, about the channel that had only begun in January and had already led to agreements, he was far from critical of the two foreign ministers. He lauded the paper presented to him and immediately informed President Clinton, gladdening the young leader who had yet to chalk up any noteworthy achievement in global diplomacy.

The next official stage was for Arafat and Rabin to separately sign letters of mutual recognition between the PLO and Israel. Holst, full of enthusiasm, flew to Tunisia and Israel to collect the leaders' signatures on their historic letters to each other.

ALONG THE ROADSIDE

Faisal Husseini was considered the "King of East Jerusalem." He was a scion of the most important family in the city, which enjoyed a position of prominence for generations. Compared to their rivals, the Nashashibi family, the Husseinis took a more extreme stance vis-à-vis the Mandatory government and Zionist immigration. Faisal's father was Abd al-Qadir al-Husseini, who commanded the Arab forces in the Jerusalem area in 1948 and was killed in the fighting at Al-Qastel, a hilltop village overlooking the road to Jerusalem. The extremist Mufti Hajj Amin al-Husseini was a family relation, as were Jerusalem's mayors, other notables and even Yasser Arafat.

Faisal was born in Iraq, grew up in Cairo, joined the PLO and arrived in the West Bank only after the Six-Day War. Almost immediately upon his arrival in Jerusalem in 1967, he was embraced as the uncrowned leader. After the signing of the Oslo Accords, he was the Palestinian Authority's representative in the city.

Hirschfeld was the one who introduced us, and we quickly formed an ongoing and open relationship. Over the years, and until his sudden death in 2000, we met many times and appeared together overseas as rivals who were ready to compromise in order to live in peace.

In 1989, I traveled to the US with Husseini on a lecture tour. Each of us presented the Palestinian-Israeli conflict from his point of view, and we made an effort not to bore each other, or ourselves.

Our largest event was in San Francisco, where we appeared before hundreds of people. At one point, an older woman stood up, walked slowly to the end of aisle, and started heading down the stairs toward the stage. We didn't understand what she wanted, but she didn't say anything, and we tried to ignore her. Her journey toward the stage began when Faisal was concluding his remarks and continued when I started to speak. And then she reached the stage, turned her back to us and simply began to disrobe, as if it were the most natural place in the world to do so. Faisal and I didn't know what to do. We hoped that ushers or security personnel would emerge from somewhere and put an end to the striptease. But no one came to the rescue. The main embarrassment was mine: Faisal had already finished his lecture, and it was my turn to speak.

The minutes seemed to last for hours. Finally, before the final stage of disrobement, two volunteers rose from their seats, approached the woman, and escorted her out of the auditorium. This episode became our shared secret.

✳✳✳

He liked to conclude our conversations by saying that his true dream was that when each if us spoke about "my Jerusalem," we'd really mean "our Jerusalem." He was always steadfast in his views, but it was clear to him that the Palestinian interest is to live alongside Israel and with Israelis, and that it was thus imperative to compromise, even in regard to Jerusalem.

He had a rare sense of humor and vast knowledge, and he was good storyteller. In one of our first meetings, for example, he told me about his first visit to Tel Aviv. He had heard a lot about the first Hebrew city and its wonders, and soon after arriving in the West Bank (by swimming across the Jordan River), he came to Tel Aviv and enjoyed strolling along its streets. A policeman stopped him, asked to see his papers, was not satisfied with what he found, and brought Faisal to a nearby police station. There he was interrogated by a police officer, who treated him with unexpected friendliness. "You're the son of Abd al-Qadir?" the officer asked. Faisal answered in the affirmative and feared that the officer's demeanor would now change. But the officer actually started to say, "I have to tell you as a Jew and as a Zionist. . . . " Faisal heard those words and burst into uncontrollable laughter.

The officer looked at him in astonishment and didn't understand what Faisal was laughing about. The laughter continued, and this was the scene in the interrogation room: A confused officer trying to understand what he had done that was so hilarious, and a man under questioning who could not stop laughing.

In the end, Faisal explained, "I couldn't believe that a man would call himself a Zionist. I grew up in places where the most horrible insult was to call someone a 'Zionist' [sahyouni in Arabic], and suddenly I meet a respectable person who tells me he's a Zionist."

Over the years, stories like these gave me insights that I couldn't have received in any other way.

28

An Engagement, Not a Marriage

AT THE NEXT CABINET MEETING, THE FESTIVE MOOD WAS ALSO MIXED with tension. The ministers found it hard to accept the fact that negotiations had been conducted with the PLO throughout the year, without their knowledge. The IDF chief of staff, Ehud Barak, who had also been kept in the dark, remarked that the agreement was as full of holes as "Swiss cheese." Motta Gur, who was then serving as deputy defense minister and was also invited to the ministerial meeting, came over to me from the other end of the conference room and asked who had participated in the weekly meetings with Rabin. I told him, and he seemed to calm down—in part, at least. I asked Barak, who was sitting next to me, how he would vote if he were a cabinet member rather than the IDF chief of staff. He responded without hesitation that he would vote in favor of the agreement.

Joel then presented the details of the Declaration of Principles. Eli Rubinstein, the cabinet secretary, raised more than twenty reservations. Rabin was asked whether the signing of the agreement was conditional upon Israel's recognition of the PLO. He immediately replied in the negative. The negotiations on mutual recognition were still underway. It was not yet clear whether the talks would lead to a signed agreement between the two sides or only an exchange of letters in which the Palestinians would make several commitments, and Israel would acknowledge receipt of the letters. Rabin wanted to believe that the two negotiations were unconnected, but it was clear that his approval to negotiate mutual recognition had made the Oslo process the only path toward an agreement with the Palestinians and the PLO the only relevant negotiating partner.

[Incidentally, several days later, about an hour before the signing of the agreement on the White House lawn and four days after the letters of mutual recognition were signed, Arafat noticed that the agreement stated that it was between Israel and the Palestinian group in the Jordanian-Palestinian peace delegation. On the spot, he announced that he would not sign the agreement if it didn't clearly state that it was between Israel and the PLO. Rabin already starting to pack his bags to leave Washington. At the last moment, a solution was found. The wording wasn't elegant, but it was enough to avoid a crisis: The document stipulates the terms of agreement between the "Government of the State of Israel and the PLO team (in the Jordanian-Palestinian delegation to the Middle East Peace Conference) (the 'Palestinian Delegation'), representing the Palestinian people."]

At the same cabinet meeting, Aryeh Deri analyzed the document in an impressive way, but said that he couldn't vote for it because the attorney general was preventing him from continuing to serve as a minister in light of the corruption charges against him, and because he and Shas were compelled to quit the government. He announced that he would abstain. Shimon Sheetrit (Labor) also stated his intention to abstain.

I did not ask for permission to speak. I felt that my work was being done by others. No one opposed the agreement. Besides the two abstentions, all of the ministers voted for the agreement, including dyed-in-the-wool hawks who had called me and my colleagues "PLO sympathizers."

It was one of those rare moments when you need to pinch yourself to make sure it's not a dream. However, though I was happy, I was not thrilled by the new consensus and worried that it could collapse just as quickly as it had coalesced. I shared this concern with Helena too.

✱✱✱

President Clinton eagerly embraced the agreement. No one had succeeded in resolving the Palestinian-Israeli conflict, and he wanted to create a sense of historic peacemaking. So, for the signing of the Declaration of Principles, he invited both Arafat (who greatly desired this) and Rabin (who was much less enthusiastic).

I flew with Rabin and Peres, and there was a graduation-like atmosphere. Rabin even revealed to me that he intended to appoint an attorney general "to my liking" (Michael Ben-Yair). But when I saw the large audience sitting in the heat and humidity of Washington the next morning, I was alarmed. On the one hand, I felt like a bar-mitzvah boy, with the whole world eager to shake his hand and embrace him. On the other hand, I realized that many people felt like they were already attending a wedding rather than an engagement party, and that they were witnessing the signing of a peace accord between Israel and the Palestinians!

What we had achieved was only an interim agreement, as important as that was, without resolving even one of the permanent status issues. We had mobilized the UN secretary-general, heads of state, and foreign ministers, as well as others I had known since my first days at the

Socialist International or had met during my seven years as Peres's advisor or my years as cabinet secretary, director-general of the Foreign Minister, or deputy minister. I wanted to tell them: Maybe we shouldn't have troubled you yet. Maybe we should have waited until we succeeded in bringing to the world a true peace treaty! But I kept these thoughts to myself.

The picture of the towering president in the center, embracing the two aging leaders, who were a foot shorter than him, remains the image most identified with the Oslo Accords. In the eyes of the world, the agreement symbolized peace between enemies and generated huge expectations that were impossible to fulfill. The ceremony responded to the natural need to witness momentous change—like the collapse of the Berlin Wall, like Reagan and Gorbachev in Reykjavik. It was another part of the "end of history," which was also accompanied by pictures of euphoria in Israeli cities and of Palestinians handing flowers to IDF soldiers.

After the event on the White House lawn, I was invited into the Oval Office for a meeting between the president's staff and the Israeli group. The national security advisor, Tony Lake, introduced me to Clinton and started to tell him about me. The president hushed him and said that he knew exactly who I was and that the whole event that took place that morning wouldn't have happened without me. "He's also the most modest person here," he added. For a moment, I wanted to tell him what I had said a few decades earlier to my teacher Galila—that I'm not modest at all, because I'm a braggart inside.

In any case, the conversation with Clinton was different from my conversations with his predecessors. I was well acquainted with Jimmy Carter, the ideologist; Reagan, who was not embarrassed to read from his cue cards and told jokes about the Soviets; and George H. W. Bush, the reserved diplomat. Clinton was the type who brings people together and befriends them. He was sort of an Ezer Weizman, but a bit less of a "wild man."

✳✳✳

On the way back to Israel, we landed in Morocco for a few hours. We met with King Hassan II, who showed us the magnificent new mosque he built in Casablanca. The mosque was indeed very impressive, built entirely of marble, with water fountains and well-groomed gardens. The king, who heaped praise on Oslo and mentioned our previous meetings, told us that the mosque, which was inaugurated just two weeks earlier and bore his name, was the largest in the world after the Great Mosque in Mecca. He took pride in the fact that it was funded by the citizens of Morocco, including the Jewish community.

I was unable to feign wonderment, and since we had already spoken a number of times in the past, I was bold enough to ask him why he had decided to invest such great resources in the mosque. He didn't take offense and frankly responded that he did this in light of the growing strength of Islamic extremists in his country. It was his belief, he added, that the construction of the mosque proved to his subjects his deep commitment to Islam. The king dismissed my contention that it would be very difficult to beat the extremists in their own home court. (Seven years later, I mentioned this conversation to the Palestinian leader Marwan Barghouti, when he told me about his ill-fated plan to defeat Hamas.)

We returned from Morocco to Israel just prior to Rosh Hashanah, with its end-of-year interviews and the anointment of "person of the year." Rabin was applauded for following through on his central election promise, even if a few months late. Several newspapers crowned me "person of the year." Yoel Marcus even wrote in *Haaretz* that I was worthy of a "person of the decade" accolade. And I recalled (without comparing) Ben-Gurion after the UN's partition decision in 1947: Everyone went out to dance in the streets, and he stayed home, fully aware of the complexity of the situation.

During the holiday, I visited Aliza and Uri Savir in Jerusalem, and we later walked together in the center of Jerusalem. People stood and applauded us, and I said to Uri, "We need to capture this moment. It probably won't return."

Of course, the reactions of the Islamic extremists on the Palestinian side, and the reactions of the political right and the Jewish settlers in Israel, were already clear to see. For both sides, it was not a regular sort of political discord. What we did in Oslo was to touch the heart of the dispute between the two peoples, and those on both sides who insisted that "it's all mine" viewed compromise as treasonous—each side with its God, and each side with its *waqf* [Islamic endowment] or sacred land. At that moment, extremists on both sides regarded democracy and majority rule as luxuries and clung to principles they viewed as far superior to such "trivial" matters as the rule of law.

In light of all this, I was convinced that failure to exploit the opportunity that Oslo perhaps offered—to skip over the interim accord and discuss a final agreement—would be a severe mistake.

ALONG THE ROADSIDE

I invited Faisal Husseini to appear before the Mashov group on July 30, 1989 at the Labor Party's legendary headquarters at 110 HaYarkon Street in Tel Aviv. The invitation sparked harsh criticism from within and outside the party.

It was one of the most crowded gatherings in the history of the headquarters on HaYarkon Street. Husseini began his speech with challenging words: "I'm your enemy," and a great silence swept across the meeting hall. He spoke about the need to begin negotiations between Israel and the Palestinians but insisted that Palestinians who were not residents of the occupied territories—that is, PLO officials—also be allowed to participate in the negotiations.

I spoke after him and acknowledged the difficulty of squaring the circle: Israel preferred to negotiate with residents of the territories, while they reiterated that they would not engage in talks with us without including PLO representatives. That is, it was possible to meet with Husseini and with Nusseibeh and with Ashrawi and others, but it was impossible to negotiate an agreement with them.

As expected, the event did not fail to stir commotion. Husseini returned home to a barrage of criticism for meeting with us. In Israel, critics bemoaned the fact that leaders of the intermediate generation in the Labor Party had provided a podium for a prominent supporter of the PLO in the territories.

In any case, the event had educational significance. On both sides, people started to realize that such meetings were not impossible, and that if people talk to the other side, it doesn't mean they endorse its views.

29

A Tête-à-Tête with Arafat

IN THE FRAMEWORK OF THE MULTILATERAL TALKS, THE REFUGEES Committee was slated to meet in Tunis in October. I decided to travel there with the Israeli delegation and use the opportunity to meet with Arafat. I met with Rabin first, and he asked me to speak privately with Arafat about Zachary Baumel and enlist his help in locating the fallen Israeli soldier's body, which was presumed to be buried in a Syrian cemetery. After the disastrous Sultan Yaqub battle in Lebanon, Zachary was declared missing in action. His father, Yona, was convinced that his son was still alive, based on photographs that ostensibly showed him in captivity. Yona came to me often, and I raised the case of Zachary and two other Sultan Yaqub MIAs in many conversations with decision makers in the world. Of course, I promised Rabin to raise this issue with Arafat.

The delegation flew in a special plane that stopped en route in Malta. In Tunis, I met with my Tunisian counterpart and with the country's foreign minister, and then with Arafat. With the Palestinian leader, the meetings were always nocturnal. The address was not provided in advance, because Arafat made a practice of frequently changing his place of residence.

The Palestinian terrorists suddenly became my bodyguards and led me to an apartment where Arafat was already waiting, along with Faisal Husseini, Hanan Ashrawi, Yasser Abed Rabbo, and Akram Haniye. I arrived with Shlomo Gur, Haim Divon (then deputy director-general of the Foreign Ministry), and Orit Shani. The room teemed with journalists from Israel and the world, until I asked them to leave. Arafat was relaxed and a generous host; he tried to persuade me to drink tea with honey because "it's very healthy."

The Palestinian group asked many questions and showed surprising knowledge of the inner workings of Israeli politics. They were interested, of course, in Israeli public opinion about the Oslo agreement, and showed special interest in Shas. I said that I also had a question, and asked Arafat why he still wore his khaki battle dress—even after the signing ceremony at the White House. I noted that in Israeli public opinion, his military dress suggested that he hadn't abandoned the option of taking up arms against Israel.

Arafat was not eager to answer, and Hanan Ashrawi interceded for him. "Without that uniform, Arafat would not be Arafat," she said, unconvincingly. After more than an hour of conversation, I asked Arafat if we could move to a corner of the room for a short tête-à-tête, and he immediately complied. I raised the subject of Zachary Baumel, and he seemed anxious to help. He mentioned a particular cemetery in Syria and said he might be able to go there and persuade the authorities to respond positively to Rabin's request. Arafat also made a request: He asked to speak with Sheikh Ahmed Yassin, saying that if the Hamas leader were released from Israeli prison and delivered to him, it would greatly help him in dealing with Hamas. Arafat claimed that he knew how to reach understandings with Hamas.

Next, I raised the subject of a final agreement. I said that the five or six years of an interim agreement was the greatest gift we could give the extremists on both sides. If we could draft a final status agreement that both he and Rabin accepted, we could save years of attempts by extremists to undermine Israeli-Palestinian rapprochement, I argued. I emphasized that this was my private initiative, and not government policy, and noted that both Rabin and key figures on the Palestinian side preferred an incremental process. However, I expressed confidence that if we somehow managed to reach a final accord, or at least the detailed principles of a peace treaty, it would be possible to persuade both sides to bypass the interim accord.

Arafat said that he was of the same opinion and believed that a process like the one I proposed could succeed. "I don't exactly understand how your system of government operates," he added, "but meanwhile your method of working without approval and then bringing something finished to your superiors has succeeded."

I asked him to name one of his confidantes to be my partner in the next stage of secret talks. Without hesitating, he named Abu Mazen. I said that Yair and Ron would continue to conduct the negotiations on my behalf, and he promised that Abu Mazen would also find appropriate negotiators.

Yair and Ron subsequently met with Arafat in Tunisia and discussed a final agreement with him. They developed a relationship with the two academics close to Abu Mazen—Hussein Agha and Ahmed Khalidi—and the four conducted a regular channel of communication under the auspices of the Swedish government. The foreign minister of the right-wing government there, Margaretha af Ugglas, enthusiastically supported this effort and appointed the diplomat Ann Dismorr to accompany the four academics. The Swedish involvement in the negotiations on the principles of a final agreement was much more limited than the Norwegian involvement in the Oslo process, but it was crucial in enabling us to conduct negotiations and complete the work.

Hassan Asfour joined some of the talks, as did Nimrod Novik on our side. After each round of discussions, I sat with Yair and Ron, offered comments and guidance, and made decisions when dilemmas arose. Abu Mazen conducted a similar debriefing with the two Palestinian negotiators.

During the course of the negotiations, I met with Abu Mazen several times to exchange assessments on the emerging document. For example, when discussing the future of the Jewish settlements, we agreed that all of the settlements in the Gaza Strip would be evacuated, while the settlements east of the new border in the West Bank could remain in the framework of the Palestinian state. He insisted that the settlements under Palestinian rule would not remain exclusively for Israelis. That is, Palestinian citizens would be allowed to make their homes in any vacant residences.

In my dealings with Peres and Rabin, I re-adopted the Oslo model because I had no doubt that Peres would ask for Rabin's approval, and that Rabin would prefer to continue with the interim approach, which had quickly proven to be very problematic. In both cases, Oslo and "Beilin-Abu Mazen," I knew that if I had asked for approval, I wouldn't have received it. I knew that I had to come to Peres—and especially to Rabin—with results in order to convince them that this was an opportunity that should not be rejected out of hand. That is, the model was to receive approval retroactively. However, this time I didn't need approval to conduct the channel and navigate toward a draft agreement.

My main fear was that Hamas would unleash violence. I was also concerned about extremists in Israel, but certainly never imagined a terror attack like the one perpetrated by Baruch Goldstein. The massacre on February 25, 1994, opened the floodgates to hell; 29 Muslim worshippers were shot to death, and many others were wounded by a physician, an officer in the IDF reserves, who came to the Cave of the Patriarchs in his uniform, armed with his rifle, intent on killing innocent people. At the end of the forty days of mourning, the first major suicide bombings were carried out, in Afula and in Hadera.

The entire negotiations with Abu Mazen and his representatives were conducted in the shadow of terrorism and violence. Rabin adopted the policy of continuing the peace process as if there were no terrorism and combating terrorism as if there were no peace process. The principle was correct and wise. In reality, it was very difficult to implement.

✳✳✳

In 1994, prior to the elections for the Riksdag (the Swedish parliament), I had a conversation with Pierre Schori—an old friend who represented the Social Democratic Party in the Riksdag and had served as his country's state secretary for foreign affairs. I told him about the secret channel and asked him to do everything he could to ensure that it would continue under a left-wing government. He promised to do so. The Social Democratic Party indeed won the elections, and Schori was appointed minister for international development cooperation, serving under the new foreign minister, Lena Hjelm-Wallén. Another old friend, former foreign minister Sten Andersson, was appointed to serve as Sweden's emissary to the Middle East, and the channel continued under his supervision.

In parallel, from April 1994 to May 1995, the Economic Cooperation Foundation (ECF) held monthly meetings with experts in various fields connected to the final agreement: the future of the settlements, the demarcation of the border, Jerusalem, security arrangements, and the refugees. We devoted a weekend or two to each issue and outlined several possible solutions. This constituted the raw material from which we drew the proposals to be presented in subsequent negotiating sessions. As the talks were in progress, I was appointed minister of economics and planning. This did not prevent me from continuing to be involved in the negotiations.

The final negotiating session was held on Rosh Hashanah at the Ministry of Economics and Planning in Tel Aviv, and we reached agreement on all of the unresolved issues. (Where each side had presented a different proposal, they were marked "I" for Israel and "P" for Palestine; every notation of "I" or "P" was now deleted.)

About a month later, in late October 1995, Abu Mazen came to the ECF's modest offices on Dafna Street in Tel Aviv, located behind the Ichilov Hospital, for a celebratory meeting. He was accompanied by Ahmed Khalidi, Hussein Agha, and Hassan Asfour. The Israeli side included Yair and Ron, Boaz Karni, Nimrod Novik, and me. We were all enthusiastic. On the one hand, we felt that it was a historic moment. But on the other hand, the signing of the Israeli-Palestinian Interim Agreement (Oslo II) had preempted us by just a few weeks.

It was an event that called for a toast, and indeed we raised our glasses—of orange juice. (Abu Mazen does not drink alcohol.) Abu Mazen spoke about the importance of the moment, about his belief that all of the disagreements between the sides could be bridged, and about his hope that our document could serve as a basis for agreement between Rabin and Arafat. I expressed hope that despite the Oslo II interim agreement, the leaders would prefer to move expeditiously toward a final accord. "If Arafat and Rabin agree," Abu Mazen said, "we could sign within a month."

In any case, he promised to promptly show the document to Arafat, and I promised to show it to Rabin immediately after the Amman Conference and after returning from a short trip to the US I couldn't have guessed that the optimism we felt that Saturday would be completely quashed the following Saturday, November 4.

✳✳✳

The subject of the Nobel Prize was the elephant in the room for about a year, from the time of the signing ceremony on the White House lawn in 1993 until the announcement of the prize recipients. The media devoted considerable attention to this, and the assumption was that only Rabin would be named the Nobel laureate. Whenever someone raised the subject with Peres in my presence, I saw that Peres grew angry at the very thought that his eternal rival would win the coveted prize. I don't remember ever talking to him about it, and I don't think he worked behind the scenes to receive the prize, but I realized it was very important to him.

As the awaited announcement drew near, the media coverage intensified, and it was hard for Peres to conceal the tension he felt. Then, I received a surprising phone call from Rabbi Michael Melchior, the chief rabbi of the small Jewish community in Norway. He told me that the prize committee intended to award the prize to Rabin, Peres, and Arafat, but that one of the five committee members, Kåre Kristiansen, a former chairman of Norway's Christian Democratic Party, refused to award the prize to Arafat and threatened to resign from the committee. The members of the committee tried to come up with an alternative on which they could all agree. And indeed they reached a consensus: to award the prize to Abu Ala and me. But the committee then checked the procedural aspect and discovered that candidates have to be nominated by January 1 of the year in which the prize is awarded. And that date was long past.

I told Melchior I was glad that this technicality had spared me a dilemma, though I would not have accepted the prize in any case. The leaders who bear responsibility for the consequences are the ones who deserve the prize, I said. Needless to say, I kept Melchior's information to myself at the time. It would have just added needless tension.

In the end, it was announced on Friday, October 14, that the prize would be awarded to the three leaders. But a more pressing matter was already on the agenda: the abduction of an IDF soldier, Nachshon Wachsman, by Hamas. For six days, Israelis were glued to the media reports on the security forces' efforts to locate where he was being held. When the Sayeret Matkal commandos finally stormed the Hamas hideout in Bir Nabala, north of Jerusalem, the terrorists killed Nachshon. The commander of the force, Captain Nir Poraz, was also killed in the operation. Soon after the failed rescue attempt, Rabin and IDF Chief of Staff Ehud Barak appeared before the media and provided details. In response to a question about the Nobel Prize, Rabin said that he'd happily give up the prize in return for the abducted soldier and the officer who tried to rescue him.

✳✳✳

Nineteen nintey-four was a busy year of negotiations to normalize relations between Israel and the pragmatic Arab states. It seemed that their leaders were just waiting for an agreement like the Oslo Accord to open up to us. In conversations with them, I was surprised to learn of their admiration for Israel and their almost magical belief in Israel's power to influence decision makers in Washington.

I took upon myself the negotiations with Oman and with Tunisia. The main question was how to normalize relations, but not completely. We worked directly vis-à-vis Oman, without a third party. Tunisia insisted that Belgium be involved in the talks and that representatives of Israel and Tunisia operate out of the Belgian Embassy in their respective states. Intensive negotiations were held in Brussels at Egmont Palace, part of the Belgian Foreign Ministry. The head of the Tunisian delegation was my counterpart, the deputy foreign minister. Though there were no dramatic disagreements between us, the talks dragged on for several months.

I arrived in Tunis in the spring as the head of a delegation that included (as requested by Peres) Aharon Nahmias, a native of Morocco and a former mayor of Safed. As part of the visit, I had a breakfast meeting scheduled with the foreign minister, Habib Ben Yahya, and Nahmias asked if he could join us. He wanted to have a photo taken of him shaking hands with the Tunisian foreign minister to brandish in his campaign to return to the mayor's office in Safed. I asked the minister's bureau to approve the request, and it was approved immediately.

Jovial and goodhearted, Nahmias joined the breakfast meeting and asked the minister's permission to have a photo taken of the two of them. The minister, who was an exemplary host, immediately replied that he'd be happy to oblige. Aharon handed his camera to one of the minister's bodyguards, who snapped a picture of the two men shaking hands, brimming with smiles.

A few hours later, I met Aharon on the plane back to Israel. He looked despondent and I asked why. He told me that while packing his bags at the hotel, there was a knock at the door; and when he opened it, he saw three local security officers. Without saying much, they asked for his camera. He tried telling them that he had packed it in another suitcase that was already being loaded onto the plane. But they didn't buy his story and acted in a way that didn't leave him much room for bargaining. He dug into his suitcase, "found" the camera and surrendered it to the security man who seemed to be the most senior of the three. They deftly removed the film in which they identified the photo of the mayoral candidate and foreign minister, confiscated it, and returned the empty camera to Nahmias.

During this period, Peres spoke about a "new Middle East." In my view, he was mistaken, and we argued quite a bit over this. The peace and normalization agreements of the 1990s did not change character of the regimes or public opinion. In his conversations with me, the Tunisian foreign minister could speak disdainfully of Arafat and say that his government was preparing a great farewell event for the Palestinian leader to make it clear that he wouldn't be returning to Tunis. At the same time, however, his security men could, as in the "old" Middle East, confiscate the photograph taken of him with the Israeli politician who wished to proudly display it in his election campaign.

30

Erekat's Astonishing Request

IN 1995, IN PARALLEL TO NEGOTIATIONS THAT LED TO THE SIGNING of the Interim Agreement (Oslo II), a Palestinian group led by Arafat met with an Israeli group led by Rabin at the Israeli Civil Administration compound at the Erez Crossing on the Israel-Gaza border. Rabin asked me to accompany him, and I was glad to do so.

During the first part of the meeting, Arafat requested changes in Israeli policy on a number of issues. One of his requests was for Israel's consent to hold popular elections for the Palestinian president instead of having the president elected by the Palestinian Legislative Council. He explained that Israel was also preparing to conduct direct elections for the prime minister for the first time, and said he saw no reason why a similar election shouldn't be held on the Palestinian side.

After talking for some time, we took a recess and each side retired to a different room for consultations. A few minutes after we sat down in the room designated for the Israeli group, a soldier knocked on the door and asked for me. He said that Saeb Erekat had an urgent message for me from the Palestinian delegation. I reported this to Rabin and went to meet Erekat.

Erekat was very agitated and told me that he had decided to take action. I asked him what he was talking about. "You know how much I appreciate Abu Ammar (Arafat) and how much I'm committed to him and loyal to him, but I'm loyal first and foremost to the Palestinian cause. And here, today, we may be severely undermining the chances of democracy in Palestine." I gazed at him in astonishment. "As a political scientist, I think as you do, that your direct elections for prime minister will be a great mistake," he continued. "But direct elections for president of the Palestinian Authority will be an utter disaster. With all of Arafat's many qualities, he has lived his entire life in a world of Arab dictators. Those are the only regimes that he truly knows.

"Arafat is very worried about having the president elected by the legislative council because it means he'd be dependent on the members of the council and would need to compromise and build coalitions that come with a price. He wants one-man rule. That's the most important request, from his perspective. If you agree, he'll achieve his objective, and the Palestinian people will live in an authoritarian regime. It's not as if we'll be living in a Scandinavian democracy if he's elected by the council, but it's a different world, from our view. The more I see how important the change is to Arafat, the more fearful I become."

I had never seen Saeb Erekat come to me "hat in hand" like this, almost begging. He could be funny, sad, embittered, angry, frustrated—but begging? I promised to immediately speak to Rabin about this. When I returned to the room, Rabin was curious to know what urgent message the Palestinian delegation had wanted to convey. And he was surprised, as I had been, to learn that it wasn't a message from the delegation, but rather a story of Saeb versus Arafat.

My relationship with Erekat did not go back many years, but it was a very intensive one. We often met privately and engaged in conversations that focused not only on concrete topics, but also on the future relations between the two peoples. He called himself "the Indian" because he felt like an outsider, someone who would never be part of the PLO leadership, even though he played an essential role for it. In his view, this was because he was from "here," from Jericho, and still lived in the house where he grew up. I understood that his words contained implicit criticism of corruption in the PLO leadership that had now relocated from Tunisia. He later became a minister in the Palestinian Authority and even served as the PLO's secretary-general, but in those days, Erekat felt he was up against a glass ceiling.

The fact that both of us were political scientists was an important common denominator. We read the same books, more or less, taught about the same political philosophers and researchers, and met each other's families. I remember that on one of my visits to his home, he expressed pride in the fact that his two daughters had participated in Seeds of Peace, an American program that brings together young Israelis and Palestinians. He later told me that during a major flood in Jericho, his daughters received twenty-three email messages with offers of assistance from young Israelis who had participated with them in the program.

Of course, we sometimes also spoke at length about Hamas. Saeb said that in his eyes the most important contribution of the Oslo process was to weaken Hamas. "From your perspective," he said, "Hamas was originally a religious organization that focused on welfare projects and then became a terror organization in the first intifada. From my viewpoint, it's an organization that will strangle us if it rises to power. If Hamas ever defeats Fatah, my wife Neameh won't be able to wear jeans and feel free. Hamas is our common enemy. You fear the tragedies it may cause. I fear the way of life it wants to impose on us."

When Fatah's Tanzim faction launched the second intifada, Saeb was furious. He told me he wasn't sending his son to school. I asked why, and he said that if his son didn't join his classmates after school in throwing rocks at Israeli soldiers, they'd taunt him for being a "coward." And if he joined them and threw rocks—he might return home in a coffin.

Erekat, like Husseini, was not an easy rival, but he was an honest and creative negotiator. His early death, in 2020, left a void that will not be easy to fill. In political negotiation, it's essential to have someone on the other side who knows the facts, doesn't rely on slogans and theatrics, and knows how to define priorities. Saeb Erekat was someone like that.

✳✳✳

In any case, when the two sides resumed the joint meeting, Rabin explained why he could not approve most of the Palestinian requests, but said that Israel did not object to Arafat's wish for direct elections. Rabin wanted to appease Arafat in the short term, even though he was aware of the potential price of directly electing the Palestinian Authority's president. Arafat's eyes gleamed. Saeb did not show any emotion. Arafat acted like he had been defeated and had been forced to accept a bitter decree. "You have the upper hand," he said and expressed disappointment over the fact that Rabin had rejected most of his requests. However, we knew that he had received the thing that mattered most to him.

ALONG THE ROADSIDE

In the early 1980s, Hirschfeld and I went to visit Husseini at his home. When we arrived at the family's large house, we found dozens of guests in the parlor, sitting with exemplary quiet, waiting patiently. We spoke with one of them. There wasn't a system of making an appointment or personal invitations. Anyone who wished to consult with Husseini or request assistance would come and sit for a few hours, waiting for their turn.

Suddenly the door to Husseini's office opened, and two people walked out; one of them had a hen in his hands. While escorting them out, Faisal saw us and invited us into his office. Of course, we had set an appointment.

I asked him to explain the scene, and he burst out laughing—laughter came easily and often to him.

"With you Israelis," he said, "a politician who wants to get elected talks about foreign affairs and social welfare plans, about housing construction and infrastructure. But a quarter of an hour from West Jerusalem, we live in a world where a leader must decide between two neighbors on the ownership of a hen that fled the chicken coop."

31

Don't Leave Us with Half a Party!

THE KNESSET ELECTIONS IN 1988 ENDED IN A NARROW VICTORY FOR the Likud. Peres was convinced that if there had been direct elections for prime minister, the votes from ultra-Orthodox and Arab Israelis would have enabled him to defeat Shamir by a large majority. In arguments between us, both private and public, Peres always returned to the story of Mitterrand. The French president once explained to Peres that General de Gaulle was the one who initiated the constitutional change that enabled the direct election of the president in France. Mitterrand was elected due to his grassroots support; under the system in place before the constitutional change, the small leftist party he headed would never have been able to bring him to power.

Professor Uriel Reichman, who founded the Movement for a Constitution in Israel, proposed a reform that included the idea of direct elections for prime minister, along with combined regional-proportional elections for the Knesset. Peres adopted the proposal and rejected my view that this mishmash was a recipe for trouble: It would focus public attention on the candidates, like in the US, rather than on the issues. In addition, the large parties would shrink, as voters would be encouraged to support their candidate for prime minister and cast their vote in the parliamentary election for the party closest to their heart. We debated this question publicly within the Labor Party, but Rabin also supported the proposal—and when Peres and Rabin agreed on something, it was difficult to mount an opposition.

On March 18, 1992, the Knesset gave its final approval to an amendment calling for direct elections. It was a "victory" for the parliamentary opposition: fifty-five MKs voted in favor of the legislation (including Netanyahu, who bucked party discipline to do so) and only thirty-two MKs voted with the government and against the proposed amendment.

The legislation was set to enter effect in the 1996 elections. Meanwhile,

I became more convinced that it was a bad idea and made efforts to revoke the new law. Most of my parliamentary allies in this fight were Likud MKs, such as Reuven Rivlin and Uzi Landau. Avrum Burg, who initially supported the direct elections system, changed his mind and backed our efforts. The Israel Democracy Institute, under the leadership of Dr. Arik Carmon, also supported my stance and provided the legislation's opponents important comparative material. Gradually, some of the advocates of direct elections for prime minister experienced a change of mind. So I decided to try to raise the subject for discussion at the Labor Party convention.

This required collecting hundreds of signatures. I feared that many members would prefer to refrain from signing, feeling that it might jeopardize their relations with the party's leaders. But I was surprised to find that it wasn't difficult to obtain the signatures, mainly with the help of members of the Mashov group. Nonetheless, some of those who signed advised me not to pursue the initiative because my appointment as minister, expected in July, was not yet final, though it had already been reported in the media. And a public confrontation with Rabin would not boost my chances.

In any event, the party convention addressed the subject on June 5, 1995. The vote was procedural: Should the convention remove the subject from the agenda or devote a substantive discussion to it? One of the arguments raised against me was that the party's first priority was to advance the peace process, and that a discussion of the elections system would divert us from that. I replied that I was the last person anyone could accuse of neglecting the peace process. Another argument was that the party had campaigned on the issue of direct elections in 1992, and that revoking the legislation now would harm our credibility.

I replied to this argument by saying that the party's credibility must be weighed against the national interest, and if we decide that the new system is against the national interest—we cannot allow ourselves to stick to a wrong decision only because we don't want to embarrass ourselves. I concluded my unusually long speech with a personal appeal to Rabin and Peres; the two had agreed in advance to prevent a substantive debate of the matter, even though Peres had already lost his enthusiasm for the new system: "The direct method may have 1,000 advantages, but it has one certain disadvantage—and all of its supporters and opponents agree on this: It will make the major parties smaller and scatter the votes. . . . The price of compromise between you was too high this time. I'm turning to you with a last-minute cry: Don't do this to yourselves. Don't leave us with half a party!"

Rabin's response focused on the obvious assertion that in order to advance policy goals, you need to win elections. But he didn't explain why the new system would ensure victory for the Labor Party. "Yossi, with all due respect for your role in Oslo, you would have been going around in circles there for three years, with nothing to show for it, if the Knesset elections had ended differently," he said. "The problem is a parliamentary reality and the ability of a political leadership to adopt the recommendations of those who sat in Oslo. You alone don't bear the consequences when there's a Beit Lid [the suicide bombing at the Beit Lid Junction on January 22, 1995, that killed twenty-one soldiers and one civilian]. You're not the target for attack."

A majority of those attending the convention voted to remove the subject from the agenda.

✷✷✷

The numerous surveys conducted before Rabin's assassination showed that the gap was narrowing between him and Netanyahu in a head-to-head contest. Some polling indicated that Netanyahu would overtake Rabin. After the assassination, Peres led in the surveys, but his lead also dwindled and disappeared on the eve of the elections. In the end, Netanyahu defeated Peres in the direct elections for prime minister by a slim 1 percent margin. The results of the separate vote for parliament painted a different picture: thirty-four seats for Labor and thirty-two for the Likud. In retrospect, it turned out that Netanyahu's vote in favor of the direct election system in 1992, contrary to his party's position, paved his way to the Prime Minister's Office four years later.

Following the elections, the effort resumed to revoke the direct election system. This time, there was more support in the Labor Party for this effort. On May 27, 1998, Uzi Landau and I submitted a bill to revoke the direct election amendment. The Knesset approved a preliminary reading of the proposal by a vote of fifty to forty-five, but we needed to mobilize a sixty-one–vote majority to get the bill through its next reading. We managed to do that on December 21, with sixty-two MKs in favor and fifty-seven opposed. It was a great victory, but despite the collaboration between MKs on both sides of the aisle, we weren't able to bring the proposed legislation to the critical second and third readings.

The direct election system remained in effect, and Ehud Barak was elected prime minister in 1999 by a large majority of the popular vote. The large parties, on the other hand, shrunk dramatically: Labor (then temporarily called One Israel) had to suffice with only twenty-six Knesset seats, and the Likud won just nineteen. Less than two years later, after defeating

Barak in the special election for prime minister, Sharon promptly advanced the legislation Uzi Landau and I had drafted—even though he personally benefited from the direct election system. In March 2001, seventy-two MKs voted in favor of revoking direct elections and only thirty-seven preferred to keep the system in effect. This put an end to the misguided attempt to combine the presidential system and the parliamentary system. However, the repercussions of the direct election system on the size of political parties and on sector-based voting are still with us today.

In practice, Israelis split their votes to support the leader of one of the two major blocs in the direct election for prime minister, while voting in the parliamentary elections for smaller parties that more precisely reflected their preferences. There seems to be little chance of returning to a system of large parties in the foreseeable future.

❋❋❋

Even though I had already worked at the Foreign Ministry, and despite the fact that the position of deputy foreign minister was not so different from the position of director-general, my three years as deputy foreign minister were a completely different period for me. I was already very familiar with the ministry, its procedures, and its personnel. I didn't have to worry about disputes over turf (as was the case when Avrasha Tamir was director-general and I was the foreign minister's "No. 2"), and I could focus on subjects that I viewed as particularly important. Peres never restricted my field of activity, despite the significant disagreements that sometimes arose between us.

As deputy foreign minister, I again chaired the appointments committee, and this gave me an up-to-date picture of the ministry's senior staff, their aspirations for appointments in Israel and abroad, and the personal issues that prevented them from accepting appointments (for example, children serving in the IDF), or which prompted them to seek particular overseas assignments. I devoted a significant part of my time to these matters.

The Foreign Ministry has a hierarchy and a certain type of formality that do not exist in other ministries, certainly not to the same extent. When I invited a ministry official responsible for a particular desk to come and provide details on a crisis somewhere, the official would always come with his or her boss. I sometimes felt at meetings that I was hearing the view the department had already formed on the relevant problem, rather than the view of the young official who knew more about the matter.

I decided to try to "break" the hierarchy by convening a group of outstanding young people, of various ranks, to discuss topics that were considered taboo in our everyday diplomatic work. My advisor, Shlomo Gur, suggested names of ministry employees, some of whom I knew. From this list of candidates, who were completely unaware of their candidacy, we chose about a dozen diplomats who seemed particularly creative to us. To encourage uninhibited discussion, we met outside of the ministry. I arranged with professor Yehuda Elkana, the director of the Van Leer Institute at the time, for the institute to host our monthly, Friday-morning roundtable meetings. I raised some of the topics, and the participants initiated other topics. Everyone invited to join the group answered affirmatively, though some were concerned that their direct supervisors would not look kindly upon their participation and asked to keep the forum's existence as confidential as possible.

It was a classic case of removing barriers of rank and formality: We all came dressed in jeans (thus inspiring the name "Jeans Forum") and we spoke in a completely different way than we spoke at the ministry. As time passed and the forum's existence remained unpublicized, the participants felt freer to express opinions that were considered heretical. The questions we discussed included, for example: a possible initiative by Israel to gradually wean itself from American financial assistance; diplomatic relations with certain countries; the ministry's structure; and international crises to which Israel should respond in word or deed (sending a field hospital, for instance). Some of the views presented in these conversations trickled into official ministry discussions.

From my perspective, it was a way to get to know members of the young and intermediate generations at the ministry who seldom expressed their views in official meetings, focusing instead on taking notes or offering some points of information. The Jeans Forum continued until I was appointed minister of economics and planning in the Rabin government in July 1995.

✻✻✻

Another framework I created, which remained active after I left the Foreign Ministry, was a seminar program ("Hutza'ir") for high school students. I was annoyed by the general impression that the Foreign Ministry's work mainly involved cocktail parties, especially when I heard this view expressed in high schools, where I often appeared. Therefore, I decided to start a program for eleventh graders; they would come for a series of sessions at the Foreign Ministry, ask questions, receive answers, and, at the end of the year, travel overseas to gain an understanding of what it meant to work at an embassy and why at the end of the twentieth century, and after the invention of the fax, there was still a need for diplomats to do "relocation" with their family.

The young participants were chosen in consultation with their schools. The demand to participate far exceeded our ability to accommodate all of the applicants. But we managed to recruit a talented group of teenagers who questioned everything and took nothing for granted. Some of them, after completing their academic studies, were accepted into the ministry's cadet course or pursued related fields.

I enjoyed speaking with them about the importance of diplomacy on the personal level and about building trust between the ambassador and the decision makers in the host country. They asked many questions. One of the questions on their minds was to what extent diplomats need to hide their true opinions on the issues they present.

There was no black and white answer to that question, I replied. The answer did not appear in the ministry's handbook that outlined the etiquette to be followed in each country—for example, not to cross your legs and turn the sole of your shoe toward your host in the Arab Gulf states. Of course, there are situations in which diplomats feel they cannot continue to represent the state due to its policies or actions, and they resign. But sometimes diplomats are permitted to say that along with the message they were asked to convey, they would like to add a personal note, off the record. In such cases, the diplomats can note what they personally find problematic in the official message, while also fully understanding the state's motive behind the message. In my view, this sort of qualified message, though problematic, is preferable to a situation in which the recipient of the message senses a discrepancy between the message and the tone in which it is delivered. Indeed, foreign diplomats have come to me on a number of occasions and explicitly told me that in light of our friendship, they wanted to let me know that they did not fully identify with the message they were obliged to deliver.

We also spoke quite a bit about the philosophical side of diplomacy, about the effect of overseas service on the spouse's career, about raising children in foreign places and in foreign languages, and about the fact that no substitute has yet been found for the personal relations between diplomats and their hosts. Through personal relations, it is sometimes possible to move mountains or, in a single moment, to destroy what has been achieved over the course of a generation.

32

Opening the Locked Door in the Palace

THE DIALOGUE BETWEEN THE VATICAN AND ISRAEL BEGAN IN THE wake of the Madrid Conference. When I arrived at the Foreign Ministry in the summer of 1992, there was already a negotiating committee with members such as Rabbi David Rosen, and Peres asked me to chair the committee in order to identify the main problems and try to reach an agreement.

Though Israel and the Vatican had maintained informal relations for decades, the relationship was highly charged and tentative. Historically, the Vatican had opposed a Jewish state in the Holy Land and the Balfour Declaration, and wanted to give Jerusalem an international character. This, of course, was contrary to official Israeli policy. After the Holocaust, there was a fundamental change in the Vatican's attitude toward Judaism and, accordingly, toward the State of Israel. In 1965, the Vatican rejected the doctrine that assigned collective culpability for the crucifixion of Jesus to every Jew, in every generation. And though the Church was still years away from establishing official relations with Israel, it began to denounce anti-Semitism.

However, it was not clear what the Vatican really wanted to achieve. Was the Vatican looking to reach understandings on tax exemptions for Church institutions? Or was it seeking to embark on a historical rapprochement with the Jewish people? And would this initiative culminate in the opening of embassies and the establishment of full diplomatic relations?

Shlomo Gur and I delved into the material. I then convened the venerable forum that was conducting the negotiations and understood from its members that their primary concern was that the Church's educational institutions would be granted a wide berth, paving the way for missionary activity. The Vatican demanded an Israeli commitment to protect the freedom of conscience and religion. The Israeli side demanded a commitment from the Vatican to combat anti-Semitism, while it preferred to place

Opening the Locked Door in the Palace | 241

this subject under the title "fighting racism." In addition, the Vatican demanded that the accord be called a "fundamental agreement" rather than just an "agreement." The Israel team opposed this. I tried to understand why and found that the team suspected that the Vatican had an ulterior motive for insisting on this particular definition. In any case, we agreed on guidelines in advance of the next meeting with the Vatican's representatives, scheduled for November 1992.

The Vatican's team was led by Monsignor Celli—a tall, bald, and cheerful man, who sought to create an impression that he had come to work and not to waste time. We started with a private meeting in my office. I told him that unlike my contemporaries who grew up in Jerusalem, for a Tel Avivian like me, the Church was like a locked room in a palace. There were no churches in the first Hebrew city, and I rarely encountered a priest, monk, or nun. Therefore, our dialogue was an opportunity for me to open the locked door. He said it was also an opportunity for him and that he hoped that despite the disagreements to date, we would succeed in reaching an accord. He didn't specify the nature of the accord, and I decided not to ask at that stage. On the other hand, I informed him that I wouldn't sign an agreement unless it included an explicit call for battling anti-Semitism.

The negotiating teams joined us, and he introduced his colleagues. One of them was David Jaeger, an expert in ecclesiastical law. Jaeger was a graduate of Zeitlin High School in Tel Aviv, a Hebrew speaker who had converted to Catholicism. The topics we discussed included encouraging Christian pilgrimages to the Holy Land, securing tax exemptions for Catholic schools and recognizing their special status. At the time, the tax breaks for Catholic educational institutions were slated to expire in accordance with a government decision. I asked my friends at the Finance Ministry to postpone this change in tax policy for a few months, until we concluded the negotiations with the Vatican. I was pleased that the treasury acceded to my request.

However, the expulsion of Hamas members to Lebanon not only aborted the talks with the Arab delegations in Washington, but also brought the negotiations with the Vatican to a halt. Celli and his delegation resumed their meetings with us only in March 1993, and then we indeed made progress on most of the issues. I informed Celli that we were willing to accept the Vatican's demand to call the emerging accord the "Fundamental Agreement" and he was very happy to receive this news.

I was living then in two parallel universes: Oslo and the Vatican. There was much similarity between the two channels: In both cases, the central question remained unresolved until late in the game. On the Palestinian side: Would there be mutual recognition between Israel and the PLO? Regarding the Vatican: Would it decide to establish diplomatic relations with Israel? In both channels, there was one side that wanted to separate the agreement from the issue of mutual recognition. The Vatican did not want to link the Fundamental Agreement to diplomatic relations, and Israel under Rabin did not want to link the Oslo Accord to recognition of the PLO. In the end, it became clear in both channels that such separation was impossible.

In a private conversation, Celli told me that the Vatican had yet to decide about establishing diplomatic relations with Israel. I asked Gur to open a channel to David Jaeger, who seemed very intent on seeing the negotiations succeed. Jaeger confirmed that no decision had yet been made, and suggested setting up a secret meeting for me with Jean-Louis Tauran, the Vatican's foreign minister.

The meeting took place in September, on the sidelines of the annual launch of the UN General Assembly session. Shlomo and I arrived late in the evening at the headquarters of the Vatican's delegation, an inconspicuous New York building. The interior of the building looked much more like a monastery than an embassy. The dim entrance hall exuded a sense of melancholy. Tauran came down from the second floor and joined us. I explained to him that our meeting was not part of the ongoing negotiations and that the other members of the team did not know about it. I emphasized that we couldn't drag out the negotiations much longer.

He congratulated us on the Oslo Accord and said that if we had managed to reach an agreement with the Palestinians, we would surely succeed in reaching agreement with the Vatican. I smiled, but I wasn't certain that he was right. My main message was the connection between the Fundamental Agreement and a commitment to establish embassies and exchange ambassadors. Tauran suggested how to word Israel's commitment to safeguard the independence of Catholic education, but said the Vatican was very hesitant about establishing diplomatic relations with Israel. In his view, the main objective was to present our agreement as an accord between two states, the Vatican and Israel, which have common interests, including the establishment of embassies; he did not want to present it as an agreement between the Christian world and the Jewish people.

I told him that I had no mandate from the Jewish people to sign anything that I personally might find acceptable and that would inevitably be subject to a range of interpretation. That is, the agreement would be signed between two sovereign states and not between two religions.

However, practically speaking, it would be impossible to prevent the world from seeing this ostensibly technical process as a historic gesture of reconciliation between Jews and Christians. He smiled and explained that the Oslo Accord had changed the picture from the pope's perspective. There was heavy pressure from Christian communities in the Arab world not to sign an agreement with Israel. Some of those communities feared becoming the target of severe violence if such an agreement were signed. But if Arafat shook Rabin's hand, who could stop Monsignor Celli from shaking Yossi Beilin's hand?

I left the meeting feeling a bit optimistic. Nonetheless, a number of seasoned Foreign Ministry officials were still convinced that the Vatican would not change its policy and would not agree to recognize Israel and exchange ambassadors. The topic made headlines, and most of the commentators were skeptical. Two weeks before the agreement was signed, Dr. Sergio (Itzhak) Minerbi (an Italian-born Israeli diplomat, considered one of the leading experts on Vatican policy), was interviewed for a long article in *Haaretz*. The title of the article declared that the Vatican would never sign an agreement with Israel as long as Jerusalem remained under Israel's control.

On December 30, 1993, the agreement was signed. Several months earlier, during the festive celebration of the Oslo Accord on the White House lawn, I had felt that the event was overblown. Now, however, I agreed with the world's description of there were some religious figures in Israel and in the Jewish Diaspora who sought to prevent it, arguing that Israel was receiving very little while granting legitimacy to the Vatican, almost free of charge. But it was very hard to attribute much weight to those naysayers.

A special plane took the Israeli negotiation team on a morning flight to Rome, and we soon found ourselves at the Vatican. The Vatican team, led by Celli, led us to a conference room where we discussed the next steps. The accord was a framework agreement, to be followed by talks focusing on financial arrangements between the Church and Israeli tax authorities.

Celli then took on the role of tour guide and led us to the Sistine Chapel and beautiful rooms (including bathrooms) full of paintings that were not usually shown to tourists. Those were magical moments. The tension that characterized our previous meetings dissipated once we knew the document was ready to be signed, and we could now allow ourselves to be tourists for a moment.

But not for much more than a moment. The members of the Vatican's negotiating team arrived in casual dress, and we flew together on an executive jet to Ben-Gurion Airport. Upon landing, they hurried off to their hotel, and later arrived at the Foreign Ministry in full regalia: shiny black garments with red sashes.

The hall in the Foreign Ministry was too small to accommodate the many guests and the Israeli and international media. The relatively short event was broadcast live on CNN. Celli and I made short speeches. He suggested that it was not just another routine ceremony of declaring diplomatic relations and spoke about freedom of worship. I noted that both sides had felt hesitancy and concluded by saying that it was "a ceremony between two states, not between two religions. Nonetheless, its significance extends beyond its legal value."

In warm friendship, we said goodbye to the Vatican team. I promised Celli that I would take him up on his invitation to visit him in the Vatican and taste some of his home cooking (his "wonderful" dishes, in his words). I later kept that promise, and when he asked me about the locked door, I replied that I felt that, indeed, the locked door at the palace had opened for me.

***

In September 2000, I was invited to meet with Pope John Paul II. He wanted to thank me for my part in the agreement, seven years after it was signed. I was told in advance that it would be a private meeting and that it would last twenty minutes. I must admit that those were twenty very long minutes, perhaps the longest of my life.

He was then 80 years old but looked much older, and I wasn't sure during the conversation whether he was really there. Recalling a similar conversation with Rabbi Schach ten years earlier, I decided to fill the silence by talking about the impression the pope had made during his visit to the Holy Land several months earlier. While I was still wondering whether he heard me, the pope suddenly grabbed my hand and asked, "Tell me please, what's happening with you lately? How could it be that Katzav defeated Peres in the contest for president? Did your Knesset lose its mind? How could someone even compare Katzav to Peres? Tell me, does that mean that Ehud Barak will also have to resign"

And then I realized—he had been there the whole time. . . .

ALONG THE ROADSIDE

Over the years, the subject of pursuing the presidency was raised in various conversations with Peres. He always looked down on that job and rejected the notion out of hand. However, in 2000, he decided to throw his hat into the ring. We hadn't discussed this, and I assumed the main reason for his decision was that he had been forced to suffice with a completely superfluous ministerial portfolio, concocted especially for him, in Ehud Barak's government: the Ministry for Regional Cooperation. He didn't want to remain there, and it never occurred to him to retire at age seventy-seven. Like many others, I was sure it wouldn't be difficult to muster a Knesset majority behind his candidacy, especially since he would be facing off against Moshe Katzav, who was not considered an alternative of same caliber.

During the vote in the Knesset, in May 2000, I was no longer an MK. I had resigned (together with Matan Vilnai) at the request of Prime Minister Barak, to make room for Colette Avital and Eli Ben-Menachem, the next-in-line on the party's Knesset list. I was at work in my office at the Justice Ministry but listened to the radio broadcast of the vote and was shocked to hear that Peres had received fewer votes than Katzav in the first round of voting.

I hurried to the Knesset, went to Peres's temporary headquarters, and asked if I could do something to help persuade particular MKs. Everyone in the room was stunned and gloomy, but Peres still believed that the battle wasn't lost. He asked me to speak with three MKs before the second round of voting commenced. I approached the three, and I realized it was a lost cause.

Katzav defeated Peres in the second round, and the Knesset shook with the loud jubilation of his supporters. I entered Peres's office. He was sad, but not broken. I left the building with him. His spokesman, Yoram Dori, was at his side. Peres turned to him while walking and said, "Yoram, don't forget to take back the letter!" He was referring to the letter of resignation he had submitted to the prime minister prior to the vote—because a government minister is not eligible to run for the presidency. However, a minister's resignation only takes effect forty-eight hours after it is submitted, and forty-eight hours had not yet passed since Peres had submitted his letter. He was thus entitled to retract his resignation and remain in his ministerial position without being sworn in again.

On the one hand, I had to admire Peres for remembering the letter at that difficult moment. On the other hand, I swore to myself that I would never find myself in such a moment.

33

Yossi, We Have a Trump Card Here!

LIKE MANY OTHER IDEAS, THE BIRTHRIGHT CONCEPT WAS BORN largely by chance. It even has a date and place of birth: January 14, 1994, at the WIZO House in Tel Aviv, where I was speaking to an international forum of about two hundred WIZO women.

It was a wintry Friday. Peres discovered that he was scheduled to address the forum that afternoon and tried to get out of it. The fact that Raya Jaglom had been leading this forum for a quarter of a century did not boost his motivation to meet with the WIZO women, to put it mildly. Though he had no real excuse to wiggle out of this speaking commitment, Peres gently inquired whether I was available. He noted that it was close to my home, so it wouldn't be a major hassle for me. I also had no good excuse to beg off, other than wanting to spend time with my young family during the daylight hours for a change. I didn't ask him whether there was a topic for his talk, but I assumed he would have spoken about the peace process if I hadn't replaced him.

After receiving a list of the WIZO women's home countries, I could say with confidence that the per capita GDP in Israel was higher on average. On the other hand, Jewish identity was on the decline in those countries, and the rate of intermarriage was climbing rapidly. I thought that it was now Israel's turn to invest in Jewish continuity in the world. Therefore, I decided to speak about the significance of a Jewish state, in my view, and about Israel's connection to world Jewry. I also promised to respond to questions about the peace process at the end of my remarks.

My main message was that Israel owed a debt of gratitude to world Jewry for the blood and treasure it invested in helping to establish the Jewish state and nurturing it during its early years, but that there was no justification for the Jewish world to continue to donate money to Israel after it had become a developed state with a sound financial footing. I told the women that truly ingenious instruments such as Israel Bonds have become a superfluous financial burden. [In the past, Israel Bonds provided the Israeli government with a security net for obtaining large-scale loans if the world turned its back and banks refused to extend loans.] Israel spends large sums on maintaining the Israel Bonds bureaucracy and pays bondholders interest rates that are much higher than market rate. We can receive loans from any bank in the world at relatively low interest but find ourselves paying large sums to our bondholders.

In addition, I said, we are continuing to send to America and other places our best spokespeople to persuade pension funds and trade unions to purchase our high-interest bonds. And every sale they make adds a superfluous cost for Israel's treasury to pay. "They say that the bond is an expression of the connection between the purchaser and Israel, but for years most of the bonds have been held by non-Jews. . . . The Israel Bonds enterprise should simply be shut down," I said.

After concluding my lecture, I felt much less popular. Many of the listeners felt personally insulted. I explained that nothing I said was intended to belittle the great importance of their organization, and that I highly valued their involvement in WIZO's educational and cultural work in Israel. However, from a monetary perspective, Israel was no longer a needy country.

"But you still have poor people!" someone in the audience shouted.

I replied that the primary reason for poverty was an unfair division of the pie, and that I wouldn't want to see wealthy Diaspora Jews donating money to support poor people in Israel. "Our job as the government is to invest much more in the weaker sectors; it is not to seek handouts," I asserted.

"So where do you expect the world's rich people to invest?" another participant asked.

"In the institutions of your community, in education, and in funding visits to Israel for young people to meet Jews here from Israel and from around the world."

I had no idea that this would cause such a stir. My remarks, as covered by the journalists in attendance, quickly made headlines. Ill-informed commentators hastened to declare that I wanted to sever Israel's ties with the Jewish world, and Jewish leaders in the world strongly denounced my words, contending that a cutoff of donations to Israel would mean disconnecting from Israel in a world in which the bank check is an expression of identification.

Executives at the Israel Bonds organization (apparently only God can explain the bloated salaries Israel pays them) and Jewish federation leaders—including both my political allies and opponents—all rejected my views. Jewish figures in Israel and the world sent urgent letters of concern to Rabin and Peres. Rabin censured me and Peres expressed his appreciation for the financial support Israel enjoys from world Jewry. Rabin also sent me the angry letter he received from Raya Jaglom, who claimed that I had criticized the organization's volunteer activity and had dismissed its importance.

The Knesset Immigration and Absorption Committee, chaired by Emanuel Zisman (who had quit the Labor Party in the wake of the Oslo Accord), invited me for a discussion-condemnation just a few days later, on Tuesday. "My aim is for every Jewish young person to know that when they reach the age of seventeen or eighteen, they will have a plane ticket to Israel and find an organized tour program here," I explained. "I don't want to rely on the fact that a young person has wealthy parents because I'm not sure they'll pay for such a visit—in part, due to a fear that their children will want to remain in Israel." I spoke at length about the fundraising for Israel that portrays it as a needy state, even though Israel has long since moved past that stage. I told them that prior to a lecture I delivered in Atlanta about six months earlier, the federation leaders asked me not to describe Israel as an economic success story because it would undermine their fundraising efforts.

Hanan Ben-Yehuda, the treasurer of the Jewish Agency, said, "If we pursue Dr. Beilin's particular proposal, and let's say they stop donating to the State of Israel in one way or another, I fear that the Jewish communities there would be the main ones to suffer, because they raise their funds there in connection to the State of Israel."

It was actually a Likud MK (and former Speaker of the Knesset), Dov Shilansky, who came to my defense. "I would like to say to Deputy Minister Yossi Beilin that during the past two days we've heard how your friends are attacking you from every side. . . . When you say things that are true, I agree with them. And to make it perfectly clear, I want to emphasize that I commend Beilin on the candor and sincerity with which he speaks on this question, as on other questions."

✳✳✳

In the following months, my work focused on the multilateral talks that flourished in the wake of the Oslo Accord. I found myself in Cairo, Amman, Doha, Muscat, and Tunis, as well as in Japan, Canada, and Russia. On the other hand, I was drawn into the Jewish world.

Evidently, when an establishment figure expresses anti-establishment views, it always stirs interest. So I was invited to numerous Jewish events to present my perspective and did countless interviews with the Jewish press. This led me to conclude that I should present my ideas in an orderly way and in greater detail. I did this with the help of Sam Norich, an expert on American Jewry who later became the editor of the Jewish-American newspaper *The Forward*.

I addressed two standalone topics: creating a new global Jewish forum that would also include Jews who are not members of the Zionist movement and initiating a program that would allow every young Jew in the world to visit Israel for two weeks, with all expenses paid by the Jewish people. My declared objective was to create a global meeting place in Israel where young Jews could get to know each other. There are always secondary goals in such initiatives, but from my perspective the time spent on the bus together was the essence, and whatever they learned about Masada was less important. I was not seeking to turn them into ambassadors for Israel in the world or intent on convincing them to immigrate to Israel. Still, even today, whenever I meet young people who say they moved to Israel because of their Birthright experience—I couldn't be happier.

✴✴✴

The stiff resistance I encountered in various places, primarily in the US and in Canada, stemmed from the Jewish federations' concern that funding would not be found to sustain the initiative of bringing young Jews on free trips to Israel—if the initiative indeed proved successful. They feared that if the money dried up, and they were forced to shut it down, it would be very difficult to persuade Jewish families to independently fund trips for younger siblings after an older brother or sister had traveled free of cost. Serious and well-intentioned people at the federations were worried that my idea would be a death blow to the existing programs (in which the costs were shared by the family, the synagogue, and the federation)—and indeed, all of those programs ceased to operate. Birthright, however, continues to stand strong. Thanks to the program, about 50 percent of the target age group of Jews in the world visit Israel each year.

When I realized that my original idea wouldn't fly, I came up with a new formula of shared funding by the Israeli government and major Jewish donors. It wasn't easy to sell the idea. The objection in Israel was mainly related to the Talmudic dictum "the poor of your own city take precedence," and Israelis were disinclined to buy plane tickets for young people from wealthy families. The reservations expressed by Jewish philanthropists mainly derived from the fact that each had already adopted another Jewish project, and it wasn't easy to persuade them that my idea was feasible.

The toughest meeting for me was with my old friend Charles Bronfman and his wife Andy. After speaking briefly about the subject, he suggested that we meet in Jerusalem, at the home of Andy's parents, the Morrisons, and that I present my ideas to them. I sat with Charles and Andy by the pool there. They were dressed in beach clothes, and I was sweating in a suit and tie. I spoke with them about creating a Jewish forum called Beit Yisrael [House of Israel] that would address matters of concern to the Jewish world; one of the organization's divisions would work on bringing young Jews to visit Israel. I estimated that the program of Israel visits would cost $200 million a year.

They rejected both ideas. Charles said (and perhaps he was right) that there was no real chance of creating a democratic Jewish organization; ultimately, it would be led by activists and politicos, and it would look just like the Jewish Agency. Andy said that it would be a mistake to bring young Jews to visit Israel without asking them to spend a dollar from their own pocket. Even if we obtained funding for the project, she argued, we'd find ourselves without participants because when people receive a gift and don't need to fork over a cent—they treat it accordingly. "They'll toss the plane tickets in the trash and fly to Paris instead," she said.

Charles agreed with her assessment and added, "You don't give things for free. That's a basic rule!" He went on to say that he did not dispute the importance of bringing young Jews to Israel, and for that reason he had been contributing to the Israel Experience program for a number of years, and many young Jews visited Israel each year in the framework of that program. He was interested in expanding that program and bringing more young people, but he was unequivocal in asserting: "The moment you give it for free, the project will collapse."

I didn't give up easily. I said that "free of charge" depends very much on the nature of the gift. I suggested the possibility of conducting a pilot program in one community in order to test the concept. Charles also opposed this idea and reiterated that once people learned that the trip was free, no one would agree to pay for a trip in the future.

Four days later, they sent me a letter. I was surprised. Had they reconsidered their initial response and changed their minds? No, not at all—the letter was intended to further substantiate their response. It stretched over several pages and included words of appreciation for the storm I had stirred in the Jewish world. However, when it came to the subject of the visits to Israel, Charles wrote:

> I don't believe that people get very enthusiastic when something is given to them for free. In our society, we are willing to pay provided there is a perceived value to that for which we are paying. I believe very much in scholarships for those who can't afford to make the trip, and Andy has come up with a terrific idea about subsidies—that the subsidy be a pre-payment for post-trip community work. The key is, though, that those who can afford to pay should do so because that payment will make the Israel Experience much, much more worthwhile.

Around the same time, I met with Michael Steinhardt, who was considered the "king" of hedge funds and was very interested in the issue of Jewish continuity. He also brought *The Last Night of Ballyhoo* to Broadway. The play portrays the tension between Jewish immigrants from Germany and their Russian counterparts, and features the formal Ballyhoo ball, where young Jews living in non-Jewish areas meet each other and fall in love.

I traveled to his estate in upstate New York. It was a Saturday, and he had just returned from feeding his animals. I told him that I intended to do something similar to the story of Ballyhoo: to create a great Jewish meeting place in Israel to promote Jewish continuity. We spoke for a long time, and at the end of the conversation Steinhardt expressed skepticism about the feasibility of the idea but said he was willing to invest $15,000 to study it. I turned down his offer. I could never have guessed that he would be the one to ultimately enable my idea to reach fruition.

I tried to take advantage of every trip to the US to talk with philanthropists who might be willing to help fund trips to Israel, but the only responses I received were complete rejection or "I'll give it some thought." I was also involved in producing brochures on the subject and was in close contact with the Redbridge community in northeast London, home to about thirty-five thousand Jews. The community offered to serve as the pilot community for the program and to provide full funding. I was inclined to accept this offer. But the icy reactions, on the one hand, and the demands of my job as deputy foreign minister, on the other hand (not to speak of the personal attacks and the constant threats against my family and me in the wake of the Oslo Accord), did not leave me much time to pursue the idea of Israel trips funded by the Jewish people.

✷✷✷

After Rabin's murder, the subject of visits by young Jews was further relegated to the back burner. I was busy advocating for a withdrawal from Lebanon and campaigning for the leadership of the Labor Party against

Ehud Barak. But one day, I received an invitation from Steinhardt to meet at the King David Hotel in Jerusalem. I didn't know whether he wanted to talk about a particular issue, but assumed he was interested in a general analysis of the situation in Israel. Nonetheless, I decided to bring with me some new material, prepared by a team led by Gidi Grinstein, on the proposal for fully funded Israel visits.

My advisor Haim Weizman accompanied me, and Laura Lauder from the San Francisco federation was with Michael. He told me that he had decided to devote his time to Jewish philanthropy and had been looking for a major new project since our last meeting, three years earlier. Various ideas at different stages of development had been presented to him, and he had concluded that the only initiative with the potential for making a dramatic difference was my "baby," as ambitious as it may be. Steinhardt added that he believed it was possible to mobilize a large group of Jewish philanthropists, with each one committing to contribute one million dollars annually for five years. Then, with the help of the Israeli government and the Jewish federations, it would be possible to meet the expected demand. He also said that he intended to speak with Prime Minister Netanyahu about this idea, and to ask him to ensure that the government plays its part in the project.

I told him that when I shared my idea with Netanyahu at an early stage, he expressed regret that he hadn't come up with the idea himself. After saying this with a smile, Netanyahu promised to help with anything I need in this context. At the time, he was serving as a deputy minister. But now, he was in a very different position as prime minister. In any case, I wanted to jump for joy after hearing that Steinhardt was on board.

I didn't do that, in part because Michael went on to say that he usually partnered with Charles Bronfman in contributing to Jewish projects, and that since Charles was also in Jerusalem at the time, he would talk to him about it. I was concerned that Charles might pour cold water on Michael's enthusiasm. But Michael phoned me on Saturday night to inform me that Charles was with him. I don't know what was said in their conversation—but in those moments, the two became the founding fathers of Birthright. In a subsequent meeting with the two philanthropists, the prime minister promised to secure state funding for the project.

∗∗

Starting in January 1998, the process of establishing the program entered high gear. Michael asked Avraham Infeld to lead the founding team. Shimshon Shoshani, a former director-general of the Education Ministry, later assumed this role. Gidi Mark, whom I had recruited for the project back when he was assisting me as a consular official in New York, was appointed the project's chief operating officer and later replaced Shoshani as CEO. Gidi Grinstein, Yoav Shapira, and Einat Wilf worked vis-à-vis the American team to update the plans. The project began to take shape.

However, there was still no government funding. The political situation was unstable; Netanyahu resigned as prime minister at the end of 1998 and Ehud Barak was elected on May 17, 1999. As minister of justice in Barak's government, I made every effort to secure funding for Birthright. The new minister of diaspora affairs, Rabbi Michael Melchior, was an enthusiastic supporter of the idea, and together we persuaded the finance minister, Beiga Shochat, to move from hesitancy to support.

On November 8, 1999, the government decided to allocate $70 million for the Birthright project over five years, including an immediate transfer of $4 million. Just over a month later, on December 14, the first planeload of Birthright participants landed at Ben-Gurion Airport. The El Al 747 was painted with huge letters: "Birthright Israel." I spoke to the excited young people—some kissed the ground and some danced. But I think I was even more excited than they were.

On February 4, 2000, I received a letter from Bronfman:

> Thank you for working, first with Michael and then with me, to convince us of the need for what became Birthright Israel. As you know, I was skeptical to begin with, mainly over the impact of something that is provided entirely as a gift. Even so, those magical ten days in January changed my mind! The gift was emotionally expressed by the students in an incredibly positive way. Yossi, we had a trump card here, and I hope that Michael also hopes to continue working with you to advance this initial success. . . . Well done to you, Yossi!

ALONG THE ROADSIDE

In the summer of 2000, immediately after the failure of the Camp David talks, I invited Faisal Husseini to meet with me. The main stumbling block at the talks involved the sacred places in the Old City of Jerusalem, and I wanted to better understand what was behind the Palestinian demand for sovereignty over the Temple Mount.

"Let's say there's an earthquake in Jerusalem," Husseini said, "and the buildings on Al-Haram a-Sharif [the Temple Mount] are completely destroyed. Let's say, Yossi, that you're the prime minister. Not Netanyahu and not Barak either. You also wouldn't allow the reconstruction of the

Dome of the Rock and the Al-Aqsa Mosque. The religious Jews would be ready to sacrifice their lives to prevent an Israeli government from rebuilding them, and that would also resonate throughout the entire Jewish world. If the mount were under our sovereignty, we'd find the financial means and rebuild the two structures. That's why sovereignty is so important."

The conversation did not end with that. My main argument was that even if he were right, we couldn't base peace accords on such improbable circumstances. However, our discussions came to an abrupt end: A year later, he died unexpectedly during a visit to Kuwait. He was sixty-one and was, according to his own definition, an enemy. But he was also a leader and a partner.

34

Turn on the TV, Rabin's Been Shot!

I HAD A LONG CONVERSATION WITH EHUD BARAK AFTER HE COMpleted his term as IDF chief of staff on January 1, 1995. We had never talked politics before, but my impression was that he was a hawk on matters of security and dovish on the peace process. The pundits envisioned a political future for him and were sure he'd make a smooth transition from the army to the political arena. (This was before the enactment of legislation stipulating a three-year "cooling off" period before top security officials are eligible to vie for a Knesset seat.)

Barak didn't dismiss the possibility of joining the Labor Party, and expressed affinity for Rabin and Peres, but said he had other plans. He told me that he preferred to secure financial independence for himself before entering politics. I argued that it was not the time for such self-indulgence and that if there was ever an "hour of need"—it was now the hour.

He had put off a minor operation on his leg until completing his military service, and now allowed himself the time to undergo medical treatment. Consequently, he was unable to wear shoes for a number of days and decided to use the time to study the history of the Zionist labor movement. I still had the materials from a course I had taught at the university on socialism in Israel (including pre-state Israel), so I wouldn't have to prepare a special course of study for him. I told him I'd be glad to volunteer to teach him the history of Poalei Zion (Workers of Zion), HaPoel HaTzair (The Young Worker), the "Unaffiliated" movement, Gdud HaAvoda (The Work Battalion) and the various offshoots of these groups. Since he was extraordinarily intelligent, I noted, we could cover this material quickly.

Thus, for a period of days, I came to his hotel room in Herzliya quite late at night and sat with him for a couple of hours discussing Ben-Gurion and Berl Katznelson, Yitzhak Tabenkin, and Meir Ya'ari and Ya'akov Hazan. I explained their different approaches, which of them defined themselves as a socialist, a social democrat, and so on. I was happy to see that he was interested in the subject, and he was undoubtedly one of the best students I ever had. It was only then that I learned that Barak was a night owl, that the wee hours of the night were his best hours, and that he liked to get up late in the morning.

I also told Barak about my doctoral dissertation and asked if he'd be interested in joining the Octet if and when he entered politics. He immediately rejected the idea—the former commander of the Sayeret Matkal commandos preferred to go it alone.

Soon afterwards, he decided to travel to the United States, and we met in Washington a few weeks later. For some reason, I remember that he wore a prominent, dark ring from Stanford University, where he had completed a master's in Engineering-Economic Systems in 1978; he was apparently now enjoying a sort of nostalgic respite. I asked him whether he was indeed building a nest egg for his family, and he said he hoped so. I outlined my analysis of the political situation in Israel and reiterated that I didn't think he could permit himself to take this timeout from public service. It was clear to me that he was weighing his options. The aura of an IDF chief of staff is not eternal, and he understood this very well. In any case, I promised not to nag him about this, and ultimately, he decided to dive into the political waters.

On July 17, 1995, at a special meeting of the Labor Party's central committee, Rabin presented Barak's candidacy for minister of interior and my candidacy for minister of economics and planning. As part of my new job, Rabin asked me to coordinate the preparations for the economic conference scheduled to be held in Amman in November. I gladly accepted the assignment. In the same conversation, I thanked him for the ministerial portfolio, but added that I was accepting it only because I thought the ministry should be shut down.

The Economics and Planning Ministry was a superfluous ministry that Menachem Begin had established in order to find a place in the government for his friend Ya'akov Meridor. A department or two were plucked from the Finance Ministry, and also from the Prime Minister's Office, to form an artificial ministry. The ministry's sixty-three employees made important contributions to the public good, but they could have done this in the previous frameworks.

Rabin laughed. He said he had never heard of someone taking on a ministerial portfolio in order to close a ministry. The prime minister was sure that I'd be coming to him in another few months to ask for a budget increase for the ministry to help it fulfill its vital tasks.

I promised him that there was no chance of that happening. I added that there was an idea I hadn't managed to implement when I was cabinet secretary and perhaps could implement now: preparing a page on each of the prioritized items on cabinet meeting agendas. I didn't have to explain to him—he knew better than me—that most of the ministers are unfamiliar with many of the topics discussed in the meetings. They receive a brown envelope on Wednesday, skim through the material, check if there are topics pertaining to their ministries or issues that might intrude on their territory—and tend to vote in favor of their colleagues' proposals or in line with the prime minister's position.

Rabin, who was uncharacteristically in high spirits during the conversation, asked with a wry smile whether it wouldn't be too dangerous if the ministers were to suddenly know what they were voting on. But he gladly accepted my proposal, and the Ministry of Economics and Planning began to prepare a page on each topic every week. The ministers embraced the new practice, except when they felt their ministry's proposal was not described in a positive and worthy manner.

In any case, I indeed kept my word and dismantled the Economics and Planning Ministry, returning the departments to their original ministries. But Rabin was no longer alive to witness this—he had already been assassinated.

The director-general of the Economics and Planning Ministry was my former policy advisor, Dr. Alon Liel. Even if he didn't like my idea of shutting down the ministry, he helped to carry it out, with a focus on protecting the ministry's employees.

Meanwhile, we worked hard to prepare for the conference in Amman. Our main partner was the Palestinian minister of planning, my friend Dr. Nabil Sha'ath, and the two of us worked in coordination with the Jordanian minister of planning, Rima Khalaf. The central task was to prepare information packets for regional entrepreneurs, primarily in the fields of infrastructure and tourism. We worked on this in collaboration with the private sector, whose key representative was Dr. Yossi Vardi.

We held frequent meetings in Jordan, which successfully met the complex challenge of hosting the conference. The feeling was that a new era was dawning in the Middle East, and that Israel was becoming a regional asset in the eyes of the Arab world. The economic cooperation was not artificial; we addressed issues that were critical for Jordan, such as the supply of water, and we saw that a shared electric grid would be very beneficial to both sides. You didn't need to be an economic genius to understand that the lack of economic cooperation imposed on us until the 1990s was very costly, and not only for us.

On the morning of the conference, I flew in the helicopter that took the prime minister from the helipad at the Knesset. I told him there was an important matter I wanted to present to him after returning from a short trip to the US later that week. He said he'd be glad to hear what I had to say and asked me to set an appointment with his office. The meeting never took place. Ever since, I've asked myself whether he would have seen the Beilin-Abu Mazen document in a positive light, as he had in the case of the preliminary Oslo document in February 1993, and whether he would have been ready to launch negotiations based on it. History doesn't provide answers to such questions.

On Friday, November 3, 1995, I arrived in New York. The next morning, our consul general in the Big Apple, Colette Avital, hosted a brunch at her home. She invited several dozen guests, most of them New Yorkers and some of them Israelis who were staying in the city, to hear my assessment of Israel's political situation and prospects for the peace process. The participants were worried that not enough people would come to the demonstration planned for Saturday night in Tel Aviv. I was confident that many people in the peace camp would be eager to express their identification with a government whose top priority was achieving peace and was unwilling to surrender to extremists.

Among the guests at the brunch was Amos Oz, who walked me back to my hotel along Park Avenue. Amos was one of the very few people who knew about my channel with Abu Mazen on a final status accord, and he agreed that we had to shorten the path toward a solution. I was familiar with his strict writing regimen at his home in Arad and came several times during hours when he wasn't writing in order to show him some of the drafts and hear his comments.

It was only on that Saturday in New York that I updated him about our "graduation party" with Abu Mazen a few days earlier in Tel Aviv to celebrate the completion of a final agreement drafted by his team and mine. He was very curious to hear how we had formulated the solutions for Jerusalem and the refugees. We arrived at my hotel still in mid-conversation, so he came up to my room, and we continued talking there. It was the early afternoon in New York. And then the telephone rang. It was my bureau chief, Orit Shani: "Turn on CNN, quickly. Rabin's been shot!"

At that moment, we obviously assumed that it was an act of Palestinian terrorism.

Shocked, we stayed glued to the TV set and thought that Rabin had only been wounded and would recover. After all, it was hard to believe that anyone could mortally wound someone who was so well-guarded. But we soon learned from the TV reports that it was an Israeli assassin and that Rabin's condition was critical.

Barak was also staying at the same hotel. I immediately called his room and found that he was also following the chilling news. And then Orit called again.

"It's over," she said. "Rabin is dead."

The news was confirmed by CNN a few minutes later.

There are undoubtedly many ways to describe the feelings that swept over us. Amos certainly could express them in a more literary way than I could, but at that moment we both sufficed with weeping. After a few minutes, Amos got up and walked to the door. We didn't say a word to each other. We hugged, silently, for a long moment. Everything was so clear and so unfathomable.

I remained alone in the room. I didn't cry at my parents' funerals, but in those moments in the New York hotel room, I simply couldn't hold back the tears. And it was Rabin—a person whose behavior I often found unbearable: his snide remarks, his bluntness, and his attitude toward me. The famous bloodstained page of the *Song of Peace* said everything for me: In the end, he paid with his life for his readiness to make peace, and I'll always be indebted to him for that.

But now? What would happen now? Everyone would say that the man was murdered, but his path would continue. But could this indeed be realized? How crucial was it that peace would come at the hands of this particular man, who had appeared with his visor cap and, unknowingly, had imbued me with confidence in the Paran desert nearly thirty years earlier?

Countless thoughts raced through my mind in the wake of the incomprehensible event that had just occurred. Besides wondering whether Israel could remain the same Israel after the assassination, I suddenly realized that Yitzhak Rabin had been the greatest challenge of my life. I wasn't fond of him, and he wasn't fond of me, but it turned out that Rabin had a greater impact on my public life than anyone else—not because I saw him as a role model and not because I saw myself following in his footsteps, but because I couldn't explain the key moves in which I was involved or initiated without his role in them.

During my seven years as party spokesman, his presence was always felt—even when he was absent. Every press statement or media briefing took into consideration how Rabin might react and the implications of the cursed conflict between Rabin and Peres: when he decided to compete for the party's leadership, when he decided not to complete, when he announced that he'd take anti-nausea pills and participate in a particular vote, when he decided to run for the Knesset as part of a team led by Peres, and so on.

In the struggle to impose sanctions on the apartheid regime in South Africa, Rabin was my main challenge, not the Likud ministers. He was the one who sought to neutralize Peres, and thus also exclude me from involvement in the bilateral peace talks when I was deputy foreign minister. And he was my greatest challenge in the Oslo process, when I feared that every facial expression or offhand comment he made signaled his intention to terminate it. He was the one for whom I tried to tailor the understandings I reached with Abu Mazen.

Peres needed me and wasn't embarrassed to show it. The work with Peres flowed and was fruitful, fascinating, and enriching. We got used to each other. We angered each other, and we knew how to overcome serious disagreements. I exploited (for the good, I believe) the freedom he gave me in the various positions I filled, as long as I operated under his authority. However, Rabin was the wall I had to eventually climb in order to achieve my goals. But he was also the wall that supported me in the most important endeavor of my life.

Nothing prepared me for the murder of a prime minister in whose government I served, and it was impossible to comprehend the unbearable ease with which someone could uproot him from the world of the living and neutralize him forever.

In my hotel room in New York, I was restless. I phoned Barak. We decided to return to Israel on El Al that night. Our security people arranged seats on the plane for us, even though it was already full. I was told that the passengers who lost their seats because of us were very understanding. I didn't sleep a wink the entire flight. We spoke about the incident and wondered whether the murder was orchestrated by an underground, like the Jewish Underground a decade earlier, or whether it was the act of a sole assassin. In any case, it was still unfathomable, and the questions it raised about the future felt endless. We discussed the murder's effect on Israel's image and the argument that Israel should be wary of signing peace treaties with its undemocratic neighbors because regime changes could overturn the agreements—while it was actually Israel where the prime minister was murdered after signing peace accords.

Meanwhile, as Barak and I were still en route to Israel, the cabinet convened in Tel Aviv and chose Shimon as acting prime minister. It was done without any dissension, as the obvious recourse. Ehud told me that, according to the law, the Peres government could serve for about another year, and added that he intended to meet the next day with Peres and recommend himself as Rabin's replacement as defense minister and me as Peres's replacement as foreign minister.

✱✱✱

Upon landing on Sunday, I went straight from Ben-Gurion Airport to Peres's office. He was grim, tired, and far from certain how to lead the state in the coming days. The entire world was slated to arrive for the funeral, and that was the only topic on the agenda at that stage. We divided between us the task of accompanying the guests, and I was assigned Prince Charles and Tony Blair, who was then the opposition leader in Britain as head of its Labour Party.

At the funeral itself, Peres eulogized Rabin and called him "my big brother." Many viewed this as the height of hypocrisy, but that wasn't true; Rabin's murder was a traumatic blow for Peres. The tensions between them perhaps never disappeared, but they were both intelligent enough to work together. The fact that Peres became prime minister in such an expected way did not allow him to feel even a bit of the optimism so characteristic of him. It felt like the end of the world, or at least the end of the State of Israel as we had known it; we had wanted to believe that it was immune to phenomena like the murder of its leaders.

There was great anger then against the political right and the national-religious camp, with which the assassin was affiliated. People said it was difficult to walk around Tel Aviv with a kippah. People blamed Netanyahu, saying that his inflammatory rhetoric, especially at the demonstration in Zion Square, had led to the murder. I was fearful of this onslaught of collective blame and didn't know where it would lead. I thought it was important to lower the flames. When asked in a CNN interview whether I blamed Netanyahu, I said I was sure that he felt as I do and that he also viewed what happened as a national tragedy—despite his fierce criticism of Rabin, of Peres and of me personally. After the interview, I received two telephone calls. The first was from Netanyahu, who thanked me for what I said; the second was from Leah Rabin, who was angry that I had "made life too easy for him."

In the meantime, Peres weighed his moves in the wake of the murder. The polls published in the media showed him leading Netanyahu by tens of percentage points in a potential election. It seemed that if he called for early elections for the Knesset and prime minister, the left-wing bloc would win in a landslide. On the other hand, Peres was well aware of the disparity between pre-election polls and actual election results and believed that events could occur within 100 days that could jeopardize the victory. He also didn't want to be accused of "dancing on Rabin's blood" by calling for early elections. On the other hand, he wanted to lead diplomatic initiatives based on a personal mandate expressed in elections, and not as a continuation of the mandate Rabin received in 1992.

Thus, in terms of the peace process, he went back to deliberating between the Palestinian channel versus the Syrian channel. President Clinton informed him about the "deposit" Rabin had given Warren Christopher—his willingness to withdraw from the Golan Heights if Israel's security demands were met. Rabin had never spoken to Peres about this, and Peres felt uncomfortable when Clinton discussed the matter with him, assuming he had been involved in making the dramatic decision. Peres admitted to the president that he was hearing about it for the first time but promised to honor Rabin's commitments.

Clinton proposed holding talks in the US between the Israeli and Syrian delegations. The Syrians were willing to do this after being jolted (like the Jordanians) by the PLO's unilateral move in Oslo, and they decided that the time had come to focus on their own interests and establish an independent channel with Israel. On the other hand, Peres wanted to continue to advance vis-à-vis the Palestinians and believed, unlike me, that it would be difficult to conduct both channels simultaneously.

On Saturday, November 11, a week after Rabin's murder, I came to Peres's home in Jerusalem (the foreign minister's residence, on 7 Rachel Street) to present the Beilin-Abu Mazen document to him. I arrived with rolled-up maps at the apartment building, which was secured from every possible corner. I told him the whole story, about the agreement I had reached with Arafat and the work we had done in the following two years. We went over each section, and he studied the maps I brought, which demarcated Israel's annexation of 4.5 percent of the West Bank in exchange for full territorial compensation, primarily in the Halutza area.

As usual, Peres didn't say a word about the fact that during most of that two-year period I was serving as his deputy and hadn't informed him about my secret project. He sufficed with saying that it was a very interesting document but didn't think the Israeli public would accept giving up the Jordan Valley. He also said he didn't think it would be right to present such a comprehensive plan prior to elections and would prefer to revisit the subject after them. I tried to persuade him that the document could serve as Labor's leading banner in the 1996 elections. This was not a convincing argument in his eyes, especially when his victory seemed so certain according to the latest polls. A two-hour conversation resulted in the suspension of two years of work. I phoned Abu Mazen and told him that if he hadn't yet shown the document to Arafat, it was important for him to know that Peres was not ready to use it at this stage.

Peres wanted to shorten his term as acting prime minister and sought to quickly reconstitute Rabin's minority government. I thought that would be a mistake and suggested that in the current circumstances the NRP might be interested in joining the coalition. That would enable us to muster a majority in the Knesset, while demonstrating to the NRP a sort of understanding that the peace camp did not hold the entire national-religious camp collectively responsible for the prime minister's assassination. I added that the agreement with the NRP could be similar to the one it made with Golda, and later with Rabin: It would not prevent the government from conducting peace negotiations, but any results would need to be approved in a referendum or elections. Peres gave me the green light to explore this option with the leader of the NRP, Zevulun Hammer.

I invited Hammer to meet with me, and we had a long conversation on the assassination, on the feelings of the national-religious camp, and on the severe and unfair accusations leveled against the entire camp. I told him that I understood the feelings of his camp and believed we could address them politically, by broadening the coalition and welcoming the NRP into a government led by Peres—provided that we could continue negotiating with the Palestinians and the Syrians. Hammer accepted my proposal and was willing to reach an agreement that would preserve the Rabin coalition with the addition of the NRP. We agreed that the new coalition would continue until the elections about a year later and would not prevent the continuation of peace negotiations.

We scheduled a three-way meeting that evening at Peres's residence in Jerusalem. The conversation was long, tough, penetrating, and essential. The result was positive and, of course, was conditional upon the consent of the coalition parties. Peres was confident about winning the support of the Labor Party, and I took it upon myself to speak with Yossi Sarid, who was slated to assume the leadership of Meretz in January 1996.

I admit—Yossi's response took me by surprise, and I certainly didn't expect its decibels. The moment he heard the idea, he rejected it out of hand. "It's unthinkable that the political consequence of Rabin's murder will be to bring the settlers' party into the government," he said. He saw no reason to present the idea for discussion in Meretz and declared that Meretz would not sit in the same government with the NRP. Later, he also expressed in the media his utter rejection of "Yossi Beilin's perverse ways."

In the end, Peres did not want to engage in a confrontation with Sarid, and the coalition he formed was an exact replicate of the one led by Rabin.

We traveled together from Jerusalem to Tel Aviv for a Labor Party central committee meeting where we needed to win approval for Peres's coalition. Peres pulled out a piece of paper with a list of the government ministries and the names of the people he wished to appoint to head each ministry. He told me that he wanted to retain the defense portfolio for himself, as Rabin had done, until the elections the following year, after which he would reshuffle the ministerial assignments. For now, he would assign Barak the Foreign Ministry. He asked me if I'd be interested in heading the Ministry of Public Security because Moshe Shahal had told him that he didn't want to be reassigned that portfolio. I replied that I wasn't interested and would prefer to complete the dismantling of the Economics and Planning Ministry and then remain as a minister without portfolio, focusing on the peace process and other issues, until the next elections. He didn't press me to change my mind.

After the central committee approved the Peres-led government, it was brought before the Knesset for a vote. It was one of the less festive events in my public life, even though Peres was now again the prime minister, and the citizenry seemed to be with us. Indeed, the opposition (led by Netanyahu) abstained in the vote to approve the prime minister—the only time in Israeli history this has occurred.

✳✳✳

Ostensibly, we could now use the time remaining until the next elections to expedite the peace process. However, the enormous shadow of the assassination made all of these factors less important. There was a profound sense that things would never be as they once were. Peres in his second term as prime minister was nothing like Prime Minister Peres of the 1980s. The energy was not the same energy, the enthusiasm was not the same enthusiasm, and, for sure, the optimism was not the same optimism. It took quite a few years for him to return to himself. This was also expressed in the opinion polls: The Labor Party started to lose Knesset seats, and Peres's edge over Netanyahu began to dwindle.

A wave of terror attacks that followed the targeted killing of Yahya Ayyash ("the Engineer") on January 5, 1996, contributed to the erosion of public support for us. More than sixty Israelis were killed in four acts of terror at that time—each incident and its particular brutality; each incident and its painful photos; each incident with those who hurried to the site and declared that the killing was spawned by the peace process; and each incident with the challenging effort to answer and be heard. In addition, the talks in the US with the Syrian delegation were suspended after the Syrians refused to denounce the wave of Palestinian terrorism.

At some point, Peres decided to call for early elections. I cannot forget our elation in the Labor Party's Knesset faction when we defeated the opposition's proposal to postpone the elections for several months, to May 29. There is no better example of a Pyrrhic victory.

Of course, it wasn't true elation. The primaries for the party's Knesset list were held in an atmosphere of mourning. All of the members of the Octet were again elected to realistic slots on the ticket after again running together and helping each other. I was elected to the eleventh slot.

✳✳✳

In the months following Rabin's assassination, heightened security measures were imposed to protect government ministers. In addition to the guard post set up outside my apartment building and a personal bodyguard, there was an "advance" team that scouted out my next destination and only then permitted my vehicle to arrive. We would leave my home via different routes in order to break routine. Some of the routes went against the direction of traffic, with one of the security officers stopping traffic to allow my vehicle to proceed.

In such moments, you want to bury yourself. You're surrounded by young people whose mission is to protect you, even with their own bodies, as if their lives were less important than yours. Other people are delayed because of you.

When you aren't home, raucous demonstrations are held outside the building. The residents, who just want to get home, are stopped by the security personnel and asked for their apartment number. You don't want to look in your neighbor's eyes and see the quiet blame for disturbing their daily routine.

In addition to all of this, despite the assassination, there were more and more telephone threats, and it wasn't uncommon to receive messages informing the members of my family that I had died in a car accident or in some other way, and this took a toll on them. On Passover eve, for example, we found ourselves at my niece's home, sitting at the *seder* with a bodyguard. On one occasion, we—my security detail and I—left Jerusalem early enough to allow me to shower at home in Tel Aviv before my next meeting, but I was informed that the "advance" team had already arrived at the next address, so I wasn't permitted to stop at home.

I also avoided going to places if it wasn't essential. I remember during visits to Arab communities that I was always asked, "Yossi, don't you trust us?" And it didn't help to explain that the security men accompanied me everywhere, in Jewish and in Arab communities alike. Each such meeting entailed a sort of insult, and each time I wondered whether the harm didn't outweigh the benefit.

Meanwhile, the gap narrowed between Labor and Likud and between Peres and Bibi. At the end of election day, the exit polls showed Peres winning by a slim margin in the race for prime minister, and we all breathed a sigh of relief. After several interviews with the Israeli and foreign media, I went to sleep feeling that we had won a victory by the skin of our teeth. But in the early hours of the morning, I heard cries of jubilation from afar and understood that they weren't coming from the Labor Party.

When I turned on the radio, I learned that Bibi had won by less than one percent of the vote.

The direct election for prime minister, which Peres had believed in so strongly, ultimately contributed to his downfall.

✸✸✸

Peres remained in Tel Aviv after the elections and, as usual, arrived early to work the next morning at the Defense Ministry in the Kirya complex. I phoned his office and was told that it was as quiet as Yom Kippur there. No one had come to speak with him, and it would be good if I came. When I arrived, I was told that he was on his daily phone call with his wife Sonia, but that I should go in. They called each other *"Buzhik."* When she asked how things were going, he would answer *"luxe de luxe"*—even when the situation was not so splendid. As he motioned me into the room, they had reached the "What's for lunch?" stage of the conversation. "Chicken is fine," Peres replied, and the phone call came to an end.

In the conversation that followed, we discussed the option of a national unity government led by Netanyahu. I told him that contrary to my traditional opposition to such governments, this time there was a deadline of critical importance for the State of Israel: May 4, 1999, the date set in Oslo for a final agreement. If Netanyahu headed a right-wing government, he wouldn't be eager to reach a final agreement with the Palestinians. But if we were inside the government, we could change the government's course of action. He agreed, and it later turned out that other Labor Party leaders were inclined to support a national unity government.

Netanyahu was much less enthusiastic about the idea and ultimately formed a government composed of right-wing and ultra-Orthodox parties. Thus, we found ourselves in the opposition.

35

No Positions, Only Principles

I was sitting in my Knesset office one evening, and Michael (Miki) Eitan knocked on the door. In my eyes, Miki was one of the most extreme hawks in the Likud. I remembered the days when he formed the "Lobby for the Land of Israel Front" in the Knesset. I was curious to hear what he had to say. He explained that he was still a Greater Land of Israel man at heart, but realized that the Oslo process had changed the reality and that the political right must adapt itself to the new situation; it must make an effort to fight for those issues it viewed as red lines in future negotiations with the Palestinians, while offering something in return to our interlocutors.

I was very pleased to hear this and asked him what he planned to do. He proposed that we convene a series of meetings with a number of left-wing and right-wing MKs to determine whether we can find any common ground. And if we do find points of agreement, we can then jointly prepare a document that can serve as a platform for future talks with the Palestinians. He knew, of course, about the agreement I had reached with Abu Mazen, though the actual document had yet to be published, and said that based on what he had read in the media, the principles in the Israeli-Palestinian document were not impossible to bridge. I told him I was very happy to learn about his initiative, though it was hard for me to imagine us formulating a joint document that could overcome the hurdle of sloganeering. After all, the two of us had never conducted an in-depth conversation on the peace process.

We made plans to meet again. Miki and I spoke about our motives and about possible solutions for ensuring Israel's existence as a Jewish and democratic state. We exchanged lists of proposed names for his initiative. Neither of us rejected the other's list, though some of the people, particular those on the political right, bowed out of the initiative after a few meetings.

I discussed the idea with my friend Dr. Arik Carmon, the president of the Israel Democracy Institute (IDI), and asked whether the IDI would host our experiment, even if its chances of success were not great. Arik replied that this was exactly the institute's mission: to examine such ideas.

Several months later, after holding meetings at least once a week after Knesset plenum sessions, a document was signed by eight MKs: Ze'ev Boim (Likud), Shlomo Ben-Ami (Labor), Eliezer Sandberg (Tzomet), Yehuda Lancry (Gesher), Haim Ramon (Labor), Meir Sheetrit (Likud), Miki Eitan, and me. Likud MKs Naomi Blumenthal and Michael Kleiner also participated in the meetings, but quit before the document was signed, as did several Labor MKs. Rumors were circulating in the Knesset about these unexpected meetings, and criticism of the initiative also reached the plenum debates. Right-wingers accused Miki of willingness to surrender national values, while the left criticized me for my ostensible readiness to embrace populist views.

The fiercest critic was the new chairman of Meretz, Yossi Sarid, who contended that it was impossible for the right and left to find real consensus on the peace process and warned that the left was ready to give up its principles for the sake of reaching a very low common denominator. The headlines quoted a hackneyed statement of his about "squaring the circle."

Nonetheless, the conversations were fascinating, especially because they revealed that neither side had conducted an in-depth internal discussion on the elements of a final agreement with the Palestinians. Instead, both sides made do with "principles" that were in fact a list of "noes" (no to a Palestinian state, no to dividing Jerusalem, no to returning to the 1967 borders, no to the return of Palestinian refugees to Israel). When we forced ourselves to sit together and examine the "yeses"—we ran into difficulty.

I recall one meeting in which our differences of opinion on a particular issue crossed party lines. Naomi Blumenthal asked one of the Likud members about the party's position, and someone replied, half in jest, "The Likud has no positions. We have principles." The same could be said about the Labor Party—and about the Palestinians too. No one volunteered to discuss possible concessions to the other side in exchange for accepting our demands. We left the discussions on the give and take for the moment of truth, which was slow in coming.

On January 22, 1997, we convened a joint press conference and distributed the final version of what is known as the "Beilin-Eitan document." The document notes a lack of consensus regarding the Jordan Valley: "A second version insists on imposing Israeli sovereignty over the Valley." The only other disagreement that remained concerned the Palestinian political framework to be established in the wake of the permanent status negotiations. Here, the document states that Israel, subject to certain limitations, will recognize "the Palestinian entity" as one that exercises self-determination in the framework of "extensive autonomy" in one version, or in the framework of "a state" in another version. (It is noteworthy that the Labor MKs who negotiated the Beilin-Eitan agreement insisted on referring to the future entity as a "state," while the party's platform in the 1996 and 1999 elections still refrained from explicit mention of a Palestinian state.) The document won praise from many MKs who were not involved in drafting it, and even the cynic Sarid told me that I had managed to pleasantly surprise him.

The joint endeavor proved to us that some of our disagreements simply reinforced the competing frameworks in which we operated. We realized that if and when a final agreement is presented for public deliberation and approval, it will not necessarily create a rift.

Those who dropped out of the group because they felt unable to sign a joint document did so sadly, without slamming the door. The collaborative work, and the fact that many of the disagreements crossed party lines, encouraged me to form the multi-party framework that lobbied for an IDF withdrawal from Lebanon.

***

Speeches by politicians, and election speeches in particular, are a breeding ground for unfounded truths and facile assertions, and it is tempting to turn them into headlines. Abba Eban's foolishness in coining the term "Auschwitz borders" in reference to the 1967 borders, Moshe Dayan's outlandish statement that "Sharm el-Sheikh without peace is better than peace without Sharm el-Sheikh" and Ben-Gurion's ill-considered disparagement of the UN as "Umm Shmum" are among the many that are initially greeted with a smile and then somehow become Holy Writ—until they eventually are put to a practical test and tossed into the trash bin of history.

The assertion that Israel's security zone in South Lebanon provided protection for the Galilee communities was just as illogical as the original name of the First Lebanon War: Operation Peace for the Galilee. It was no coincidence that the IDF refrained from deploying reservists in the security zone, preferring to send young soldiers for whom the nightly battles with Hezbollah fighters was a sort of fascinating challenge. Those confrontations endangered the communities of northern Israel by triggering barrages of Katyusha rockets. Yet the defense establishment and political echelon convinced themselves that withdrawing from the security zone would not only fail to put an end to the rocket fire but would further expose the Galilee to rockets.

Of course, not everyone shared that view. There were those in the IDF, especially among the senior officers in the Northern Command, who believed that the security zone was a source of insecurity. However, those who held such beliefs were wary of expressing them in formal meetings. Occasionally I could tell by the tone of senior officers in meetings of the government plenum or inner cabinet that they harbored misgivings about the official line, yet that line became all-powerful.

Many soldiers spent the majority of their military service in South Lebanon, alongside the complex phenomenon called the South Lebanon Army (SLA). This gave rise to a group of parties with vested interests: NCOs and non-senior officers who played roles in maintaining the security zone and viewed their deployment there as a sort of career assignment. This also fostered close relationships between those stakeholders and SLA fighters in an area that was under Lebanese sovereignty but completely controlled by Israel. It was neither occupied territory nor annexed territory, but rather a sort of no man's land, with all of the implications this entailed.

The large slogans hanging in the dining room at each military post, assuring the soldiers that they were defending the Galilee communities, were aimed to quell the doubts of anyone who questioned this article of faith. As time went by, it became more difficult to see our deployment in the security zone as something temporary. It also became harder to share with the soldiers—many of whose comrades had been killed or injured in Lebanon—the doubts that existed in the government and in the army regarding the wisdom of remaining in Lebanon. The conventional wisdom was that the IDF would leave Lebanon in the framework of a future peace accord with Syria, because Syria was the dominant actor in Lebanon. However, a peace accord with Syria did not seem imminent.

As someone who remembered the genesis of the security zone as a sort of political compromise and who had opposed it from the start, I didn't conceal my opinion that we should get up and leave—regardless of whether the world views it as a smart move by a strong state that was not forced to do so, or whether the Arab world portrays it as a sign of weakness. It was foolish to continue to do the wrong thing only to avoid being seen as weak. As soon as I joined the government in the summer of 1995, I called for an in-depth discussion of our deployment in Lebanon. I thought that a decision to withdraw without linking it to Israeli-Syrian peace might serve as an incentive for the Syrians to engage in serious negotiations with us. The linkage between the withdrawal and peace with them turned the withdrawal into a card in their hands, and I believed that the Syrians would be in no hurry to relinquish it.

Rabin did not summarily reject my remarks, but the real surprise at my first meeting as a minister was a note I received from the legendary coordinator of Israel's activities in Lebanon, Uri Lubrani. He had been waiting a long time to hear this voice in the government, he wrote. So it became increasingly clear to me that there was a gap between the public utterances of those responsible for this issue and what they really thought. However, an in-depth discussion was not conducted. The Lebanon routine continued, with its clashes and casualties.

After Rabin's assassination, it did not feel like the right time to re-examine accepted truths. And then Operation Grapes of Wrath occurred: In April 1996, Hezbollah escalated its firing of Katyusha rockets at northern communities in Israel, in violation of the understandings reached (indirectly) following the previous operation in Lebanon—Operation Accountability. A barrage of Katyushas was fired at Kiryat Shmona on April 9. Peres, as prime minister, tried to do the best he could. Renewed conflict in Lebanon was the last thing he wanted. Hezbollah did not respond to our efforts and acted like it wanted a confrontation. We had no diplomatic recourse, so Peres's moderate government found itself compelled to approve the operation proposed by the IDF chief of staff, Amnon Lipkin-Shahak.

Three days later, I entered Peres's office and told him that now was the moment to withdraw from Lebanon: The IDF had achieved its objectives, and Israel was in a position of strength. The best way to exploit the fruits of the operation was to declare it a military success and announce a dramatic decision that Israel had reached the conclusion that it no longer needed the security zone.

Peres invited the chief of staff to a three-way conversation, and I repeated my proposal. Amnon, a smart, practical, and moderate man, rejected it out of hand. "However you frame it, it will look like an admission of defeat, even though it's a victory," he said. I agreed with him that Hezbollah would try to portray it as such, but I thought that the results on the ground would prove Hezbollah wrong. My arguments didn't help. Peres didn't want a confrontation with the IDF chief of staff and said that we'd revisit the subject after the elections.

On April 19, 1996, a force from the IDF's Maglan unit in Lebanon came under fire and requested artillery support. Our cannons fired shells to provide cover for the force's escape. Four errant shells landed next to a

UN compound in Qana, where refugees from the ongoing operation were encamped. Nearly 100 Lebanese refugees, some of them children, and four UN soldiers were killed by the shells.

I was shocked by the scope of the carnage and was angry that Peres had been unwilling to end the operation promptly. The world was also shocked and angry, and we felt the heat from Washington in particular. Peres asked me to travel to the US capital and meet with White House officials and members of Congress. They all understood the situation, and no one accused us of deliberately targeting civilians. But all we could do was apologize and end the operation with our tail between our legs.

I also appeared on television networks to define a case that was impossible to defend. Instead of explaining Israeli diplomatic initiatives, I had to explain for the thousandth time that I didn't mean to kill children. It wasn't easy.

When I returned to Israel, I worked on the Grapes of Wrath understandings, which essentially focused on defining actions that do or do not justify a violent response. The French foreign minister, Herve de Charette, came to my home on Saturday, and we sat for a long time drafting the document. The objective was to reach understandings on the conduct of the IDF and Hezbollah in the future, and for the US to present these understandings as the world's position, based on conversations with the governments of Israel and Lebanon and in consultation with Syria. Uri Savir also worked on this in the Washington channel.

On April 25, the UN General Assembly condemned Israel's actions in Lebanon and called for a cessation of hostilities. Indeed, we concluded the operation two days later with an interesting agreement that managed to hold up (more or less) for several years and included significant UN involvement.

The miserable conclusion of the operation, along with the four suicide attacks precipitated by the targeted killing of "the Engineer," were the primary factors that enabled Netanyahu to quickly close the gap in the contest for prime minister. The elections, as noted, took place a month later, on May 29.

ALONG THE ROADSIDE

In retrospect, the two years between the signing of the Oslo Declaration of Principles and Rabin's assassination were full of abrupt transitions between great hopes and exciting precedents, on the one hand, and bitter disappointments and violent precedents, on the other hand. To a great extent, the hopes sprang from the opening of the Arab world to us and the alacrity with which yesterday's enemies treated us like old friends. That was true of Jordan, the Gulf states, and North Africa.

From my perspective, the connection with Oman was very special. I arrived in the capital city, Muscat, for a discussion on water, which ultimately led to the construction of a desalination plant. I was impressed by the country and met with the movers and shakers there. There were live broadcasts of the unprecedented meetings, and there was a lofty feeling in the air.

One evening, Oman's minister of state for foreign affairs, Yusuf bin Alawi, took me on a short tour of the city streets. As a gesture of friendship, he drove the vehicle, and we discussed various topics, including Iran. I asked him where he thought Iran would be in another ten years, and he responded by asking me whether I had ever visited there. I replied in the negative. "That's the difference between us," he said. "Those who've seen the satellite dishes in Tehran understand that the citizens are exposed to what's happening in the world."

It turned out that his analysis was overly optimistic.

Soon afterwards, I returned to Muscat at the head of an interministerial delegation to sign bilateral agreements with Oman. Again, it was exciting to fly to Cairo, and from there to Doha in Qatar, and arrive in the late evening in Muscat. The Omani chief of protocol welcomed me and informed me that the meeting to discuss the agreements was scheduled for 1:00 p.m. the next day. He then asked whether I wanted to do anything special in the morning, before the meeting. I remembered being impressed by the city's beautiful fish market and said I'd be happy to show it to my colleagues.

The chief of protocol was thrilled by my choice. The next morning, a line of official vehicles awaited us, and we left the hotel, all dressed in suits, and rode to the fish market. The new market was built as a long corridor along the sea. The fish were displayed on marble tables, and the fishermen sat and waited for customers. They looked at us in astonishment, but nothing more, until we reached the heart of the market and saw a man in Western dress, unlike most of the customers. He looked at our delegation and asked whether we were French. I answered in the negative. He asked whether we were from Italy. After again answering "no," I felt compelled, as the head of the delegation, to express Israeli patriotism and told the man we were from Israel.

His face turned ashen, on the spot, and he started to deliver a speech—as if prepared in advance—about the expulsion of the Palestinian refugees in 1948 and about the injustices of Zionism. The Omani security men who accompanied us silenced him and moved him aside. I asked them to let him be, but they didn't take their orders from me.

For me, it was a clear illustration of the gap between the pragmatic leadership and public opinion. It was clear to me that even if there is normalization with Arab states, the Palestinian question, if left unresolved, will make normalization hard to implement.

36

How Do We Get Out of Lebanon?

THE SHIFT TO THE RANKS OF THE OPPOSITION DID NOT TAKE THE wind from my sails on the Lebanon issue. On the contrary, I read everything I could about Hezbollah and spoke with key figures in Israel and in the world. Most of them concurred that the organization would do its utmost to depict our withdrawal as its victory but believed that an IDF withdrawal from Lebanon would not encourage Hezbollah to fight for objectives within Israel. I also met with foreign scholars who had interviewed Hezbollah leaders. According to these scholars, the overwhelming majority of Hezbollah's leaders had affirmed that the goals of the organization (which was formed in the wake of our invasion in 1982) centered on Lebanon, and that the rhetoric about conquering Jerusalem was empty talk, even in the eyes of those who engaged in such rhetoric.

I then initiated a meeting with MKs from Labor, Likud, The Third Way, and Shas to form a parliamentary lobby for ending Israel's presence in Lebanon. I assume that the participants came to the meeting for two main reasons: Some were intent on blocking any agreement with Syria that included a withdrawal from the Golan Heights, and others thought our continued deployment in Lebanon posed a danger to Israel's northern communities rather than protecting them; the latter realized clashes between our soldiers and Hezbollah fighters led to rocket fire on those communities, and not vice versa. It was important for me to clarify that Hezbollah's threat will end only by a peace treaty with Syria, but we cannot depend on Syria forever. Whatever the motives, the common denominator mattered most, and we agreed remaining in Lebanon was detrimental to our national interest.

It was February 1997, soon after we published the Beilin-Eitan document. Miki was again a partner in the new initiative, along with his Likud colleague Gideon Ezra. The two were among the most vehement opponents of prolonging our quagmire in Lebanon. We made plans to meet again on Saturday night in Kochav Yair.

And then, on February 4, 1997, two helicopters transporting soldiers to IDF outposts in the security zone collided midair above She'ar Yashuv, killing all 73 soldiers aboard. Naturally, the horrendous accident raised the question of our long stay in South Lebanon, even though the crash occurred in Israeli airspace. If not for the deployment in Lebanon, those helicopters would never have taken off. The helicopters were also reportedly flying without lights to avoid being detected en route to Lebanon, and this further intensified the criticism about remaining in the security zone.

We decided not to cancel the meeting in Kochav Yair. For us, the accident —as chilling and tragic as it was—only underlined the absurd situation that had to be terminated. The media was waiting outside Gideon Ezra's home, and we were asked whether it was an appropriate time for such a meeting. Most of us responded that the tragedy was a dreadful expression of the heavy price we were paying to maintain a security strip that was only causing us harm. But it was not easy for any of us.

The meeting itself was emotional and gloomy. The helicopter tragedy reinforced our view, but it was clear that we would become a target of criticism. The TV news showed the gathering and presented the participants' comments on the timing of the meeting. In any case, we decided to create an extra-parliamentary framework called the Movement for a Peaceful Withdrawal from Lebanon, and I served as chairman of the movement.

On Monday afternoon, when each Knesset faction routinely convened, the MKs who had participated in the Saturday night gathering were peppered with criticism from their party colleagues. Some even accused us of "dancing on the blood of the fallen." The Likud members were pressured to quit the new movement, and they did so with heavy hearts. The others remained, and we were joined by important figures who had served the state in the IDF, Mossad, Shin Bet, and Foreign Ministry. We received many inquiries from citizens, including a letter from a group of women from Galilee kibbutzim who were very impressed by our initiative and asked to meet with me. A few days later, I traveled to Kibbutz Gadot and had long conversations with the women, who later formed the Four Mothers movement. We made plans to collaborate and hold joint events, and we followed through on those plans.

During those tumultuous days, I was interviewed on Menashe Raz's Saturday morning program on Channel 1, and I presented my opinion about the need to leave Lebanon with or without an agreement. I was surprised by the results of a public opinion survey presented on the program regarding a withdrawal from Lebanon: Only 18 percent of the respondents were in favor, with the rest opposed or undecided.

I met with bereaved families from the helicopter tragedy, but only with those who were interested. Most of the families responded positively, but some expressed reservations, and I could certainly understand that. The parents and siblings I met strongly encouraged me to persist. My main message to the families was that the soldiers' job was to carry out orders and to ensure the implementation of decisions. Their job was not to assess the wisdom of the decisions—that was the job of the general public and elected officials. As long as the decisions were made in a legal and democratic way, their implementation ensured the democracy's existence, and the fallen soldiers thus died in the service of democracy.

We formally registered the Movement for a Peaceful Withdrawal from Lebanon in 1997. My advisor Amir Abramovich coordinated this effort, and Reuven Merhav, a veteran of the Mossad and Foreign Ministry, served as the movement's director. Approximately six-thousand people signed on as supporters, including writers such as David Grossman, performers such as Orna Porat and Hanna Meron, scholars such as Shlomo Avineri, former security personnel such as Shlomo ("Chich") Lahat and Brig. Gen (Ret.) Uzi Keren, and others. We held protest vigils by the Defense Ministry and demonstrations in various places; we distributed informational materials and appeared quite often in the media. At each public event we held, we felt the mood gradually shifting in our direction.

A Labor Party convention was held in April 1997, soon after the helicopter tragedy, and Lebanon was a central topic. I had decided to compete for the party's leadership against three other candidates—Barak, Shlomo Ben-Ami, and Ephraim Sneh—and I called for the convention to call for a full withdrawal from the security zone. Barak and Sneh were strongly opposed and managed to prevent the convention from adopting my proposal.

At least at the beginning of the leadership contest, Barak thought it would benefit him electorally to support Israel's continued presence in Lebanon. (This was completely contrary to his original stance in 1985, when he opposed the creation of the security zone and advocated for a full withdrawal from Lebanon.) He published an article arguing against a withdrawal and claiming that the unilateral pullback I was proposing would be an act of "irresponsibility" that was liable to bring harm to Israel's northern communities.

In an attempt to elevate the dispute from the level of slogans, I decided to publish a detailed plan on how to withdraw from Lebanon. The document was prepared with the assistance of two retired IDF colonels, Yonatan Lerner and Asher Sadan. The main idea was a "back to back" withdrawal, coordinated with Lebanese entities, but not as part of an agreement. The pamphlet was sent to leading opinion makers and journalists in April 1998. Based on this document, I also published a pamphlet for the general public entitled "A Guide to Leaving Lebanon."

I placed the pamphlet on the desks of every member of the Knesset Foreign Affairs and Defense Committee, on which I served, prior to a meeting with the defense minister at the time, Yitzhak Mordechai. This infuriated the defense minister, who called me a "gambler." I walked out of the meeting, slamming the door behind me. The media got word of the confrontation, and most of the reactions I received were favorable.

The feeling that the army was once again (as in the prelude to the Yom Kippur War) stuck in a particular "conception" continued to spread.

∗∗∗

During that period, I visited the security zone several times and met with officers and soldiers. I listened carefully for nuances. The GOC Northern Command at the time, Amiram Levin, expressed a firm opinion that the IDF should leave Lebanon, but only after delivering a mighty blow to Hezbollah.

On February 22, 1998, I visited the Karkom outpost in the security zone together with three other MKs (Nissim Zvili, Dedi Zucker, and Naomi Chazan). I repeated my message to the soldiers about their essential role in ensuring democracy, regardless of political disagreements. "Your job is to follow orders that are backed by an elected Israeli government. Our jobs, as politicians, is to never stop weighing the question of whether it's the best way to defend the northern communities," I said.

At the end of the meeting, an officer accompanied me and asked questions he had refrained from asking in the meeting hall: How will Hezbollah act if we withdraw? What will Syria do? And does the Lebanese government have any standing? His name was Assaf Rosenfeld, a resident of Acre. He knew that I was well acquainted with his father, an activist in the Labor Party. Four days later, there was a Hezbollah attack on the Karkom outpost, and three IDF soldiers were killed. Lt. Assaf Rosenfeld was one of them. Consumed by sadness, I traveled to Acre for the *shiva*. I knew in my bones that that we should have, and could have, prevented his needless death. I told his parents about our conversation and the questions he had asked. I felt that I owed him some answers.

There was also an IDF general who came with his wife one day to my home for a heart-to-heart conversation and implored me to continue my push for a withdrawal from Lebanon. He added arguments to those I already knew. In his assessment, there would be no massacre of SLA personnel after we leave. He also urged me not to be swayed by those who argue that Israel's moral commitment to the SLA prevents us from unilaterally withdrawing. The SLA, he said, is doing what it believes is best for the future of Lebanon, just as we are driven by Israel's interests. "There's a meeting of interests, but not an identity of interests. And we must not decide to give up our interests just because the SLA wants us to stay with them in the security zone," he added. The general also complained that unspeakable acts were being committed at the Khiam detention center in the no man's land of the security zone. Though the prison was under the SLA's command, Israel bore indirect responsibility, he noted.

Each such meeting and new piece of information only reinforced my sense of mission and determination not to let up. I felt more convinced with every passing day. I recall that in one of our meetings in 1998, Arafat warned me against a unilateral withdrawal from Lebanon, saying that it would prove that Israel relinquishes territory only if you threaten it, and clings to territory if you enter into agreements with it. According to Arafat, my campaign to withdraw from Lebanon was perceived as a campaign against Palestinians who were pro-peace. I told him that I was aware of that, but that I was unwilling to let our soldiers die in order to strengthen the standing of the pragmatic Palestinian camp.

✱✱✱

As time went by, support for a withdrawal rose in the opinion polls, reaching 72 percent in early 1999. The support crossed party lines and sectors. When I was invited to participate in Dan Margalit's "Popolitika" program, I saw Barak enter the TV studio behind me. After my segment was over, I remained in the makeup room to listen to what Barak had to say. He declared that the IDF would withdraw from Lebanon within a year of the formation of a government under his leadership. I couldn't have wished for better news.

Following Barak's victory on July 9, 1999, and the formation of his government, we focused quite a bit on the question of a pullout from Lebanon. Since Barak preferred to concentrate on the Syrian channel, there was growing speculation that he would link the withdrawal from Lebanon to peace with Syria. The IDF chief of staff, Shaul Mofaz, often spoke about leaving Lebanon in the framework of an agreement. Barak remained vague on this subject. To meet his campaign promise, the IDF would have to leave by July 2000. When the negotiations with the Syrians went sour, Barak decided to pull out of Lebanon unilaterally.

The government approved the decision in May. On May 24, I was sleeping in a Jerusalem hotel when the telephone rang in the middle of the night. It was Danny Yatom, the prime minister's political-security chief of staff, on the other side of the line.

"Yossi," he said, "I have news for you that you'll be glad to hear, even in the middle of the night. We're out [of Lebanon] and everything is okay."

After that phone call, I couldn't fall asleep.

37

Hoo Ha—Look Who's Coming

NETANYAHU'S VICTORY IN 1996 MARKED THE END OF PERES'S LEADership of the Labor Party. He was already seventy-four years old, and one would never guess that his future still lay before him as the revered president of the state. Barak made it clear that he saw himself as Peres's successor, and Shimon also saw him as a worthy candidate. I viewed Barak as a born leader, but his experience in civilian life was very limited, no more than a few months. So in my assessment, Haim Ramon was more qualified to lead the party. In conversations between Ehud and Shimon at Peres's home in Tel Aviv, Barak pressed to schedule the primaries for Labor's leadership as soon as possible. Peres described this pressure to me and didn't understand why Barak was hurrying him so. In the end, the primaries were set for June 2, 1997.

I spoke with Ramon about putting forward his candidacy. He said he would do this only if the party held open primaries (that is, primaries that would also be open to non-members who paid a nominal fee to participate in the process). Haim believed that open primaries would be his only path to victory, as many party members had not forgiven him for forming a new framework with Amir Peretz ("New Life") that defeated the Labor Party in the Histadrut elections in 1994 and for the reforms he then initiated as chairman of the labor federation.

I strongly supported the idea of open primaries because they were designed to express the preferences of the general public and not only those of party activists, and I tried to persuade central committee members to back the proposal. Unfortunately, most of the members were opposed and the election system in place when Rabin defeated Peres in 1992 remained unchanged.

After the open primaries option was rejected, Ramon told me he wouldn't run for the party leadership but would support me if I decided to run. I told him that the role of top honcho was not on my wish list. I wasn't sure I was cut out for that role, and I had proven to myself that it was possible to exert influence without necessarily sitting in the front row. On the other hand, I thought the party could not allow itself to elect Ehud, despite his talents and leadership ability, because he didn't know the ropes.

A prime minister must be very familiar with the Knesset and know how to operate vis-à-vis the opposition—and just as importantly, vis-à-vis the coalition he leads. He should be familiar with the various governmental systems, including what to expect from them and what to demand of them. In addition, he must have an in-depth understanding of the roles played by the system's senior officials: the attorney general, the state comptroller, the accountant general, the police commissioner, and so on. It's a complex system, and Ehud Barak was connected only with limited parts of it. The parliamentary area almost completely unfamiliar to him, just as it had been with Rabin during his first term.

I decided to consult with some of the Octet members. Avrum Burg, who was serving as chairman of the Jewish Agency, urged me to throw my hat into the ring. Yona Yahav, who had joined us in the 1996 elections, immediately declared his support for me. I told other Octet members that I'd understand if they supported Barak. Membership in the Octet did not obligate us to support a fellow member who decided to compete for the party leadership.

Helena did not like the idea of me becoming party chairman and everything it entailed. Peres told me that he had promised to support Barak as his successor when the latter joined the Labor Party and the government, but that he was severely disappointed in him and would support me. Publicly, he remained neutral, and his support was expressed in a number of personal conversations he conducted with party members who were close to him.

My possible candidacy sparked considerable media interest, and quite a few positive articles. Opinion polls showed Barak leading me among Labor Party members, and both of us outpolled Netanyahu, though Barak led Bibi by a larger margin. It was an opportune time for me to announce my decision to run.

Barak asked to meet with me. At our meeting, he said he had no doubt that he would emerge victorious but that he believed it was "very important" (a phrase he often used) for him to win a sweeping victory in the lead-up to the fateful race against Netanyahu. I replied that he may or may not be right, but that the most important thing was for the losing candidates to pledge their full support for whoever wins the primaries. We exchanged some words of mutual appreciation, which were heartfelt I think.

He noted the efforts I had made to convince him to enter politics and said my decision to run against him was surprising. I told Barak that I didn't regret those efforts, but believed his political experience was too modest for a leap to the top of the pyramid at this stage, and I mentioned Rabin's first term as prime minister to illustrate this point. I also reminded Barak that he and I had some disagreements regarding the peace process and a withdrawal from Lebanon.

A few days later, I convened a press conference at Beit Sokolov in Tel Aviv and announced my candidacy for the party leadership. This was followed by a wave of public statements and letters expressing support for my candidacy, which drew considerable press coverage. Most of the pundits predicted a sure victory for Barak, but a number of columnists applauded my decision to run and expressed public support for my candidacy.

I immediately began to look for a campaign manager who could direct the campaign's organizational side as well as its messages. A number of people offered to take on this role, including a former general whom I had never met. His interest in this role flattered me, but it turned out that he was motivated by hostility toward Barak. I told him that I didn't belong to the anti-Barak camp, considered him a friend, admired him, and believed that he was a worthy person. The general withdrew his candidacy on the spot.

For several months, I worked nonstop on the campaign. I felt obligated to personally engage in fundraising, and these efforts bore fruit. I was similarly responsible for appointing the members of my campaign staff. The meetings at party branches and parlor gatherings were very important, and unlike general election campaigns, there were no surrogates who could replace the candidate in intensive appearances.

The campaign staff opened branches throughout Israel, and I met activists who invested time and effort in promoting my candidacy, including some who had never been in close contact with me previously. Some of these new connections developed into enduring friendships. I tried to maintain emotional composure but wasn't always successful. At a certain point, a group of young supporters was formed under the leadership of Michal Aharoni from Rehovot, and they accompanied me to all of my appearances, adding a lot of color and the familiar chant (which rhymes in Hebrew): "Hoo ha, look who's coming! The next prime minister!" Bumper stickers appeared on cars declaring: "Beilin—he's the head [*rosh*]." (The Hebrew word *rosh* can also mean leader, brains or prime [minister].) I must admit that I felt a bit uncomfortable with some parts of the campaign, but there was also something magical in it. It was exciting to see how people identified with the campaign and viewed my victory as the victory of their path. At some stage, I felt the need to win if only to avoid disappointing them.

Nonetheless, I failed in an effort to form an alliance under my leadership with the two other MKs vying for the party leadership, Shlomo Ben-Ami and Ephraim Sneh. The three of us, along with Barak, ran separately till the end. It was a fair and friendly contest, with nothing like the bad blood between Rabin and Peres. The debates we held at party branches and in the media were also respectful. All of the candidates were of high quality and had impressive life experience. Ehud had not only served as IDF chief of staff but was also the most decorated soldier in IDF history and had a graduate degree in Engineering-Economic Systems from Stanford. Ben-Ami was a professor, a brilliant intellectual, and a former ambassador to Spain. Sneh, a physician, was a brigadier general in the IDF reserves, a man of letters, and the son of Moshe Sneh. We enjoyed excellent relations before the primaries, and they remained so during and after the campaign.

Barak was expected to win in the first round. My hope was that he wouldn't cross the 40 percent threshold and that the supporters of Sneh and Ben-Ami would vote for me in the second round. Perhaps if the two had joined me, it would have been possible to defeat Barak in the first round.

The primaries were held on June 3. The number of party members eligible to vote was 163,330, and 113,981 ballots were tallied. Barak won 50.33 percent of the vote; I received 28.51 percent (32,496 votes), Ben-Ami 14.17 percent and Sneh 6.6 percent.

I met with Ehud the next day. The media wanted to know whether I intended to maintain my group of supporters as a camp within the Labor Party. I had no such intention. I told Barak that the contest, the candidates, and the way it was conducted had boosted the image of the Labor Party, giving him an excellent starting point in preparation for the general elections. "My entire political life has been in the shadow of the uncompromising battle between Peres and Rabin, so I won't lend a hand to forming a Beilin camp versus a Barak camp," I told him. He seemed relieved to hear me say this.

Indeed, the Octet no longer convened. Perhaps this was because we had already become a "political establishment," or perhaps because of the disagreements that had arisen between us in the contest for party leadership.

After Barak's unequivocal victory over Netanyahu, Ehud invited the candidates for ministerial appointments. He had postponed this for several weeks, and meanwhile speculation ran rampant. In the end, he offered Shlomo the public security portfolio and me the Justice Ministry. Haim Ramon was offered the role of minister without portfolio, with responsibility for Jerusalem affairs. Avrum was not offered a place in the government and was elected Knesset speaker with the help of his Octet colleagues and contrary to Barak's wishes.

It's hard to understand what led Barak to choose the ministries he offered us. The expectation was that since Shlomo and I had won the top spots in the Knesset primaries, one of us would be foreign minister, and the other would be finance minister. Barak never asked for our preferences and presented his proposals as the only options.

I suggested to Shlomo and Haim that the three of us inform Barak that we'd forego joining the government. With all due respect for the importance of the portfolios he offered us, we all had relative advantages that made us better suited for other roles. They rejected my suggestion, and I accepted the majority decision. The justice portfolio was challenging and important in my eyes, but I believed it would be preferable for an attorney to be minister of justice, and I wasn't thrilled to set a precedent as the first justice minister in Israel who was not an attorney.

38

Pursuing Justice

BARAK'S LACK OF POLITICAL EXPERIENCE WAS ALREADY EVIDENT A few weeks after forming a new government, which lacked any common denominator. It included right-wing and left-wing parties, and ultra-Orthodox and secular factions; special efforts were needed to keep it intact. As part of the perennial gamesmanship between Shas and United Torah Judaism (UTJ), the minister of national infrastructure, Eli Suissa (Shas), posed a challenge to UTJ when he announced that the Israel Electric Corp. was planning to transport a huge turbine part on the Jewish Sabbath. The transport was timed for the weekend, in accordance with a police directive, to avoid creating a major traffic jam during the workweek. Such turbine parts had been transported on the Sabbath in the past and had caused little stir. This time, however, it made headlines in the ultra-Orthodox press. Suissa's attempt to provoke UTJ worked, and indeed the ultra-Orthodox leadership demanded that the transport be rescheduled to avoid violating the Sabbath.

Barak was spending a quiet weekend with his wife at Moshav Beit Hillel in the Galilee. He asked Rabbi Melchior (his minister of Diaspora affairs), Isaac Herzog (his cabinet secretary) and me to try to resolve the problem. We studied the matter, conducted discussions with UTJ leaders, checked the technical options, and finally found a solution: En route to its destination—the southern coastal city of Ashkelon—three temporary parking lots would be prepared. The Electric Corp. vehicles would travel on weekday nights to avoid blocking traffic, and then park for the day at one of the three lots before the morning rush hour.

I was pleased with this simple solution and updated Barak. To my surprise, he said the solution was unacceptable to him. I asked him why. His reply stunned me: "If we cave in to the ultra-Orthodox parties, Hafez al-Assad will think that I'll cave in to him in negotiations."

"Ehud," I said, "by that time, you'll no longer have a government. UTJ finds itself in an idiotic situation that compels it to quit the government, even if it doesn't want to. And it's liable to be the first of others to leave. The solution is a compromise; it's not a matter of caving in. The turbine part will be transported, and there will be no Sabbath violation!"

He persisted in rejecting the compromise, and UTJ quit the coalition in record speed, just weeks into the new government.

※※※

I was familiar with the Justice Ministry primarily through Helena, who served many years as a senior criminal attorney. My top priority agenda at the ministry was to cancel the emergency situation that had been in effect since the establishment of the state and to replace some of the emergency-based laws with new legislation that was not conditioned upon an emergency footing. I also wanted to focus on civil rights and examine court reforms. Of course, the reality forced me to devote time and energy to other topics that dictated the agenda.

Elyakim Rubinstein had been serving as attorney general since 1997, following Netanyahu's failed attempt to appoint Roni Bar-On. I liked Eli, despite our divergent worldviews, but I assumed there was always an elephant in the room—his frustration over the Oslo process, which took place while he was leading the Israeli contingent that negotiated with the Jordanian-Palestinian delegation in Washington. Edna Arbel was the state prosecutor. I had known her for many years and valued her judgment, which was not always in line with Rubinstein's. The best-known expression of their different views arose in regard to indicting Netanyahu in the Amedi affair: Arbel was in favor of prosecuting Netanyahu on corruption charges, but Rubinstein opted not to do so. I defended the attorney general's decision, recognizing his right to reject the system's recommendation; the only higher legal authority was the High Court.

I appointed Shlomo Gur to replace the ministry's esteemed director-general, Nili Arad, because I didn't see eye to eye with her and didn't want my term to be marked by continual disagreements between us. Senior ministry personnel were not happy about my decision.

On September 30, 1999, soon after assuming my new ministerial post, the High Court handed down a historic decision banning the torture of suspects, including the "moderate physical pressure" approved by the Landau Committee in 1987. The court spent several years discussing this issue, and its ruling was not unanimous. The ruling made waves in Israel and abroad: The world applauded it, and Israeli opinion was divided. I personally welcomed the decision and spoke about its historic importance. Some warned that the Shin Bet would have to shut down if it couldn't use force in interrogating suspects. The security establishment demanded legislation that would explicitly permit the use of "moderate physical pressure" in special cases in order to enable effective interrogations.

Ami Ayalon, the head of the Shin Bet at the time, asked to urgently meet with me, and we met later that day. Ami explained that the ruling took a very important tool out of the hands of Shin Bet interrogators and argued that it was essential to remedy the situation as quickly as possible via legislation. I told him that if the government decided to promote such legislation, it would need to find another justice minister. He asked if he could "torture" me, and I immediately consented. Using a chair, Ami demonstrated several methods of "moderate physical pressure" on me in an effort to convince me that they did not really constitute torture. "You didn't persuade me," I told him.

After failing to win my support, the pressure was aimed at Barak to initiate legislation that would permit "light" torture. I told the prime minister that the only possible option was to claim the "necessity defense" after the fact, in the case of a "ticking bomb," but that the use of force in interrogation should never be allowed in advance, through legislation or any other way. Ehud noted that the attorney general supported such legislation. I advised him not to take upon himself responsibility for legislation that has no parallel in democratic countries, even if he received the green light from Rubinstein.

In the end, Barak decided to form a committee to examine various aspects of the problem. I told the prime minister that he was entitled to form any committee he wished, but that if he was ultimately persuaded that such legislation was needed, I would be out. My stance was unequivocal: In a democratic state, even in a "defensive democracy," torture in police or military interrogations must not be allowed because of the need to protect human dignity and rights. Israel, which claims such great pride in being the only democracy in the Middle East, cannot behave like the worst of authoritarian regimes. A modern interrogation system can extract information from suspects without torturing them. Moreover, a person seeking relief from torture is likely to mislead his interrogators, thus creating a boomerang effect.

There is still no law in Israel that allows the use of violence in Shin Bet interrogations. Nonetheless, according to Israeli and foreign sources, such violence still occurs. But any interrogator who resorts to violence is committing an illegal act.

***

As noted, I do not have a law degree. There were some advantages in the fact that I wasn't from the legal profession: I didn't come with preconceived notions and didn't intend to return to the courtroom and appear before judges whose appointment I had supported or opposed. Nonetheless, I still had to learn a lot and needed to learn quickly. Therefore, I decided to devote the Passover vacation week to an intensive seminar on the principal fields of law. I was tutored by members of the Bar-Ilan law faculty, as suggested by professor Dudi Schwartz, the dean of the faculty, and funding was found to offer me this accelerated course at no expense to the taxpayers.

The six-day course was conducted in my Tel Aviv office, twelve hours a day. My instructors were senior faculty members, including Schwartz, professors Yaffa Zilbershats, Yedidia Stern, Gidi Sapir, Shaḥar Lifshits, Ron Shapira, and others. I soaked up every word and loved being a student again. I also recorded the lessons so that I could refer to them later when preparing for discussions on relevant topics. I'm not sure how the lecturers felt in what was defined as "the continuing education program for Minister Beilin," but I felt obliged to remain alert throughout all of the long hours of study.

Of course, I didn't become a legal expert in one week, but I did gain a lot of important knowledge that helped me during my short term as justice minister. I created several forums to help me manage my work in an organized way. One forum was a regular meeting with former justice ministers to discuss issues of current public interest. The forum sometimes met at the home of Haim Cohn, the legendary Supreme Court justice. Another forum was a regular gathering of law school deans, with whom I'd consult regarding the dilemmas I faced. I would share some of the insights from these forums at the weekly meeting I scheduled with the attorney general and state prosecutor, which focused on matters of principle and current issues.

In addition, I made a practice of meeting with each candidate for a judicial position, from Magistrate's Court to the Supreme Court. The conversations were time-consuming, but very important to me. Thus, when their names came up for discussion at the committee responsible for selecting judges, I didn't suffice with perusing the page with their resume. From my perspective, the two most important things were the candidate's wisdom and judicial temperament. A candidate's wisdom does not appear in a resume or in the recommendations of the subcommittees that interview candidates. And judicial temperament is particularly difficult to gauge and is liable to erode over time. Thus, in collaboration with Supreme Court President Aharon Barak, we developed a framework, including psychologists, that observes the candidates' conduct and reactions to different situations over the course of several days.

Quite a few attorneys complained to me about the courtroom demeanor of judges—about their disrespectful treatment of attorneys and witnesses, and their impatience. So I visited some courtrooms, but soon realized there was no point in doing this, because everything changes the moment the justice minister enters with all his entourage. In order to see what it was really like in court, I decided to do something outlandish: to come in disguise and sit in one of the back rows. It wasn't easy to pull this off, especially because it made things difficult for my security detail. But I thought it would be a serious mistake to give up the effort to gain a first-hand impression. I had a list of judges against whom complaints had been raised and after watching them preside, I was able to confirm that the complaints about their rude conduct were indeed justified.

Unluckily, on one of my visits in Tel Aviv District Court, a former MK, attorney Akiva Nof, immediately recognized me despite my disguise. Reports about the masquerading justice minister appeared in all the news media the next day. The judges' representative body, headed at the time by Judge Micha Lindenstrauss, asked for an urgent meeting with me. Micha, a hot-tempered man, protested my disguised appearances in court and argued that such conduct was unbefitting for a justice minister. I told the judges attending the meeting that no one appreciates their work more than I do, and that the Israeli judicial system is one of the best in the world. However, in order to maintain its excellence, we have to remove those judges whose conduct diminishes our judicial system. I said that in light of my visits, I was convinced that the attorneys' complaints were genuine. In some cases, I simply couldn't believe my eyes or ears. I expected their assistance in addressing such indefensible cases, I said. In the end, Aharon Barak joined forces with me in removing the judges whose behavior had shocked me.

✳✳✳

In parallel, I devoted time and effort to canceling the emergency situation that had been in effect since Israel's creation. The idea was to replace it with a cluster of laws that would enter effect if an emergency situation is declared in the future. I discovered an entire system of regulations predicated upon the existence of an emergency situation, especially when it came to controlling the prices of agriculture and entertainment. Yehoshua Schoffman, the deputy attorney general for government and legislation, helped me a lot in this area. An inter-ministerial committee was formed, and most of the ministers cooperated in the effort to create a set of norms via legislation rather than regulation. I was able to convince the government to ask the Knesset to extend the emergency situation for only six months (instead of the usual twelve months) in order to signal our determination to end the anomaly of Israel being the world's only democracy to maintain an emergency situation for decades.

Several justice ministers who succeeded me continued this effort, but the fact is that—as of the writing of these lines—the emergency situation in Israel remains in effect, and only a few regulations have been replaced by stand-alone legislation.

✻✻✻

The remarks I made on my first day as minister about the need to provide an option for civil marriage and for separating religious marriage laws from the civil legal code did not go unnoticed by my ultra-Orthodox colleagues and, as expected, drew harsh criticism. I realized that we might need to wait a long time before instituting civil marriage and divorce in Israel, but I also learned about civil partnership agreements. After conversations with religious and ultra-Orthodox figures, I reached the conclusion that it would be possible to institute a "spousal covenant"—that is, a civil union that confers the status of common-law spouse in advance (rather than retroactively), granting the same rights as those of a married couple.

I worked on this proposal with Shahar Lifshits, who later served as the dean of the law school at Bar-Ilan University. Shahar sought to combine civil family law with Jewish religious law. We prepared a legislative proposal, but there was no majority for it in the Knesset. Nonetheless, I still think it is the most realistic proposal for allowing couples to be recognized by the state outside of a religious framework. The proposal is occasionally re-introduced but is ultimately blocked by the ruling coalition.

Another issue we tackled was administrative detention. There was no place in a democratic regime for the intolerable ease with which hundreds of people (at the beginning of my term) were incarcerated without informing them, or their attorneys, of the charges against them. This practice of administrative detention was rooted in the British Mandate's emergency regulations, designed for use against Jewish underground groups. Menachem Begin addressed these regulations when he was prime minister but didn't uproot them.

I did not manage to mobilize a majority in the Knesset to cancel this form of detention, but I used every possible platform to denounce it. I found that this campaign had some positive impact: In one case, when the prosecution sought to place a particular person in administrative detention, the judge complained that the situation was impossible—in the morning, the justice minister declares that administration detention is an anti-democratic measure, and the prosecution appears in the afternoon asking for this measure.

At the end of my term, only seven people remained in administrative detention.

39

The Horses Have Already Left the Stables

ON SATURDAY NIGHT, OCTOBER 2, 1999, PRIME MINISTER EHUD BARAK and I had a private conversation about the peace process. We sat in his home in Kochav Yair, and he outlined his optimistic ideas on reaching peace agreements with the PLO and with Syria. I had never conducted a similarly detailed discussion on these matters with Peres or Rabin. Barak wanted to skip over the interim stages that we hadn't completed due to Netanyahu's "If they give, they'll receive" policy (a slogan he used to justify the lack of progress in implementing the Oslo process). Barak found it problematic that Israel was obliged to pay in territory in the interim stages without knowing how the final agreement would look, or if there would even be one. Therefore, he preferred to seriously examine the chance of reaching a final accord, and then implement it incrementally. I said that I agreed with him in principle and told him about my conversation with Rabin about a final agreement. Nonetheless, I added, we already have a signed interim accord with the Palestinians and must not follow in Netanyahu's footsteps in violating it.

Barak's vision was to demarcate an Israeli-Palestinian border that would be about half as long as the Green Line and could be crossed swiftly via technology-based identification. There would be an overpass bridge between the West Bank and Gaza Strip, and no Israeli settlements would remain east of the agreed border. In regard to the Jordan Valley, Barak wanted to leave both the army and the settlements in place until a later stage. He said he had made some calculations and found that a future Palestinian state could be contiguous (with the help of bridges and tunnels) with just 48 percent of the West Bank. I told him that there was no such animal and that it would mean enclosing the Palestinians in a sort of giant prison that would become a powder keg.

At that stage, Barak asked that I present the Beilin-Abu Mazen agreement to him. I explained all of the solutions we had found, and I showed him the map. Barak, as usual, asked many questions. However, he was mainly interested in learning how much "wiggle room" the Palestinians really had on each issue. That's the million-dollar question, I replied. I didn't have a clear answer but offered to write up an assessment. In general, I added, we should come to negotiations with a defined set of red lines and refrain from demanding much more than we really need. If we follow this approach, I argued, the Palestinians would be more inclined to do the same—to discard the things that were less important to them and to discuss their red lines with us.

Near the end of our meeting, we returned to the question of Jerusalem. He asked me whether the ECF or the Jerusalem Institute for Israel Studies could prepare a paper with proposed options for a solution. "You're the prime minister and the defense minister. Why don't you ask the IDF Planning Directorate or a research agency under your direct responsibility to prepare the document?" I asked. "The institutes don't leak," he replied. At the end of the meeting, we agreed to meet again soon to continue the discussion.

✻✻✻

Barak, who lived in a sort of perpetual jet lag, would always call at night. I got used to not getting alarmed when the phone rang as late as 1:45 a.m. He would call to continue a conversation we had during the day, and not necessarily on urgent matters.

I remember one day commenting to him about the fact that he didn't ask for others' advice. "Perhaps that's possible in the army, but it's unthinkable in any civilian system," I asserted. Barak truly didn't understand what I was talking about. "I speak with you almost every evening, and not only with you. Believe me, Yossi, there hasn't been a prime minister who consults with others more than me since Levi Eshkol!"

That's not what I meant, I explained. Those conversations are indeed important and beneficial, "but by consulting I mean discussing an issue of importance to you with people you value, or at least whose presence you can tolerate. You pose the question and ask others to express their opinion, and especially to argue with you and with the other participants in the discussion. In this way, you can really understand angles that perhaps you've overlooked and draw from the experience of others, and then you can decide whether you want to stick with your original direction or revise it," I explained. "You engage in two-way conversations. Instead, you could conduct multi-sided conversations, even by telephone."

"You may be right," he said. "But I can't allow myself to do that. The chance of something leaking from that kind of multi-sided conversation is much greater than the chance of something leaking from a conversation with each one individually."

✱✱✱

Barak managed to persuade Arafat to try to advance toward a final agreement, and Israel made several "redeployments" during the process. The prime minister initially focused his peacemaking efforts on the Syrian track, which culminated in the Shepherdstown talks in January 2000, with President Clinton's participation. The Syrian delegation to the talks was led by Foreign Minister Farouk al-Shara. The failure of those talks convinced Barak to unilaterally withdraw from Lebanon and to accelerate discussions with the Palestinians.

The Palestinian side felt that Barak was dragging his feet, just playing for time, and they were wary of engaging in real negotiations. In talks with the PLO, the Israeli side offered to withdraw to an area comprising 33 percent of the West Bank, and there was no way the Palestinians were going to agree to that. On May 14, the day the Palestinians mark the Nakba, there were violent clashes between Tanzim fighters and IDF soldiers. A day earlier, Israel and the PLO had agreed in principle to sign a framework document, but ultimately failed to agree on the terms of this framework.

Arafat met in Cairo with the Egyptian president, Hosni Mubarak, and complained that the negotiations were fruitless. Marwan Barghouti—a former prisoner who was expelled from the territories by Israel, returned with the Tunis-based PLO leadership in the wake of the Oslo Accord and was then considered one of the leading supporters of the peace process with Israel—asked to urgently meet with me. We met that evening at the Laromme Hotel in Jerusalem, on a day when Palestinians and IDF soldiers had clashed in the West Bank. Marwan, a fluent Hebrew speaker, was pragmatic and always looked at his years in prison as military service and as a source of pride. I had met with him and his colleagues several times since his return to the West Bank, and at the beginning of each meeting he would calculate their cumulative number of years in Israeli prisons.

This time, he came to the meeting with his close friend, Qadura Fares, a Tanzim leader and member of the Palestinian Legislative Council, and with Mamdouh Nofal from the Democratic Front. I was accompanied by Ron Pundak, Shlomo Gur, my political advisor Daniel Levy, and my friend Boaz Karni from ECF. The meeting was difficult and grim, but in retrospect its importance was enormous.

Marwan said that the Oslo process had changed the direction of the two national movements and that most of his contemporaries had gladly accepted the decision to put violence aside and focus on building the future Palestinian state. Rabin's murder had left them dumbfounded. They couldn't believe that something like that could happen in Israel. And if that wasn't enough, Netanyahu's victory had shocked them because it indicated a change of heart in Israel after Oslo. On the other hand, Barak's victory had renewed their hopes and led them to think that Netanyahu's days were a short blip in an inexorable march toward peace. "But what has happened during the past year is Israeli foot-dragging," Marwan added. "And it proves to many Palestinians who were skeptical about Oslo that they were right in their assessment, and that Israel is not really willing to accept the creation of a Palestinian state."

Barghouti also spoke at length about Hamas. He didn't belittle its power and said that Fatah's rivalry with Hamas reflected a profound and longstanding ideological dispute between a secular national movement and a religious movement that sees itself as part of a larger stream; he described Hamas as sort of an Islamist branch that believes in turning back the wheel and regards peace with Israel as contrary to the will of Allah. According to Barghouti, unless it soon became apparent that it was possible to make progress in negotiations with a pragmatic government in Israel, support for Hamas would grow, and Fatah, which saw many advantages in peace with us, would lose strength. He noted that the prisoner release Israel had promised was also not proceeding as planned, and that this was an issue that enflamed the Palestinian street more than anything else.

The Tanzim had organized the Nakba incidents that day to demonstrate Faitah's true patriotism, Marwan said. The Hamas threat to Fatah's standing was indeed real, and the way to thwart it was to reach a negotiated solution. If Barak's government was unable to do this, he warned, the Tanzim would have to take the struggle to the streets in order to overcome Hamas, and this meant a confrontation with Israel.

I replied that the way to defeat Hamas was to reach essential compromises that swiftly pave the road to peace. Those who try to fight Hamas with the Islamic organization's own weapons will lose to those who have already specialized in wielding them. I added that if there was a chance for peace, it was with a government like ours, with a leader like Barak, who was determined to achieve an accord and understood the price this entailed.

He remained very skeptical and noted that during Netanyahu's term he and his colleagues had reassured their supporters that Israel's right-wing government would be replaced by a government representing the peace camp. Today, however, "We have nothing to say to the street. Everything is stuck and it's your government. Barak has made a laughingstock of you. He dressed you in lawyer's garb, made Shlomo Ben-Ami a policeman, invented a non-existent ministry for Peres, didn't give any portfolio to Ramon, and runs foreign affairs and defense with David Levy." Barghouti went on to say that Arafat's goal is to reach a peace agreement by September 13, 2000—the seventh anniversary of the Oslo Accord. If that doesn't happen, he added, Israel could calm the Palestinian street by releasing prisoners, freezing settlement activity, and implementing the interim accord (Oslo II).

"If those things don't happen—there will be a confrontation!" he said in conclusion.

Mamdouh Nofal also complained about Israel's failure to implement the terms of the interim accord and noted that Barak had also reneged on his promise to transfer three villages—Abu Dis, Alazariya, and Anata—from Area B to Area A (that is, to the Palestinian Authority's full control).

At this stage, a security officer who had been waiting in the hotel lobby entered the room and told me that the prime minister was on the phone. I left the room and told Barak about the grim conversation with Barghouti and his colleagues. He told me that he had decided to ask the Knesset the following day to approve the transfer of Abu Dis to Area A and that he had called to ask me to ensure that we had a majority in the Knesset plenum. He asked me not to speak about the subject for the time being.

I returned to the room and said that I had just spoken with Barak, who was planning to announce an important decision concerning one of the issues raised earlier in our discussion. I added that a resumption of clashes would put the prime minister in an impossible position. Barghouti shrugged and said the horses had already left the stables.

The clashes indeed resumed with a fury the next day: twelve IDF soldiers were injured, five Palestinians were killed and another 188 were injured. The Knesset approved the transfer of Abu Dis, with fifty-six MKs voting in favor of the decision and forty-eight opposed. In the context of escalating violence, however, the decision was never implemented.

A few days later, the US national security advisor, Sandy Berger, arrived on a rare visit to Israel. Ambassador Martin Indyk invited Abu Mazen, Haim Ramon, and me to join him and Berger for dinner. Sandy asked Abu Mazen whether we still stood behind the Beilin-Abu Mazen Agreement. Abu Mazen had been dodging this question when asked of late. With half a smile, he suggested that I answer first.

I said that though I was serving in the government, I couldn't speak on its behalf on this matter. However, if he was asking me for my personal view—there was no reason for me not to stand behind our joint document.

"That's precisely my response," Abu Mazen said.

✳✳✳

At this stage, Barak's next major effort was to persuade Clinton and Arafat to participate in a summit like the one held by Carter, Begin, and Sadat at Camp David in 1978, which led to the peace treaty with Egypt. He said that if he sat opposite Arafat, he could induce him to make "a Ben-Gurionish act." Barak managed to persuade Clinton, and the question was how to convince Arafat, who was signaling that the time was not ripe. But Barak was eager to take advantage of the short time that still remained in Clinton's presidency.

On Saturday evening, June 24, I found myself with my family, browsing stacks of books at the Hebrew Book Week event, when suddenly the telephone rang. It was Barak, asking me to fly the next day to meet with Mubarak and persuade him to convince Arafat to participate in the proposed summit. He noted that Dennis Ross told him that only I could persuade the Egyptian president. I appreciated the compliment and agreed to take on the mission.

After the Sunday morning cabinet meeting and before my flight, I told Barak that I needed some sort of message from him for Mubarak. The message he wished me to deliver was clear: Compromises and concessions can only be achieved at a summit of this type. If it turns out there's common ground, he'll pursue a peace agreement. If not, he'll form a government with Sharon and pursue an interim accord. I asked Barak to specify the scope of the West Bank pullout he envisions, and he immediately replied, "We'll withdraw from 87 percent."

Straight from the meeting, I flew with Shlomo Gur to Cairo. Dr. Osama El-Baz, the president's long-time advisor, welcomed us at the airport and said that the president wanted to speak with me privately. Just four months earlier, I had met with Mubarak at the same palace, and we had spoken at length on the peace process and its prospects. This time I came with very concrete details. He was glad to see me, and the conversation lasted for two hours. I explained my mission to him, and he said that Arafat was wary of such a summit. But Mubarak's explanation surprised me. According to the Egyptian president, if there were three-way conversations between Arafat, Clinton, and Barak, the PLO leader might not understand certain terms in English. Therefore, he'd prefer to meet in a broader forum, with Nabil Sha'ath or Saeb Erekat sitting at his side. Arafat's greatest fear, Mubarak emphasized, was that the other two sides of the triangle would gang up on him.

Mubarak asked about Israel's negotiating stance, and I passed on Barak's message about our readiness to withdraw from 87 percent of the

West Bank. His response was very positive. He said he had never heard such specific readiness and that he believed it was a good basis for negotiation. Mubarak asked me for a list of the Israelis who'd be participating in the summit so that he could relay it to Arafat and reassure the latter that he could bring a similar delegation.

The conversation with Mubarak, as always, was like chatting over a coffee with your neighbor and complaining about the government. He brimmed with self-confidence but wasn't haughty. Each time he said something funny, he lightly slapped me on my thigh, as if to ensure that I got the joke. More importantly, however, he spoke at length about the benefits the Middle East would gain from peace between Israel and the Palestinians and promised to speak with Arafat after receiving the list from me.

When I got up to leave, he stopped me and said that he wanted to tell me something about Al-Haram a-Sharif. I was certain that he was going to say that no Muslim entity would ever consent to Jewish sovereignty over the Temple Mount, or something similar, but then Mubarak stunned me by saying: "You must not assume that the best solution is a religious solution—for example, to fly Islamic flags over the site or grant sovereignty to a group of Muslim states. Don't go for a religious solution and don't give the keys to religious entities. It's a political issue that must be resolved politically. Any solution you reach with the Palestinians will be accepted by the Arab world," he promised.

I had long been waiting to hear this message from the Arab world. It was hard for me to contain my excitement, but I tried not to show how thrilled I was to finally hear this. En route to the airport, I called Barak, and we made plans to meet the moment I land in Jerusalem, at the Knesset helipad. I asked him for the names of the delegation members who would accompany him to the Camp David. He gave me several names, and I immediately passed them on to Osama.

When I met Barak, he told me that the magic had already worked: Mubarak had called Arafat, and at the end of their conversation, Arafat had announced his readiness to come to Camp David. I was overjoyed. Of course, at that moment I couldn't have known how premature my joy was.

I also told Barak what Mubarak had said about the Temple Mount. Like me, he was happy to hear that the Egyptian president preferred a political solution to a religious solution. This was also a case of premature happiness.

***

July 23 is Revolution Day in Egypt, commemorating the coup executed by the Free Officers group in 1952. Important state events are held on this holiday, and the president plays a central role in them. The Camp David talks were in full swing on July 23, 2000, and then the news reported that President Mubarak had flown to Saudi Arabia. I suspected that this development was not a good omen—Mubarak did not travel to Riyadh unless summoned to do so.

I waited impatiently for a statement following the conversation between Crown Prince Abdullah and Mubarak. The statement was unequivocal: Al-Haram a-Sharif was not a topic for bilateral discussion between Israel and the Palestinians, but rather an issue for the entire Muslim world to address. I was devastated. My conversation with Mubarak was just between the two of us. No one took any notes. I wasn't the one to broach the subject of the Temple Mount, so why had Mubarak raised this issue? And why did he backtrack? And now it turned out that I had misled Barak with incorrect information!

In retrospect, I understood from the Camp David participants that Arafat asked Clinton to mobilize support from Arab leaders for the proposal raised vis-à-vis the holy places in Jerusalem. But Barak was not willing to reveal the details of the proposal to the Arab leaders, so Clinton had to ask for their support, in principle, for a solution that hadn't been presented to them—and Clinton failed to win their support. The Saudi crown prince was apparently furious and summoned Mubarak in the middle of an Egyptian national holiday in order to present a united front against Clinton's request for blind support.

In any case, to the surprise of many, the long summit at Camp David ended in resounding failure. As usual, each side shared some of the blame. President Clinton cast most of the blame on Arafat for not being ready to go far enough. In one of my meetings with Clinton, he told me that at one stage the Palestinian leader told him that if he accepted the proposal offered him, Clinton would have to come to his funeral. I asked the president how he had replied.

"What more could I say to him?" Clinton said, and asked me, "What would you have said to him?"

After hesitating for a moment, I replied: "Leaders who want peace should know that their lives are in danger. If they're not willing to endanger their lives, there will never be peace."

Criticism of the Clinton administration's conduct at Camp David included criticism from the Americans themselves. One of the claims was that their identification with Israel was so strong that the Palestinians didn't believe that any American idea really came from the American side and assumed that it was actually an Israeli idea.

But Clinton also had some critical things to say about Barak. He said that at the beginning of the summit, he wanted to put on the table a document that was very similar to my agreement with Abu Mazen, based on Berger's meeting with the two of us. But Ehud said that if Clinton did that, the Israeli delegation would pack up its bags and leave.

It is important to note that on the eve of the Israeli delegation's departure for Camp David, Barak convened a final consultation with his ministers at the Prime Minister's Residence. I was the last to leave, and I pulled out a large envelop from my bag and handed it to Barak. I told him that he had my full support to lead us toward a final agreement, but that he must not allow himself to return home empty-handed. Therefore, it would be good for him to have an alternative ready: another interim agreement with Arafat, drafted with the assistance of ECF staffers.

Barak handed the sealed envelope back to me without opening it and made me swear not to tell anyone about it. He feared that if the Palestinians got wind of an alternative option, they would set their sights on it from the outset—and the Camp David summit would fail.

Barak had ostensibly covered all his bases: If he reached an agreement at Camp David (and I have no doubt that this was his goal), he'd bring it to a referendum and win a majority. If he didn't reach an agreement, it would clearly be attributable to the Palestinians' refusal to compromise—and then he could say that he had left no stone unturned in his effort to reach a historic accord and had revealed the Palestinians' true intentions. Indeed, Clinton and most of the free world were ready to accept Israel's explanation of why the talks failed. In practice, however, the world—and Barak himself—didn't give up trying to reach an accord with Arafat.

✳✳✳

During the Camp David talks, Ehud Olmert, then mayor of Jerusalem, asked to meet with me. In the late evening, we met in my office on Saladin Street in East Jerusalem. Olmert, who had voted against the Camp David Accords in 1978, was considered one of the most extreme hawks in the Likud party. As mayor, he often spoke about the successful unification of Israel's capital city. Olmert told me that he also believed there was reason to divide East Jerusalem, with Jewish neighborhoods on one side and Arab neighborhoods on the other. "The problem is that in reality it's an impossible mission," he added. I later recalled his words when negotiating the Geneva Initiative, and my colleagues and I made great efforts to prove, down to the level of individual houses, that a division of East Jerusalem is indeed feasible.

However, the main issue that led to the failure of the Camp David talks was sovereignty over the Temple Mount.

***

Soon after his return from the Camp David summit, Mohammed Dahlan, a Palestinian security chief, asked for a meeting and said he'd be coming with Mohammed Rashid, Arafat's financial advisor. Both Dahlan and Rashid were considered Palestinian moderates. Shlomo Gur joined me for the meeting, which began with a discussion of what happened at Camp David. But soon Dahlan asked to speak privately with me.

Dahlan criticized me for my unforgiving attitude toward Aryeh Deri's criminal conduct and my unwillingness to consider recommending clemency for the former government minister. Without any sugarcoating, he got straight to the point: "The peace camp in Israel is foolish. There are people in Israel like Deri and like Avigdor Lieberman who are actually part of you. Why do you reject them? After all, Yossi, there's nothing more important than peace with us, so why are you being tough on Deri?"

I gave him a lecture on "the system of government in Israel" and said that we don't mix criminal law and ideology. If a person accepts a bribe, he belongs in prison—even if he's talented and seeks peace.

"That's why you always lose," Dahlan replied curtly.

I asked him how he could possibly associate Lieberman with the peace camp, and he said, "Trust me."

The Deri issue remained a hot topic. Many feared that his imprisonment could spark a civil war, and various efforts were made to prevent his incarceration. Immediately after he entered prison in September 2000, legislation was drafted to enable his early release after serving just half of his sentence. The third reading of the "Deri Law," sponsored by my friend Rubi Rivlin, was approved by a margin of one vote. I found this unacceptable and introduced what was later dubbed the "Beilin Law"—though work on it had begun much earlier. This legislation reinstated the possibility of early release only after serving two thirds of a sentence and specified the conditions in which early release could be granted in the future.

Thus, just after my conversation with Dahlan, I found myself in a fierce confrontation with the young and brilliant ultra-Orthodox man who had aligned with us a decade earlier to topple Shamir and was full of praise for the Oslo Accord before being forced to resign in 1993.

In the waning days of the Barak government, the legislation I initiated was approved by the Knesset, much to the dismay of Deri and thousands of other prisoners.

***

In retrospect, Barak gave the political right an unintended gift: support for the belief that Israel has no partner and thus is entitled to do whatever it wants. Barak's insistence on not allowing any note-taking during the Camp David summit spawned a rash of rumors and reports of concessions he supposedly made on Israel's territorial demands, Palestinian refugees, and Jerusalem.

The rumors concerning the Temple Mount led Ariel Sharon, who was then serving as opposition leader, to make his provocative visit to the mount on September 28, 2000, as an expression of fidelity to the site. Sharon did not come to the Temple Mount that day, with other Likud MKs in tow, to commune with the memory of the destroyed Temple. He was accompanied by about one thousand security personnel due to the fear of a violent outburst from Muslims gathered at the site.

The ensuing riots on the Temple Mount, which only started the following day, triggered the second intifada. Sharon's provocation was not the substantive reason for the intifada, and it is reasonable to assume that it would not have erupted had we reached an accord at Camp David. But there is no doubt that Sharon provided the match that ignited the flames.

In late November 2000, about two months after the intifada erupted, I arrived in Washington for meetings at the Justice Department. I took advantage of the visit to also meet with Secretary of State Madeleine Albright and Sandy Berger. At the entrance to Berger's office stood the president. I was surprised to see him in that wing of the White House, and he said he had been waiting for me. It was a sort of unofficial "drop-in" meeting that the president conducts outside of his written schedule.

Clinton thanked me for everything I had done to promote peace between Israel and its neighbors, and especially between Israel and the Palestinians, and urged me not to give up. He had another fifty days in office, he said, and only one international commitment: a three-day visit to Ireland. Otherwise, he was available and ready to be at our service in any way we deemed relevant. "There's nothing more important on my international agenda," he said.

Clinton was very concerned about the intifada and feared it would put a halt to the entire process. In regard to the situation in America—the uncertain results of the presidential election and prolonged recounting of votes—he feared that despite Al Gore's victory in the popular vote, George W. Bush would be the next president of the United States. He was right to be concerned on both fronts.

Upon returning to Israel, I updated Barak on Clinton's willingness to continue to work on our mission, but we failed to take advantage of this before his term came to an end. In practice, the coalition was very narrow. We remained a small number of ministers with responsibility for multiple ministries. I assumed responsibility for the Ministry of Religious Affairs, with the declared intention of dismantling the superfluous ministry. I figured that my experience in dismantling the Economics and Planning Ministry would help me in divvying up the functions of the Religious Affairs Ministry among the ministries of Education, Culture, and Justice. Shlomo Ben-Ami served as foreign minister while continuing as public security minister, and also headed the Israeli delegation at the joint meeting of Israeli and Palestinian negotiators who received the "Clinton parameters" on December 23.

Perhaps if the two sides had been ready to discuss these parameters as a basis for an agreement at the Camp David talks, they might have reached an accord. Now they played a much less significant role. The context was quite strange: The principles were not presented as an American plan, but rather as a summary of the sides' respective positions, along with American bridging suggestions dictated to the sides word for word. Clinton stated that the document was not subject to negotiation and it was up to the two sides to decide whether to accept or reject it as is.

At this stage, the elections for prime minister were approaching. Barak was campaigning in northern Israel and the first meeting we held to discuss the parameters Ben-Ami brought from Washington took place in a small forum. Shlomo read the document, and the forum was inclined to accept it. On December 28, the document was approved by the government as a basis for negotiation, with Barak adding several pages of reservations to the decision.

A few days later, Arafat met with Clinton at the White House, but his list of reservations led to the rejection of the document, at least according to Clinton. The principles were ostensibly deleted from the agenda, but in fact remained relevant in all subsequent efforts to renew the peace process between the adversaries.

Already on January 19, a day before Bush entered the White House, the parameters were unofficially applied when the Taba talks began, though none of us intended to reach agreements and evacuate or annex territory in the short time (less than three weeks) that remained before the special elections for prime minister in Israel. (The attorney general had, however, given the green light for conducting the Taba talks.) Perhaps Barak hoped to reach an agreement on principles he could present as part of his election platform, but in interviews he said that he didn't regard the Taba conversations as a real part of peace negotiations and that his intention was to prove to people like Yossi Sarid and Yossi Beilin that "at this time" there was no Palestinian partner.

I was sure that Barak was too smart to go through these motions only to prove to his camp that there was no partner on the other side. If that was indeed his intention, he completely failed in my case, because the Taba talks paved the way to the Geneva Initiative, which proved to me beyond any doubt that there was and still is a partner.

40

Like a Fellini Film at Taba

WE WERE A MIXED GROUP OF MINISTERS, MKS WHO NO LONGER served in the government, an attorney from the private sector and military men. We sat opposite the Palestinian negotiators we had come to know: Abu Ala led the delegation, with Saeb Erekat, Yasser Abed Rabbo, Nabil Sha'ath, Mohammed Dahlan, and others alongside him. Barak asked me to take responsibility for the refugee issue. I gathered all of the material I had on this issue at home and in the office and flew to Taba with Daniel Levy, my political advisor, and Gidi Grinstein. It was like we were in a Fellini film: The intifada was raging, and we all quoted Rabin paraphrasing Ben-Gurion, vowing to fight terrorism as if there were no peace talks, and continuing to pursue the path of peace as if there were no terrorism. But we realized this wasn't realistic. For example, a terror attack occurred in the middle of the week we spent in Eilat and our delegation returned home for two days. It was almost impossible to focus on negotiating when innocent people were being killed in the streets.

The Taba talks were held between old acquaintances. Most of the discussions were conducted in committees, each assigned to one of the issues deferred in the Oslo Accord to permanent status negotiations. On the refugee issue, I found myself opposite Nabil Sha'ath, dubbed by his colleagues the "Palestinian Abba Eban" because of the eloquent English he spoke. He was born in Safed, grew up in Egypt, studied at universities in the US and taught at the American University of Beirut.

I told him that I thought we were each familiar with the other side's arguments on the refugee issue but proposed that we start by switching roles: Each of us would present the other's positions, and then we could comment on the accuracy of the presentations. Nabil was pleased by the idea but wanted to ask a question before commencing with the role-playing: "You speak all the time about a Jewish majority. Why is that so important to you?"

Surprised by the question, I replied by telling him the story of the clandestine immigrant ship *Struma* that sank in the Black Sea in 1942 with nearly eight hundred Jewish refugees on board. No state had been willing to take in the refugees, who had fled from the Nazis. "I need a state that will accept any Jew, and only Israel can ensure that," I explained.

"And how many Jews are living in the United States?" he asked. "Less than 40 percent, right?" I told him that the percentage was much lower—Jews accounted for only 1.8 percent of the US population.

Sha'ath was thrilled to receive this information. When I asked him why it made him so happy, he said that it proved his theory: If there are so few Jews in America and their influence is so great, then there's no reason for the Jews in Israel to want to be a numerical majority—even as a minority, they would be the dominant factor.

In any case, after I responded to his questions, he tried to present the Israeli case, while I endeavored to present the Palestinian case. We both received no more than a "passing" grade. We spoke about the number of Palestinians who might be absorbed in Israel, and though our positions were not far apart, we were unable to reach an agreement on this question or on other topics such as compensation. On the subject of the "narrative," we agreed that each side would write its story, while refraining from provocation vis-à-vis the other. And we lived up to that commitment. Though we could not accept the document composed by Sha'ath's Palestinian team, it enabled us to better understand the Palestinian perspective. And we realized that even after achieving peace, we'd need to live with the realization that their perspective differed from our historical perspective, and vice versa.

In the end, we didn't agree on the number of Palestinian refugees Israel would be prepared to absorb, but we did agree that a future peace agreement would include two narratives, Israeli and Palestinian, with each side recognizing the other's narrative without the need to reach consensus on a single narrative.

After a week in Taba and Eilat, including a joint Friday evening ceremony to usher in the Jewish Sabbath and similar gestures, the two sides concluded that the talks had led to an unprecedented level of agreement and that we'd meet again after the elections.

But everyone had read the public opinion polls and knew that optimism also had its limits. Some of us (though not everyone) felt that if we had continued the talks a bit longer, we could have bridged the gaps. In a conversation with the Palestinian minister of culture, Yasser Abed Rabbo, we concurred that those who claimed that the gaps between us were impossible to bridge were mainly those who realized that concessions would be necessary and were unwilling to make them.

Barak later tried to convene a summit meeting under Swedish auspices prior to the elections, but no salvation came from Scandinavia. The main accomplishment we presented to the public on the eve of elections was the withdrawal from Lebanon, but that could not outweigh the intifada.

The killing of thirteen Arabs demonstrators, including twelve citizens of Israel, in early October engendered rage and distrust in the Arab community in Israel. The immediate response included flashes of violence, but also led many Arabs to boycott the elections held four months later. I was assigned responsibility for getting out the vote in the Arab sector, which refused to work with Barak's staff. When I met with the mayor of the Arab town of Nahf at his home, young people besieged the place and prevented me from appearing at the town hall. Some of them were armed, and additional security forces were required to clear an exit route for me.

Barak clearly understood the situation. On the night before the elections, he invited me to his home. I told him I was at campaign headquarters, making phone calls. He asked me to come anyway. When I arrived at his apartment on Balfour Street, I saw that he had already come to terms with the defeat and had only one question—what did I think about a unity government under Sharon.

"The only advantage of a joint government with him is the possibility of blocking him here and there," I replied. "And I don't think that's our role. Personally, I could never imagine serving in a government led by Sharon, and from the Labor Party's perspective it would be political suicide."

✷✷✷

Voter turnout the next day was lower than ever. Sharon trounced Barak, winning 62 percent of the votes. Yet Barak was keen on serving as defense minister in Sharon's new government and urged me to join him. He noted that since I had acceded to his request and resigned from the Knesset when he appointed me justice minister, I would be left with neither a government portfolio nor a seat in the Knesset. I told him that it was not a relevant consideration for me, that he didn't owe me a thing, and that I wouldn't serve in Sharon's government.

A few days later, my friend Dov Weisglass, who was later appointed Sharon's bureau chief, came to my office with an invitation from the newly elected prime minister to join his government. I thanked Dov but said I wouldn't even consider the offer. "I won't bear collective responsibility for the actions of Sharon's government. We simply have opposing worldviews," I said.

On the Palestinian issue, I scheduled a meeting with Yasser Abed Rabbo at the offices of the *Al-Quds* newspaper in Jerusalem. I told him that what he had said to me in Taba about the possibility of reaching an agreement was still echoing in my mind, and that after concluding my term as minister in a few days I could devote my time to concerted work on a final agreement. I added that in the context of a growing discourse on the seemingly unresolvable nature of the Israeli-Palestinian conflict, it was important for me to examine—first of all, for myself—whether it was still possible to prove the opposite.

Yasser said that I had described exactly what he was feeling. He had been asking himself whether our sense of nearly reaching a peace agreement was a sort of Fata Morgana, or whether we really had been just weeks away from agreeing on a permanent status accord in Taba.

We agreed to embark on a collaborative effort and decided to adopt an approach that was very different from the Beilin-Abu Mazen negotiations. The idea was not to prepare a document for Arafat and Sharon, but rather to conduct negotiations between two delegations that are as representative as possible and to present the document as proof that pragmatic elements from both sides can reach agreements. We talked about forming a group of ten to twenty people on each side, conducting discussions only in the full forum and covering all of the permanent status issues noted in the Oslo Declaration of Principles. Yasser agreed to head the Palestinian team and to recruit partners.

In assembling the Israeli negotiating team, it was important for me to include people who had served at the highest echelons of the defense establishment, intellectuals and academics, along with politicians from various parties—just as we had done in the Beilin-Eitan project, the Movement for a Peaceful Withdrawal from Lebanon, and the Beilin-Lubotzky Covenant (a set of agreements on issues of religion and state drafted with professor Alex Lubotzky, then an MK from The Third Way party.)

The positive response was almost immediate. The only one who asked for a more in-depth conversation before joining was Amnon Lipkin-Shahak, the former IDF chief of staff who served in ministerial posts in Barak's government. We met at his home for a long conversation. After I explained that we aimed to offer a detailed draft of a final agreement, he conditioned his participation on one thing: that we wouldn't demand the inclusion of Ariel as part of the settlement blocs Israel wished to annex in a land swap arrangement. Amnon said that he had come to know politicians and that politicians are liable to make unreasonable security demands in an effort to pander to their voters. Ariel was built in the heart of the West

Bank, and its annexation to Israel would unreasonably harm the contiguity of the future Palestinian state. In order to defend Ariel, Israel would have to secure a wide swath of territory stretching far into the West Bank. It would make a Palestinian state a joke, he asserted. I promised Amnon to honor the condition he set.

We got to work. I transferred my small staff to the ECF's offices, and Daniel Levy drafted the agreement on the Israeli side, working opposite Ghaith Al-Omari on the Palestinian side. Most of the meetings between the two sides were held at the World Bank offices near the Qalandiya Crossing, which both sides could access even during periods of violence. We felt like we were swimming against the tide, but firmly believed in the goal we had set for ourselves.

※※※

I was invited in October 2001 for two evenings of debate with professor Edward Said on the two-state solution at the University of Geneva. A young professor from the university, Alexis Keller, greeted me at the airport. His academic expertise focused on the Middle East; he had read my books and followed the work I had done in recent years. En route to the hotel, he said he was sure I hadn't given up working on the peace process and was interested in knowing what I was doing now. I told him about the talks with Abed Rabbo and his team, and our effort to draft a final accord. He told me that he was a scion of generations of bankers and would be glad to help cover the administrative costs of the project. In addition, he asked that I meet his father, who had worked in diplomacy as well as banking, and promised to contact Micheline Calmy-Rey—the head of Geneva's Council of State who later served as foreign minister and president—so that Switzerland could become for us what Norway was in the Oslo process.

Alexis managed to secure the Swiss patronage and the banking support, and thus the new channel became the "Geneva Initiative." Alexis also accompanied some of the discussions and played an important role in the process, at one stage, when the level of violence made meetings impossible, even preventing Yasser and me from meeting, Alexis arrived on the scene to conduct "shuttle diplomacy" between the ECF's offices and Yasser's home in El-Bireh, with the barrel of an Israeli tank peeking in from the balcony. For Alexis, it was a once-in-a-lifetime experience.

The talks went on for about two and a half years. Many drafts were exchanged, and the negotiations were not easy, especially when we focused on the refugees and Jerusalem. Often, someone would propose leaving two options in the document when we found it difficult to compromise. I strongly opposed that approach. I contended that one of the most intractable problems in the negotiations between the two sides, including the failed Camp David talks, was the feeling that differences could be worked out later and that the negotiators had not yet reached the moment of truth. I asked everyone to treat our negotiations as the moment of truth and that's what ultimately occurred. We did not offer more than one version on any issue. Clearly, this prolonged the negotiations, along with the terrorism and violence that continued much longer than we had imagined.

ALONG THE ROADSIDE

During the negotiations, Yasser and I were invited for a week of joint appearances in the United States, mainly before Jewish audiences. We spoke quite a bit about the different narratives, about the effort to find common ground and about the official and unofficial talks in which we had participated. As always on such tours, I tried my best to vary my presentation in order to avoid boring my partner and myself. On the second day of the tour, Yasser said that he wanted to tell me a story but would save it for the end of the tour. As an expert in deferring gratification, I didn't prod him to tell me sooner, but I was obviously curious.

Before we said goodbye, he indeed honored his promise, and here's the story he told: A well-educated Palestinian fell in love with a beautiful young Jewish woman in the early 1900s. They lived together in Jerusalem and had fourteen children—seven girls and seven boys. They all spoke Hebrew and Arabic fluently. In 1948, when fierce clashes erupted between Jews and Arabs, and after personally experiencing hostility from Jews, the Palestinian father proposed splitting the family: He would move with the girls to the eastern part of Jerusalem, and the Jewish mother would remain with the boys in the western part of the city. Both were certain that the separation would be temporary and that after the violence died down, they would reunite. But Jerusalem was divided, and the family was unable to meet. The girls were raised by the father as Muslims, citizens of Jordan, and married Muslims; the boys were raised as Jews in Israel and served in the army.

At the end of the Six-Day War, when the wall in the heart of the city was torn down, the girls came to meet their mother. The father had passed away. At this stage, each side carried on with their lives—the Jewish brothers and their families in Bat Yam, Jerusalem, and other places in Israel, and the Muslim sisters and their families in East Jerusalem and in various places in the West Bank. On the Jewish and Muslim holidays, the Jewish brothers and Muslim sisters would try to get together.

Chapter 40

Yasser's wife, Liana Badr, a patriotic Palestinian, author and woman of culture, is the daughter of one of the seven girls born to the Jewish-Muslim couple. When they arrived in Ramallah from Tunisia in the wake of the Oslo Accord, they would meet with Liana's Jewish uncles in the various cities where they made their homes in Israel.

After hearing this story, my wife Daniela joined Liana on a visit to her elderly aunt in East Jerusalem. The erect and elegant woman, in her late eighties or perhaps even older, lived in a handsome stone house. The aunt's Muslim husband had died quite a few years earlier. She served Liana and Daniela afternoon tea in fine china and spoke with Daniela in fluent Hebrew. Liana felt a bit left out as the conversation went on and on.

A small world.

41

There's Someone to Talk with

IN A MEETING WITH FORMER PRESIDENT CARTER IN ATLANTA, I TOLD him about the ongoing Geneva Initiative talks Yasser and I were leading. I knew Carter well from his term as president and from a number of meetings with him in Jerusalem and in Atlanta. He had kept tabs on the Oslo process and my negotiations with Abu Mazen, and said he'd be happy to take part in the new process. I told him that when we finished, we'd organize a public event and would be happy to have him participate as a guest of honor. He immediately agreed, and we were in regular contact leading up to the Geneva ceremony. I was also in contact with other figures in the US, including the actor Richard Dreyfuss, who volunteered to come wherever I asked to emcee this sort of event.

I thought we'd be able to conclude the work by the end of 2002 and hoped we could connect the Geneva ceremony to Carter's acceptance of the Nobel Peace Prize in December 2002. But unresolved issues prevented us from meeting that timeline. The signing of the Geneva Accord finally took place on October 12, 2003. What delayed it was the lack of agreement, up to the last moment, on East Jerusalem. We had prepared the public relations campaign long in advance, in anticipation of concluding the agreement a year earlier, as noted.

✳✳✳

The Geneva Initiative offered a precise mapping of the border between Israel and the Palestinian state, and between Israeli Jerusalem and Palestinian Al-Quds. According to this map, Israel would annex 2.25 percent of the West Bank, including the areas where most of the Jewish settlers lived, while compensating the future Palestinian state with similar territory, most of it on the Israeli side of the Gaza Strip. The Palestinian state would be nonmilitarized. A multinational force would provide security assistance along the borders and in Jerusalem. Israel would annex the Jewish neighborhoods in East Jerusalem, and its Arab neighborhoods would be part of the Palestinian capital. Israel would have sovereignty over the Western Wall, and the Temple Mount would be in the hands of the Palestinian state, without any change in the status quo. The Old City would be an open city. Both sides would recognize that the two states as the national homelands of the two nations.

After we agreed on the map, only in the fall of 2003, we believed we could overcome the remaining disagreements on Jerusalem and the refugees in several days of marathon negotiations. We arranged to meet during the Sukkot holiday week in Jordan, on the eastern side of the Dead Sea. On the eve of our journey, I watched the news on TV and saw Sharon speaking to a Likud municipal election rally. He suddenly surprised his audience and the viewers of the live TV broadcast by revealing that some Israelis were planning to travel to Jordan the next day to conclude a subversive agreement involving Israeli concessions to the Palestinians. He presented this as an act of treason, and for a moment I too was angry at those Israelis—until realizing that he was referring to me and my colleagues, and that the traitorous act was the attempt to draft a peace treaty acceptable to both sides.

We immediately phoned each other and fumed about the prime minister's remarks, but the truth is that Sharon became the best PR man we could have ever hoped for. Now, the media in Israel and the world prepared to cover the final stage of our negotiations. In parallel, we recruited the advertising entrepreneur Dror Sternschuss, who orchestrated an impressive campaign. The main message was: We have someone to talk with and something to talk about, and that there was no "devil in the details." Dror also came up with the idea of sending a copy of the agreement to every household in Israel, and not to place the document in mailboxes anonymously. This was an unprecedented undertaking by a nongovernmental entity.

***

When we arrived at the hotel in Jordan, correspondents from the world's media were already waiting for us, and we could barely take a step without the press on our tail. In the wake of Sharon's attempt to portray us as traitors, we were thrust into the public spotlight after having kept a low profile during our two and a half years of talks. This newfound publicity also increased the pressure on us not to repeat the failure of Camp David. From Sharon's perspective, there was a real boomerang effect: When the names of the Israeli negotiators were disclosed, no serious person could describe us as a group of subversives hostile or indifferent to Israel's national interests. In addition, the global coverage of our initiative led Sharon to explain to *The New York Times* in an interview a few months later (April 16, 2004) that one of the reasons behind his decision to unilaterally withdraw from the Gaza Strip was his fear that many Israelis would support the "dangerous" Geneva Initiative.

In any case, the two days in Jordan were difficult. Voices were raised and tears were shed. There was a crisis that almost led the delegations to pack their bags, and there were reconciliations. In the end, the fact that we signed a document of understandings, the fact that well-known figures were involved on both sides, and the fact that we were proposing solutions for everything that had never been resolved combined to make our achievement worthy of headlines around the world.

Earlier in the year, we had met at the same hotel for a weekend of talks. At the end of our discussions, we were invited to the home of Karim Kawar, Jordan's ambassador in Washington, to meet with King Abdullah and Queen Rania. This gave me the opportunity to tell the king about the Geneva Initiative, and he asked for our okay to inform President Bush, with whom he was scheduled to meet in a few days. We later learned that the king attributed great importance to the fact that we had signed the agreement in Jordan.

A few days after the signing, the main headline in the *Yedioth Ahronoth* daily declared that 39 percent of Israelis supported the Geneva Initiative. Despite the ongoing intifada and the disappointment about the peace process, it turned out that many Israelis still wanted to believe that it was indeed possible to reach peace with the Palestinians. The fact that such a high percentage of the public supported the initiative and its proposed solutions reflected a desire to reinforce the belief that peace was possible.

The fact that the signatories and supporters of the initiative, whose names appeared in the booklet distributed to the public, represented different streams in Israeli society apparently also contributed to this support. They included retired IDF generals such as Amnon Lipkin-Shahak, Amram Mitzna, and Gideon Sheffer; authors such as Amos Oz, A. B. Yehoshua, and David Grossman; Dave Kimche, a former deputy director of the Mossad and director-general of the Foreign Ministry; and political figures such as Yuli Tamir, Uzi Baram, Colette Avital, Dalia Rabin, and Avrum Burg from the Labor Party, Nehama Ronen from the Likud, and Haim Oron from Meretz.

When the Oslo Accord was published a decade earlier, a government system stood behind me to help field the requests and questions, handle the invitations, and address the various dilemmas that arose. Now, however, I was no longer in the government or Knesset, and the flood of inquiries was incredible. Abed Rabbo and I found ourselves prioritizing meetings with prime ministers, foreign ministers, and important parliamentary committees on foreign affairs. We held meetings with the prime minister of Britain, Tony Blair; the king of Morocco, Mohammed V; the Russian foreign minister, Igor Ivanov; the chancellor of Germany, Gerhard Schröder; the leaders of Brazil, Argentina, and Chile; and many others. It seemed that the world was embracing our document as proof that it was possible to achieve peace.

The next stage was the ceremony, which took place in Geneva on December 1, 2003. The Swiss made every effort to ensure that it would be a stately event. Two special planes transported Israelis and Palestinians from Ben-Gurion Airport. Jibril Rajoub represented Yasser Arafat. Jimmy Carter arrived with his entourage, and Richard Dreyfuss served as emcee. The assembled guests included Lech Walesa, the former president of Poland, and Nelson Mandela appeared in a video. The level of the participants expressed the importance the world attributed to our informal endeavor, and the major TV networks broadcast live from the ceremony.

The amazing attention the international media gave to the Geneva Initiative prevented the anticipated right-wing assault against the unofficial document formulated by "has-beens." The world's desire to see progress in the Israeli-Palestinian channel was apparently stronger than any other consideration.

Arik Sharon was astonished by this wave of interest and support. His attempt to belittle what we had done and present it as unpatriotic now looked entirely pathetic. When we were invited to meet at the State Department with Secretary of State Colin Powell (whom I knew well from his days as President Reagan's national security advisor), Sharon clumsily tried to prevent the meeting from taking place; he asked President Bush to instruct Powell to cancel the meeting. But Bush brushed off the request and encouraged his secretary of state to meet with us. At a press conference during an overseas visit, the president noted that he was very pleased by the Geneva Initiative and welcomed every effort by "civil society" to advance the peace process.

Amnon Lipkin-Shahak joined me at the meeting in Washington, and Yasser Abed Rabbo represented the Palestinian side. Powell asked many questions and was interested in how the Sharon government could be persuaded to support such a plan. Participating in the meeting alongside Powell was Elliot Abrams, a member of the National Security Council who was considered a hawk and a Sharon supporter, but he didn't present any views of his own.

It was a snowy Washington day. The snowstorms led to flight cancellations, so the trains were packed, including the train that was supposed to take us to New York to meet with Kofi Annan, the UN secretary-general. It turned out that Bill Clinton had also planned to fly from Washington to NY, and he too arrived at the train station. Since there were no reserved seats, the former president and his team were seated in the buffet car. One of our people who saw the president's team informed them that I was on the train, and Clinton asked me to come to the buffet car.

Yasser and I immediately joined him, but not for the horrifying meal of junk food he bought for himself. Clinton knew about the meeting at the State Department and was interested in hearing how it went. Naturally, he complimented us on our work and expressed special appreciation for the level of detail in the agreement. He told us that he had read every word in the Geneva Initiative and admitted that in at least one area—the solution for the Temple Mount and Western Wall—it improved upon what he had proposed in his parameters. "If you need my help in promoting the initiative, don't hesitate," he said.

The easy part of the journey was from Washington to Penn Station in New York City. Snow had piled up in the Big Apple, and the streets were impassable. We were in contact with Annan's office and at one point, not wanting to keep the secretary-general waiting any longer, we suggested that he cancel our meeting. But he rejected our suggestion and waited three hours for us to make our way across town to the UN building.

***

During that period, we received hundreds of letters from around the world. One such letter was from Richard C. Goodwin, a Jewish-American real estate magnate, who wrote to congratulate the signatories and offer a $1 million donation to cover the costs of preparing the professional appendixes we planned to prepare on issues including security arrangements, the refugee problem, Jerusalem, water, borders, and the environment. When we opened Geneva Initiative offices in Ramallah and Tel Aviv, Goodwin came to the area and fulfilled his promise.

Within a few years, all of the Geneva Initiative's appendixes were completed, with the assistance of experts from both sides on each issue. These appendixes, which added about five-hundred pages to the original document, made the initiative the most detailed and consensual document ever written in the history of Israeli-Palestinian peace planning. It was not easy or simple, but we felt confident that if we made a determined effort to close a deal (as opposed to looking for excuses to explain why it was impossible), we would find solutions and reach an agreement.

Some people speak disparagingly about the multiplicity of peace plans and the failure of the two-state solution. However, except for the Geneva Initiative and the short, important Statement of Principles signed by Ami Ayalon and professor Sari Nusseibeh in 2003, there have been almost no peace plans that both sides have dared to sign. Other plans, as original and creative as they may be, are all from one side. Similarly, the two-state solution, which was first proposed in 1937, has never been tried, and it remains, as of the writing of these lines, the most widely supported solution in both Israel and the West Bank.

In 2015, I published an article in *The New York Times* proposing an Israeli-Palestinian confederation as a vehicle for implementing the two-state solution. In recent years, I've devoted considerable effort to developing this idea, which offers, among other advantages, a way to avoid evacuating the Jewish settlers who remain east of the new border in the West Bank. A group of Palestinians led by attorney Hiba Husseini and a group of Israelis under my leadership are continuing to work together to design this additional floor on the foundations of the Geneva Initiative, viewing it as an enabler of the two-state solution.

42

Two Farewells

In 2001, Helena and I decided to separate after thirty-two years of marriage. We felt we had concluded one chapter and were both entitled to start a new personal chapter. These feelings almost certainly would not have led to divorce in our parents' generation, when people only chose this recourse when marital life became intolerable. We told ourselves that at the beginning of the twenty-first century, we had a privilege that our predecessors lacked, and that starting a new chapter did not mean that we regretted the chapter that was coming to an end, and that it could end in true friendship and not just "amicably" or without rancor.

It wasn't simple or obvious, and no divorce is without some hard feelings. Gil was already married and had started a family of his own, and Ori had completed his military service. I was not serving in a public role and could focus for a moment on my personal life in my sixth decade.

A few months later, I married Daniela Sielski, whom I had known since joining the Labor Party's Young Guard in 1975. Daniela, a Zionist from birth who attended a Hebrew day school in Argentina, immigrated to Israel on her own when she was not yet eighteen. She studied history at Hebrew University and became active in the Labor Party's Young Guard; her relative advantage was her fluency in languages, along with her familiarity with the international arena. While most of us spoke halting English and perhaps understood a bit of French and Arabic, she was a native speaker of Spanish and German, having learned those languages in her parents' home, and was fluent in English, Portuguese, and other languages. She volunteered to work in the party's international department and accompanied various VIPs who visited Israel and met with Ben-Gurion, Golda Meir, and other Israeli leaders, while her fellow Young Guard members only saw such iconic figures from afar. We had been ideologically and politically close for years. Daniela was one of the party's prominent activists who worked with me in various battles, including the campaign against Barak for the party's leadership. When we married, she was working at the Tel Aviv Foundation, with responsibility for relations with German-speaking countries. Since the work at the foundation required her to spend much of the year abroad, our marriage led her to resign from her job there.

Helena got married soon afterwards to attorney Yaacov Yisraeli, a founding partner of the Shibolet law firm where she was a senior partner. Our five grandchildren—Gil's and Ori's children—were born after we had both remarried, so the third generation received a supplement of grandparents.

Gil worked for a number of years as a chief editor of current events programs at Keshet and Channel 10, while also completing a master's degree in political science at Tel Aviv University, and Ori worked in advertising. After Ori completed his academic studies, the two formed an advertising firm named "The Beilins." Ten years later, Gil embarked on a political journey in the Labor Party and competed in the primaries, while Ori continued working at the advertising firm and producing music.

✶✶✶

In 2003, I left the Labor Party, which had become a party that clung to power at any price. The creation of the Kadima party (which has since vanished, as is the lot of all Israeli centrist parties) expressed the ideological bankruptcy of the Labor Party's leading figures. I moved to Meretz, was elected party chair in 2004, and, two years later, headed the Meretz list in the Knesset elections. I remain a member of Meretz and really feel at home with its platform.

After four years as party chair, I decided not to run for reelection. I clearly recalled the promise I made to myself: to wrap up my political career at age 60, without looking for excuses to continue. Thus, I resigned from the Knesset and, together with Daniela, formed Beilink, a firm that connects Israelis engaged in business and other enterprises with relevant contacts in the world. Since 2015, our main focus has been to help save Jewish cemeteries in Eastern Europe by documenting and fencing them.

In the public sphere, I've taken on the role of chairman of the Hillel student organization in Israel. Hillel, the world's largest Jewish student organization, is active on eight campuses in Israel. From my perspective, its primary mission is to foster Jewish continuity in the world via the connection with Israel. In addition, I still chair the steering committee of the Geneva Initiative, and our office in Tel Aviv continues to operate in coordination with the office in Ramallah. Our main activity is peace education, and we organize meetings with different groups to discuss ways to return to a real peace process that can ensure Israel's future as a Jewish and democratic state. I continue to work with the ECF, and since 2015 have focused mainly, but not only, on the idea of an Israeli-Palestinian confederation as a means of facilitating the implementation of a two-state solution.

In the political sphere, I suffice with writing opinion pieces, especially in *Israel Hayom*, where I'm able to express my views to a readership mainly comprised of people from the opposing political camp. In the academic arena, I accepted an offer to teach overseas for the first time. As a visiting professor at NYU, I taught graduate students during the spring semester of 2020 and it was an extraordinary experience.

✳✳✳

As far as I know, there are no tenders for agents of change. A person earns this designation only in retrospect, after playing a key role in changing perceptions or organizational structures. Sometimes the agent of change is the person at the top of the pyramid; sometimes it's someone working within the system; and sometimes it's someone operating outside the formal hierarchy. Agents of change usually find themselves up against people who operate within the system and see no reason for change; they are accustomed to the way things are and fear that change may adversely affect them, their status, and their entitlements. People who resist change may also be afraid that they will fail to adapt to the change. Often, they claim that the agent of change has ulterior motives—after all, if the change is so essential, why didn't they initiate it themselves?

People I've worked with have called me an agent of change. I wasn't keen on adopting this designation, mainly because I didn't feel that I had been obsessive in changing the systems I encountered, or had sought to do so only for the sake of making a change.

In retrospect, however, I must admit that it is an apt description. I can think of many changes for which I was an agent, and I referred to some of them in this book. In my eyes, the two biggest changes were the Oslo process, which led to the historic mutual recognition of the Zionist movement and the Palestinian national movement, and the Birthright project, which made Israel the most significant meeting place for young Jews and is still bringing about half of the relevant age cohort to Israel each year. There is ostensibly no connection between the two, but I see a very clear connection: the enormous importance I attribute to Jewish continuity. If we wish to ensure Israel's future as a democratic state, a state of the Jewish people and of all the citizens living in it, we must secure a Jewish majority. And this majority can only be achieved by setting a clear border, based on the 1967 borders.

Oslo, which was an important step toward setting that border, was derailed by extremists from both sides, who viewed the partitioning of the land as religious or national heresy. Despite the criticism leveled against it from both the Israeli and Palestinian sides, it created a new situation on the ground, where the large majority of Palestinians live under self-rule, and in which the Palestinian national movement recognizes Israel and coordinates with it on security and other matters. It is not the longed-for peace, but it is an unparalleled achievement in the century-long conflict.

In any case, establishing the border between Israel and its Palestinian neighbor, and tightening the connection between Israel and world Jewry (and American Jewry in particular) are two sides of the same coin, in my view. The victory of Zionism is not in trampling or ignoring the Palestinians, but rather in finding a way toward a shared victory, without treading upon and harming the other. I've devoted most of my life in pursuit of this objective, and I'll continue to do whatever I can. And if the objective is not achieved in my lifetime, someone else will carry the torch.

Afterword

THIS MEMOIR CONCLUDES FOLLOWING THE SIGNING OF THE GENEVA Initiative, some twenty years ago. Nevertheless, I felt that such a book cannot be published today without referring to the catastrophe which happened to my country on October 7, 2023.

The event itself was totally unexpected, and—much like 9/11 in the US—caused an enormous blow to our self-confidence. The ramifications were many and upended the views of both Israeli political camps. Among the supporters of the Two State Solution there have been voices which reconsidered the possibility of peace between Jews and Palestinians, while on the other side, people have been raising questions about the feasibility of "managing the conflict." Others, on the hawkish side, would like to rebuild Jewish settlements in the Gaza Strip, and endorse capital punishment in Israel.

I cannot say that the current situation is obviously conducive to peace, but I do believe that it may turn many toward a more realistic solution, for courageous Israeli and Palestinian leaders.

Leaders, even if they are brilliant, behave, in most cases, like fire fighters. They extinguish a fire, but if there is no urgent need they prefer to kick the can down the road. In the context of the Palestinian-Israeli conflict, the violence was tolerable in the eyes of the world for many years. When JD Hiba Husseini and I presented our work on a Palestinian-Israeli Confederation (The Holy Land Confederation) to top decision makers in the world, explaining that such a structure may be the only way to implement the Two State Solution, we understood that our issue was not on the agenda. People were very nice to us and promised to support any such idea once adopted by the political parties, but they couldn't believe that the leadership on both sides were ripe for that.

Today we are in a different situation. The Middle East is on fire. President Biden, unlike his predecessor who was indifferent to the conflict and its possible solutions ("one state, two states"), is publicly committed to the Two-State Solution and isn't shy about mentioning it often as the only solution. I've known President Biden closely since he became the chair of the Senate Foreign Relations Committee. He is one of the most knowledgeable leaders about the Middle East, and his support for the Two State Solution isn't new, but nowadays he is determined, more than ever, to promote it intensively. The issue is back on the international agenda.

In Israel, before 10/7, the policy of the longest serving Prime Minister, Netanyahu, was to "manage the conflict" and to focus efforts on normalizing relations between Israel and the maximum number of Arab States. He has said, publicly, that once there is a big enough coalition between Israel and Arab countries, it would be much easier to negotiate peace with the Palestinians, and to prevent them from fulfilling or achieving some of their main demands.

Today, more and more Israelis understand how pathetic these two aims were. It is impossible to manage such a conflict when both peoples live on a boiling lava. The Arab street's support for the Palestinian cause will not allow the Arab leaders, even if the wish so to join Israel establish in a coalition which should weaken the Palestinians.

So now, when the Israeli-Palestinian conflict is high on the international agenda, when there is only one relevant Palestinian address, when non-peace options proved to be totally unrealistic, and the Israeli government is (hopefully) ready to negotiate the Two State Solution, and the American Administration is pushing the parties to negotiate the Two State Solution, there is a new chance for peace.

The solutions for all the major issues are known. Since we signed the Oslo Agreement (which—according to the invites to the Madrid Conference—dealt only with a five-year interim agreement, and just mentioned the main issues which should be dealt with in the negotiations for the permanent agreement) we've negotiated, formally and informally, the permanent solution (The Beilin-Abu Mazen understandings of 1995; the Clinton Parameters of 2000; and the 2003 Geneva Initiative, led by Yasser Abed Rabbo and myself). Those who support these solutions know exactly what they support, and those who oppose them are aware of what they negate.

But the situation on the ground has changed a lot during the last thirty years, especially in reference to the Jewish settlements in the West Bank. If in 1993, when we signed the Oslo Agreement, about nintey thousand settlers lived in the Occupied Territories, today the number is about half a million (not including the Israelis who live in East Jerusalem), and this has become the major obstacle to peace. No Israeli Prime Minister will evacuate about one hundred and fifty thousand settlers who may find themselves in the new Palestinian State.

One of the main reasons for offering our confederation idea (beside the need for close cooperation between the two states) is that we agreed that such a structure may allow the settlers who will prefer to remain in their homes, as Israeli citizens, and Palestinian permanent residents, to do so. The same number of Palestinian citizens will be allowed to live in Israel, in the same legal status.

If we take off the table the need for a mass evacuation, and allow the settlers to decide whether to leave, and be compensated, or to stay, we remove the major impediment from the path to peace. There is no reason why not to do it, why should both sides continue to pay such a high toll, and why should the Jewish state lose its Jewish majority.

Acknowledgments

THE PERSON TO WHOM I OWE THE PUBLICATION OF THIS BOOK IS DANIEL Waterman, the editor in chief of the University of Alabama Press. I would like to thank professor Mark Raider, from the University of Cincinnati, who connected me with the University of Alabama Press, and to my loyal translator, Ira Moskowitz.

Index

Abbas, Mahmoud. *See* Mazen, Abu (Mahmoud Abbas)
Abdel-Shafi, Haidar, 195, 208
Abdullah, Crown Prince, 300
Abdullah, King, 315
Abed Rabbo, Yasser, 306, 307, 309–13, 316, 317, 324
Abramovich, Amir, 277
Abrams, Elliot, 316
Abu Ala. *See* Qurei, Ahmed (Abu Ala)
AbuZayyad, Ziad, 169
Admoni, Nahum, 115, 139
Agam, Yaacov, 18
Agha, Hussein, 224, 226
Agudat Yisrael party, 148–49, 179–81
Ahad Ha'am School, 26, 46
Aharoni, Michal, 283
al-Assad, Hafez, 196, 215, 286
Albright, Madeleine, *159*, 303
Alexander II, 174
al-Husseini, Abd al-Qadir, 216, 217
al-Husseini, Mufti Hajj Amin, 216
Alignment (*HaMaarach*), 81; and Camp David Accords, 91; in Knesset, 74, 82, 92, 102, 147; and Peres, 94, 95, 105
al-Kurd, Maher, 204
Allon, Yigal, 81, 91, 93, 114
Allon Plan, 114
al-Masri, Taher, 115
Al-Omari, Ghaith, 310
Alon, Menachem, 43
Alon, Shimon, 43
Aloni, Shulamit, 193, 203
al-Shara, Farouk, 295
Altalena, 17, 44
Alter, Pinhas Menachem, 179
Amir Peretz ("New Life") party, 281
Andersson, Sten, 226
Annan, Kofi, *162*, 317
Arab League, 116
Arad, Nili, 287
Arafat, Yasser, *158*, 229; Beilin meeting with, 223–24; and Camp David talks, 298–301; and expulsion of Palestinians, 189; and Geneva Initiative, 316; and interim peace agreement, 227; and Jordan confederation, 112, 113; on Lebanon withdrawal, 279; and letter of recognition of Israel, 216; and Madrid Conference, 125, 196; and Nobel Peace Prize, 227; and Oslo Accords, 127, 169, 205–6, 212, 215, 218–20; and peace negotiations, 295; and presidential elections, 230–32; and Rabin, 243; support of Iraq by, 185, 211; and Washington talks, 195, 298, 299, 304; and West Bank, 262–63
Arbel, Edna, 287
Arbeli-Almozlino, Shoshana, 91
Arel, Moshe, 145
Arens, Misha, 140
Arens, Moshe, 106, 123, 128, 141, 177

Argov, Shlomo, 99
Arian, Asher, 77, 93, 101
Arlozoroff, Haim, 17
Aronoff, Mike, 93
Asfour, Hassan, 176, 204, 225, 226
Ashkenazi, Motti, 81
Ashrawi, Hanan, 100, 169, 201, 212, 222–24
Assaf, Ami, 38
Avineri, Shlomo, 277
Avital, Colette, 245, 258, 315
Ayalon, Ami, 288, 318
AyalonRubinstein, Elyakim (Eli), 125, 195, 196, 218
Ayyash, Yahya ("the Engineer"), 264, 272
Azania, Baruch, 28

Badr, Liana, 312
Bahrain, 200
Baker, James, 177, 178, 184, 185, 188
Bank Leumi, 15–16, 24, 28, 41, 74
Bank of Israel, 114, 168
Barak, Aharon, 131, 203, 289–90
Barak, Ehud, 260–61; and Foreign Ministry, 264; as IDF chief of staff, 203, 218, 228, 255, 284; and Labor Party, 126, 251–52, 281–84; and Lebanon withdrawal, 277, 279, 295; and peace talks, 185, 293–96, 298–99, 301–4, 306, 308; and politics, 255–56; as prime minister, 236–37, 244–45, 253, 284–86, 288, 294–97
Baram, Uzi, 85, 148, 149, 190, 315
Barenboim, Daniel, 16
Barghouti, Marwan, 221, 295–97
Barkat, Mordechai, 96
Bar-Lev, Haim, 79, 86, 88, 99, 140
Bar-Lev line, 79, 80
Barnea, Nahum, 72
Bar-On, Hanan, 138
Bar-On, Roni, 287
Bar-Zohar, Mickey, 189
Bassiouni, Muhammed, 189
Baumel, Yona, 223

Baumel, Zachary, 223–24
Begin, Menachem, 17, 109, *152*; and Camp David Accords, 88, 91, 211, 298; and Herut party, 183; in Knesset, 28, 48; and Lebanon, 99; and national unity government, 74, 81; policies of, 21, 111; as prime minister, 86, 95, 101, 256, 291
Beilin, Aliza, 27–28, 48, 75
Beilin, Daniela Sielski, 82, 83, 312, 319–20
Beilin, Gil, 76–78, 319, 320
Beilin, Helena Einhorn, 136, 184, 204, 219; law career of, 73, 77, 97, 287; and Peres, 87, 134; and Yosef Beilin, 14, 53–54, 71, 74, 80, 282, 319–20
Beilin, Ori, 90, 319, 320
Beilin, Rachel, 31, 33–34
Beilin, Talia, 28
Beilin, Yinon, 4, 6, 18, 22, 30, 48; and Aliza, 27–28; as caregiver for Yosef Beilin, 24–26; military service of, 26–27, 41, 62, 63, 66
Beilin, Yosef, *153–67*; and ambassadorship, 132–33; and Arafat, 223–24; and Barak, 255–56; bar mitzvah of, 35–36; and Birthright Israel, 248–53; and Bus 300 Affair, 129–30; as cabinet secretary, 103, 105–9, 124, 129–30; and Camp David Accords, 91; and chess, 40, 42–43; childhood of, 5–8, 13–14, 16–23; and direct elections, 234–37; education of, 12, 38–40, 43–45, 50–51, 53–54, 71, 77, 87, 90, 93, 101–3; in France, 121–22; and Geneva Initiative, 131, 301, 305, 310–18, 320–21, 324; and government formation, 183–84; and grandparents, 30–34; and Holocaust survivors, 37–38; and Holy Land Confederation, 212–13; and Husseini, 216–17, 232–33; and informal peace talks with PLO, 175–77, 194–95, 200–202; on Israel Bonds, 246–48; and Israeli-Egyptian talks, 88–90; as

journalist, 47–52, 81, 84, 135–36, 204; as journalist for *Davar*, 71–73, 77–78, 86–87; and King Hussein, 112–18; in Knesset, 146–48, 150–51, 186, 267–69; and Labor Party, 70, 76, 81–82, 192–93, 277, 281–84; as Labor Party spokesman, 86–88, 92, 105, 259–60; and Labor Party Young Guard, 82–83, 94; and Lebanon withdrawal, 268–72, 275–80; and London Agreement, 119–20, 123–24; and Madrid Conference, 197–98; and Mashov group, 97–98, 186, 188, 190; and Meretz party, 320; military service of, 14, 54, 55–61, 67–70, 99; military service of during wars, 62–66, 78–80; and Ministry of Economics and Planning, 238, 256–57, 264, 303; and Ministry of Finance, 168, 175; and Ministry of Foreign Affairs, 133–34, 136–38, 150, 195–96, 237–40; and Ministry of Justice, 285, 287–92, 295; and Ministry of Religious Affairs, 304; in Morocco, 120–21; and music, 25–26, 40–42; and no-confidence vote, 179–80; in Oman, 273; and Oslo Accords, 125–26, 169–70, 198–99, 203–4, 209–11, 218–20; and peace talks with Oman and Tunisia, 228–29; and peace talks with Palestine, 293–99, 309–10; and Peres, 86–88, 92–95, 103–4, 109–10, 244–45, 260; and Peres's 100-days team, 101–2, 105; and Pollard Affair, 131–32; and Rabin, 256–60; Rabin on, 138, 140, 149, 177; and rapprochement with Palestine, 168–69, 303; and Sharon, 308; and Shultz, 119–20; on Sinai Campaign, 41; and Socialist International, 100–101; and South Africa, 135–44; and Soviet Jews, 170–74; and Sweden peace talks, 224–26; and Taba talks, 306–7; and theater, 42, 46, 48–50; threats to, 251, 265–66; United States tour by,

97; and Vatican, 240–44; and War of Attrition, 79; at Western Wall, 66–67; and Yinon Beilin, 24–26
Beilin, Ze'ev, 31–34
Beilin, Zehava Bregman, 2–5, 9–14, 18, 20, 22–26, 30, 53, 76
Beilin, Zvi, 4, 15–16, 18–23, 29, 41, 50, 67, 76–77; military service of, 17, 24, 25, 41
Beilin-Abu Mazen Agreement, 293–94, 297, 301, 324
Beilin-Eitan document, 268–69, 275, 309
Beilin-Lubotzky Covenant, 309
Beinisch, Dorit, 129
Belgium, 228
Ben-Aharon, Yossi, 196
Ben-Ami, Shlomo, 126, 268, 277, 284, 285, 296, 303
Ben-Avraham, Nehemia, 20
Ben-Elissar, Eliyahu, 86
Ben-Gurion, David, 17, 41, 44, 306, 319; Bible study group of, 10; in Knesset, 28, 48; and Peres, 84, 149; and "Unfortunate Affair," 72; and United Nations, 221, 269
Ben-Menachem, Eli, 193, 245
Ben-Yehuda, Baruch, 9, 50
Ben-Yehuda, Hanan, 248
Berger, Sandy, 297, 303
Bernstein, Leonard, 18
Bertonov, Shlomo, 49
Bertonov, Yehoshua, 49, 50
Biden, Joe, 323–24
bin Alawi, Yusuf, 273
bin Shaker, Zayed, 113
Birthright Israel, 246–53, 321
Bishop, Maurice, 98
Blair, Tony, 261, 316
Blumenthal, Naomi, 268
Bochbot, Shlomo, 172
Bograshov, Haim, 9, 50
Boim, Ze'ev, 268
Boneh, Solel, 82
Botha, Pieter Willem, 141–42
Botha, Pik, 143

Boutros-Ghali, Boutros, *155*, 189
Brandt, Willy, 89
Braslevi, Yosef, 10
Bregman, Baruch, 2, 9, 24, 27, 39, 74–75
Bregman, Levana, 24, 25, 74, 75
Bregman, Oded, 74, 75
Bregman, Rivka Shapira, 2, 5–8, 28, 30–31
Bregman, Shula, 74, 75
Bregman, Yosef, 1–5, 25, 53, 74
Bregman, Yossi, 74–75
Bregman, Zehava. *See* Beilin, Zehava Bregman
Bronfman, Andy, 250–51
Bronfman, Charles, 250–53
Burg, Avrum, 188, 282; in Knesset, 147, 235, 285; and Labor Party, 191, 193; and peace talks, 169, 315; and Peres, 102
Bus 300 Affair, 128–31
Bush, George H. W., *154*, 177, 188, 220
Bush, George W., 303, 304, 315
Bussel, Hayuta, 31
Bussel, Yosef, 31
Buthelezi, Mangosuthu, 137

Callaghan, James, 89
Calmy-Rey, Micheline, 310
Camp David Accords, 88, 91, 211, 301
Camp David talks, 253–54, 299–304, 311
Carmon, Arik, 235, 268
Carter, Jimmy, 220, 298, 313, 316
Caspi, Ram, 129–30
Celli (monsignor), 241–44
Chabad-Lubavitch movement, 181
Charles, Prince, 261
Chazan, Naomi, 278
China, 132
Christopher, Warren, 208, 215–16, 262
Clinton, Bill, *166*, 317; and Camp David talks, 298, 300–301, 303–4; and Oslo Accords, 127, 216, 219–20, 262; and Syrian peace talks, 295
Clinton Parameters, 304, 324

Cohen, Eli, 132
Cohn, Haim, 289

Dahlan, Mohammed, 302, 306
Davar, 6, 10, 11, 204; Beilin as journalist for, 71–73, 77–78, 86–87
Dayan, Moshe, 17, 80, 81, 84, 93, 269; as defense minister, 61, 79; as IDF chief of staff, 41; on King Hussein, 113; in Knesset, 48
Dayan, Yael, 147, 193
de Charette, Herve, 272
de Gaulle, Charles, 234
Degel HaTorah party, 179, 181
Deir Yassin massacre, 86
de Klerk, Frederik Willem, 143
Democratic Movement for Change (Dash), 91–92, 95
De-Nur, Yehiel, 47
Deri, Aryeh, 177–78, 181, 219, 302
Dichtwald, Arie, 59
Dinitz, Simcha, 172
Dismorr, Ann, 225
Divon, Haim, 223
Dizengoff, Meir, 32
Djerejian, Edward, 201
Dor, Muli, 82
Dori, Yoram, 245
Dreyfus, Alfred, 16
Dreyfuss, Richard, 313, 316
Dror, Yehezkel, 107

Eban, Abba ("Aubrey"), 84, 88, 114, 269; in Knesset, 48, 146, 150–51
Eban, Suzy, 150–51
Economic Cooperation Foundation (ECF), 226, 294, 295, 301, 310, 321
Egeland, Jan, 196–97
Egypt: and Israel, 80, 88–90, 114, 145–46, 188–89, 200, 213, 298; and Taba, 210; and Yom Kippur War, 79
Einhorn, Helena. *See* Beilin, Helena Einhorn
Einhorn, Irena, 78
Einhorn, Yitzhak, 51

Eisenstadt, Beno, 25
Eisenstadt, Shmuel Noah ("Mulik"), 26
Eisenstadt, Zippora (Tante Zippa), 25
Eitan, Michael (Miki), 267, 268, 275
Eitan, Rafael (Raful), 185
Eitan, Rafi ("Smelly"), 131
Elazar, David (Dado), 79
El-Baz, Osama, 189, 298, 299
Eldar, Reuma, 48
Eliav, Lova, 190
Elisar, Eliahu Ben, *152*
Elitzur, Yehuda, 10
Elkana, Yehuda, 238
Elyashiv, Yosef, 179
Emunim, Gush, 99
Erekat, Saeb, 143, *164*, 230–32, 298, 306
Erlich, Simha, 91
Eshkol, Levi, 60, 82, 294
European Union, 175
Ezra, Gideon, 275–76

Fares, Qadura, 295
Fatah, 232, 296
Finkel, Shimon, 50
Four Mothers movement, 276

Gabay, Yoram, 168, 175
Gafni, Moshe, 180
Gahal alliance, 183
Galilee, 99, 105–6, 269–70
Galili, Yisrael, 80, 88, 91
Gavish, Moshe, 168
Gaza Strip, 323; and bridge, 293; evacuation of, 225; and Geneva Initiative, 313; and Oslo Accords, 204–5, 207, 209, 230; and peace talks, 99–100, 113; and Sinai Campaign, 41; uprising in, 125; withdrawal from, 188, 315
Gdud HaAvoda (The Work Battalion), 255
Geneva Initiative, 53, 131, 301, 305, 310–11, 313–18, 321, 324
Gere, Richard, *165*
Gilad, Amos, 112

Givton, Hanoch, 48
Glazer, Shiye, 20
Godard, Yossi, 48
Golan, Menachem, 42
Golan, Tamar, 100
Golan Heights, 64–66, 80, 215, 262, 275
Goldberg, Yossi, 183
Goldmann, Nahum, 80
Goldreich, Arthur, 135–36
Goldstein, Baruch, 225
Goldstein, Pinhas, 183
Goodwin, Richard C., 317
Gorbachev, Mikhail, 119, 120
Gordon, Uri, 190
Gore, Al, 303
Gorodish-Gonen, Shmuel, 79
Gotthelf, Yehuda, 72
Greenbaum, Rina, 46–47
Greenbaum family, 46
Greenberg, Rivka, 39
Greenberg, Uri, 39
Grenada, 98
Grinstein, Gidi, 252, 253, 306
Grossman, David, 277, 315
Grupper, Pesah, 183
Gulf War, 185–86, 188, 211
Gur, Efraim, 184
Gur, Motta, 99, 218
Gur, Shlomo, 237–38, 287, 302; as ambassador, 137–38; and Oslo Accords, 196, 204, 210, 223; and peace talks, 295, 298; and Vatican, 240, 242
Guterres, António, *167*
Gvaryahu, Haim, 10

Haaretz, 99, 120, 221, 243
Ha'avoda, Ahdut, 101
Habib, Philip, 99
Hadar, Amos, 91
Hadas, Yossi, 196
Haddad, Ibrahim, 100
Hakham, Amos, 10
Halevy, Efraim, 115, 117
Halpert, Shmuel, 148–49
Hamas, 221, 225, 231–32, 296; abduc-

tion of IDF soldier by, 228; and expulsion to Lebanon, 202–3, 207, 241; leader of in Israeli prison, 224
Hammer, Zevulun, 263
Hanegbi, Tzachi, 177
Haniye, Akram, 223
HaPoel HaTzair (The Young Worker), 255
Harish, Micha, 85, 179
Harish, Yosef, 130
Hassan II, King, 89–90, 220
Hazan, Ya'akov, 255
Heiberg, Marianne, 208
Hendler, Chanale, 50
Herut party, 28, 183
Herzl, Theodor, 1–2, 7
Herzog, Chaim, 60, 130, 181, 182
Herzog, Isaac, 286
Herzog, Isaac Halevi, 77
Hezbollah, 269–72, 275, 278
High Court of Justice, 130–31, 202–3, 287
Hill, Charles, 120
Hillel, Shlomo, 91
Hillel student organization, 320
Hirschfeld, Yair, 100; and Husseini, 216, 232; and informal meetings with PLO, 175, 194–96, 201–2; and Oslo Accords, 198–99, 201, 203–7, 209, 212, 224–26; and peace talks, 168–69
Histadrut labor federation, 71, 281; Afro-Asian Institute of, 137; criticism of, 73, 82; members of, 5, 17, 31, 190, 192, 194; ownership of companies by, 97, 98, 139, 146–47
Hitler, Adolf, 37
Hjelm-Wallén, Lena, 226
Hodorov, Ya'akov, 20
Hollander, Asher, 40–41
Holst, Johan, 208, 209, 214–16
Holy Land Confederation, 212–13
Hoover, J. Edgar, 207
Hosid, Yossel. *See* Bregman, Yosef
Hourani, Abdallah, 176
Hovav, Moshe, 48

Hoz, Dov, 43
Hushi, Abba, 25
Hussein, King, 66, 185; Jordan severed from West Bank by, 125, 212; at Mayo Clinic, 126–27; and peace talks with Israel, 80, 111–20, 123, 125–26
Hussein, Saddam, 185, 186, 188
Husseini, Faisal, 212, 216–17, 232–33; and Hirschfeld, 100; on Jerusalem, 253–54; and Mashov group, 221–22; and Oslo Accords, 168–70, 197–99, 208, 223; and Rød-Larsen, 194–95
Husseini, Hiba, 318, 323

IDF. *See* Israel Defense Forces (IDF)
Indyk, Martin, 297
Infeld, Avraham, 252
International Union of Socialist Youth (IUSY), 83
Iran, 89–90, 273
Iraq, 95, 185–86, 188
Isaak, Chaim, 71
Ish-Shalom, Michael, 22
Israel Air Force, 63–64, 112
Israel Bonds, 246–48
Israel Defense Forces (IDF), 24, 115, 295, 297; Barak as chief of staff of, 203, 218, 228, 255, 284; and Bus 300 Affair, 128; and child allowances, 190–91; Dayan as chief of staff of, 41; Eighth Brigade of, 59; and Goldreich, 135–36; and Hamas, 228; and helicopter accident, 275–77; induction center of, 32; International Law Department of, 210; and Lebanon, 61, 99, 106, 269–72, 275, 278–80; on PLO, 200, 218; and Sinai Campaign, 41; and Six-Day War, 62–65; and "temporary" extension, 57; and Yom Kippur War, 78–80
Israel Democracy Institute (IDI), 235, 268
Israel Experience, 250
Israel-Jordan Common Agenda, 126
Israel Navy, 115

Israel Radio, 10, 47–48, 51–52, 60
Ivanov, Igor, 316

Jaeger, David, 241, 242
Jaglom, Raya, 246, 248
Jarring, Gunnar, 80, 145–46
Jerusalem, 176; and Camp David talks, 300, 303; division of, 268, 301; and ECF, 226; and Geneva Initiative, 310, 313–14; and Hezbollah, 275; IDF capture of Old City in, 63; Jordanian banks in, 114; Knesset in, 16; "no man's land" in, 169; Old City of, 253–54; Palestinian leadership in, 99–100, 197, 198, 216–17; Palestinians in, 194; Sadat visiting, 109; and sovereignty, 253–54; and Vatican, 240, 243; Yinon Beilin in, 27–28, 48, 221; and Zehava Beilin, 3–5, 53
Jerusalem Institute for Israel Studies, 294
Jewish Agency, 31, 140, 171–72, 250, 282
Jewish National Fund, 3, 4
John Paul II, Pope, *156*, 244
Johnson, Lyndon, 207
Jordan: economic conference in, 257–58; and Geneva Initiative, 314–15; and Israel, 80, 111–20, 123, 169, 200, 212–14, 273; and Palestinians, 112, 125–26, 149, 212, 218–19, 287; severed from West Bank, 125, 212; and Six-Day War, 114; and Washington talks with Palestinian delegation, 196, 287
Jordan Valley, 262, 268, 293
Jumblatt, Walid, 100
Juul, Mona, 194, 196

Kahane, Meir, 99
Kaplan, Mendel, 140
Karni, Boaz, 169, 226, 295
Karp, Yehudit, 129
Kashash, Yosef, 72
Katzav, Moshe, 109, 244, 245
Katznelson, Berl, 255

Kawar, Karim, 315
Keller, Alexis, 310
Kennedy, John F., 101–2
Keren, Uzi, 277
Kessar, Yisrael, 192
Kessary, Ouri, 16
Khalaf, Rima, 257
Khalidi, Ahmed, 224, 226
Khatib, Ghassan, 169
Khomeini, Ruhollah, 90
Khouri, Saman, 169
kibbutz, 23, 25, 27, 31, 80, 91, 147, 276
Kimche, Dave, 315
Kleiner, Michael, 268
Klieman, Aharon, 77
Knesset: and Alignment, 74; and ban on PLO meetings, 199, 200; and Camp David Accords, 88, 91; and direct elections, 234; and extension of emergency situation, 291; factions in, 183; in Jerusalem, 16, 22, 28, 48; and Mapai, 25; and no-confidence vote, 179; and peace process consensus, 267–69; and prime minister, 282; and Progressive Party, 32; and Rabin, 78; and Russian Jews, 173; and transfer of Abu Dis, 297
Kofman, Ehud, 102
Kol, Moshe, 32
Kolodny, Misha (aka Moshe Kol), 32
Koning, Henk, 175
Kreisky, Bruno, 89
Krinitzi, Avraham, 7
Kristiansen, Kåre, 227
Kurtzer, Daniel, 201, 202
Kuwait, 185, 188

Labor Party: and Beilin, 17, 70, 81–82, 320; Beilin as spokesman for, 86–88, 92, 259; and Camp David Accords, 91; and direct elections, 235, 236; and government formation, 184; and Histadrut, 147; and Husseini speech, 221–22; in Knesset, 102, 146, 191, 193, 195, 236, 264–66; leaving gov-

ernment, 177–78, 185; and Lebanon withdrawal, 106, 277; and Mashov group, 97–99, 186, 190; and Meir, 81; merging with other parties, 88, 95, 147–49, 178–80; and national unity government, 95, 147–48; and no-confidence vote, 178–79; and peace process consensus, 267–69, 275–76; and PLO meeting ban, 199; and Rabin, 78, 93; and rotation of prime minister, 102, 105, 116, 132, 133, 147; and South Africa, 139–41; Young Guard of, 82–85
Lahad, Antoine, 106
Lahat, Shlomo ("Chich"), 277
LAKAM (Science Liaison Bureau), 131
Lake, Tony, 220
Lancry, Yehuda, 268
Landau, Uzi, 235, 236
Landau Committee, 287
Lapid, Tommy, 73
Lauder, Laura, 252
Lavi, Nissim ("Cushi"), 69–70
Lavon, Pinhas, 72
Lebanon: and expulsion of militants, 202–3, 207; and peace talks, 196, 213; Sultan Yaqub battle in, 223; withdrawal from, 105–6, 251, 269–71, 275–80, 283, 295, 308
Lebanon War, 99, 101, 102
Leibowitz, Nechama, 10
Lerner, Yonatan, 277
Levac, Alex, 128
Levanon, Chaim, 32
Levin, Amiram, 278
Levine, Alon, 59, 60–61
Levy, Daniel, 295, 306, 310
Levy, David, 106, 109, 191–92, 297
Levy, Gideon, 93, 94
Levy, Moshe, 106
Liberal Party, 183
Lieberman, Avigdor, 302
Liel, Alon, 137, 142, 257
Lifshits, Shahar, 289, 291
Likud party, 107, 133, 177, 193; and Agudat Yisrael party, 148; conflict within, 109, 115; and direct elections, 235; in Knesset, 95, 102, 147, 234, 236, 266; and Lebanon withdrawal, 105–6; and Liberal Party, 183; and peace process consensus, 267–69, 275–76; and peace talks with Egypt, 189; and peace talks with Jordan, 119, 123; and South Africa, 140, 141; spokesperson for, 86
Lindenstrauss, Micha, 290
Lipkin-Shahak, Amnon, 271, 309, 315, 316
London Agreement, 112, 120, 123–25, 191
Lubotzky, Alex, 309
Lubrani, Uri, 271

Madrid Conference, 125, 169, 185, 191, 197–98, 200, 324
Magen, David, 109
Malka, Gaston, 109
Mandela, Nelson, 135, 142, 143, *161*, 316
Mandler, Albert, 59
Mansdorf, Amos, 142
Maor, Galia, 114
Mapai party, 3, 25, 31, 38, 72, 94
Mapam party, 72, 147
Marcus, Yoel, 221
Margalit, Dan, 279
Mark, Gidi, 252–53
Mashov group, 97–99, 146, 169, 186, 188, 193, 221–22
Massalha, Nawaf, 147
Matkal, Sayeret, 128
Mazen, Abu (Mahmoud Abbas), 53, 224–27, 258, 262–63, 267, 297, 313
Mbeki, Thabo, 142–44, *164*
Medzini, Moshe, 18
Meetings Law, 186, 199–204
Meir, Golda, 74, 80, 82, 319; and Egyptian peace accord, 80, 145–46; on King Hussein, 113; and Labor Party, 81, 88; and NRP, 263; rejection of

Index | 337

mutual recognition by, 214; and Yom Kippur War, 114
Melchior, Michael, 227, 253, 286
Meretz party, 53, 193, 199, 202–3, 263, 268, 320
Merhav, Reuven, 277
Meridor, Dan, 203
Meridor, Ya'akov, 256
Merom, Hagai, 147
Meron, Dan, 73
Meron, Hanna, 277
Meshel, Yeruham, 73
Meshulah, Yehoshua, 73
Meskin, Aharon, 50
Meyrovna-Friedman, Mina, 22
Michaeli, Rivka, 48
Miller, Aaron David, 202
Milo, Roni, 109
Minerbi, Sergio (Itzhak), 243
Mishcon, Victor, 111, 113, 116–19, 126
Mitterrand, François, 234
Mitzna, Amram, 315
Mizrahi, Eliezer, 180
Moda'i, Yitzhak, 108, 130, 183–84
Mohammed VI, King, 316
Mohar, Eli, 72
Moledet party, 185
Mordechai, Yitzhak, 128, 278
Morocco, 89
Mosensohn, Ben-Zion, 9
Mossad, 90, 132–33, 139, 276; and Jordan meetings, 111, 112, 115
Moussa, Amr, 189
Movement for a Peaceful Withdrawal from Lebanon, 276, 277, 309
Mubarak, Hosni, 295, 298–300
Murphy, Richard, 170–71

Nahmias, Aharon, 228–29
Namir, Ora, 139, 192
Nasser, Gamal Abdel, 60, 63, 67, 68, 80, 146
National Religious Party (NRP), 185, 263
Navon, Yitzhak, 140, 149
Neeman, Yuval, 185
Netanyahu, Benjamin, *154*, 234, 264; and attorney general, 287; and Birthright Israel, 252–53; and Madrid Conference, 191–92; and Oslo Accords, 127, 293; and peace negotiations, 324; as prime minister, 236, 266, 272, 281–82, 284, 296; and Rabin's assassination, 261; on West Bank, 125
Neubach, Amnon, 102, 114
Nidal, Abu, 99, 100
Nissim, Moshe, 123
Nobel Peace Prize, 227
Nof, Akiva, 290
Nofal, Mamdouh, 295, 297
Nordau, Max, 7
Norich, Sam, 249
Norway, 195, 197, 202, 204–9, 212, 215. *See also* Oslo Accords
Novik, Nimrod, 102, 169, 225, 226
NRP. *See* National Religious Party (NRP)
Nusseibeh, Sari, 169, 185, 222, 318

Ofri, Arye, 169
Olmert, Ehud, 108, 301
Oman, 200, 228, 273
Oron, Haim, 315
Osirak nuclear reactor, 95
Oslo Accords, 198–99, 203–12, 221, 243, 302, 321–22; beginnings of, 194–97; and Declaration of Principles, 126, 272, 309; finalization of, 215–16, 219–20, 266, 315–16; and interim accords, 297, 324; and Israeli-Palestinian Interim Agreement, 226–27, 230; and Jordanian-Palestinian delegation, 287; and Palestinian opinions of, 295–96; and PLO, 169–70, 176, 214, 242, 262; and Rabin, 125, 213, 215, 218–19, 260
Owen, David, 89
Oz, Amos, 50–53, 258, 315
Oz, Galia, 53

338 | Index

Oz, Nili, 52

Pakistan, 132
Palestinian Liberation Organization (PLO): and informal peace talks, 175–77, 209, 214, 218; and Jordan, 112; leadership of, 231; and London Agreement, 124; and Meetings Law, 100, 186, 190, 195–96, 198–200; and Oslo Accords, 126, 169–70, 198, 204–8, 218–20, 242; and Palestinians, 100, 116; and peace talks, 222, 293, 295; and Rabin, 192, 199–200; and recognition of Israel, 98, 168–69, 208, 213–14, 216; and Washington talks, 195, 201, 207, 298–99; weakness of, 189
Palestinian National Council (PNC), 168, 169
Palestinians, 220, 273–74; and annexation of settlement blocs, 309–10, 313–14; and Barak, 185, 293–97, 301–3, 308; and border demarcation, 146; and Bus 300 Affair, 128; and Camp David talks, 299–301, 303, 304; and common grounds with Israel, 267–69; and conflict with Israel, 97, 148, 187, 219, 295, 297; expulsion of, 92, 189; and informal meetings in Oslo, 194–95, 198–99, 204, 205, 212–13, 215; and Israeli citizenship, 89; and Israeli talks at international conference, 177; and Jordan, 112, 116–18, 125–26, 149, 218–19, 257; and leadership, 100, 197, 216; and Lebanon withdrawal, 279; and Mashov group, 99; and Netanyahu, 266; and Peres, 262–63; and PLO, 116; and presidential election, 230–32; and Rabin, 198, 200, 207–8, 210–14, 224–25, 232, 262; and rapprochement with Israel, 168–70, 224; and self-government, 84, 114, 188, 204–5; separation of Israel from, 188; and Shamir, 178, 191; and Sharon, 314; and Six-Day War, 67; and South Africa talks, 142–43; and Taba talks, 306–9; and Temple Mount, 253–54; and terrorism, 265; and two-state solution, 176, 186, 190, 192, 204–5, 209, 225, 269, 318, 321; and Washington talks, 195–97, 201, 205, 207–8, 212, 213, 215; and Washington talks with Jordan delegation, 196, 287
Party for the Advancement of the Zionist Idea, 183–85
Patt, Gideon, 106
Paz, Yehuda, 137
Peerce, Jan, 19
Peleg, Yisrael, 97
Peres, Shimon, 84, *154*, 297; 100-days team of, 101–2; and ambassadorship to Egypt, 109–10; and Begin, 81; and Beilin, 86–88, 98, 108, 133–34, 138–39; and Bus 300 Affair, 128–30; and Camp David Accords, 91; and conflict with Rabin, 81–82, 92–93, 188, 196–98, 259–60, 284; and direct elections, 234–36, 266; election campaigns of, 85–86, 94–96, 101–2, 244–45; as finance minister, 168, 171; as foreign minister, 195, 206; in France, 121–22; government formed by, 181–84; and informal peace talks with PLO, 175–77; and Israel Bonds, 248; on Israel Bonds, 246–47; and Labor Party, 81, 147, 148–49, 178, 192, 281–82; and Madrid Conference, 197–98; on media, 103–4; meeting with King Hussein, 111–18; in Morocco, 120–21; and national unity government, 147–48; and Nobel Peace Prize, 227; and no-confidence vote, 179; nominating Beilin as ambassador, 132–33; and Oslo Accords, 197, 201, 205–6, 209–11, 213, 215, 219; and peace talks with Jordan, 119–20, 123; and peace talks with Tunisia, 228–29; and PLO, 214; and

Pollard Affair, 131; as prime minister, 148, 260–66, 271, 293; on retirement, 94; and Sartawi, 100–101; on separation of religion and state, 191; and Socialist International, 88–89, 100; and Swedish peace talks, 225; and Vatican, 240
Peres, Sonia, 110, 182, 266
Peretz, Amir, 147, 192
Peretz, Yitzhak, 109, 172
Pickering, Thomas, 119
PLO. *See* Palestinian Liberation Organization (PLO)
Poalei Zion (Workers of Zion), 255
Pollard, Jonathan, 131–32
Pollard Affair, 131–32
Porat, Leah, 48
Porat, Orna, 277
Poraz, Nir, 228
Powell, Colin, 316
Preuss, Teddy, 86
Primor, Avi, 138
Progressive Party, 32
Progressive Socialist Party, 100
Pundak, Nahum, 204
Pundak, Ron, 203–7, 209, 224–26, 295

Qurei, Ahmed (Abu Ala), 194, 200–202, 204–5, 209–12, 214, 215, 227, 306

Ra'anan, Natan, 82
Rabbo, Yasser Abed, 223
Rabin, Dalia, 315
Rabin, Leah, 86, 210, 261
Rabin, Yitzhak, 3, 78, 82, 306; and Arafat, 243; assassination of, 126, 127, 236, 251, 257–65, 271, 272, 296; and Beilin, 138, 140, 149, 177, 238; and Bus 300 Affair, 128–29; coalition of, 264; and conflict with Peres, 81–82, 92–93, 188, 196–98, 259–60, 284; as defense minister, 106, 111–12, 148; and direct elections, 234–36; and expulsion of militants, 202–3; and government formation, 183–85;

as IDF chief of staff, 61; and IDF soldiers, 223–24, 228; and interim peace agreement, 211–12, 219, 225, 227; and Jordan, 115–16, 119, 126; and Labor Party, 81, 88, 101, 148–49, 178, 192, 195, 281; on Lebanon, 99, 271; and Madrid Conference, 125, 196; ministry appointments by, 256–57; and national unity government, 124, 147–48; and Nobel Peace Prize, 227; and no-confidence vote, 179; and NRP, 263; and Oslo Accords, 197, 200–201, 205–13, 215, 218–20; and PLO, 186, 199, 214, 216, 242; and Pollard Affair, 131; and presidential elections, 230–32; as prime minister, 185, 283, 293; on separation of religion and state, 191; and Six-Day War, 60, 61; and South African, 136; unpopularity of, 82, 84, 85
Rabinovich, Itamar, 196
Rafi party, 74, 88, 101
Raful, 193
Rajoub, Jibril, 316
Ramon, Haim, 285, 297; in Knesset, 147, 177–79, 268; and Labor Party, 82, 146, 190, 193, 281
Randel, Dov, 194
Rania, Queen, 315
Rashid, Mohammed, 302
Rattok, Lily, 73
Ravitz, Avraham, 180
Raz, Menashe, 276
Raziel-Naor, Esther, 28
Reagan, Ronald, 117, 220, 316
Reichman, Uriel, 234
Reno, Janet Wood, *163*
Rifa'i, Zayed, 115, 117–18
Rivlin, Reuven, 235
Rivlin, Rubi, 302
Rivlin, Ruby, 191
Rodensky, Shmuel, 50
Rød-Larsen, Terje, 194–96, 199, 201
Rokach, Israel, 4
Ronen, Nehama, 315

Index

Rosen, David, 240
Rosen, Meir, *154*
Rosenblum, Doron, 72
Rosenfeld, Assaf, 278
Ross, Dennis, 298
Rovina, Hanna, 50
Rubinstein, Arthur, 18
Rubinstein, Danny, 72
Rubinstein, Elyakim (Eli), 196, 218, 287, 288

Sabra and Shatila massacre, 101
Sadan, Asher, 277
Sadat, Anwar, 80, *153*; and Camp David Accords, 211; and peace agreeement, 113, 145–46; and Socialist International, 89; visit to Israel by, 88, 109
Sadeh, Yitzhak, 59
Safieh, Afif, 176
Said, Edward, 310
Sandberg, Eliezer, 268
Sapir, Gidi, 289
Sapir, Pinhas, 81
Sarid, Yossi, 186, 269, 304; and Labor Party, 81, 85, 99; and Meretz party, 263–64, 268
Sartawi, Issam, 100–101
Saudi Arabia, 89, 200, 300
Savir, Aliza, 221
Savir, Uri, 102, 209–10, 221, 272
Sayeret Matkal, 228
Schach, Elazar Menachem Man, 179–81, 244
Schneer, Menachem Mendel, 181
Schoffman, Yehoshua, 290
Schori, Pierre, 226
Schröder, Gerhard, 83, 316
Schwartz, Dudi, 289
Segal, Yehiel, 32
Sella, Aviem, 131
Selman, Galila, 39–40, 43, 220
Serry, Robert, 176
Sha'at, Nabil, *160*
Sha'ath, Nabil, 257, 298, 306–7
Shahal, Moshe, 264

Shai, Nachman, 186
Shalom, Avraham ("Avrum"), 128–31
Shamgar, Meir, 203
Shamir, Yitzhak: and Bus 300 Affair, 128–29; and expulsion of militants, 203; government formation by, 184–85; and Iraq war, 186; and Jordan, 113, 114; and Lebanon, 106; and Likud party, 109, 184; and London Agreement, 119, 120, 123–25; and Madrid Conference, 125, 191–92; and national unity government, 147–48; and no-confidence vote, 179, 180, 183; and PLO, 169, 176–77, 200; and Pollard Affair, 131; as prime minister, 101, 102, 116, 132–33, 196, 234; and South Africa, 140–42; and ultra-Orthodox parties, 147, 148, 178, 183, 234
Shani, Orit, 184, 204, 223, 258
Shapira, Ron, 289
Shapira, Yoav, 253
Sharett, Moshe, 17, 43, 92
Sharir, Avraham, 183, 184
Sharon, Ariel ("Arik"), 298; as defense minister, 99; on Geneva Initiative, 314–16; and Likud party, 109; as prime minister, 237, 308; and Temple Mount, 303; and Yom Kippur War, 79
Shas party, 177–81, 219, 223, 275, 286
Shavit, Uzi, 73
Shazar, Zalman, 10
Sheetrit, Meir, 268
Sheetrit, Shimon, 219
Sheffer, Gideon, 315
Shemer, Naomi, 99
Shem-Tov, Victor, 214
Shilansky, Dov, 248
Shilon, Dan, 184
Shimoni, Yitzhak, 48
Shin Bet, 111, 132, 133, 276, 287–88; and Bus 300 Affair, 128–31
Shochat, Beiga, 253
Shoshani, Shimshon, 252–53
Shultz, George, 119, 120, 123

Sielski, Daniela. *See* Beilin, Daniela Sielski
Simhoni, Asaf, 41
Sinai, 41, 56, 91, 146, 210
Singer, Joel, 210–11, 213–14, 218–19
Six-Day War, 57, 59, 61–64, 70, 74, 79, 80, 114
SLA. *See* South Lebanon Army (SLA)
Sneh, Ephraim, 126, 169, 277, 284
Sneh, Moshe, 17, 284
social-democratic party (SPD), 82–83
Socialist International, 88, 100–101, 220
Sofer, Esther, 48
South Africa, 135–44, 260
South Lebanon Army (SLA), 106, 270, 278–79
Soviet Union, 170–74, 211
Steinhardt, Michael, 251–53
Stelmach, Nahum, 20
Stern, Isaac, 18
Stern, Yedidia, 289
Sternschuss, Dror, 314
Stoltenberg, Thorvald, 196, 197, 208
suicide bombings, 225, 236, 272
Suissa, Eli, 286
Sweden, 215, 224–26
Switzerland, 310, 316
Syria: Baumel in, 223–24; and Cohen, 132; and Lebanon withdrawal, 105, 270–71, 275, 278, 279; and peace talks, 196, 213, 262, 265, 293, 295; and Six-Day War, 114; and Yom Kippur War, 79, 80

Tabenkin, Yitzhak, 255
Tamir, Avrasha, 133, 237
Tamir, Yuli, 315
Tauran, Jean-Louis, 242
Tawil, Raymonda, 100
Tehiya party, 95, 185
Tel Aviv Foundation, 320
Temple Mount, 253–54, 299–301, 303, 314, 317
terror attacks, 264–65, 306
Thatcher, Margaret, 116

Third Way party, 275, 309
Toledano, Nissim, 202
Topaz, Dudu, 95
Tucker, Richard, 19
Tunisia, 223, 228
Tuval, Mario, 82
Tzapir, Tuvia, 150
Tzomet party, 185, 193
Tzur, Yehudit, 129

Ugglas, Margaretha af, 225
"Unaffiliated" movement, 255
"Unfortunate Affair," 72
United Jewish Appeal (UJA), 171–72
United Nations, 84, 272; Security Council Resolutions of, 74, 98, 117–18, 145, 168, 176, 188
United States: and Israel, 186, 238, 272, 303; and Israeli-Palestinians talks, 195–97, 201–2, 205, 207–9, 211–13, 215; and Madrid Conference, 196–98; and Palestinian-Jordan delegation, 196, 287; and Pollard Affair, 131–32; and South Africa, 138, 141, 142; and Soviet Jews, 170–71
United Torah Judaism (UTJ), 286–87
Uri, Abba, 27
Ussishkin, Menachem, 1–2
USS Liberty, 112

van der Stoel, Max, 175–76
Vardi, Yossi, 257
Vatican, 240–44
Verdiger, Avraham, 180
Verwoerd, Hendrik, 136
Vilnai, Matan, 245
Vinokur, Yosef, 43–45
Vorster, John, 136

Wachsman, Nachshon, 228
Walesa, Lech, 316
War of Attrition, 79
War of Independence, 11, 16, 17, 56, 59, 92, 135
Weisglass, Dov, 308

Weizer, Asher, 51, 53, 54
Weizman, Ezer, 133, 140, 142, 190, 220
Weizman, Haim, 252
Weizmann, Chaim, 1, 2, 7
West Bank, 113; elections in, 169; and Israeli annexation, 262–63; and Israeli settlements, 293, 324–25; Jordan's relinquishment of, 212; and Oslo Accords, 204–5; and Palestinian state, 225; and settlement blocs, 309–10; and two-state solution, 205, 318; uprising in, 125; withdrawal from, 295, 298–99
Western Wall, 16, 22, 63, 66–67, 314, 317
Wilf, Einat, 253
Wilson, Harold, 83
WIZO, 10, 246
World Jewish Congress, 80

Ya'ari, Ehud, 72
Ya'ari, Meir, 255
Yadin, Yigael, 32, 91
Yahav, Yona, 193, 282
Yahya, Habib Ben, 228
Yariv, Aharon, 214
Yariv-Shem Tov formula, 98, 116
Yassin, Ahmed, 224
Yatom, Danny, 280
Yavin, Haim, 48
Yehoshua, A. B., 315
Yisraeli, Yaacov, 320
Yizhar, S., 110
Yom Kippur War, 21, 59, 74, 78–79, 84, 114, 136, 145, 146, 204
Yones, Eli, 168
Yosef, Dov, 7
Yosef, Ovadia, 178, 181
Yugoslavia, 208

Zadok, Haim, 81, 131
Zakai, Yehezkel, 91
Zamir, Yitzhak, 128–30
Ze'evi, Rehavam, 185
Zelniker, Shimon, 137
Zemer, Hanna, 72, 73, 87, 110
Zilbershats, Yaffa, 289
Zisman, Emanuel, 248
Zmora, Ohad, 72
Zucker, Dedi, 278
Zvili, Nissim, 146, 147, 193, 278

Also by Yossi Beilin

Israel: A Concise Political History
Touching Peace: From the Oslo Accord to a Final Agreement
His Brother's Keeper: Israel and Diaspora Jewry in the Twenty-first Century
The Path to Geneva: The Quest for a Permanent Agreement, 1996–2004
Birthright: The True Story